Nobody Said Not to Go

Nobody Said Not to Go

The Life, Loves, and Adventures of Emily Hahn

KEN CUTHBERTSON

FABER AND FABER
BOSTON · LONDON

First published in the United States in
1998 by Faber and Faber, Inc.,
53 Shore Road, Winchester, MA 01890

Library of Congress Cataloging-in-Publication Data

Cuthbertson, Ken.
Nobody said not to go : the Life, Loves and Adventures of Emily Hahn / Ken Cuthbertson.
p. cm.
Includes bibliographical references.
ISBN 0-571-19950-X
1. Hahn, Emily, 1905–1997—Biography. 2. Women novelists, American—20th century—Biography. 3. Women environmentalists—United States—Biography. 4. Women journalists—United States—Biography. 5. Women travelers—United States—Biography. I. Title.
PS3515.A2422Z62 1998
813'.52—dc21
[B] 97-43687
CIP

Jacket design by Ha Nguyen.
Interior design by Will Powers
Typesetting by Stanton Publication Services, Inc.
Printed in the United States of America

Dedicated to
the memory of Emily Hahn
and also to
my daughters, Laura, Hayley, and Skye—
may they be free to soar as high as
their dreams will take them

Contents

Preface

THIS BOOK GREW OUT of some research that I did in the late 1980s and early 1990s into the life of the late American writer John Gunther (1901–1970), the creator of the popular series known as the "Inside" books. At that time, Emily Hahn and her sister Helen, who had known Gunther for many years, were especially helpful and encouraging to me. Like most people, I was dazzled by these two Hahn sisters; they were not sedentary octogenarians, content to while away their days playing cards or knitting. They radiated life.

The first time I visited the Hahn sisters at the cozy, book-lined flat they shared on 12th Avenue West in lower Manhattan was one morning a week before Christmas 1986. "All of these boxes belong to a nephew who has run away to join the circus," Emily Hahn informed me. It seemed plausible. In fact, *anything* would have sounded possible where this family was concerned.

Helen was busy building a harpsichord that she told me she intended to learn to play. In one corner of the living room stood a large wooden Victorian dollhouse Helen had built; it was complete with miniature furnishings and working lights. Even as Helen and I spoke, her sister Emily was beetling out the door. That day, as she did most workdays, she left the apartment at about 9:30 A.M. to hike to her office at the *New Yorker*, a bustling half-hour distant. She was eighty-three.

The more I learned about these two free-spirited Hahn sisters and their amazing family, the more awed I became. Their energy and zest for life were absolutely contagious.

When my Gunther book was published in the spring of 1992, I sent Emily Hahn a copy along with a note asking if she'd consider talking with me about an idea that I had for a book: *The Emily Hahn Story*. To my surprise—and delight—she responded quickly and with an enthusiasm that I was to learn was characteristic. "Yes," she announced. "Let's do it!" With those words ringing in my mind, we were off and running.

Emily Hahn once told an interviewer that given the choice, she always chose the uncertain path in life. I had no way of knowing when I began my research for this book just how true were those words or that it would take me almost five years to retrace the "uncertain paths" that Emily Hahn had followed in her peripatetic life. (If I have any regret about having spent so long working on her story, it is that Emily did not live to see this book's publication, although she did read and offer her comments on much of the manuscript.)

I found the scattered bits and pieces of the Emily Hahn story in far-flung places in Japan; Portugal; Hong Kong; Canada, England, and the United States. In the course of my research, I met scores of people who were invariably welcoming and accommodating. I'd like to thank the following individuals and groups for their kind help: Linda Belford, Senior Manuscript Specialist, Archives, University of Missouri–St. Louis, St. Louis, MO; H. T. ("Alf") Bennett, London, England; Virginia Black, Berkeley, CA; Anne Boxer, Melton, Suffolk, England; Grace Clowe, Albuquerque, NM; Ron Claircoates, Kingston, Ontario, Canada; Alvin D. Coox, Department of History, San Diego State University, San Diego, CA; Virginia Dajani, American Academy and Institute of Arts and Letters, New York City; Danys Delaques, Reference Archivist, National Archives of Canada, Ottawa, Ontario, Canada; the late Agnes G. DeMille, New York City; Stephen Endicott, Department of History, York University, Toronto, Ontario, Canada; Valerie Feldner, New York City; Martha Gellhorn, London, England; Alice Gibb, London, Ontario, Canada; Brendan Gill, New York City; Philip Hamburger, New York City; Muriel Hanson, Chatham, MA; Gulbahar Huxur, Vancouver, British Columbia, Canada; Bertha Harvell, Berkhamsted, Herts., England; the late Barbara Ker-Seymer, London, England; Janet Lorenz, Margaret Herrick Library, Academy of Motion Picture Arts and Sciences, Beverly Hills, CA; Tamas McDonald, London, England; Joan Mark, Peabody Museum of Archeology and Ethnology, Harvard University, Cambridge, MA; William Maxwell, New York City; Cynthia Miller, History and Genealogy Section, St. Louis Public Library, St. Louis, MO; Dorothy Miller, Salt Lake City, UT; Carl Mydans, Larchmont, NY; the reference staff of the New York Public Library, New York City; J. Kevin O'Brien, Chief, Freedom of Information-Privacy Acts Section, Information Management Division, Federal Bureau of Investigation, Washington, DC; Takio Oda, Tokyo, Japan; Coralee Paul, St. Louis, MO; Carolyn Reese, Albuquerque, NM; Jennie Rathburn, Houghton Library, Harvard University, Cambridge, MA; Dr. Xiohong Shao, Nanjing, People's Republic of China; Clio Smeeton, Calgary, Alberta, Canada; Britton C. Smith, Kingston, Ontario, Canada; Robert Spindler, Archives, Hayden Library, Arizona State University, Tempe, AZ; E. C. Taylor, Dorset, England; Craig Tenney, Harold Ober Associates, New York City; Lisa Tetrault, Assistant Archivist, University of Wisconsin–Madison, Madison, WI; Edgar Whitcomb, Hayden, IN; Geoffrey Wilson, Viana, Portugal; E. P. (Bill) Wiseman, St. Albans, Herts., England; Hyacinth Wilkie, Brooklyn, NY; Peter Yeung and the staff of the Canada–Hong Kong Resource Centre, Joint Centre for Asia Pacific Studies of the University of Toronto and York University, Toronto, Ontario, Canada; and Frances Zainoeddin, New York City.

Thanks, too, to Fiona Batty of Peters, Fraser and Dunlop, London, England, literary executors of the late Rebecca West (for permission to quote from Rebecca West's letters to Emily Hahn) and to James Benét, Sebastopol, CA, literary executor of the late William Benét (for permission to quote from his father's letters to Emily Hahn).

At the Lilly Library, Indiana University, Bloomington, IN, a sincere thank-you to Saundra Taylor, Breon Mitchell, and former Lilly Librarian William Cagle, for their courtesy, diligence, and professionalism during the long days that I spent sifting through Emily Hahn's papers. Hahn was herself a meticulous gatherer who kept vast quantities of old letters, manuscripts, photos, and press clippings; the staff at the Lilly Library have done a superb job of cataloguing and preserving all of this material for posterity. The Hahn papers are a treasure trove of information for scholars and literary historians whom I hope will delve further into Hahn's life and work.

Also at Indiana University, special thanks to the Ball Brothers Foundation for their kind financial support in the form of a Ball Brothers Fellowship. The money helped me to pay expenses when I visited Bloomington to do my research at the Lilly Library.

Closer to home, thanks to my wife, Marianne and daughters, Laura, Hayley, and Skye, for their understanding and patience in putting up with "daddy's" early mornings, late nights, and absences from family gatherings as I worked on "the book."

At Queen's University in Kingston, Ontario, Canada, thanks to my colleagues and friends Mary Lou Marlin, Dianna Bristol of alumni affairs, former *Alumni Review* editor Cathy Perkins, and Geoff Smith of the history department for their encouragement and for feedback on those portions of the manuscript that they read.

In New York, thanks to Emily Hahn's longtime friend and confidante Sheila McGrath, who with patience and endless good humor, shared with me her memories of Emily Hahn and her encyclopedic knowledge of the *New Yorker*; and thanks to my agent Laura Tucker, Richard Curtis Associates, for seeing the potential in this book, sharing in my passion for it, and believing in my ability to see it through to a successful completion, and to my editor Valerie Cimino and copy editor Sharon Hogan at Faber and Faber for their expert guidance in producing a final text.

Special thanks to Emily Hahn's late sister Josephine ("Dauphine") Arthur, Chapel, NE; "very best" friend J. S. ("Jimmy") Cummins, London, England; nephew Gregory Dawson, New York City; nephew Charless Hahn, Winnetka, IL; late sister Helen Hahn, New York City; niece Hilary Schlessiger, New York City; and cousin Richard Schoen, Falls Church, VA.

Special thanks also to Emily Hahn's beloved husband Charles Boxer,

Berkhamsted, Herts., England, for his hospitality and his patience in answering my questions and letters. "The Major" is one of the most remarkable, complex, and charming men I've ever met (or am ever likely to meet!), and to Emily Hahn's daughters Amanda Boxer, London, England, and Carola Vecchio, Jackson Heights, NY. Both Amanda and Carola graciously shared with me their memories of their mother and their candid insights into her life. In them, Emily Hahn lives on.

Last, and most important of all, my heartfelt thanks to Emily Hahn. Her friend Muriel Hanson insisted that Mickey was a woman without pretensions. "What you saw was what you got. That's who she was," Muriel said. She was right. Emily Hahn was beautiful, intelligent, funny, charming, boundlessly generous, and selflessly loyal to those who were dear to her. Like all of us, she had shortcomings: by times, she could be stubborn to a fault, uncompromisingly and maddeningly independent, and she did not suffer fools gladly.

Emily Hahn was also an enormously talented writer. Whenever I read her writings, I'm struck by how much the person that you meet on paper is the same person that her family and friends knew. Emily Hahn's literary voice, so disarmingly casual and engaging, was uniquely hers. The ability to write so effortlessly is neither common nor easy; it is a rare and wondrous gift.

When I first met Emily Hahn she was eighty-one years old. I really got to know her starting in the autumn of 1992, when she agreed to cooperate with me on this book. For a time, I referred to her as "Ms. Hahn" or "Mrs. Boxer," sometimes as "Emily." I asked her one day, "What *should* I call you?" She appeared puzzled at first and then flashed that wry smile of hers. "Well, my friends call me Mickey. You can call me that, if you like," she said.

I feel privileged to say that I did, and also that Mickey Hahn has permitted me to share her amazing story with you.

Kingston, Ontario, Canada
January 1998

Introduction

Afoot and light-hearted I take to the open road,
Healthy, free, the world before me,
The long brown path before me, leading wherever I choose.
"Song of the Open Road," Walt Whitman (1819–1892)

DURING THE GREAT DEPRESSION, a male colleague cautioned Emily Hahn to "be careful" when she quit her $25-a-week teaching job, left New York, and went looking for adventure in the African jungles. "I still don't know what he meant," she said sixty years later.

Her uncertainty was genuine, for "careful" was not a word that was part of the Hahn vocabulary. She was the quintessential rebel without a pause. At the height of her career in the years 1940 through to the late 1970s, she was also one of America's most irrepressible and prolific female writers, yet today Emily Hahn is largely unknown and her writings are seldom read. The reasons for this are as complex and varied as the woman herself.

When Hahn died in New York City on February 18, 1997, she left behind an astounding literary legacy. During her sixty-eight years as a contributor to the *New Yorker*, she wrote hundreds of articles, short stories, and poems; Hahn was one of a handful of writers who worked for all four of the legendary magazine's editors—Harold Ross, William Shawn, Robert Gottlieb, and Tina Brown; however, what has often been overlooked is that Emily Hahn also wrote fifty-two books, many of which were years ahead of their time. Hahn's informal, highly personal prose style was a precursor of the "new journalism" that revolutionized the media world in the 1960s. The fact is, Hahn was an exceptional writer who made the impossible look easy. British writer Rebecca West, her good friend and one-time mentor, never doubted that Hahn's lack of public recognition had as much to do with her gender as with her personality. "Like you," West once told Hahn, "I'd have a far higher reputation if I were male."[1]

There was another reason for Hahn's relative obscurity: her writing—like the woman herself—had a quicksilver vitality that defied easy categorization. She resolved early in her literary career never to become predictable or to play it safe; in that she succeeded. For better *and* worse, no one ever knew what to expect next from Emily Hahn. She dismayed her literary agents and publishers by moving effortlessly from fiction to journalism or the casually elegant first-person essays that were her trademark. The Hahn bibliography includes a dazzling smorgasbord of literary genres: history, biographies, humor, women's issues, bohemianism, travel, cooking, children's stories, zoology, natural history, and fiction.

When coupled with her gender, Hahn's refusal to be pigeon-holed or to generate self-promotional sound bites for the literary marketplace carried a steep price. She seldom achieved the mass readership or adulation that she so richly deserved.

If Emily Hahn was bitter about this or about anything else in her life, it never showed. To the end, she preferred to focus on positives, of which there were many in her life. She derived a profound sense of satisfaction from the lofty reputation that she enjoyed among those who knew good writing. In 1987, Hahn's literary colleagues accorded her one of the greatest honors any writer can receive when they elected her to the American Academy of Arts and Letters. The Academy members were well aware of Hahn's myriad literary accomplishments.

She rose to prominence in the early 1940s with two books about China. *The Soong Sisters* (1941) was a biography of the Middle Kingdom's illustrious "first family" of the day, and *China to Me* (1944) was an irreverent, tell-all memoir that chronicled Hahn's life, loves, and freewheeling wartime adventures in the Far East. She wrote about her experiences with a candor that was at once bewildering and beguiling, and readers responded to what she had to say. Both China books were best-sellers, and Hahn received a torrent of letters as a result. Some praised her. Others reviled her. One indignant reader sent her a piece of soiled toilet tissue, another wished her dead.

Emily Hahn was never surprised when her writing provoked passionate reactions; she had an instinctive feel for the power of words and the impact that they can have on people's lives, including her own.

The great irony was that when Emily Hahn left home in Chicago in 1922, it was not to become a writer, but rather a geologist—a decidedly unorthodox occupation for a woman at that time. After more than her share of travails, Hahn became the first female ever to graduate in mining engineering from the University of Wisconsin. Sadly, she never got a chance to use her skills in a profession that was almost exclusively male. This was neither the first time (nor would it be the last) that Emily Hahn clashed with "the system" in a male-dominated world.

If you define a feminist as someone who believes women can do anything that men can, there's no doubt that Emily Hahn *was* a "feminist" long before the term was coined. Yet she scoffed at that notion. "Feminists belong to clubs. They collect money for causes," Hahn would declare with a knowing smile. "I wish feminists well, but I've never wanted to be one."

Her response was hardly surprising, for Emily Hahn was the archetypal American individualist; she preferred to act first, ask questions later. "My younger daughter [Amanda] once rebuked me for not being the kind of mother one reads about," Hahn once told an interviewer. "I asked her what kind that was, and she said, the kind who sits home and bakes cakes. I told her to go and find anybody who sits at home and bakes cakes."[2]

Emily Hahn led an astounding life; she was a 1990s woman born a generation too soon. She came of age in the 1920s, at a time of great emotional and intellectual ferment. Despite the laissez-faire mentality of the Jazz Age, which was personified by the carefree, sexually liberated flapper, most Americans still subscribed to the philosophy that gender roles should be clearly defined: a man's job was to work and provide for his family; a woman was expected to tend the home, bear children, and "love, honor, and obey" her husband. That may have been fine for others, but Emily Hahn was far too free-spirited, far too intelligent to ever become a slave to social convention. She burned with a restless intensity that bedazzled most people.

Hahn traveled to nearly every corner of the globe. She worked as a horseback trail guide in New Mexico in the 1920s. She lived with Congo pygmies and hiked across central Africa on her own in the 1930s. For a time, while it suited her, she was an opium addict and the concubine of a Chinese poet. She rubbed elbows with beggars and kings, missionaries and prostitutes, headhunters and government heads, poets and cowboys, spies and soldiers. The famous and the infamous.

When Hahn had her first child, a daughter, she was already thirty-six years old and still single. Her scandalous love affair with a married British army intelligence officer named Charles Boxer, the father of that child, scandalized Hong Kong and was one of the greatest love stories of the war years. Disregarding her own safety, Hahn convinced the Japanese that she was Eurasian, all so that she could spend two years in occupied Hong Kong working to save Boxer's life when he was wounded in battle and thrown into a hell hole POW camp; Emily Hahn truly was one of the most fearless people you would ever meet.

When she did eventually marry Boxer, their fifty-one-year marriage was the fairy-tale ending to a fairy-tale romance. It also defied all conventional wisdom that said it could not work or endure. "Conventional wisdom" never applied to Emily Hahn. She was a larger-than-life character with a flair for the dramatic and for the grand entrance; whether you met her in person or in her prose, she had an unequalled knack for memorable opening lines. Her 1970 memoir *Times and Places* begins, "Not long after my family moved from St. Louis to Chicago, I ran away from home."[3]

Hahn went right on running for most of her ninety-two years of life. "I wanted desperately to be noticed, and equally desperately to be let alone," she once explained.[4]

A *New York Times* reporter has described the life of Emily Hahn as "a ground breaking, breathtaking [one] in which she has thumbed her nose at convention all the way."[5] That summation is an apt one. Hahn was a woman who lived life at full tilt and always on her own terms. Sometimes she loved and won; sometimes she loved and lost. No one could ever say that her life was always pleasant or genteel. Nor was it mundane.

This is a book about the literary career of Emily Hahn, an enormously gifted writer whom one of her young colleagues at the *New Yorker* correctly describes as "a great lost American literary treasure." But even more important, this is also a book about the remarkable life, loves, and adventures of an inimitable, larger-than-life woman who dared to walk the uncertain paths that others fear to tread.

Emily Hahn went out into the world and lived life on her own terms because, as she so succinctly put it, "Nobody said *not* to go."

I

In the Beginning

1

The afternoon of September 22, 1943, was sultry and overcast in Hong Kong, the kind of liquid afternoon when Emily Hahn loved nothing better than to sit in the shade among the flowers on the terrace of her flat high up on the Peak. There she would while away the hours, sipping a cool drink as she chatted with friends, read, smoked a good cigar, or leisurely watched the comings and goings of ships in the harbor far below. Today there were no cool drinks. No friends. No books. The memories of those genteel afternoons in this outpost of the British Empire were growing as faded and dim as watercolors in the rain.

This was Day Four Hundred and Sixty-Eight of the Japanese occupation of Hong Kong. For Emily Hahn, her two-year-old daughter Carola, and for one hundred and twenty other foreign nationals, this day would be different. They were being repatriated in an International Red Cross prisoner exchange. More than a thousand Japanese nationals who had been in the U.S. when the war began were being shipped to Lourenço Marques, a neutral Portuguese port on the coast of East Africa. (Now known as Maputo, Mozambique.) Here, they were to be exchanged for American and Canadian civilians who had been taken prisoner by the Japanese in Shanghai, Hong Kong, and Saigon. Emily Hahn's mind was a welter of conflicting emotions as she thought of all this.

She had dreamed of freedom each and every day of her ordeal in occupied Hong Kong; it had been a struggle to survive, let alone maintain her dignity and sanity. Emily desperately wanted to escape the madness and hardship, yet she had felt a duty to stay. In truth, for once in her life she did not know what she really wanted. She felt dazed and numbed by a sense of resignation borne of knowing her fate was no longer in her own hands.

The day had begun at first light, with tearful good-byes to her faithful Chinese houseboy Ah King and to Carola's *amah* Ah Yuk. Then, with Carola snuggled into her shoulder, Emily had taken up her suitcase and made her way through a drizzling rain to a park in downtown Victoria. Here the Japanese searched the refugees and checked their travel documents. Then they were herded onto a leaky fishing trawler for the journey to Stanley on the south coast of the island. The choppy waters of the harbor gave way to rolling ocean swells as the boat rounded the western tip of Hong Kong Island, chugging past Victoria Peak on the left. They turned directly into the wind and the driving rain. The waves breaking over the bow of the boat soaked those who were crammed together on the deck. The weather and sea conditions mattered little, for like Emily and Carola, most of the bedraggled passengers who huddled close were too seasick to care.

After ninety minutes, they arrived at Stanley Bay on the south side of the island. Here the refugees were unloaded on the quay and made to line up inside a large, empty terminal building. Japanese soldiers rechecked their papers and combed through everyone's belongings. Emily and Carola waited with the hundred and twenty other ragged, dirty, and hungry civilians being repatriated this day. They stood for several hours. While the Japanese worked slowly and methodically, the smell of unwashed bodies and the sobbing of children grew almost unbearable in the heat and humidity.

When the paperwork was done, the refugees were hustled out onto the quay. There in Stanley Bay awaiting them lay the *Teia Maru*, an exchange ship that was to carry them on the first leg of their journey home. Emily saw the Japanese had painted a large white cross on the hull; there was one on each side. "Now we stood some more, looking at the ship, while the people [on board], repatriates from Japan and Shanghai, looked at us," she later wrote, "and, thronging the top of the stone wall at Stanley prison camp, our friends who had to stay behind stared at our backs."[1]

Eventually, the Hong Kong repatriates were loaded into launches to be ferried out to the *Teia Maru*. On board, they were met by a welcoming committee of "bossy Americans," who assigned them to cabins. Emily Hahn and Carola were put in a long, narrow cabin with two other women. Carola promptly fell asleep. Emily lay down beside her, sobbing into her pillow. She cried for Carola, for herself, and for her beloved Charles in a Japanese POW camp. The man she loved, the father of her child, was the husband of another woman. He was also a British intelligence officer who had been marked for death by his captors.

As Emily Hahn lay there in her bunk aboard the *Teia Maru,* she recalled their tearful last meeting. Knowing she and Carola would not visit the POW camp again, Emily had ignored all the rules. She looked longingly at Charles through the barbed-wire fence as the rickshaw in which she and Carola rode passed along the adjacent roadway. They had been so tantalizingly close, yet so far apart; speaking and all physical contact were strictly forbidden. Then suddenly Carola, who was sitting on Mickey's lap, stood up and waved. "Daddy bye-bye! Daddy bye-bye!" she shouted, her words trailing out in the air like escaped balloons. These were the only two words of English that the little girl knew; her *amah* had taught them to her just for this occasion.

At that moment, Emily had been frozen with terror. She knew people had been shot for far less in occupied Hong Kong. But the guards did not shoot at them this day, and so Emily too turned and looked directly at Charles for one last time. She saw that the man she loved was hungry, dirty, and clad only in a ragged pair of shorts and tattered shirt. His left arm hung uselessly in a sling, almost two years after he had been wounded in the battle for Hong Kong. Despite his haggard appearance and the raw emotions clawing at his heart, Charles was a British officer and he stood firm. As their eyes locked in one hurried final embrace, Emily thought she saw a glistening in Charles's eyes. Or was it the light? She could not tell through the torrent of tears cascading down her own cheeks. As her rickshaw drew away, Emily stared back at Charles until she could see him no longer. Then he was gone. Would she ever see him again? She did not know.

After more than thirteen years abroad, Emily Hahn was going home to the U.S. She had reached a crossroads in her life. She was thirty-eight years old and a single mother. Although she was a published author, she had been out of touch with her agent and with the New York literary marketplace for several years. Everything that Emily Hahn owned was in the battered suitcase she carried with her. Where would she and her daughter go now? What would they do? How could she ever begin all over again?

Hahn hugged her daughter close as the two of them lay in their bunk. Then she wiped the tears from her eyes and pulled a blanket over them. She joined Carola in the sleep of the exhausted.

• • •

Mickey Hahn's life began at 4858 Fountain Avenue, a quiet downtown residential street in the north-central St. Louis neighborhood known as Grande Prairie. A suburb sprouted there in the years just after the Civil War on the old common fields farmed by the first French settlers in the region. By 1876, when the Grand Prairie was annexed by the city, it was a bustling community of Irish and German immigrants. Bounded on the north by St. Louis Street, on the west by Kingshighway Boulevard, on the south by Delmar Street, and on the east by Grande Boulevard—all busy commercial thoroughfares—the neighborhood was no different from countless others that grew up in cities across the American Midwest in the late nineteenth century.

Dr. Edward Saunders, the family's physician, "brought babies in his black bag," as the Hahn children were told. He obviously had one in there as his motorcar came to a halt in front of the house on the morning of January 14, 1905. Saunders's hat and muffler were pulled snug against a biting northwest wind. He hurried up the front walkway, for he was late. He was also chilled to the bone after having fumbled around for several minutes to thaw out the motor of his car. The weather report on page 1 of the day's *St. Louis Post-Dispatch* promised the cold snap would continue. It further cautioned, "Those who have ears and noses to save should prepare to save them now, for Jack Frost will continue abroad in the land."

Dr. Saunders arrived at Hannah Hahn's bedside with not a moment to spare, for she was already laboring mightily to bring her fifth daughter into the world. It was not an easy birth, for the baby was coming feet first, a breech birth. As Hannah struggled with the pain, she could hear the Hahn and Schoen families, who had gathered in the parlor to await the outcome of Hannah's labors. Isaac Hahn, her husband, reveled in the bustle of a big house filled with the sights, sounds, and smells of family life. Although he himself was the eldest of seven children, these were sensations fate had largely robbed him of as a child.

• • •

Isaac's parents, Rosa (nee Hyman) and Emmanuel Hahn, were German Jews. Rosa was born July 15, 1832, at Felheim, Bavaria. Isaac knew little about her youth, other than that she had emigrated to the Philadelphia area with her parents and eight siblings in the early 1850s. Later, at least some of the family migrated west to Memphis.

Isaac's father, Emmanuel Hahn, was born April 15, 1826, near Darmstadt, Hesse, a town in southwest Germany, about 80 miles from the French border. According to a family history that Isaac penned in 1925 at his children's urging, Emmanuel had been apprenticed to a locksmith. However, because he was the youngest of four children and was not supporting his family, he left for America at age seventeen. He settled in Memphis, Tennessee. "Naturally, his education was limited," Isaac wrote. "His mother died when he was very young, and he never knew a father's love, being a posthumous child."[2] Like many Jews who emigrated to the American Midwest in this period, Emmanuel found work as a peddler.

Once he had established himself and put a roof over his head, Emmanuel sent for his brother and two sisters. Many of the other details of the Hahn family's early years in America have been forgotten, but it seems likely that Rosa Hyman and Emmanuel Hahn met and were married about 1855, for as Isaac explained, "In the Prayer Book is inscribed in German by my mother, 'My son Isaac was born August 18th, 1856, on Monday morning at three o'clock.' . . . This was in Memphis, Tennessee, on the northwest corner of Second and Exchange Streets."[3]

Four Hahn siblings followed in the years between 1856 and 1865: Isidor (who was known as "Bud") in 1858; Pauline in 1860; Moses in 1862; and Rebecca ("Beckie") in 1865.

Isaac's father, exempted from service in the Confederate Army during the

Civil War because of his large family, served in the home guard. He earned a living by making and selling ice cream to the Confederate troops stationed at Fort Pickering, just south of Memphis. After the war, he worked as a clerk in a dry goods store. Life was not easy, and Emmanuel was just forty-one when on July 26, 1867, he died of yellow fever.

Rosa Hahn, pregnant with twins, was left to face the daunting task of raising seven children on her own. She did what she could. She rented the house in Memphis, packed up her family, and moved back east to be with her family in Philadelphia. Following the birth in late 1867 of the twins Emilie and Amelia, Rosa found it difficult to make ends meet. In fact, the story of her family's life for the next few years is right out of the pages of a Dickens novel. The baby Emilie took ill and died at age seven months. However, even with one less mouth to feed, Rosa still could not make a go of it; her situation was desperate. In 1868, when a cousin in Cleveland sent word that the Independent Order of the B'nai Brith (a fraternal order to which Emmanuel had belonged) had opened an orphanage in the Ohio city, Rosa made a tearful decision: she committed Isidor, Moses, and Pauline to the institution in the hope that there they at least would be fed and educated. Rosa kept the two youngest children, Rebecca and Amelia, while Isaac, still just twelve years of age, was thrust into the role of family breadwinner.

When Pauline returned to live with her mother in 1869, Isaac was sent to Tennessee to attend school and work in his Uncle Ben's dry goods store in La Grange, a busy commercial town just east of Memphis. Here the boy fell into the life of the community and began attending the local Methodist Sunday school. "Uncle Ben didn't want anyone to know we were Jews," Isaac recalled in his memoir, "but I confided the fact to Parson Fife, who took particular pains to convert me."[4] Fife's plan to have Isaac—"a brand plucked from the burning," as he described him—attend a Methodist seminary might have succeeded if not for two obstacles: Uncle Ben forbade it, and Rosa Hahn counseled her son to wait until he was older before making such an important decision. Isaac never attended the seminary.

His flirtation with Methodism was just one of many sources of tension between Isaac and his uncle Ben, for the young man had developed a fiercely independent streak, which he would pass on to his daughter Mickey. Isaac became an outspoken atheist, and he and his uncle clashed often. As a result, in June 1870, Isaac went to live with his great-aunt Sophie, thirty miles southwest of La Grange in Holly Springs, Mississippi. He worked there at a variety of jobs, one of which was selling newspaper subscriptions and books. Although Isaac did not make much money, he had the opportunity to read and became familiar with the classics; Shakespeare, Dickens, and Twain were favorites. Even more important, Isaac developed an insatiable appetite for ideas and the "show-me" skepticism of the self-educated man.

His life changed abruptly in February 1873 when he received a letter from a cousin informing him that his mother had died; like her husband, Rosa Hahn fell victim to yellow fever. Isaac, now seventeen, decided the time had come to make something of himself and to reunite his family. He returned home to Memphis, finding work as a clerk in a dry goods store. He was a quick learner and became a proficient bookkeeper and salesman. In this latter capacity, Isaac traveled far and wide throughout the Midwest and South. His memoirs provide a vivid sense of daily life in the America of the latter decades of the nineteenth century, for Isaac recorded the vicissitudes of his own struggles in the kind of gritty detail no history book ever could.

In those days, most people stayed close to home. Life was precarious, for health care and public sanitation were primitive or nonexistent. As a result, terrible epidemics swept the land with the regularity of the changing seasons. Yellow fever, spread by mosquitos, was among the worst. Isaac contracted the disease, but unlike his parents, he recovered and thus became immune. Others in his family were not as lucky; Isaac's brother Moses died from the disease during a summer visit to Memphis in the late 1870s, and their great-aunt Sophie succumbed a year or two later. His sister Amelia got sick and died in 1886, and although the cause of her death was not recorded, yellow fever was probably to blame.

Even as such epidemics ravaged the population, a series of severe depressions plagued the farming-based economy of the areas where Isaac worked and traveled. Many farmers went broke, and Isaac was fortunate to hang onto his job. He made the best of his situation, and through Horatio Alger pluck and luck he prospered. In the summer of 1881, Isaac joined the St. Louis–based S. A. Rider & Company, purveyors of dry goods, groceries, jewelry, and just about everything else people in the small towns and isolated farms of the American Midwest and South needed or wanted.

With money in the bank and a secure job, Isaac was ready to settle down. His opportunity came when he chanced to meet Caroline Godlove, the daughter of a business associate. As he recalled in his memoir, "I never expected to be married until my sister did, but I was nearly 31 years old, and changed my mind thinking that we could give [my younger sister] Beckie a good home and she would be happy with us until she found a home of her own."

Isaac and Caroline—"Carrie" to her family—were wed in a Jewish ceremony on January 5, 1888, at the Harmonie Club on Chateau Avenue in St. Louis. Intriguingly, what Isaac remembered most vividly about his wedding day was dancing the first dance at the reception with Carrie's bridesmaid and best friend, Hannah Schoen; this, "they say, is not the usual thing," he later acknowledged.[5] Isaac would come to wonder if that dance had not been an omen. So, too, would Hannah, for during the wedding she had eyed Isaac wistfully and whispered to Carrie, "I only hope that I can marry one just like him one day."

Isaac was on a sales trip in February 1889 when he arrived in Lincoln, Nebraska, to find a telegram awaiting him. The message read: "Wife deathly ill. Come home at once." Carrie Hahn suffered from "consumption"—now known as tuberculosis. Isaac rushed back to St. Louis to find his wife "listless and [taking] no interest in anything at all."[6] A month later, Carrie was dead. She and Isaac had been married just over a year.

• • •

In an effort to forget his sorrow, Isaac immersed himself in work. By 1892, he was making the princely sum of $3,000 a year, and he had been promoted to the position of vice president of S. A. Rider. He had a good job, a loving family, and many friends, yet there was a void in his life. Isaac began courting Carrie's friend Hannah Schoen, who had comforted him and shared his loss at Carrie's passing.

Born October 25, 1866, in St. Louis, Hannah was the third of six children. Her parents, Fredericka (Linz) and Leopold Schoen, were Bavarian Jews. Leopold followed in the footsteps of his older brother Aaron when he emigrated to the United States in 1849. Fredericka arrived two years later. The couple met and were married on March 1, 1858, in St. Louis. Hannah, their eldest daughter, was pretty, dark haired, bright, and opinionated. She was a strong personality who in many ways was years ahead of her time. "Mother was not a career woman only because career women had not yet been developed," Emily Hahn explained in a 1970 memoir entitled *Times and Places*.[7]

By necessity as much as by design, young Hannah became a vocal advocate of equal rights for women. While Hannah's older brothers, Isaac, Joseph, and Meyer, were given the opportunity to attend college, Hannah's parents adamantly refused to allow her or her sisters, Minnie and Ella, to do likewise. The Schoens' rationale was as simple as it was typical of the time: money was tight, so why bother with the expense and effort of educating daughters? Chances were they would marry and spend their working lives raising children.

While Hannah bristled at such inequities, she had no choice but to comply with her parents' dictates. Naturally, that was not the end of the matter. "Mother always did exactly what she wanted to do, but she always richly justified herself in advance," Emily Hahn noted in *Times and Places*. "For example, there was her job before she married, which I loved to hear about. Mother had gone out and got herself a business training and worked in an office long before most girls dared to have such excitement in their lives."[8] Hannah argued that a woman had as much right to earn a living as a man did. Besides, she added, she *hated* housework. Forsaking pots and pans for pencils and papers, Hannah Schoen became a stenographer. For a time, she worked in Chicago. Family members admired her proficiency as a typist. They also marveled at her dogged insistence that no young woman should ever be short-changed educationally, as she had been. Come what may, Hannah was determined that any daughter of hers would have the same opportunity as any son.

Most men would have been cowed by Hannah's vehemence and probing intellect. Not Isaac Hahn. He had been raised by strong women, and he found himself inexorably drawn to Hannah. Isaac proposed one starry autumn evening as the couple strolled arm in arm through Forest Park in St. Louis. Pausing beside a park bench, Isaac gallantly spread out his handkerchief on the seat for Hannah. Then he popped the question. When the happy couple rushed off to share their news with family and friends, Isaac's handkerchief was left behind on the bench. "Whenever we were walking in Forest Park and we passed the spot where Daddy had proposed to Mother, he'd always go over, stop, and ask if we could help him find his handkerchief," Emily Hahn remembered. "That was typical of Daddy's wit."[9]

Isaac Hahn and Hannah Schoen were wed on December 21, 1892. The bride was twenty-six, the groom ten years her senior, so they wasted no time in starting a family. Hannah gave birth to the couple's first child in October 1893, a baby girl they called Caroline ("Taddie"). She was followed two years later by Emmanuel ("Mannel"), by Rose in 1897, Frederic in 1899, Dorothy ("Dot") in 1901, Helen in 1903, Emily in 1905, and Josephine ("Dauphine") in 1907.

Taddie never knew her siblings. She was just a month short of her second birthday when, in September 1895, she fell victim to scarlet fever. Baby Frederic died in the fall of 1899 from a bowel ailment.

• • •

By the time of Emily's arrival, Isaac was carrying a few extra pounds and suffering from the diabetes that ran in the Hahn family. At age forty-nine, Isaac was at ease with his role as a father. "I was the fifth of six children [who lived], and by the time I was born both my parents had got used to being parents," Emily explained.[10]

One can imagine the scene as Isaac awaited the news from the second floor master bedroom that cold January day in 1905. It being a Saturday morning, the children were home. Grandfather Schoen was there, too, pacing the floor as he tugged anxiously on his beard. From time to time, he was joined in his perambulations by the various cousins, aunts, and uncles who wandered in and out. As Isaac sat in his favorite leather armchair reading the newspaper, the four children playing at his feet occasionally scrambled up and over him. Isaac glanced anxiously at the stairs as Grandmother Schoen or the family's two young maids Dora ("Doda") and Catherine ("Taffy"), who lived in the attic, scurried up and down with supplies for Dr. Saunders.

The exact details of the birth of the baby Emily have been forgotten; in all the excitement no one remembered to report her arrival to the vital records office of the St. Louis health department. Ninety years later, Emily Hahn noted, "They haven't got my birth certificate. When I needed it for my first passport we discovered this omission, and Mother had to come with me to the passport office to declare formally that I did indeed exist."[11]

Hahn also explained why her entry in *Who's Who in America* is not exactly correct. "I was originally named 'Amelia' after one of my father's sisters: the twin who died young," she said. "The minute I was old enough to hear about it, I changed my name to the other twin's 'Emilie.' People called me 'Millie' anyway, so I changed that, too, and the spelling of 'Emilie' to 'Emily.' Why? Oh, girls always change their names. But I *still* don't like Amelia."[12]

It probably would not have mattered what name Emily Hahn was given, for Hannah nicknamed her "Mickey" because of her resemblance to a popular comic strip character of the day. Mickey Dooley, a matey Irish saloon keeper, was the creation of Chicago newspaperman Finley Peter Dunne. The Hahns had not one drop of Irish blood in their veins, but in Hannah's mind the nickname fit. From a young age, Mickey Hahn dreamed of one day becoming a sculptor, a scientist, or a naturalist, all of which were "unladylike" vocations.

Mickey's childhood was an idyllic one, filled with scenes that might have been snipped right out of the Norman Rockwell paintings.

Mickey would always recall her early years in St. Louis as "unfashionably happy." This was one aspect of her life she was obliged to accept and enjoy, even if she did not do so quietly.

2

St. Louis has long been known as the gateway to the West, yet the city is southern in its temperament, customs, and climate. The winters are cool, the summers, hot and humid. In Mickey's day, the schools closed whenever the thermometer hit ninety degrees Fahrenheit. The children would race home to cool off any way they could, often under a spray of water from a garden hose.

While the city's steamy weather wilts people, it is ideal for plants. Another St. Louis image that was etched into Mickey's memory was the lushness of the vegetation. "Foliage played a large part of my childish life," she recalled, "though it had at least as much to do with eating as with beauty in the eye of the beholder. I was always nibbling at flowers."[1]

Sometimes Hannah would pack up her three youngest children and take them on a summer holiday in the country. They traveled by train to Lake Mendota, in Madison, Wisconsin, or to a farm in Michigan. As they grew older, Helen, Dauphine, and Mickey were shipped off to summer camp on their own. Otherwise, they idled away the endless summer days rocking on the front porch swing, rambling around the neighborhood, or lolling about the house reading.

Wherever she was, whatever she was doing, until she was well into her teens, Mickey could be found clinging to her best friend: Teddy (named after President Roosevelt) was a miniature brown teddy bear that Mickey bought with her allowance when she was eleven. "Probably I wouldn't have been so wacky about him if I'd been permitted to keep live pets," she explained.[2] This love of animals would be a recurring theme throughout Mickey's life.

Like Mary's little lamb, Teddy followed his owner to school one day. Miniature bears were still something of a novelty, and so the grade six classmates made a great fuss. In an effort to restore order, the teacher snatched the bear away. Mickey panicked. Unable to decide whether to laugh or cry, what came from her mouth was a loud braying that startled everyone. Embarrassing though it may have been, the outcry evoked the desired result; the teacher immediately promised to return Teddy after school.

Mickey made clothes for her beloved furry friend, talked to him, drew pictures of him on her school books, and read him stories. Reading was a favorite pastime. Mickey's kid sister Dauphine recalled, "[Mickey] didn't like to play rough games. She'd disappear and read as much as she could."[3] Unfortunately, Teddy Roosevelt himself had something to say on the matter. "I wish to preach, not the doctrine of ignoble ease, but the doctrine of the strenuous life," he had proclaimed. Hannah Hahn and millions of other Americans of the day subscribed to the same muscular philosophy. She insisted her daughters spend their days playing in the fresh air. After all, too much reading ruined young eyes. Mickey, Dauphine, and Helen were restricted to just thirty minutes of pleasure reading each day, an hour once they got older.

This proved to be a particular hardship for Mickey. She was an indifferent student, and she admitted, "I was good in subjects I liked, lousy in others, such as French and Latin. I flunked each once."[4] Nevertheless, she was a voracious reader, having taught herself to sound out words when she was a toddler. Until she was three, Mickey had been slowed physically by a brace that she wore to compensate for the twisting of one of her legs during her breech birth—or so family legend had it. However, the presence of the brace also gave her an excuse to spend endless hours browsing through her father's library. She loved to thumb through the big *Webster's Dictionary* that was always open on a lectern in the parlor. Mickey fell in love with books; it was as simple as that. Her notion of luxury as a child was to be allowed to read at the table during meals, a pastime her parents strictly forbade.

Despite her general aversion to physical activity, Mickey was a self-described "natural wanderer." As she grew older and her reading skills improved, she roamed far and wide in the boundless universe of her imagination. Her companions and friends on these literary ramblings were such popular authors of the day as Dickens, Kipling, and Twain; she adored them all. Writing more than half a century later in her book *Times and Places*, she confided, "I found playing outdoors boring until I learned to hide books under the back porch or in a peach tree's cleft. After that, it was simply a matter of finding some spot out of sight where I could read in peace."[5]

• • •

"People were always telling us how lucky we were to be a big family," she wrote. "The world we grew up in was secure; our brother and sisters were always our champions. Though we might have our little spats, who didn't? In the end, the family was the important thing, cemented by love and loyalty. I have never doubted the fundamental truth of that concept, but I'm not so sure the spats were all that trivial."[6]

In later years, the three younger girls would remember how it was their mother who refereed family squabbles. It was also Hannah who raised them. What Mickey recalled best about her mother was her fiery temper. Hannah was "a door slammer" who was as quick with a slap on the backside when one was needed as she was with a hug. Once, after being spanked for some misdeed, a sobbing Mickey cautioned her mother, "You just wait until you're little and I'm big!"

It is unlikely that Hannah Hahn worried. She lost none of her feistiness as she grew older. During her working days, she had created a mild scandal in St. Louis by wearing bloomers as she rode her bicycle. Hence, Hannah was puzzled and somewhat disappointed when her own two youngest daughters, Mickey and Dauphine, refused to go to their public school in knickers. However, by the time the girls reached high school they were sufficiently rebellious to be attracted to the prospect of doing so.

To say their outfits attracted attention would be an understatement. The first morning they wore their knickers Mickey and Dauphine drew stares on the way to school and attracted the scorn of their teachers. As Mickey and Dauphine crossed the schoolyard on the way home, two newspaper photographers awaited them. A photo and an article dealing with "immodest attire" appeared in the next day's papers.

Hannah Hahn backed her daughters in their defiance. In fact, if they had wavered in their convictions, they would have faced the daunting prospect of explaining why to their mother, who delighted in the refusal of her offspring to back down from the fight.

By contrast, Isaac Hahn's presence in the household was muted. He trav-

A Hahn family portrait, circa 1917. Pictured are (back row, l–r) Helen, Rose, Mickey, (front row, l–r) Dauphine, Isaac, Dorothy, Hannah, and Mannel.
Courtesy Charless Hahn

eled a lot on sales trips, and his homecoming was usually an event. When Hannah knew Isaac was coming, she dispatched Helen, Mickey, and Dauphine to the streetcar stop to greet him. The three girls made a fuss as he got off, but Mickey's enthusiasm was mostly perfunctory. The truth was, she was frightened of her father. For one thing, he disliked the noise that the three young sisters were wont to make. For another, it was obvious to everyone that he played favorites. Pretty, red-haired Dot was his pride and joy. "I carried on . . . only because the others were doing it," Mickey admitted in *Times and Places*.[7] It was not until she became much older that Mickey really came to love and understand her father.

The sibling rivalry that was a constant underlying theme of life in the Hahn household goes a long way toward explaining the hows and whys of Emily Hahn's early life. Long after she had grown up and had left home, Mickey carried with her a burning desire to succeed and a nagging sense of insecurity. Her self-image was defined almost as strongly by who she was *not* as by who she was. Mickey would never forget how her parents treated her older siblings, Mannel, Rose, and Dot, as adults who were permitted to live their own lives. "Helen, Dauph(ine), and I were cut off . . . not by age, but by euphony, I suppose," Mickey once wrote. "We had our supper in the kitchen, while the three older ones dined [with their parents]. Helen longed to make that jump, and she did. Then she found out that she was bored stiff and wanted to come back. We didn't let her." [8]

All five of the Hahn girls were bright and attractive, but it was Helen who was graced with the kind of "knockout good looks" that set male hearts aflutter. Mickey one day chanced to overhear her parents discussing Helen's beauty. Physical appearance was not a measuring stick that Hannah and Isaac Hahn normally used to compare their daughters, and their offhand comments had a profound impact on Mickey. She had always felt superior to Helen, whose dark curly hair had to be painstakingly combed out and glossed each morning by "the upstairs girl." Now Mickey began to regard Helen's appearance with a mixture of envy and despair. She also began studying the illustrations in the fairy-tale books that Dot collected. What she saw distressed her. The fairy princesses bore a striking resemblance to Helen. "I didn't repine over my shortcomings or refuse to believe they existed; I conceded them," Mickey wrote. "If the world wanted graceful, blue-eyed princesses with curls, it would have to make out with Helen. I had *Webster*."[9]

While that was true enough, the dictionary's therapeutic powers proved limited. As the three younger Hahn sisters began dating, a spirited rivalry developed for clothes and for the boys they started bringing home for inspection. The Hahn household became a busy place.

Both Hannah and Isaac Hahn took a keen interest in meeting the young men their daughters dated. Since all visitors were considered "public property," the parents, the older sisters, and sometimes even big brother Mannel would "pounce," as Mickey put it, anytime a new "gentleman caller" appeared. "As soon as a stranger was led into the parlor—which is what we called our sitting room—the place got terribly crowded, because everybody piled in, curious and full of hospitality. En masse, the family took over, and it was just like a party."[10] Everyone in the Hahn household played the piano or violin, and of course Isaac loved to sing, so it was never long before passersby on Fountain Avenue would hear "Whispering Hope" or "Sweet and Low" wafting from the house as a family sing-along began.

Painfully aware of the hazards of bringing home for inspection any young man whom she favored, Mickey was determined to find a way around the ritual. Inevitably, her first date raised parental eyebrows. For one thing, it occurred during her sophomore year at high school, when she was just fifteen. For another, she ignored family protocol by announcing one Saturday evening that she was going to the movies with a boy named Charlie Waugh, who sometimes walked her partway home after school. Mickey recalls two things about her first date. One was how her older sisters lined up as she was leaving and chanted, "Be home early! Be home early!" The other was that she and Charlie talked mostly about books and poetry. By this point in her life, Mickey was growing more interested in literature, and the arts generally. "My writing just happened," she said, "and it was still very private."

On Saturday mornings, Mickey joined Helen in attending art classes at Washington University. Mickey sketched, painted, and sculpted. After class, she and Helen received extra guidance and encouragement from their sister-in-law. Nancy Coonsman Hahn was a noted sculptor who had married Mannel during the war. "Helen preferred to paint, but I would be a great animal sculptor, or a poet, or a violinist, or an exceedingly intellectual courtesan: the world was wide and lovely," Mickey wrote in her book *Kissing Cousins*. "And then we moved to Chicago."[11]

3

A LITTLE MORE THAN A CENTURY after its founding as the frontier outpost called Fort Dearborn, the city of Chicago was still hustling for respect. Chicago in the third decade of the new century bristled with ferocious, unbridled energy. The city of Al Capone was also the home of a world-renowned symphony and the site of the world's first skyscraper, built in 1885 by architect Frank Lloyd Wright. "I will" became the city's unofficial motto—or as newspaper columnist Mike Royko quipped: "I will, if I don't get caught."

All roads converged at Chicago. A steely spider's web of railway tracks that spanned the western half of the continent in the late nineteenth century terminated in the city's sprawling rail yards. Chicago's wharves, factories, and grain elevators hummed with activity. The South Side stockyards and slaughterhouses were the world's largest and busiest. Poet Carl Sandburg's "City of Big Shoulders" exerted a magnetic pull for people hungry to savor the fruits of the American dream; three out of every four residents were either foreign-born or first-generation Americans.

None of this escaped the attention of Isaac Hahn and his business partners at S. A. Ryder in St. Louis, three hundred miles to the south. Hoping to take advantage of "a golden opportunity," the company opened an office and warehouse in Chicago in 1920. When Isaac agreed to act as manager, he and Hannah sold their house in St. Louis and moved north. Isaac left for Chicago in January, leaving Hannah, Mickey, and Dauphine behind to finish out the school year. They lived for a few weeks in a hotel, then stayed with Mannel and his wife Nancy.

The Hahn's move to Chicago came as a jolt both to Mickey, who had just turned fifteen, and to Dauphine, now thirteen. Dot was away at college in Wisconsin; Mannel was married and working; Rose was studying psychiatric social work in Boston; and Helen was attending Smith College in Northampton, Massachusetts. Mickey and Dauphine had the family home to themselves, and they enjoyed being free of what Mickey termed "the crushing mass of sisters." For Mickey, who was finally starting to feel comfortable at Soldan High School, a move could not have come at a worse time. She had started making friends and dating. She was also becoming more intent on writing.

Mickey's literary interests led her to strike up a friendship with Ralph Crowley, a University of Wisconsin student who she met through her sister Dot. Although "The Kid," as he had dubbed himself, was a few years older than Mickey, the two of them had a lot in common. Ralph, too, had attended Soldan, spent summer vacations in Wisconsin, and loved books and writing. Mickey and Ralph began corresponding in the autumn of 1919. "Send me your story," he had urged in response to a query in one of Mickey's letters. "I'll send you some as I write them. (I've given myself the task of writing one each week.)"[1]

Mickey's surviving correspondence from this period indicates that by now she was asking family and friends to read and critique her writing. She had sent several humorous articles to Dr. Miner Evans, one of Rose's teachers in Boston. In a note dated December 7, 1919, Evans offered praise. "I have read [your] articles with interest and think they are very clever," he said.[2]

Such encouragement gave Mickey the confidence to continue her literary endeavors; she needed it. For all her feistiness and independence of spirit, at heart Mickey was no different from any other teenage girl. She lay awake nights wondering if she would ever grow up. She was acutely, painfully conscious of her appearance. She was also emotionally vulnerable and utterly lacking in self-confidence. "I was what they still call young for my age," she once recalled, "not boy-minded, and well padded with puppy fat."[3] Mickey was certain she could never be as pretty or as popular as her older sisters; visions of beautiful, popular Helen lingered in her mind's eye.

Many years later, Rose would remember Mickey as the "chubby and serious" girl in the family. That assessment was revealing, for it indicated how adept Mickey was at masking her emotions and her true temperament, even where her own family members were concerned. When she took pen in hand, or sat at her mother's old battered manual typewriter, the "chubby and serious" girl exhibited a precocious and deliciously naughty wit. Writing became an outlet for her adolescent emotions.

It is evident from reading the letters she received from friends and from her own writings many years later that the prospect of moving to Chicago left Mickey distraught and angry. Her reaction was as understandable as it was predictable. With its population of 2.7 million people—about four times that of St. Louis—Chicago was terrifyingly large, violent, dirty, and threatening. Initially, at least, Mickey did not want to live there. "I had never dreamed that it would be necessary to like that city, much less live in it," she wrote in *Kissing Cousins.* "We had always sniffed scornfully when we passed through Chicago on our way to or from the summer in Michigan. A horse-drawn cab took travelers from one railway station to the other, and above the smell of the horse and the straw you could often detect the stockyard stink. The downtown streets were big and noisy enough to terrify provincial children."[4]

However, there was another uncertainty in the move, one that went unarticulated for reasons that were unique to the Hahn household. Public schools in St. Louis were racially segregated, and whites did not socialize with "coloreds." Not so in Chicago. When Mickey's schoolmates learned she was moving there, some of them began teasing her. "Some of the children said, 'Mickey's going to live in Chicago, and she'll have to sit next to niggers,'" she remembered. "I cried."[5]

These concerns were not ones Mickey dared raise at home, where racism was not countenanced. By any measure, her parents' attitude toward blacks was more tolerant than that of their white neighbors in St. Louis. Being Jewish had sensitized both Hannah and Isaac to racism, and they refused to subscribe to the bigotry that was inherent in Southern racial mores of the day. For example, they did not hesitate to scold their children "for minding about Negroes," as Mickey said. "We weren't at all typical Southerners where race was concerned."[6]

Where most whites shunned blacks socially, the Hahns harbored no such reservations—although the opportunities for interaction in St. Louis were admittedly limited. Neither Mickey nor her siblings actually knew very many blacks. Not so in Chicago, where the Hahns' liberal views were put to the test. There had also been violent race riots in Chicago in the summer of 1919, during which hundreds had been injured and entire neighborhoods looted and burned. On one memorable occasion, Rose came home for Sunday dinner accompanied by a handsome young "colored" man. Jean Toomer was a poet who hailed from Washington, D.C. Born to a well-to-do family, his father had been a mulatto who "passed" for white. His dusky-skinned son struggled with his racial identity, describing himself as having been "born of chaos dressed in formal attire."[7] In 1923, Toomer's first book, a dazzling collection of verse entitled *Cane*,[8] would lead some people to compare him favorably to fellow poet and friend Sherwood Anderson, who praised the book. One black critic went so far as to praise Toomer as "a bright morning star of a new day of the race in literature."[9] Unfortunately, the author of *Cane* never lived up to his early potential. In large part that was because he could not deal with the ambiguities in his life nor accept the fact that in some people's eyes he was not white. Hannah and Isaac Hahn and other family members treated Rose's guest cordially. However, their black maid adamantly refused to wait on him. "That was a great scandal in our house," Mickey recalled.[10]

When school ended in June 1920, Mickey went with Mannel and his wife Nancy to New York, where Helen was living after having dropped out of college. Mickey then spent the rest of her vacation at a summer camp in Michigan. The holiday was anything but relaxing; Mickey's correspondence from this period reveals her continuing anguish over her family's move to Chicago. She poured out her resentments in letters to former boyfriends and classmates back in St. Louis.

Mickey was surprised to learn that she and Dauphine were not the only family members unhappy in Chicago. Isaac Hahn had not consulted with his wife when he leased a flat in a redbrick apartment building at 841 Lawrence Avenue, a busy commercial street on the city's north side. Hannah hated the place, and she let her husband know it. So the family moved at least twice during its first two years in Chicago, each time to a slightly more spacious quarters. The one constant in their lives was that Mickey and Dauphine attended Nicholas Senn High School.

Being in her junior year, Dauphine fit in more easily than Mickey, who was two years older and more set in her ways. Nonetheless, it was a struggle for both the Hahn girls to make new friends. Dating was a major concern. At age thirteen, Dauphine was too young to go out with boys in St. Louis. Things were different in Chicago. Isaac grumbled, and Hannah growled. Initially, Mickey looked on in awe. Then, she too began "going out." It all seemed so perfectly natural.

This Side of Paradise, a first novel by a young Princeton University dropout, had appeared in bookshops in April 1920. The book created an instant sensation because it chronicled the coming of age of the so-called Lost Generation—the disaffected and confused young people who came to adulthood in the years just after the First World War. "I read and loved it," Mickey recalled. "Here, I thought, was a writer who really knew the score!"[11]

Most adults were much less impressed. In fact, many older people were appalled by Fitzgerald's depiction of America's changing sexual and social mores. The same socioeconomic forces that had given rise to the movement for an end to discrimination against blacks had also fueled demands for gender equality. The suffragette campaign, in full swing at the time, culminated in the passage of the 19th Amendment by Congress in August 1920.

Hannah Hahn watched these developments with interest, for she was a keen supporter of the right of women to vote. As Mickey recalled, "I remember Daddy saying to Mother, 'But don't you realize that if you vote for *him*'—I don't recall who *him* was—'you are simply cancelling my vote?' Mother actually did realize it, and she liked the fact. She just smiled."[12]

• • •

The same people who railed against female suffrage were adamantly opposed to the demands of the new breed of free-thinking women known as "flappers." Flappers smoked in public. They drank alcohol, used lipstick and rouge, and flaunted their sexuality. What's more, they dared question the traditional "double standard."

Despite parental objections, many of Mickey's female classmates at Senn were aspiring flappers. In July 1920, a fashion writer for the *New York Times* observed that "the American woman . . . has lifted her skirts beyond any modest limitation." Mickey and Dauphine had caused a stir in St. Louis by wearing knickers to school; now, just a few years later, the sisters marveled at how some schoolgirls in Chicago wore skimpy black satin dresses, silk stockings rolled to the knee, and "painted their faces." Mickey's only bow to bohemianism was a beret she had taken to wearing ("Because artists wore berets, that's why!"). She remembered her mother musing aloud about why her daughters no longer brought any of their schoolmates home to visit, as they had in St. Louis. Mickey could only chuckle to herself, for she had no doubts where her peers went after classes. "It was my private opinion that they were out cracking safes somewhere or rolling around on the floor of some opium den," she wrote.[13]

Begrudgingly, Mickey began to fit in at Senn. She joined the staff of the student magazine, ate lunch at the same lunch counter where the "glamor boys and girls" hung out, and slowly made friends in what had seemed initially like a closed society. Still, she was not happy. She often spent her allowance on solitary rides on the city buses. What she liked most about her new city was Lake Michigan, with its sun-dappled expanses that stretched away to the eastern horizon. The autumn breezes blowing in off the lake were scented with a heady aroma of distant places. The lumbering lake freighters and passenger ships that came and went from the port of Chicago were a source of endless fascination, for they fed dreams of one day sailing away. "Even I could not claim that there was something like [the lake], but better, in St. Louis," Mickey wrote. "Even I could not imagine anything better to do at dusk than bowl along by Lake Michigan in the front seat of the top of a double-decker bus. The wind from the great sea was never quite like ordinary air. It had a delicious foreign smell. But the most enchanting thing about the lake was that you couldn't see to the other side."[14]

One Friday evening, she ran away from home after one of her frequent disagreements with Hannah. Mickey emptied out a box of coins that she had saved and went to spend the weekend at the home of a girlfriend. It was not until Saturday evening and after many anxious telephone calls that Hannah Hahn tracked down her wayward daughter. When she did, she was livid. "Come home right now!" she demanded. Mickey did. As she wrote many years later, "There was no reason *not* to go home. Mother was right about that. I had escaped. I'd had my wish."[15]

That one fleeting taste of freedom was the balm needed to soothe Mickey's restless spirit. After the experience of "running away," she grew more amenable to her new life in Chicago. For one thing, Mickey was reassured to learn that her English teacher, Miss Peterson, "knew a thing or two about poetry." For another, she discovered the joys of a downtown bookshop named Kroch's, which had a wider selection than anything she had ever seen before. Then there were other appealing aspects of life in Chicago: the Art Institute, the lakeshore, the awesome architecture, and the reassuring sense that Chicago was not some sleepy provincial backwater, but rather a place where important things were happening. "Little by little I gave in," Mickey wrote in *Kissing Cousins*. "Even if Rose hadn't come back home and met and married Mitchell Dawson, I would have got used to Chicago. Mitchell only speeded it up."[16]

• • •

When Rose Hahn returned home from the East after studying to be a social worker, she found work in north Chicago. Mickey could not help but notice that Rose and Hannah now quarreled more than ever. Both were headstrong, opinionated women. None of that mattered to Mickey. What was important was that her favorite sister had returned. Her mere presence was reassuring and soothing.

As Rose began to look up old friends from her university days, a steady stream of gentlemen callers appeared at the door of the Hahn's apartment. One of them was a thirty-year-old lawyer named Mitchell Dawson. What Mickey remembered most about him was his red hair and softspoken manner.

Born in Chicago on May 13, 1890, Mitchell was the third of the four sons of Eva (Manierre) and George Dawson. Mitchell's eldest brother, George Jr., had drowned at age seventeen, and his younger brother, Lovell, died in his early twenties of spinal meningitis. The two surviving Dawson boys achieved distinction in their chosen fields; Mitchell's older brother Manierre became a painter of some renown, and Mitchell became an attorney. He earned his B.A. at the University of Chicago in 1911 and a law degree two years later. He then went to work in his grandfather's thriving law office where he earned a comfortable living. But Mitchell had other ambitions. In his spare time he wrote poetry and prose for various literary journals.

Mitchell Dawson was also an avid reader. He brought the Hahns the latest books by popular American authors; Mickey adored him for it. She liked him, too, for his reaction on the day when he found her reading a copy of Nietzsche's *Thus Spake Zarathustra*. If Mitchell was surprised to find Mickey reading such difficult material, he did not show it. Nor did he laugh, as many adults might have. He asked Mickey if the book was "a good translation." Then he recommended that she look at Schopenhauer as an introduction to Nietzsche. "So I trotted downtown and bought Schopenhauer," Mickey recalled. "It was intoxicating being treated as an equal by such a man, and the delightful sensation was repeated over and over because he and Rose took to including me in their dates."[17]

Mickey and Mitchell became fast friends. It was not long before she was asking him to read what she was writing. He was eager to do so, for he had sensed her talent. "I once wrote a poem that went, 'People who can say things make me sick,'" Mickey remembered. "[Mitchell] read it and said, 'Well me too, and you're one of them!'"[18]

Mitchell and Rose encouraged Mickey's literary dreams. They took her to plays, concerts, and poetry readings. They also let her come along on visits with Mitchell's friends in the Chicago literary community. These friends included poets Marion Strobel, Glenway Wescott, and future Pulitzer Prize winner Carl Sandburg, who was in the early 1920s the unofficial poet laureate of the American Midwest. Like many people who met Sandburg, Mickey was mesmerized.

Beetle browed, with unruly thatches of white hair that hung down over his ears and collar, Sandburg was his own man. He usually wore a battered old baseball cap from his days as a semi-professional ballplayer. On his feet were a pair of half-laced, stub-toed shoes that had been out of style since long before the turn of the century. When he socialized or attended poetry readings, Sandburg took along his banjo or guitar, which he loved to strum as he crooned the American folk songs that he collected.

Like many others who met him, Mickey was puzzled by Sandburg's verse. "'Hog butcher of the world,' indeed," she mused, "What a peculiar way to write poetry! But I liked it."[19] Mickey also liked the giddy sense of freedom she got from being around Mitchell and his literary friends. Her life in Chicago no longer seemed so unbearable.

• • •

In the spring of 1923, Helen returned home from New York. Her reappearance upset the routine the Hahns had settled into. Helen was a presence to be reckoned with. "Talented as she was at bowling over adults, our young men didn't stand a chance. It was hell, but I would never admit that it was hell for *me*," Mickey wrote. "I would say indignantly, 'Dauph's so young, it isn't fair. A kid like that can't possibly hold her own against an older woman like Helen.'"[20]

Helen had no shortage of gentleman callers, which provided her younger sisters with a couple of unexpected benefits. For one, it brought a steady stream of promising young men to the door. Mickey would remember two of them well. One was an aspiring young actor named Melvyn Hesselberg. He went on to achieve great things on Broadway and in Hollywood as a dapper leading man named Melvyn Douglas. Mickey sometimes dated his younger brother Lemarr, who was one of her high-school classmates at Senn.

The other was an energetic *Chicago Daily News* reporter named John Gunther. Big, fair haired, and gregarious, he had been born in 1901 on Chicago's north side. Gunther approached courting with the same exuberance with which he approached all things in life. He announced that he planned to marry Helen. Although they dated seriously for about a year, she had already decided she had no interest in becoming his wife. In the fall of 1924, Helen broke the news. Gunther responded by running away to Europe. He was intent on becoming a famous foreign correspondent and then returning to claim Helen's hand. It was not to be; Helen was already married by 1936, when Gunther wrote an international best-seller entitled *Inside Europe*. That book, the first popular look at the European dictators who were edging the world toward war, became a best-seller on both sides of the Atlantic. The term "inside" subsequently became a part of the world's lexicon, and Gunther went on to write a series of *Inside* books. In the process, he earned what a writer for the *New Yorker* once described as an exalted place alongside Franklin D. Roosevelt and Charles Lindbergh, "one of the half dozen or so international celebrities of the day."[21]

Dauphine Hahn remembered how Gunther continued to call on the family whenever he was in Chicago. One New Year's Eve he came by and finding neither Helen nor Mickey at home, he invited Hannah out for a drink. "Daddy had been resting, and he came and asked me, 'Where is your mother?'" Dauphine recalled. "I told him John Gunther had come by and they'd gone out for a while. He looked at me and said, 'Let me hang onto you, baby, or he'll take you, too.'"[22]

4

As a typical fifteen-year-old when her family moved from St. Louis to Chicago in 1920, Mickey Hahn was groping for identity and despairing of ever growing up. Within a year, though, she had leaped headlong into adulthood. "Though that word [sex] was not permitted to be spoken in our house above a whisper, the awful fact of it pervaded the entire group," Mickey wrote.[1] Where matters of the heart were concerned, she had learned well the lessons that her older sister Helen had taught her. A steady stream of letters from lovesick admirers found its way to Mickey's mailbox.

No one was more surprised by this than Mickey, whose mental image of herself at age sixteen was of an earnest, plump young woman. Photos taken at the time suggest otherwise and offer compelling evidence why young men were draining their inkwells writing to her. These fading black-and-white images show that Mickey had inherited her mother's graceful good looks. They also document that the moon-faced schoolgirl from St. Louis had lost her girlish "puppy fat" and grown into an attractive young woman. In one striking head-and-shoulders photo, Mickey is stylishly dressed, her dark hair is cut in the kind of bob that was fashionable at the time, and there is an alluring delicacy to her features.

Despite her good looks, Mickey remained painfully self-conscious and bedeviled by self-doubt. Behind the air of defiance, hints of the uncertainties and despair that she often felt—and evidently shared with friends—punctuate the letters she received. Most of the time, Mickey was as taciturn as a sphinx. Only when she sat down at a typewriter was she at ease revealing herself. When she was not composing poems, articles, or short stories, Mickey wrote letters. "We all scribbled in my family," she once explained. "Writing was something I did as naturally as playing games, but I never really said to myself I'm going to be a writer."[2]

Mickey had an abundance of material to include in her letters. One evening, she accompanied Rose and Mitchell to a meeting of the Poetry Society. Afterward, as they stood at the bus stop, Mickey noticed that Rose and Mitchell were unusually passionate when they embraced and said good-night. Mickey was embarrassed, even disgusted, by this public display of affection on her sister's part. A few days later Mickey learned the reason for Rose's amorous behavior: she and Mitchell had been secretly married. They had spent their wedding night with Mickey at a poetry reading.

When the couple eventually broke the news to their families, most of the

Hahns were delighted, although they were taken aback by the brevity of the courtship. Mickey was confused and filled with dismay by the realization that her relationship with her favorite sister had been forever altered. In letters she wrote to friends, Mickey claimed that while she had come to like Mitchell very much, she was skeptical where marriage was concerned. That was probably true, for it was fashionable in bohemian circles to argue that monogamy and conjugal bliss were as hopelessly outdated as the horse and buggy.

As a young woman coming of age in the early 1920s, Mickey Hahn was well aware of the national debate about the morality of birth control and the future of the institution of marriage. Wedding bells, she concluded, were not in her own future. Outwardly, at least, Mickey maintained an attitude of cool cynicism, vowing never to follow her sister Rose to the altar. On the occasions when Mickey's fashionable cynicism slipped, she revealed hints that at heart she was no different from other young women her age: she was emotionally vulnerable and fearful of the world and her place in it. Mickey professed indifference to marriage while secretly dreading the possibility that no suitor would ever ask for her hand.

• • •

During her senior year at high school, Mickey announced that she intended to study art and become a sculptor, like her brother Mannel's wife, Nancy. Rose

Mickey as she looked as a high-school senior, circa 1921.
Emily Hahn Estate

and Mitchell supported her in these plans and argued on her behalf, but the Hahn elders had other ideas. Isaac and Hannah insisted that Mickey follow her sister Dorothy to the University of Wisconsin in Madison. That was easier said than done, for Mickey was an indifferent student.

Despite a recommendation from her high-school principal, Mickey had to write a series of last minute entrance examinations in order to qualify. This was even more arduous than it might otherwise have been, because Mickey neglected to provide the Wisconsin registrar with her mailing address. As a result, she did not receive notification until just nine days before the examinations were scheduled. Despite the handicap, Mickey scored well, and in late September 1922 she began first-year studies in Madison.

Mickey initially enrolled in a general arts program. That changed after she took a half course in geology to fulfill her science requirement. When Mickey did well, and after she chanced to hear a lecture on inorganic chemistry given by Professor Louis Kahlenberg, one of the more popular teachers on campus at the time, she decided to take another science course. In an article she wrote in 1946 for the *New Yorker*, Mickey recalled what happened next:

"When I tried to get into [Kahlenberg's] class, I ran into a trifling technical difficulty. Kahlenberg's course, the dean explained, though it exactly paralleled that of the Letters and Science brand of chemistry, was usually taken only by engineering students.

"Now, the dean may have fought with his wife that morning, or maybe he was worried about his bank account, or perhaps it was necessary that he say no once in a while, just to prove he was a dean. I'm sure that he never intended thus carelessly to mold my future life with one hasty word, but that is what he did. 'No,' said the dean rudely, and turned back to his desk.

"His manners hurt my feelings, but that alone wouldn't have done the mischief. Like many young people in my day, I was bristling with principles, eager to find abuses in the world and burning to do away with them. In five seconds I had condemned the dean's decision as an abuse."[3]

Mickey marched into the registrar's office, where she transferred into the College of Engineering and enrolled in the forbidden chemistry course. Her intention was to transfer back into the College of Letters and Science after completing this one course, and she probably would have done so had the engineers not upped the ante. So she decided to study mining engineering.

The University of Wisconsin had been coeducational for many years. Women studied medicine, agriculture, and the pure sciences. Engineering alone remained a males-only bastion; the mining engineering program, established in 1904, had never had a female enroll. Many of the faculty and students were stunned that a woman, a seventeen-year-old at that, had the audacity to challenge this tradition. What to do about it was the question. "To a man, they wore stiff corduroy trousers, and looked down haughtily on the other colleges, which they condemned as highbrow," Mickey wrote. "It was not in them to be diplomatic, and I maintain that they brought upon themselves what followed."[4]

First, the engineers appealed to the state legislature to expel the only female student in the College of Engineering. When their petition was denied—rightly so, for the school was a publicly funded institution with a coeducational nature that had been spelled out in its charter—they adopted a new approach, no less ill-conceived. Professor Shorey, the mining engineering teacher who was assigned to be Mickey's academic advisor, decided to "reason" with her. Shorey surely must have found blasting hard rock to be easier than dealing with the determined young woman who stood before him in his office for their first meeting.

Shorey explained there was no point in Mickey studying mining engineering because no mining company would ever hire her. When Mickey said she didn't care, Shorey lost his cool. "It's a waste of time, anyhow—your time and mine—because you won't get your degree," he blurted. When Mickey demanded to know why, Shorey got to the nub of it. "The female mind is incapable of grasping mechanics or higher mathematics or any of the fundamentals of mining taught in this course," he said.[5] Like many men of the day, he genuinely believed it.

If Shorey hoped such blunt talk would discourage Mickey, he was mistaken. His words were like gasoline poured on a burning ember. Mickey would forever recall that it was at that precise moment in her academic career that she abandoned any idea of becoming a sculptor. Instead, she would become a mining engineer—no matter who or what stood in her way. It had come down to a question of wills; whose was strongest, Mickey Hahn's or that of her teachers and the fifteen young men who were to be her classmates? There was never any doubt.

. . .

One afternoon, not long after the confrontation with Shorey, Mickey attended her first surveying class. As the professor scribbled instructions on the blackboard, it was obvious that a woman in the classroom was as unwelcome as water in a hiking boot; no one wanted or dared to make eye contact with her, let alone befriend her. When the students paired off for a term of fieldwork, no one chose Mickey as a partner. Not a word was spoken to her until a few minutes later, as seven pairs of surveying gear were being handed out in the equipment storeroom. Mickey, the fifteenth student, remained defiant. All eyes were on her as she walked over to claim a surveying level and a tripod for herself. The professor rubbed his chin and muttered that he was "sure" there was supposed to be an even number of students in the class. "I guess Bemis has dropped out," he sighed.

At that moment, as if appearing on cue, a tall, lanky young man entered the room. "Aw, I'll take her. What the hell!" he said.

Had Reginald Bemis not been late for class that day, he would have known he had just chosen his work partner for the entire term, and Mickey's experiences as a first-year engineering student might well have been much less successful. Fortunately for her, Bemis was a few years older than his classmates and had worked in open-pit mines before coming to school. He was already a proficient surveyor. Bemis was also stubborn enough not to allow himself to be intimidated by his classmates, regardless of whether or not he shared their antipathy toward the only female in the class. When the others took to calling him "Her Choice" (unbeknownst to Mickey until long afterward), Bemis slugged it out with the most vocal of his tormenters. And to spite them, he set about teaching Mickey all he knew about surveying, which was a lot. Although the Hahn-Bemis team achieved top marks in the class for their reports and field drawings, doing so was not easy.

Mickey related details of a typical geology field trip in one of her letters home to Dauphine. All mining and engineering students were required to go out and find various rock formations, old mines, and other topological features. The going was difficult in the rugged Wisconsin countryside. Naturally, it became a matter of pride for Mickey to take part and to go everywhere the guys went. "Twenny led our division," she told Daphine. "He doesn't walk as fast as Emmons, but he takes you up cliffs and hills that the devil himself would balk at. And I stuck it out because he was watching, only the road home was one big climb of about two miles, and that's worse than a hill. In climbing I almost stopped four times but didn't. Then all of a sudden my legs disobeyed and stopped. . . . Twenny just smiled, and I flashed past him and came second into the station. I don't know how. . . . Well, today I got flowers: violets, and a rose, and a card in strange writing. 'To a game sport,' and I don't know who it is."[6]

Mickey had resolved to follow the advice of a sympathetic geology professor who had told her that she should never look for special treatment, and should never complain, no matter how angry, upset, or tired she got. Mickey was determined to follow that advice. Displaying the patience of Job, she adhered doggedly to a self-imposed vow of silence. Most of the time. And she did whatever she could to fit in.

Mickey began wearing a pair of baggy khaki coveralls to classes. She smoked cigars and even tried chewing tobacco, which made her ill. She took her turn lugging the heavy surveyor's equipment on field trips and acquiesced when classmates began calling her Mickey. Her siblings, friends, and schoolmates had called her Emily or Millie, while her father's pet name for her was Bill, for reasons only he knew. "[Mickey] was a nursery nickname of mine which had been more or less forgotten by everyone but Mother," she wrote. "The engineers heard it and adopted it as a more acceptable, masculine-sounding name than my real one, which was hopelessly ladylike."[7]

Although Mickey was precluded from a few activities, including one summer-long expedition to some mines in Montana (where women were barred by law from working underground), inevitably she earned the begrudging respect of her classmates. In their eyes, she had become "one of the guys." Almost. That goes a long way toward explaining what happened on one of the few noteworthy occasions when Mickey's emotions overcame her stoicism. The incident occurred during her senior year, when she decided the time had come to attend a meeting of the males-only Geology Club. Ostensibly her purpose was to hear a visiting professor's lecture; in reality, she had resolved to show that she had as much right to be in the club as anyone.

The evening went smoothly until it came time for all newcomers to pay their membership dues. When the student who was collecting the money refused Mickey's dollar, she stepped outside to discuss the situation with the club president. Clyde Strachan was embarrassed, but adamant: the club was a social group, and as such it did not have to abide by the rules that had opened the engineering program to a woman. Mickey, frustrated and flush with rage, shocked even herself by breaking into tears. "I ran down the hall, completely routed," she wrote many years later. "This was disaster. I had committed the one unforgivable sin: I had been feminine. I wanted to kick myself for shame. I wanted to die."[8]

She need not have felt so sheepish. Her reaction to the snub caught the club members completely off guard. They had grown so used to Mickey enduring their taunts that to a man they were chagrined at the pettiness of what they had done. A few minutes later, Strachan sought out Mickey to share some good news with her. He found her sitting red eyed and dejected in a study room. Strachan announced that the members had reconsidered the matter and voted unanimously to accept her membership after all.

The Geology Club incident was a none-too-subtle reminder that try as she might, Mickey *was* different from her classmates. By day, she wore coveralls and studied mining engineering. By night and on weekends, she lived a conventional coed lifestyle. She roomed with a group of young women in one of the many large old student boardinghouses near the campus.

When she was not studying or chumming with girlfriends, Mickey wrote poetry and stories, some of which appeared in the student literary magazine. Two of her first published pieces, a poem and a literary sketch, appeared in June 1923 (under the byline "Emilie Hahn").The former was "Dust and Ashes," a poem that conveyed Mickey's dark, fatalistic view of life.

Sunrise and sunset are cries of fear.
At dawning all that goes to make the day,
All life beneath the clouds, is swayed in clear
And momentary passion. Then the near
Indifferent doom once more is swept away.
Once more the spotless color of the trees
Is bearable. Once more the trees forget,
And all their breathless tearing ecstasies
And all destroying half-discoveries
Must hide and wait until the sun has set.
At night, perhaps, they pray. But who can hear?
Sunrise and sunset are two cries of fear.

The other item, "Table Talk," was a short literary sketch that reads like the writing exercise that it no doubt was: "The low ceiling was roughly beamed, and the shadows of the room crept up to it only to be swallowed in its vague pattern of light and dark. Through the thick, sluggish atmosphere of rising cigarette-smoke and steady low talk, an iron lantern glowed red. . . ."[9]

Mickey's contributions to the student literary magazine further heightened her campus profile and her mystique. As a result, her social life was a busy one. "I must have been a pest as an undergraduate, restless and complaining most of the time," she remembers, "but there were fewer coeds than male students at the University of Wisconsin in those days, so I had dates anyway."[10]

Dorothy Raper, one of Mickey's housemates and closest friends at the time, confirmed that recollection. What she remembered best was that Mickey was the sort of person "everybody took to; she was attractive, and she knew how to talk to people."[11]

Mickey conveyed the details of her social life in letters she wrote to her sisters. The picture that emerges is one of a young woman who was enjoying campus life despite her struggles to prove she could hold her own in the College of Engineering. When she was not studying or writing, Mickey attended Saturday night dances and did all the silly things that were done by university students of the day. Much of it seems harmless by today's standards. In a letter to Dauphine, Mickey reported on a memorable date she had with a young man whose nickname was Squirrel. "I like Squirrel," she announced. "He and I went out in a canoe last night and smoked cigars and got sick."[12]

On another occasion, Mickey borrowed a girlfriend's party dress, pinned on as many fraternity pins as she could borrow, and rode on a throne in the engineering students' raucous St. Patrick's parade. "They put a sign on her throne that read 'Gold digger of 1923,' or whatever year it was," Dauphine recalled. "The engineers always had a fight with one of the other faculties, and this time the other students got all the rotten eggs they could find and pelted the engineers. There was an awful scuffle. Mickey felt very badly about the dress, even though she had it cleaned. But she was happy because she loved to stir things up."[13]

Mickey's irreverence came through at other times, too, and no doubt helps explain how she survived in such an antagonistic environment. In another letter to Dauphine, she related how, in English class, "The young man next to me corrected [me] when I wrote 'Freshman' on [a] card. 'Freshwoman', he suggested. 'Not *that* fresh,' I chirped, and he retired for a while. But we got chummy, and he seems quite clever. Still, I said no dates until I knew if I liked him and his eyes are pink."[14]

Mickey's popularity had been boosted by dint of her older sister Dorothy having attended Wisconsin a few years earler. In the time-honored Hahn tradition, when Mickey arrived on campus in the fall of 1922, she inherited one or two of her sister's boyfriends who had not graduated by the time that Dorothy went on to study journalism at the University of Missouri. It did not bother Mickey that these young men and many of the others on campus whom she dated were several years older than she was. "I just liked older fellows, and they seemed to like me," she explained with a shrug.[15]

One of these "older fellows" was a geology professor named Noel Stearn. He was in his early thirties when he met Mickey. Lean, fair-haired, and handsome, he set coed hearts aflutter. Noel was also an accomplished amateur poet, and he hit it off with Mitchell Dawson when Mickey introduced the two of them. When Mitchell learned that Noel had been unsuccessful in getting his poems published in *Poetry*, the influential journal started in Chicago in 1912 by Harriet Monroe, Mitchell suggested a new approach. He knew of Monroe's fascination with offbeat romantic characters. Mitchell advised Noel to visit her dressed in the clothes that he wore on geology field trips. The affectation worked. "After that, Noel had all sorts of poems published in *Poetry*," said Mickey. "You know, the interesting thing is that Mitchell never did think Noel's stuff was any good."[16]

Another of Mickey's boyfriends was Donald Parker Hanson, a Milwaukee native who was four years her senior. Helen and Mickey had actually met him several years earlier on a summer vacation in Wisconsin. Donald and Helen dated for a time, and when Mickey arrived in town, he asked her out. Donald liked to write, was fun to be around, and Mickey enjoyed his company. He had inherited his distinguished family's zest for life. He was a restless bundle of energy, possessed of a quick mind, a burning creativity, and a gregarious nature. Donald was also notoriously undisciplined, was not a very good student, and was in the habit of carrying a hip flask of bootleg liquor, despite Prohibition. Six months before Mickey's arrival in Madison, Donald and another student had been thrown into jail overnight and fined a total of $15 for drinking in public. The dean of men asked them to "withdraw," but Donald appealed and won a reprieve.

Unfortunately, student informers saw Donald imbibing at a fraternity party the following November. More seriously, they reported how he had "offered drink to young women." This time, there would be no more chances. Donald was banished from the university for good. Mickey shared the news in a letter to her sister Dorothy. "Don is expelled," she reported. "He is going to New York, and it will kill his mother. She is coming up (from Milwaukee). I am to talk to her. He cried. I was embarrassed."

Donald followed through on plans to go to New York when staying in Madison became impossible. "Everybody talked about going there," Mickey explained. "It was our Mecca."

He found work with an advertising agency before breaking into the magazine industry. He eventually carved out a career for himself, founding the mass circulation magazine *Woman's Day,* which was enormously popular with American women on the homefront during the Second World War. Mickey and Donald Hanson maintained their friendship long after he left Wisconsin, and they kept in touch until his death in 1978.

Mickey's own restlessness found an outlet in the nightly conversations she began having with her housemate, Dorothy Raper. ("That's the old English pronunciation for Roper—a maker of rope," she explained. "Some people wonder."[17]) A year older than Mickey and one year ahead of her in school, Dorothy was outgoing, energetic, and athletic; she was a competitive swimmer. Dorothy came from a prominent family in Cleveland, where her father was a well-known liberal newspaper columnist. Dorothy had been encouraged to think for herself, had done some traveling, and had even been to New York. She and Mickey shared an interest in geology. When Dorothy suggested they go on a trip to the Belgian Congo in Africa, Mickey was enthusiastic; one of her maternal cousins, Jean Schoen, had traveled to the Dark Continent on her own in 1924 and afterward had presented a series of public lectures. "Mickey and I chose a place called Lake Kivu to visit," Dorothy said. "I picked it out on a map because the water was supposedly too cold for crocodiles, and so we could swim there."[18]

As a warm-up to the African expedition, in the spring of 1924 Mickey and Dorothy decided to travel to New Mexico and California. After rejecting the idea of hitchhiking or riding the rails, Dorothy came up with a novel idea: they would go by car. "Roads generally were unpaved and risky, motels had not yet been invented, and most people who made long trips overland went by train," Mickey wrote many years later in *Times and Places.* "So I realized that [Dorothy] had suggested an adventure of respectable proportions. The West!"[19]

5

Mickey and Dorothy were giddy with excitement as they studied maps and made plans in the weeks before their departure from Madison. "My first trip West was a tremendous affair," Mickey later wrote. "I don't think I ever got so steamed up again, not even when I went to Africa or China."[1] Yet when the day of departure arrived, the great cross-country highway adventure the young women were so eagerly anticipating began somberly.

They loaded the car the morning of June 19, 1924, said a few hasty and tearful farewells, and then set off for Chicago. Here they were to leave some of their belongings with the Hahns and have lunch with Dorothy's parents, who were coming over from Cleveland for the occasion. Ultimately, Mickey and Dorothy planned to visit Dorothy's uncle in Albuquerque, New Mexico, and then to motor to Los Angeles before returning home.

Now, with their suitcases packed, the wind whipping their hair, and the car puttering away beneath them, the prospect of the journey suddenly seemed daunting. Mickey and Dorothy had dubbed their vehicle "O-O" for two reasons: its license number was 94005, and each time the engine coughed or emitted one of its other ominous sounds, they muttered in unison, "Oh oh!" There was no turning back once O-O was on the road, no matter what sober second thoughts they may have had.

Even on today's highways, the 2,400-mile cross-country drive from Wisconsin to California is a major undertaking. In 1924, the same trip posed a much bigger challenge, physically and mentally. Almost all of the 2.9 million miles of paved highways in the continental United States lay east of the Mississippi. To the west, conditions were often difficult and rude. Only a generation earlier, this whole area had been popularly known as the "American frontier." Not a lot had changed in the years since. Many roads were little more than dirt pathways, sunbaked in summer, ankle-deep in mud when it rained, and virtually impassable in winter. Roadside accommodation was scarce. Gas stations were also few and far between, and the likelihood of finding emergency repairs or tow trucks was slim. Were Mickey and Dorothy worried about the hazards of the trip? "I guess," Mickey recalled. "But we didn't know any better. Like every other car owner, I took it for granted that sometimes you had to push."[2]

A "proper" young lady did not go driving. Nor did she motor across the country without her husband or a parent accompanying her. Therefore, quite apart from all of the other challenges Mickey and Dorothy faced in making their trip, the matter of their gender was also a key concern. But they were adamant, so Dorothy's father bought them a shiny new black Model T Ford for their trip. It cost $290. "[Dorothy's] parents bore the brunt of its cost," Mickey remembered in *Times and Places,* "pointing out to my parents by letter that she was their only child, whereas I was one of six."[3]

Isaac and Hannah Hahn were understandably not enthusiastic about Mickey's plans. However, nothing she did surprised them anymore, and they knew they had little say in the matter. They also knew that unlike her classmates (most of whom had summer jobs in mining), Mickey faced the embarrassing prospect of finding another kind of work or of spending three idle months at home in Chicago. Neither alternative was appealing, so Hannah and Isaac agreed to help Mickey pay her share of the trip expenses.

They also offered her some introductory letters. Isaac, who knew many people across the West from his days as a traveling salesman, wrote to relatives, friends, and customers along the route Mickey and Dorothy had mapped out. "Of course, I just mention the different ones you can see in case you might *accidentally* need advice or help," he explained in a letter mailed to Mickey after she had left on the trip.[4]

While Mickey welcomed the paternal assistance—and actually called on some people whom Isaac suggested—she and Dorothy had resolved to place their faith in their wits and in the reliability of their Model T. The first thing they did upon taking delivery of the car was run it over to a garage for what Mickey termed "a major operation." The two-person bench seat was customized to fold down flat and to serve as a makeshift bed. "If we kept our feet still, so as not to kick the steering wheel or the other controls, the car was long enough," Mickey wrote. "Privacy was to be afforded by the car's rain curtains, of cloth and isinglass, and we bought a mosquito net that fitted nicely over the entire equipage."[5]

In preparation for the trip, the women had purchased some durable blue cotton shirts and khaki trousers. Dorothy had her hair buzzed short and styled into what passed for sideburns. In a peaked cap, from a distance she looked like a man. Dorothy and Mickey knew that two women driving alone risked attracting attention, mostly of the unwelcome variety. As a further precaution, Dorothy stowed a small-caliber handgun in the space under the driver's seat. Neither young woman knew much about the weapon, but its mere presence was a source of reassurance to them and to their worried families.

"For the first hour or so [after leaving Madison] we were very quiet," Dorothy noted in the journal she and Mickey kept for part of the trip. "I think that we were paying our debt of homesickness and doubt and thoughtfulness all at once, so that we could be through with it. . . . Soon, of course, we started to giggle."[6]

After spending a night with the Hahns in Chicago, Mickey and Dorothy set off for St. Louis on Sunday, June 22, 1924. Their progress was swift that first morning, despite rain squalls. The highway was still paved, except for the main streets in many small towns through which they passed. In one such town "completely lined with fine black mud," Mickey raced along without braking. O-O "whirled around until it sank to rest in a puddle. Several little boys shouted: 'Slow down! You'll get yours!'"[7]

Their prophecy came true, and sooner rather than later. That same afternoon, less than a hundred miles out of Chicago, Mickey and Dorothy ran into a violent thunderstorm. It soaked them, O-O, and all their belongings. Faced with the prospect of sleeping in a wet vehicle in soggy clothes, they stopped that first night on the road at an overnight cabin in Bloomington, Illinois. It was an ignominious beginning to their great adventure, but there was at least one positive aspect to the experience: everyone they met seemed genuinely interested in knowing more about their trip.

By July 2, after ten hard, dusty days on the road, the seemingly endless expanses of the prairies were finally behind them. Apart from a few minor breakdowns and some scares from menacing-looking migrant farmworkers they encountered in campgrounds along the way, Mickey and Dorothy were motoring through Colorado and northern New Mexico's scenic Capulin Mountains. "The change of landscape that greeted us . . . was magically sudden," Mickey wrote years later in *Times and Places.* "It was like straying off one colored postcard onto another. Here, with no gentle transition, was the true West, with mountain ranges trailing their long blue-and-purple skirts, right-angled mesas standing sharply against the great sky, and under our wheels arid, yellow ground that bristled here and there with grudging greyish shrubs. Tumbleweed moved with us, the tangled combings of a giant caught in the wind."[8]

They celebrated the July 4th holiday in Santa Fe, the state capital of New Mexico. In a letter to her parents, Mickey reported that the "streets are about two yards wide, and everybody is drunk." The cowboys, she noted, were all remarkably good looking "until they take off their hats."[9]

Mickey and Dorothy arrived at the door of Dorothy's uncle in Albuquerque on July 6, having completed the 1,600-mile drive from Madison in just seventeen days. All things considered, everything had gone surprisingly smoothly. Writing many years later in *Times and Places*, Mickey mused, "I must be wrong to recall the trip as long. . . . Nevertheless, that is the impression I have kept."[10]

Dorothy's uncle Howard, a prominent radiodontist and part-time author, was well connected socially in Albuquerque. The six days Mickey and Dorothy spent in town were a whirl of parties, dinners, dances, and other happy social events. The Rapers took their young guests on a tour of the area; they visited a traditional adobe Indian village and were introduced around the town as celebrities. A journalist friend of the Rapers even included mention of Mickey and Dorothy in the social notes column of the *Albuquerque Morning Journal*; the fact they had "driven overland from Madison" on their own was deemed newsworthy. "Several delightful affairs have been planned for their entertainment during their brief visit in Albuquerque," the *Journal* article reported.[11]

Refreshed and renewed, Mickey and Dorothy left Albuquerque for Los Angeles on July 11. Along the way, they visited the Petrified Forest and the Grand Canyon and crossed a worrisome 150-mile expanse of searing desert. Mickey confided in a letter to her parents that after all this California was an anticlimax; they had fallen in love with the Southwest, and after three weeks on the road, Dorothy was growing homesick.

Back in Albuquerque again on July 24, Mickey wrote her parents a long letter in which she catalogued O-O's growing list of mechanical ailments. "[The car] has been acting funny at last," she wrote. "She developed a choke or a jerk yesterday on a hill, nothing to worry about, but she wasn't the same little car that used to leap so bravely at a touch. So we took her to a garage. The man filed the points on the coils, greased the timer, changed the spark plugs, and told us his life's history, and charged us too much."[12] Fifteen minutes after leaving the garage, they had a flat tire. It was becoming apparent to Mickey and Dorothy that it was time to head for home.

Their return trip to Chicago retraced the route they had driven a few weeks earlier. This time, it was hard, steady, but smooth, driving. There were few sight-seeing stops, for both of them were impatient to get back. Dorothy had broken a tooth and needed to visit her dentist, and she longed to see her family and her boyfriend. Mickey was impatient to complete her studies and find a career.

"My parents complained that I was never the same after that summer in the Model T, and no doubt they were right," she wrote in *Times and Places*. "I was restless and discontented at home, and, as they said, anything served as an excuse to get away anywhere, even if it was only a weekend in Libertyville [Illinois] or Milwaukee. But now that I think it over, I don't think it was fair to blame [O-O]. It wasn't the car that did it."[13]

The essence of "it" was a hunger to see and experience whatever it was that lay beyond the horizon. When Mickey was a little girl growing up in St. Louis, "it" had been a curiosity to learn where Daddy traveled on his western sales trips. In Chicago, "it" had been a curiosity to follow the steamboats that sailed off into the vastness of Lake Michigan. On the trip west with Dorothy, "it" had been an itch to learn what lay around that next bend in the road, or over that next hill.

• • •

Mickey's final two years at the College of Engineering at the University of Wisconsin in Madison passed quickly, almost quietly. By the third year, many of her engineering classmates had come to respect her gritty perseverance. Most, if not all, begrudgingly accepted that Mickey would not and *could* not be forced to quit. Not that it mattered anyway, for to a man they shared the opinion of Mickey's academic advisor. Professor Shorey had chided her, arguing that even if she proved herself to be the exception to the "rule" that a woman could not grasp the essentials of engineering, no mining company would ever hire her. Initially, at least, it seemed he was right, although not for the reasons he had anticipated.

The mining industry is cyclical, and 1926 was one of its lows; the job market for mining engineers was bleak. During her final year, Mickey sent off dozens of unsuccessful job applications. She consoled herself by concentrating on her studies, dating several of the many young men who pursued her, and daydreaming of the distant places she would visit once she had earned her degree. Mickey's fantasies were fueled by the vague plans that she and Dorothy Raper had made to visit Lake Kivu in Africa and by the encouraging letters she received from her old friend John Gunther.

Mickey also had no shortage of gentlemen callers. The most persistent was Noel Stearn, who made no secret of his intention to win Mickey's heart. They had dated for two years in Madison before Noel took a job with a mining company in early 1924. He had continued writing to her as he traveled up and down the West Coast and into Mexico and sent her copies of the poems and stories he was writing. The introductions that Mitchell Dawson had given Noel opened doors for his verse at various literary magazines, and with Mickey's help he began selling stories to a men's magazine called *Adventure*.

Noel was jealous and demanded that Mickey stop seeing other men. She refused. Her emotions were unsettled, and she was uncertain of whom, if anyone, she really loved. While the prospect of marriage appealed to her vanity, she really had no intention of settling into a safe, conventional life as a wife and mother. There was too much else Mickey wanted to do and see. Even if she did not find work as a mining engineer, her prospects seemed as varied as they were intriguing.

Mickey contemplated continuing her education, either at the University of Wisconsin or at Bryn Mawr College in Pennsylvania, where she had applied and been accepted into a graduate program in English literature; she had proved her point at Wisconsin and was ready to study or work at something other than engineering. Helen, Donald Hanson, and other friends were living and working in New York and urging Mickey to join them and look for work there.

Travel abroad was another possibility. Even after Dorothy announced plans to find a job and get married, Mickey still dreamed of visiting Lake Kivu on the border of Uganda and the Belgian Congo. She was convinced she could make the trip to Africa on her own and could do so cheaply. Her family and friends said she was crazy. Maybe so, she said, but what did it matter? She would go mad if she did not go somewhere.

Paris was another possibility. Mickey heard the siren call of the city where F. Scott Fitzgerald, Ernest Hemingway, Gertrude Stein, and Pablo Picasso were living gloriously bohemian lives. John Gunther was there, too, working in the *Chicago Daily News*'s bureau. He had vowed to help Mickey find a job as a newspaper reporter. This was the first time that *anyone* had ever suggested she write for a living. Mickey did not yet consider the idea seriously. "I would have liked [to do so]," she recalled, "but it didn't seem possible to me at that time."[14]

Still another possibility was returning home to live with her family in Chicago. Of all her choices, this would have been the easiest and most conventional had Mickey's temperament been different. "We all knew that you didn't say anything to [her] about what you thought she should do," Dauphine explained.[15] The reality was that Mickey and her parents disagreed about *everything*. Hannah was as headstrong and opinionated as ever, and Isaac's old-fashioned notions clashed with Mickey's sense of what a young woman with a college education could and should do with her life. Her fondness for smoking "stovepipes" (cigars), a habit she had acquired at Madison, and her footloose ways especially troubled her parents.

While Mickey was away at university, Hannah and Isaac had reluctantly adopted a laissez faire attitude, accepting the realization that it was fruitless to argue with their daughter. That they did so was as much a matter of necessity as of prudence. Now in his late sixties, Isaac was in agony with the diabetes that ran in his family. In the summer of 1925 his feet were so tender that he could not walk without canes. Isaac would be hobbled the rest of his life. "[Daddy] was an invalid . . . and spent his days on the sofa, with the radio turned on," Mickey wrote in her 1958 book *Kissing Cousins*. "He liked company, which was fortunate, because he got plenty of it."[16]

For all their differences, what is apparent from the correspondence between Mickey and her parents was the love and concern that they felt for her. Both Hannah and Isaac managed to keep things in perspective and to maintain a sense of humor. At one point in June 1926, Isaac wrote to tell Mickey he had received a letter from her and was reassured "to know that you still like me even if we are related."[17]

As graduation day approached, Mickey continued to weigh her options. Who can say what might have been had she married, continued her education, gone abroad, or gone to New York? Mickey's decision was made for her the morning a letter arrived in her mailbox. Many of her classmates and professors were shocked and outraged—not to mention embarrassed. Mickey was ecstatic. The letter contained a job offer from a mining company in St. Louis. She was going to work as a mining engineer, after all.

6

No one was more surprised than Mickey Hahn when she received a job offer from Penzoil Company in St. Louis in the spring of 1926. But when Mickey's brother Mannel "made inquiries" about Penzoil, he concluded, "they are a false concern," as Helen informed Mickey.[1] For that reason and because she shared her classmates' snobbishness toward oil geology, which was not considered work for a *real* geologist, Mickey did not pursue the Penzoil job offer when something else turned up.

A letter from McBride Incorporated, a St. Louis–based lead and zinc mining company, brought a second job offer. This vindicated Mickey's refusal to drop out of the engineering college despite all of the hostility she had endured and her own family's skepticism. It now seemed that she was destined to have the proverbial last laugh after all. "It was intoxicating to feel that I would go home this time with my status improved, and I must have strutted around quite a lot when I got there, between bouts of packing for St. Louis," Mickey wrote in *Times and Places.*[2]

For all her feistiness and bravado, Mickey doubted that she really wanted to work in mining, but she was too proud to admit it. Friends sensed her uncertainty, for they saw her unhappiness about leaving Madison. But there was no turning back. Mickey's college days were done. She started work in St. Louis as planned in mid-June. True to her word, she found a furnished room, not far from the neighborhood where she had grown up. Within a matter of weeks, she had moved into a small walk-up apartment that she shared with another young female geologist named Gertrude Bissell, who also had been hired by McBride. Although Mickey's domestic tendencies were weak—she freely admitted that she loathed housework—she agreed to do the cleaning and dishwashing if Gertrude cooked.

It did not take long for the two women to realize that they had little in common. Yet they became friends; Mickey needed to confide in someone how miserable she was in her job and in her life generally. "Looking back, I can't understand why I was so sure that working [at McBride Incorporated] would afford me so much bliss," Mickey wrote in *Times and Places.* "I must have envisioned the place as a super-laboratory where I would be able to work at research the rest of my life. . . . Instead of a place at a table full of retorts and Bunsen burners, I was put at an ordinary green metal desk that stood in an ordinary office."[3] To make matters worse, Mickey discovered the company had abandoned zinc and lead mining to concentrate on oil exploration in the U.S. Southwest.

As they sipped glasses of homemade gin (for Prohibition remained in effect), Mickey and Gertrude often talked late into the night. Mickey revealed how discontented she was with her nine-to-five routine, especially after she learned the company was paying her less than her male colleagues. Mickey complained too about not being allowed to go on geological explorations; the company's new surveyor was one of Mickey's classmates from Wisconsin. He took great delight in reminding her over and over, "We told you so!" His jibes were like salt in a wound, and Mickey seethed.

Her aggravation underscored the cause of Mickey's rancor: she hated her boss, Mr. Mylius. He was, she told Gertrude, "an exploiter of science and a sweater of female labor."[4] Gertrude listened calmly to all of this and a lot more, seldom offering any comment of her own.

Mickey's growing frustration was echoed in a poem that she wrote about her first job. More than seventy years later, she could still recall and recite it verbatim. "I have an extraordinary memory for things that do not matter," she quipped. The poem went:

At the twelve o'clock whistle, I went out to eat.
I had a brown handbag, slippers on my feet.
A silly big hat, and a silly big coat
And a very silly muffler wrapped 'round my throat.
I looked in a mirror that hung in a shop
And said to myself, 'I'm going to stop.'
I went very fast, and I went quite far.
I was nearly run over by a yellow street car.
Everybody yelled at me, 'Get off the track!'
So I ate a cheese sandwich, and I never went back.[5]

The whimsical tone of those lines belied Mickey's desperate unhappiness. She grew increasingly depressed at the prospect of spending the rest of her life in St. Louis, getting up at the same time each morning, taking the same streetcar to the same office, and doing the same job day after day, week after week, year after year. Mickey felt trapped; she was twenty-five years old, college educated, attractive, talented, and ambitious. She had the terrible feeling life was passing her by.

Noel Stearn urged her to "go somewhere," and offered her a loan of $500 to help.[6] The problem was to decide where to go. On visits home, her mother became exasperated whenever Mickey tried to explain her uncertainties. "But what *is* it that you want?" Hannah demanded. At this point, Mickey had to admit that even she did not know. And it was gnawing at her.

Mickey's restlessness was accentuated by the letters she received from various friends and relatives. Her brother Mannel was visiting South America. Noel was traveling throughout the western United States, Canada, and Mexico. John Gunther was roaming the Middle East on behalf of the *Chicago Daily News,* and he continued to urge Mickey to move to Paris. Then there were the letters from Dorothy Raper.

After graduating, Dorothy had broken up with her boyfriend and gone to Santa Fe. Here she found work with the Fred Harvey tour guide company. "I don't suppose you'd consider coming out here and working with me," she wrote. "You're doing so well in mining that you're probably happy where you are."[7] Reading Dorothy's words was torture, but Mickey still refused to admit she had erred in going to work at McBride. As she had done at the College of Engineering, she tried to tough it out by compartmentalizing her life. She refused to let work intrude on her private life. Mickey spent her spare time reading, writing poetry and short stories—none of which were published—and fantasizing about trips to faraway places.

Mickey's roommate Gertrude, who was cordial toward Mickey's other friends, always seemed to have another date whenever they invited her to join them. She had her own social life, which was understandable given that she was "very pretty in a blond, blue-eyed way," as Mickey put it.[8] What was puzzling was that Gertrude never talked about where she went or whom she was dating. At first, Mickey thought nothing of it, just as she thought nothing of Gertrude's silence whenever work-related topics came up during their gin-fueled late-night chats. That all changed abruptly one day in early May 1927, when Mickey chanced to overhear a conversation at the office between Gertrude and the boss.

Mylius made a passing reference to "our discussion last night." That otherwise innocuous remark might have gone unnoticed if not for the sidelong glance Gertrude shot Mickey. In that instant, the light clicked on in Mickey's brain. Instantly, it became clear why Gertrude had received two pay raises in her first few months on the job, while Mickey was still struggling on her starting salary. It also became clear why Gertrude was always "busy" whenever Mickey and her gentlemen friends had asked her out. Gertrude was dating Mylius. Mickey wondered how much of what she had told her roommate had been relayed to the boss as pillow talk. Her anger quickly gave way to indifference. "Anyway, what did I care?" Mickey later wrote. "I repeated this to myself, over and over. Angrily, I said to myself, 'You listen to office gossip, and suddenly you're in the midst of horrid intrigues. This is what comes of letting life break in.' "[9]

The following Saturday, Mickey and two male friends who worked as reporters at the *St. Louis Post-Dispatch* filled up on gin and went out for dinner;

they did not ask Gertrude to join them. As they listened to the band and sipped the "near-beer concoction" the restaurant sold, Mickey's mind began to drift. Her thoughts were interrupted by a lively discussion her companions were having about someone named Charles Lindbergh. The name meant nothing to Mickey, who had no time to read the newspaper. Her companions informed her Lindbergh was trying to become the first man to fly across the Atlantic Ocean in a single-engine airplane. It was only when one of them mentioned that the daredevil flyer had studied engineering at the University of Wisconsin that Mickey sat up and took notice.

The eyes of America were on the twenty-five-year-old Lindbergh as he took off from Roosevelt Field, on Long Island, New York, early on the morning of May 20, 1927. The next evening, as Mickey and her companions debated Lindbergh's chances of survival, he was still in the air, alone in the darkness somewhere over the vastness of the North Atlantic. The more that Mickey heard about this, the more intrigued she became, particularly as she learned that Lindbergh, too, had rebelled against the system at the University of Wisconsin College of Engineering. He had stubbornly refused to write up the results of the same physics lab experiments as his classmates, arguing that to do so was a waste of time. When his professors insisted he comply, Lindbergh quit. His decisiveness and his determination to live life on his own terms struck a responsive chord with Mickey. In that instant, Charles Lindbergh became her hero—not because of his bravery in the air, but rather because he had the courage to shun the very system she had fought so hard to become part of. Her own victory suddenly struck her as hollow.

That night, Mickey went to bed dreaming of long processions of young geologists marching past her four abreast. The searing look of contempt one of them shot her left her feeling shaken and ashamed. When she awoke early the next morning, she realized it was Sunday, May 22. As she slept, Mickey had come to an important decision in her own life: if Lindbergh had made it safely to Paris, she would quit her job. If he was lost at sea, she would tough it out.

With tears streaming down her face, Mickey dressed and then raced down to the corner drugstore to buy a newspaper. The front-page headline proclaimed: "Lindbergh Does It!" Mickey read how the aviator had landed safely at Paris's Le Bourget Airport the previous night, May 21, 1927. Lindbergh had flown 5,800 kilometers—3,600 miles—in thirty-three and a half hours in his fragile single-engine plane, the *Spirit of St. Louis.* (Surely the name was symbolic to Mickey!) It was a feat of unprecedented derring-do.

As she read the newspaper that bright Sunday morning, Mickey Hahn cried like a baby. She resolved then and there to quit her job. Like Charles Lindbergh, she would soar above the crowd in pursuit of her dreams, the consequences be damned.

• • •

Isaac and Hannah Hahn were bewildered by these developments, especially by the news that their daughter was going to New Mexico to work part-time for the summer as a Fred Harvey tour guide; Dorothy Raper had gotten her the job. What disturbed the Hahns most of all was that Mickey seemed intent on wasting all she had learned in four years of college; she was leaving a good job to work at what they regarded as menial labor.

In the days before trains had dining cars, an entrepreneur named Fred Harvey had established a chain of restaurants in railway stations across the country. He made a fortune out of his monopoly, and his female employees—Harvey Girls, as they were called—were turn-of-the-century versions of the 1990s "Hooters girls," chosen for their comeliness as much as for their waitressing skills. For that reason, the stay-at-home spouses of the traveling salesmen, who made up a sizeable portion of the eateries' clientele, viewed Harvey Girls with a mixture of suspicion and scorn.

By 1927, Fred Harvey was dead and so were his restaurants. They were doomed once the railways saw there was big money to be made in having dining facilities aboard trains. Harvey's heirs continued trading on the reputation his restaurants had enjoyed, setting up a tour business in New Mexico. There were no trains to Santa Fe, which is located in the Sangre de Cristo Mountains. The tracks ended fifty miles to the east at Las Vegas—the New Mexico Las Vegas, *not* Nevada's—and seventy-five miles southwest at Albuquerque. The Harvey company tour guides met trains at both stations, and buses carried tourists on the so-called Santa Fe Detour. These low-cost trips proved so popular that Harvey began offering private tours farther afield. This necessitated hiring new staff.

Isaac Hahn knew all about Harvey Girls. He had ridden the railways in his days as a traveling salesman. "To think that you're going to be a Harvey Girl!" he had quipped in a letter to Mickey. "You've heard Fred Harvey's last words, haven't you? 'Slice the ham thinner, boys!'"[10]

Mickey was not waiting on tables, but Isaac could not resist the chance to poke fun. Hannah was less good-natured. She began to worry after Mickey wrote with news that someone in the Harvey Girls' Santa Fe dormitory had stolen $60 she had brought with her from St. Louis. Money had become a major concern at home after the bookkeeper at S. A. Ryder Company, the business in which Isaac was a partner, embezzled $16,000 to cover some gambling debts. With Mickey temporarily broke, Hannah fretted about what would happen if her daughter needed money for an appendix operation, or some other emergency. Mickey made light of her mother's fears. "Why should

I have a faulty appendix, for goodness sake?" she scoffed. "Only other people have operations."[11]

Mickey could not have been happier in Santa Fe. Initially, she had been taken aback to discover she was obliged to undergo a training course and to don the uniform of the Harvey Girls: a khaki skirt, a baggy velveteen blouse, a wide silver belt, and a Stetson cowboy hat. Mickey enjoyed the lectures on local history and archeology, and she did not mind wearing the outfit. Nor did she mind being paid just $6 per day on a part-time basis; in a good week, she would have six days of work. If she met a group of tourists at the train station in Las Vegas, she accompanied them on a dusty three-day excursion to Albuquerque. There she met another train coming from the other direction, and she would then retrace her route with this new group. Mickey showed the "dudes" the local sites, took them to nearby Indian villages, accompanied them on trail rides, and gave them a taste of the romance of "the old West." Mickey loved every aspect of this demanding work—meeting people, traveling, horseback riding, and being free to come and go with no time clock to punch.

She was also intrigued by Santa Fe. The town was rough-and-tumble by Midwestern standards. However, as the state capital and a burgeoning artists' colony, it served to moderate the frontier influences. Visitors came from all over the world to savor the area's natural beauty, history, and climate.

Mickey found Santa Fe exhilarating. Like many people here, she played as hard as she worked. Mickey joined the local amateur theater group, having discovered that being on a stage provided her with an opportunity to indulge her innate exhibitionism. Mickey's flair for the dramatic landed her a lead role in a play called *Down the Black Canyon*. The critic for the *Santa Fe New Mexican* newspaper hailed the production and Mickey's role in it. "She was a charming heroine," the critic enthused. "When she wept for her sweetie there was not a dry eye in the house, and groans of sympathetic English were heard in the audience, which was prodigal in appreciation of her splendid acting."[12]

Summer being high season, Santa Fe was a whirl of parties, dances, and other social events. Mickey attended them all. "I simply never got tired," she wrote in *Times and Places*, "even when the party went on all night, as Santa Fe hijinks were apt to do. It was all right with me whether or not I got a good night's sleep."[13]

Drinking was an integral part of the Santa Fe lifestyle, despite Prohibition. Growing up, Mickey had never been much of a drinker until she began work in St. Louis. There she had discovered hootch—the homemade gin she and Gertrude Bissell concocted in their bathtub. In Santa Fe, everybody drank. It was part of the casual, carefree lifestyle, and Mickey joined in. She acquired a taste for tequila and corn liquor. The former was downed with a pinch of salt before and followed by a bite of lemon; the latter was diluted with Coca-Cola or chased with beer. Mickey drank both mixtures, usually in combination. Miraculously, the term "hangover" was not part of her vocabulary. Mickey found that she could drink, ride a horse, and smoke cigars like "one of the guys."

These talents came in handy, for like many western towns in 1927, Santa Fe was a man's world. There were many more bachelors than single women; cowboys were as plentiful as sagebrush, and equally restless. Judging by her letters home, many a wistful male was frustrated by his inability to break Mickey's independent spirit or to corral her heart. Most of the men she met were infuriated when she refused to behave like a "nice girl"—to be compliant, demure, and (above all), chaste. In 1927 it was considered improper for a young, unmarried woman to smoke cigars, drink, or spend time alone with a man who was not her relative or fiancé. The father of one of the other Harvey Girls posed a familiar question about Mickey when he asked his daughter, "Must she date *everyone* she meets?"[14]

• • •

The physical demands of her work and the strains of her carefree lifestyle inevitably wore Mickey down. In August of 1927, she fell ill with dysentery. "I might have known something was the matter," she told Helen in a letter, "because I was so crabby, and I was also worrying about money and business being slow, and nobody loves me, and so forth. I think I'm over it."[15]

Mickey's moodiness was also symptomatic of her general disillusionment with life. During her first few months in Santa Fe, Mickey had savored all the town had to offer. What intrigued her about life there was the blurring of familiar social distinctions. "Everyone fitted in, I reflected comfortably—and then discovered to my dismay, that *I* didn't fit in at all," Mickey later wrote. "None of the couriers did, for lots of the people who lived in Santa Fe didn't like or want the Detour."[16]

That dawned on Mickey one evening at a party in the home of a prominent local painter. The hostess and several of her guests began discussing the Santa Fe Detour in unflattering terms. Their chief criticism was the age-old one echoed by the residents of tourist destinations everywhere: commercialization was ruining the town. Santa Fe's visitors brought money, jobs, and prosperity, but they also meant crowds, high prices, pollution, unscrupulous real estate developers, and social disruption.

Such comments were a revelation for Mickey, who for the first time began to reevaluate her life in Santa Fe. The morning after the party, she poured out her doubts to Dorothy, who rejected the idea that tourism was ruining the town. Feeling confused, Mickey got a horse out of the dude ranch corral and went for a long ride alone. Several hours of musing reinforced a decision she had already made: she needed a change. Mickey's mother had been pressing her to return to school in the fall. Friends were urging her to do the same thing or else to find another job as a geologist. Mickey was not ready to do either. She surprised Dorothy and other workmates in mid-September when she suddenly packed her bags and moved to Taos, a picture postcard village about sixty miles to the northeast.

Frederic Remington, the famous American artist, had come to Taos in 1902 to savor the unspoiled scenic mountain grandeur and the splendid isolation. When other artists, writers, and photographers followed, a rivalry developed between Taos and the much larger Santa Fe. Among the newcomers who came to Taos were the painter Maurice Stern and his wife Mabel. They arrived in 1915, and Mabel made her presence known almost immediately.

Born in Buffalo, New York, in 1879, she was the only child of well-to-do parents. This was a woman used to getting her own way in most things, and she lived what was considered a "bohemian lifestyle." Mabel married four times and championed the view that love and sex should be "untrammeled" for men and women alike. True to her philosophy, she began a torrid love affair in Taos with a married native man named Tony Luhan. The locals were scandalized, but Mabel had enough money that she did not care. When Luhan left Taos in 1918, she stayed on and built an artists' retreat, a sprawling hacienda replete with parrots, porches, and dovecotes.

At Luhan's urging, the English author D. H. Lawrence and his wife arrived in 1921 searching for a wilderness utopia. Luhan traded Lawrence some land and a cabin for the manuscript of his 1913 autobiographical novel *Sons and Lovers.* Before long, the writer had a falling out with his hostess, for he quarreled with almost everyone. But other writers, artists, and photographers also came to "Mabeltown," as Lawrence had dubbed the Luhans' ranch. Among those who came and stayed for varying lengths of time were the painter Georgia O'Keeffe, photographer Ansel Adams, music critic Carl Van Vechten, and writers Lincoln Steffens and Willa Cather.

Mickey, who became acquainted with Mabel Luhan (and would one day write a biography of her), was also drawn to Taos by its scenic grandeur and spiritual freedom. Mickey was introduced to the village by a free-spirited young Mexican-American woman named Maria, whose father was a prominent local businessman. Like Mickey, Maria was a dreamer who heard the siren call of faraway places. Her mother hailed from Boston, and Maria talked of one day going there to live. "She was incorrigible," Mickey later wrote, "but she did find me a job of just the sort I wanted—without a future."[17]

Mickey went to work at a greeting card factory in Ranchos de Taos. She stencilled designs on the handcrafted cards and sometimes wrote corny verses.

("This little card I'm sending/Is very small, it's true,/But no card could be large enough/To hold my love for you.")[18] The menial work barely paid enough to live on, but Mickey was content. She had everything she needed for now: an adobe hut with a bed, a cooking stove, a fireplace, a pile of piñon wood for fuel, enough food, books to read, and the peace and quiet to write. She kept in the yard a horse she named Tom, and on weekends Mickey rode into town to attend dances and parties with Maria.

As fall gave way to winter, Mickey slipped into an easy routine. She might have remained in Taos indefinitely had she not written to her parents to let them know she was not coming home for Christmas. One day not long afterward, Mickey's mother appeared unexpectedly at the cabin door. Hannah's surprise visit was Mickey's wake-up call. Faced with the need to justify her life in Taos, Mickey realized she could not do so. She had to agree that her life in Taos, which had seemed so idyllic, really was pointless.

As a way out, Hannah offered a proposal: If Mickey would agree to return to university for graduate studies, her parents would pay her tuition. The Hahn family rule had been that once the children completed school, they were on their own. The enormity of the proffered break with tradition was not lost on Mickey. After mulling it over, she agreed to comply. The time had come to resume her love affair with geology. And where better to do so than in the cavernous streets of New York City?

II

"First, We'll Take Manhattan"

7

True to her word, Mickey began graduate studies at Columbia University in New York in January of 1928. Her older sister Helen was also in town, working as the crossword puzzle editor at the *Herald Tribune*. She was living with her husband Dwight Haven in an apartment in the suburb of Bronxville. Mickey declined to stay with the Havens and instead rented a hotel room near Times Square.

To help earn her keep, she taught geology two mornings per week at Hunter College for Women. The $500 Mickey earned for the term was enough to pay her bills. What's more, the experience proved exhilarating, for she now found herself facing a classroom full of young women her own age. "It was a funny feeling to look at them from behind a desk—the bright ones, and the hopelessly dumb ones, and the ones that try to make an impression," she told her mother. "The first thing they want, of course, was a set definition that they could write in their books and memorize. I keep expecting them to put apples on the desk."[1]

When she was not teaching or attending classes at Columbia, Mickey delighted in the adventures of everyday life in the Big Apple. By 1928, New York had eclipsed London as the world's intellectual and financial epicenter. It was a city bursting at the seams with possibilities, and Mickey was giddy with the excitement of it all. "I have walked around Times Square thousands of times, and lost myself on the subway and seen the Village and the Palace, and the [Broadway play] *Connecticut Yankee* . . . oh, and written a sophisticated poem," she told Helen.[2]

At night, Mickey sometimes joined her sister and the throngs of other white revelers who took the "A" train uptown to Harlem. Here they partook of the great black cultural awakening that was underway there. "Harlemania" was sweeping the city; as entertainer Jimmy Durante put it, "You sort of go primitive up there." Like many other whites, Mickey toured the Jim Crow speakeasies along 133rd Street's "Jungle Alley." She danced the Charleston at the Cotton Club, Connie's Inn, and Small's Paradise. She also attended several of the celebrated mixed-race parties at the apartment of Carl Van Vechten, whom she remembered from his visits to Taos. Van Vechten, a friend of Herbert's, was one of the first influential white literary critics to hail what was happening in Harlem as a great American cultural "happening." Mickey met prominent black entertainers, writers, and artists at Van Vechten's parties. Among them were the opera singer Taylor Gordon, cabaret crooner Jimmie Daniels, an

Ebony magazine editor named Alan Morrison, whom she dated briefly, and writer Walter White, a leader of the National Association for the Advancement of Colored People (NAACP) and author of *The Fire in the Flint*, one of the first books about the Harlem renaissance. It was White who introduced Mickey to the legendary W.C. Handy, the "Father of the Blues." Handy, nearly blind, earned his living as a composer and music publisher. He gave Mickey an autographed copy of a caricature of himself by the Mexican artist Miguel Covarrubias; the picture became one of her prized possessions. Handy sometimes sang for Mickey, treating her to a new verse he had written for "St. Louis Blues," one of his most popular tunes. "Let me be your little dawg till your big dawg come (*repeat*)," the song went. "When your big dawg come, tell him what your little dog done."

Despite the presence in New York of some old friends, among them Wisconsin drinking buddy Donald Hanson and Chicago-born Melvyn Douglas, who was making a name for himself as a Broadway actor, it was apparent to Mickey that life on the streets of Manhattan could be as mundane and difficult as it was anywhere else. For one thing, she found the cool, damp winter weather disagreed with her. Mickey constantly complained of a sore throat and other assorted health ailments. "It's the climate," she told Hannah. "Everybody always has a cold . . . just like St. Louis. They keep their houses so hot, it's no wonder. I feel awfully crabby."[3]

An even more significant concern was Mickey's precarious financial situation. When classes ended at Columbia in June, so did Mickey's job at Hunter College. What she desperately craved—and at the same time dreaded—was the very thing thousands of other young people who flocked to New York wanted: a career. She had no idea what she wanted to do. All she knew for sure was that she was terrified by the prospect of another mind-numbing, life-sapping office job. "There was [Manhattan] waiting for me," Mickey wrote. "I had only just come and I was a little afraid. . . . I made a rule never to eat lunch twice in succession at the same place."[4]

She applied unsuccessfully for work at the Museum of Natural History, hoping to put her knowledge of geology to good use there. Other applications also proved fruitless. "My sense of humor only works in flashes these days, and I've developed the most sickening tendency to tears—any time, any place," Mickey confided in a letter to Rose and Mitchell back home in Chicago.[5]

Despite her dark mood, she maintained an active social life. Helen's presence in New York provided Mickey with a ready-made social circle. She fell in with a crowd of artists, writers, editors, and photographers. Among them was a droll twenty-nine-year-old St. Louis native named David (Davey) Loth. Mickey remembered him visiting the Hahn's house in St. Louis with one of Mickey's cousins. "[Davey] impressed me when he was sitting there once,"

Mickey says. "Dorothy came in and gave a whoop about something, 'I'm a new woman! I'm a new woman!' she yelled. Davey said, 'Thank God!' That's when I first noticed him."[6]

After graduating from the University of Missouri Journalism School in 1920, Davey found work as a reporter at the *New York World*. His dream, he informed Mickey, was to become an author. With that in mind he was working on his first book, a biography of Robert and Elizabeth Barrett Browning.[7] Over the course of the next six decades, Davey Loth fulfilled his literary dreams, writing or coauthoring nearly fifty books, most notably a history of graft in America and a 1949 analysis of the groundbreaking report by Kinsey on human sexuality.

Davey was short and pudgy, with eyes shaded by thick spectacles. Mickey found him agreeable company, and they began spending a lot of time together. As a result, Mickey finally decided to end her long-distance relationship with Noel Stearn once and for all. That phase of her life was over; her priorities had changed. Spending time with Davey and the other friends in New York spurred Mickey to take her own writing more seriously. Her lack of purpose had always gotten in the way whenever she had tried to do so in the past. Now, for the first time, Mickey began to consider the prospect of harnessing her creative urges for a far more pragmatic reason—putting food on the table.

She sought encouragement from one of Helen's *Herald Tribune* workmates, a heavyset, personable reporter named Herbert Asbury. After reading some of her poems and articles, he urged Mickey to try her hand at freelance journalism. The idea was intriguing. After all, being paid to write, a skill that came to her so naturally, was appealing. Mickey decided to give it a try.

Her first opportunity came the day Davey asked her to cover for him on a story assignment. The task was simple: write a short feature article about a popular singer named Helen Morgan. The prospect of being paid to meet Morgan, one of the stars of the hit Broadway musical *Show Boat*, was too good to resist. "With Davey's invaluable aid," Mickey sold the resulting article to the *Sunday World*.[8] The $25 she was paid for her "professional debut" was as much as she earned in a week of teaching at Hunter College. Furthermore, the editor who bought the article encouraged Mickey to submit others. "It came at just the right time," she told Helen. "I was all worked up about what a useless bum I turned out to be, and I was already [sic] to accept that gracefully. I had a mental picture of myself as a picturesque and beautiful beachcomber dying all over Honolulu of a combination of hashish and theosophy."[9]

Despite her success, Mickey remained doubtful that she could earn a living with her writing. She thus made plans to return to Santa Fe in the summer of 1928 to work once again as a Harvey Girl. Doing so would also provide an opportunity for some time away from New York, where life had taken an unhappy turn when Helen and her husband Dwight split up. Mickey advised her sister that while it was "none of my business," Helen should not return to him; he was an alcoholic who got mean when he drank.

Mickey had finalized her travel plans and would have returned to New Mexico to live had it not been for one of her reporter friends, who dampened her enthusiasm when she called him to say good-bye. "What would I do out there [in New Mexico] anyway but play around with a lot of fairies [homosexuals] and wish I was back?" Mickey told Helen that her friend had demanded. "Whenever things seemed to be breaking right, I ran away, and so forth. He talked very loud. I finally decided I needn't go just yet, after all. So I spent all day yesterday writing some things which I will now attempt to market. Some of them are good. I'm doing a book, which Herbert Asbury thinks might be good."[10]

Asbury, one of New York's fastest and best newspaper rewrite men, was as deft in his courting as he was with his typewriter. Following Helen's divorce in late 1928, he convinced her to marry him. "Helen liked to be reassured," Mickey explained with a knowing smile.[11]

Mickey recalled that when Helen and Herbert decided to get married, Herbert insisted Mickey accompany them everywhere they went in New York. This was to avoid the possibility that Helen's estranged husband would name Herbert as a party in the divorce proceedings. One day Mickey, Helen, and Herbert were strolling along the street arm in arm when they encountered playwright Carl Van Doren. "I went away for a bit," Van Doren laughed, "and came back to find my old friend Herbert married to not one, but two beautiful young women!"[12]

Mickey later accompanied Helen and Herbert when they traveled to Chicago to finalize Helen's divorce. Hannah Hahn met her daughters and their new male friend at the train station. As they were walking out to the car, Hannah whispered in Mickey's ear, "Yes, but whose *is* he?"[13]

Mickey acted as Helen's witness in the divorce hearing, testifying how she had seen bruises Helen suffered at the hands of her estranged husband. "A lie," Mickey later admitted, "but that's how people got divorces in Chicago."[14] Committing perjury did not trouble her. Mickey had not *seen* Helen's bruises with her own eyes, but she accepted her sister's word that Dwight had beaten her. Besides, Mickey was keen to have Helen marry Herbert; she was fond of him and admired his writing. Herbert, like Mitchell Dawson before him, grasped that Mickey was an enormous raw literary talent. Mickey welcomed Herbert's words of praise, for he was someone to whom she could relate. Throughout his life he displayed the same independence of mind and irreverence that fueled Mickey's own passions. Here was a man who marched to his own beat.

Herbert Asbury burst onto the American literary scene in 1926, when a short story he wrote for H. L. Mencken's magazine *American Mercury* was banned in Boston after a complaint by the moralists of the Watch and Ward Society. "Hat Rack" told the story of a small-town prostitute who serviced her Protestant clients in the local Roman Catholic cemetery. When Mencken went to Boston and sold a copy of the magazine with the offending story, he was promptly arrested. When sales of that issue of the *American Mercury* soared, the author of the controversial story became an instant celebrity.

Asbury shocked America again with a series of books on criminal gangs, murders, bootlegging, and prostitution. His best-known book was *The Barbary Coast: An Informal History of the San Francisco Underworld*,[15] which he wrote in 1933. Two years later, director Howard Hawks and screenwriters Charles MacArthur and Ben Hecht, both of whom had worked alongside Asbury in the newspaper business, used the book as the basis for a movie starring the young Edward G. Robinson, one of Hollywood's hottest new stars.

Taking her cue from Herbert's irreverence, Mickey began writing a satirical "how-to" handbook on the principles and practices of the art of seduction. The book consisted of a series of nineteen seduction scenarios, each one described and footnoted as a scientific experiment. "The idea actually came from Herbert," she explained. "I dropped by Helen's office one day to pick her up for lunch, and he happened to overhear me talking about some of the boys I'd been dating. 'Why complain about them?' Herbert asked. 'Write about them!'" Mickey realized he was right. She put her technical education to use, formulating a set of scientific rules and regulations. "You see, I have four sisters, and we used to talk about [such] things," Mickey later told a newspaper reporter who asked her about the genesis of the book. "We discovered that the same methods had been practiced on us time and time again. The man who's successful with women is the one who can but doesn't—you know what I mean. The least successful is the fellow who pretends to be so wicked. The most primitive is the cave man who uses brute force."[16]

Mickey's book also included a bibliography, albeit one with a difference. She invented the names of some of her "sources." Others were actual books with such intriguing titles as *An Elementary Treatise on Curve Tracing* and *How to Get a Good Position*. While the humor was at times crude, even sophomoric, Mickey's choice of subject matter had been shrewdly calculated. In an era long before television talk shows and supermarket tabloids, seduction was not a subject that was commonly addressed in public, let alone probed or made light of—especially not by a woman. Seduction was one of those things about which every adult thought, yet that propriety dictated no one should discuss in mixed company. Satirizing the masculine libido was the literary equivalent of a tweak of the nose—or some other appendage of the male anatomy. Mickey knew this; she also knew her book would attract lots of media attention.[17]

She spent the next several months working on the manuscript, portions of which Mitchell and Herbert read and critiqued. The writing began in New York and continued that summer in New Mexico, where she went for a holiday with Harry Block, a boyfriend who worked as an editor with Bobbs-Merrill, and with Mexican artist Miguel Covarrubias and his girlfriend Rose Rolando. The foursome spent a memorable August in Taos, renting novelist D. H. Lawrence's house. Unfortunately, the trip ended in acrimony when Rose, "a fiery Hispanic," became convinced Mickey was trying to "bewitch" Miguel. "Honest, I wasn't," she said. "I just listened to him talk. I was surprised by all the fuss."[18]

Upon her return to New York in September, Mickey resumed her relationship with Davey Loth. She moved in with him in his apartment on West 11th Street in Greenwich Village. The arrangement was to save money, not because they were romantically involved.[19] If Mickey told her parents about her new accommodations, it is not evident from her correspondence; the issue was not even raised. That was just as well, for Mickey soon realized that dating Davey was preferable to living with him. However, she agreed to go along when he offered to pay her way to Italy if she would help with research for his biography of the Brownings. Mickey had no job and had finished work on her own book. The editors at Brewer Publishing in New York were considering the manuscript on October 3, 1928, the very day that she and Davey sailed for Europe aboard an Italian freighter.

• • •

Their ship reached Lisbon the evening of October 10. The next day at about noon, eight days out of New York, the vessel passed through the Strait of Gibraltar and into the placid blue waters of the Mediterranean Sea. Mickey was fascinated to discover that just by walking from one side of the ship to the other she could view two continents—Europe and Africa. To the port side, Spain looked arid and mountainous, not much different from the New Mexico landscape around Taos. On the starboard side, the African coastline loomed "dark and bumpy," and Mickey strained her eyes looking for the jungles. Common sense told her that they were "too far away" to be seen with the naked eye.[20] For a few minutes, at least, that fleeting glimpse of Africa revived in Mickey's mind the crazy plans she and Dorothy Raper had devised to visit Lake Kivu in central Africa.

That expedition was forgotten anew when the ship put in at the Adriatic seaport of Trieste the morning of October 17. From there, Mickey and Davey took the train west to Venice, traveling second class as a prelude to eventually moving into the even more frugal third-class carriages. So exhausted from the journey was Mickey that she fell asleep aboard the train and awoke to find an Italian lady staring at the inside of her mouth.

Mickey and Davey paused for four days in Venice, behaving like typical tourists. They rode in a gondola, and they gawked when they encountered Italian Fascist leader Benito Mussolini on the street. Despite the sights and the beauties of Venice, relations between Mickey and Davey continued to deteriorate. Mickey later admitted, "I treated him badly—neglect and worse." She reported in a letter to her mother how she "was always yipping" at Davey and had told him "to stop following [me] around."[21] To escape him, she rose early each morning and went for a long walk. The rest of the time, she closeted herself in the hotel to work on her novel. She did little research.

Although her own writing went much better after they settled into a small hotel in Florence, the city where Davey hoped to do most of his research on the Brownings, Mickey's disposition did not improve. She complained about the cold and about chilblains, which made it painful for her to type. Mickey amused herself by visiting the Medici chapel and other tourist attractions or horseback riding with an English girl she had met. "I couldn't get any boots in a hurry because they're all made to order here. I bought puttees and high shoes. Now from the knees down I look like a Fascist," Mickey said.[22]

In late November, she traveled solo to Paris to visit John Gunther. In March of 1927 on impulse he had married a twenty-nine-year-old New Yorker named Frances Powell Fineman. Mickey had Thanksgiving dinner with the Gunthers and with the wife of John's boss, Paul Mowrer, head of the *Chicago Daily News*'s European service. Mrs. Mowrer invited Mickey and Frances to visit her, but when Frances fell ill, Mickey stayed in her hotel room and wrote. "John is in London, which is rather a relief," she informed her mother, "for [Frances], too."[23]

Having decided Paris was to her liking and being in dire need of money, Mickey found temporary work as a tourist guide. She made $100 that first week. It was enough to pay for a room where, as she put it, she "could read poetry aloud or stand on my head or anything else that might occur to me without my neighbors staring aghastily."[24] Before long, Davey had joined Mickey in Paris, and the pair spent a couple of relatively carefree weeks there. They hung out at the cafés frequented by American expatriates. Here they met several interesting people through the Gunthers. One of them was the English writer Rebecca West, with whom John Gunther had had an affair soon after his 1924 arrival in London. Mickey had read West's book *The Judge* (1922) and wrote to John telling him how much she enjoyed it. When John showed the letter to West, she told him, "If that young woman ever comes to London, have her look me up." West was fascinated by Americans, and despite their thirteen-year age difference—Rebecca was thirty-six and Mickey just twenty-three—the two women became friends.

Rebecca, a journalist-turned-author, had made a name for herself with her novels and literary criticism. Her stormy relationship with H.G. Wells, at that time one of the world's best-known writers, had been the talk of London's literary salons. Being an outspoken feminist, Rebecca cared little what the gossips said. She encouraged Mickey, too, to think for herself.

Mickey was flattered to receive Rebecca's attention and was in awe of the older woman's wit, although she was taken aback by the verbal cruelties that Rebecca and her sixteen-year-old son Anthony hurled at each other—and at anyone else who incurred their scorn. Mickey and Rebecca developed a fondness for one another that was sustained by mail and by periodic visits. In the late 1940s, when both were living in England, they began having lunch regularly. Rebecca confided in Mickey the details of her bitter family problems. Outwardly, Rebecca was a formidable personality; in reality she was a vulnerable, lonely woman. A chronic insomniac, her mind raced in the wee hours of the night. As she grew older, Rebecca filled those long, empty hours by pouring out her soul in the rambling letters she wrote to Mickey and other friends. On one occasion, Rebecca implored Mickey, "For goodness sake burn this letter. I have an awful feeling that my epistolary sins will find me out."[25] Mickey and Rebecca remained close friends until Rebecca's death in 1983.

Mickey bid adieu to Paris and her friends there on December 17, 1928. She and Davey sailed from Italy on Christmas Eve aboard a French ship bound for Southampton, England. From there, they traveled on to New York aboard the RMS *Ausonia*. Mickey was relieved to be returning home after three months abroad. She was tired, homesick, and broke. Even a few days' stopover in the North African city of Tunis was of little interest to her. "This town is full of red caps and palm trees and dirty feet," she wrote Helen.[26]

Any joy that Mickey felt at heading back to New York was dulled by a rough midwinter crossing of the North Atlantic in spartan steerage accommodations. What's more, the prospects of being unemployed and penniless again did not inspire optimism. Nor did the uncertainties in her personal life. By the time the *Ausonia* sailed into New York Harbor on the morning of January 24, 1929, Mickey's mood matched the cool, gray weather. It was not a happy homecoming.

8

Her relationship with Davey Loth having cooled, Mickey moved into a rooming house upon her return to New York in January 1929. Her antipathy toward Davey heightened a few weeks later when his biography of the Brownings was published to good reviews; critics praised the book's easy, readable style and the quality of the research. Some of Mickey's friends urged her to confront Davey over his failure to acknowledge her contributions. Mickey did not. She had other concerns.

Still unsure of her ability to earn a living as a writer, she took a day job as a switchboard operator at an advertising agency. It was a skill that she had learned as a teenager in Chicago, when she had sometimes worked in her father's office. "I thought for a while maybe I would get married," she joked in a letter to Isaac, "but nobody asked me that week, and then I got this job. . . . I cut only two or three people off a day, and that's almost professional. Of course people get annoyed, but I think it's because New York keeps you at such high tension that you get irritable over almost nothing."[1]

Mickey's new career was itself disconnected when she fell ill with tonsillitis; she was laid off after only a month. Although the prospect of being out of work again was worrisome, Mickey discovered there were unexpected positives. For one, she now had both the time and the urge to write. She labored hard on her New Mexico novel and on some articles for the *Sunday New York World*. They included a two-part series on opium trafficking in New York and an interview with Floyd Dell, the prominent leftist writer. Dell, a transplanted midwesterner and close friend of poet Carl Sandburg, had made a name for himself as editor of a radical magazine called *Masses* and as the author of some sexually charged novels about disillusioned bohemians in the years after the First World War. "The (interview) was supposed to go on for an hour," Mickey told Helen, "but [Dell] could not tear himself away from me and my intellectual conversation until about eleven that evening, by which time everybody was not so serious."[2]

The money Mickey earned from newspaper articles boosted both her bank account and her self-confidence. Now that she "felt like a writer," she was determined to live like one. Mickey hung out in the city's chic cafés and speakeasies, and because she had always wanted one, she bought a Capuchin monkey. Herbert named him "Punk," because that's what the tiny creature looked like. When Mickey discovered how much attention the monkey attracted when she went out with him perched on her shoulder, they became constant companions—for a few weeks, at least.

Mickey still taught when she could, supplementing her income with what she made by writing. Eventually she hoped to be able to live by her typewriter alone. Mickey's priorities changed abruptly the day she learned that one of her articles had been accepted for publication by a New York magazine called the *New Yorker*. While she had no way of knowing it at the time, of course, the appearance of that article would mark the beginning of an incredible sixty-eight-year association that in many ways redefined her life. The great irony was that Mickey's role in selling that first article to the *New Yorker* was minimal. It was her brother-in-law Mitchell Dawson who was responsible.

Mickey had long been an inveterate letter writer. As a schoolgirl in Chicago, she corresponded with classmates or boyfriends when they moved away. When Mickey herself left home to go to college in Wisconsin, she wrote to her parents and siblings, particularly to her favorite sister Rose and Rose's husband Mitchell. "[He] took my writing seriously, but he didn't enter the circle until I was fourteen or fifteen, and he took it in hand as soon as I was grown up enough for him to do so," Mickey recalled. "I would write him long letters."[3]

Mitchell relished the mail from Mickey. The more he read, the more certain he was that she should be a writer. She had a natural gift for storytelling; her prose was witty, fluid, and filled with insight beyond her years. If he could find

Mickey with her pet monkey Punk, early 1929.
Courtesy Emily Hahn Estate

the right publication, Mitchell was convinced excerpts from Mickey's letters would work as literary vignettes. One day in 1928 he decided that the magazine he was looking for might be the *New Yorker*.

Founded three years earlier by editor Harold Ross, his wife Jane Grant, and financier Raoul Fleischmann, Ross's poker buddy, the *New Yorker*—as the name suggests—was aimed primarily at readers and advertisers in the twenty-six square miles of Manhattan Island. Writing in the now-famous prospectus that he drafted for potential investors in the fall of 1924, Ross stated that the magazine was not for "the old lady in Dubuque." He added, "This is not meant in disrespect, but the *New Yorker* is a magazine avowedly published for a metropolitan audience and thereby will escape an influence which hampers most national publications."[4]

Ross gambled that the approach would be the key to the magazine's survival. Initially, at least, it looked like he was wrong. When the *New Yorker* made its debut on February 19, 1925, it was, in the words of James Thurber, an "outstanding flop."[5] From an original press run of 15,000 copies, by August circulation had plummeted to 2,700. When the $20,000 Ross and his wife had invested and the $25,000 that Fleischmann had anted up was all long gone, it looked as though F-R Publishing Corporation (named for Fleischmann and Ross) was finished. It was only because Fleischmann continued to pour good money after bad that the *New Yorker* stayed alive. If not for Ross's determination, Fleischmann would have pulled the financial plug. In fact, he did so on one occasion, only to be convinced by Ross to change his mind.

Despite its narrow focus (and also because of it!) the magazine eventually found its niche in the New York market as well as a small but dedicated national audience. The *New Yorker* tapped into this vicarious urge, finding a receptive audience in Mitchell Dawson and other like-minded souls. To them, New York was a wondrous place indeed, and the *New Yorker* was a unique literary magazine, unlike anything else being published in America at the time.

Harold Ross had vowed the *New Yorker* would be "a reflection in word and picture of metropolitan life." He also offered readers assurances that it would not be "radical or highbrow. It will be what is commonly called sophisticated." In a typical Ross gesture, he emphasized his intentions with a verbal exclamation point: "It will hate bunk."[6] That overt pragmatism, a pointed reminder of Ross's own small-town journalistic roots, underscored the fundamental incongruity in his role as the founder of the magazine that became synonymous with big-city lifestyle and sophistication. It also ensured that the *New Yorker* would connect with readers far removed from the city's six boroughs and in a way that glib New York–based monthlies such as *Vanity Fair* and *American Mercury* did not and could not. Mickey always recalled how on the day she left Chicago for New York, Mitchell had given her a copy of the *New Yorker* to read on the train. "This is an interesting magazine that's published in New York," he had said. After reading it, she agreed.[7]

The one thing the *New Yorker* did have in common with its small-circulation cousins was its lack of cash flow. Ross could not afford to pay his editorial contributors well in the early years. It was only by virtue of his persuasiveness and a dogged persistence that he was able to find enough quality articles to keep the magazine going. Few of his friends shared his dream. Some people thought Ring Lardner had lost his senses when he stated, "I'd rather write for the *New Yorker* for five cents a word than for *Cosmopolitan* at one dollar a word."[8]

Financial constraints also dictated that Ross take chances on unknown writers. It was fortunate that he did, for doing so paid off handsomely on several occasions. For example, in 1926 a young debutante named Ellin Mackay (the future Mrs. Irving Berlin) submitted an article entitled "Why We Go to Cabarets: A Post Debutante Explains." Ross did not know what to make of Mackay's ideas, nor did he much care for the writing. He changed his mind only after newly appointed managing editor Ralph Ingersoll urged him to do so. When Ross agreed, the decision proved to be one of the wisest he ever made. The Mackay article caused a sensation when it appeared in November 1926, at the height of the debutante season. That issue of the *New Yorker* was the first to sell out, and even more important, it got people talking about the magazine. The *New Yorker* quite literally became "the talk of the town."

Ross and his staff built upon that success. Circulation and advertising revenue increased dramatically. "[The magazine's] fundamental success is based on the simple mathematics that a merchant can, at $550 a *New Yorker* page, call his advertisement to the attention of some 62,000 active and literate inhabitants of the metropolitan area," Ralph Ingersoll explained in an anonymous article in the August 1934 edition of *Fortune*. "While to reach the same group, either through a national medium or through a local paper, would cost him several times that amount."[9]

The *New Yorker* was one of the few major magazines in America to continue making money during the Great Depression. In fact, when weekly readership topped 125,000 in 1935, Raoul Fleischmann expressed concerns that the publication was becoming *too* successful. His solution was simple: the office phone number was unlisted to discourage subscribers.

From his vantage point in Chicago, Mitchell Dawson applauded the *New Yorker*'s progress and wondered if it might not be an ideal publication for Mickey's writing. After removing the salutations and signatures, he submitted some of her 1927 letters from New Mexico as possible articles. Mitchell hoped his sister-in-law's youthful irreverence might attract Ross's attention as Ellin Mackay had done. Mitchell was only partly successful. Literary editor Katharine Angell (who later married *New Yorker* coworker E. B. White) liked the letters so much that she brought them to Ross's attention. Although the *New Yorker* editor was also impressed, he rejected them, saying the subject mattter was "too far west of the Hudson."

Ross offered encouraging words in his rejection letter. Even more important, he and Katharine Angell earmarked young Emily Hahn as a writer to watch. For that reason, they were receptive when in early 1929 Mitchell submitted more of Mickey's letters, these ones dealing with her life in New York. Mickey, oblivious to all this, was surprised when Mitchell called to say Ross had accepted one of them for publication.

"Lovely Lady" appeared in the May 25, 1929, edition of the *New Yorker*. This 550-word literary vignette echoed the celebrated Ellin Mackay article in that it offered a snapshot of life in New York's trendy cafés and nightspots. "Lovely Lady" related the essence of a lunchtime conversation between the narrator, who was actually Mickey, and an unidentified woman, who was Leslie Nast, the lesbian wife of *Vanity Fair* magazine publisher Condé Nast. The story was reminiscent of others that Mickey had written during her student days at Wisconsin. The crucial difference was that four years and a wealth of life experience later, her prose style was infinitely more polished and mature. The dialogue crackled with wit and vitality, and she was beginning to display her trademark flair for dramatic opening lines. "'You know,' I suddenly said, much to my own horror, 'you're a funny person to be married to him,'"[10] Mickey's first *New Yorker* article begins.

Having sold one story to Ross, Mickey promptly submitted several others. The *New Yorker* bought two, which dealt with life in the rooming house where she was now living. The next story by Mickey to be published in the magazine appeared in the July 6, 1929, issue. At first glance, "Roommate" seemed like an account of a mundane conversation between the narrator and a young female housemate. It was and it was not. There was a lot more going on in the story than first met the eye. Once again, Mickey displayed her extraordinary ability to sketch in a few words complex characters acting out a scene rife with underlying social relevance. In this case, Mickey focused on the roommate, but there was certainly a large element of self-portraiture in the story. The woman tells the nameless narrator how her boyfriend speculated one night, "'When you met me you were intrigued because I talk rather well. The second time you saw me you weren't so interested. From now on you'll be bored until you meet someone else.'" The woman responds by quipping, "'And do you know, it's true. I told him so. I'm bored with people right away. It's a disease, a mental disorder.'"

The roommate was little different from Mickey, who, despite her recent successes, had been gripped by a renewed sense of aimlessness bordering on desperation. The 1920s had been a decade of momentous social and economic change in America, and like a lot of young people, Mickey was groping to find meaning in her life as the roar faded to a whimper. That theme recurred in the last of those initial three articles Mickey sold to the *New Yorker.* "The Stranger," published on August 3, 1929, also dealt with a quirky relationship between a nameless narrator and her lesbian housemate. The two women live in a big, drafty old house where they are the only residents on their floor. The narrator has come to New York in search of work, while the other woman is employed in a mind-numbing, dead-end office job. Day in and day out, her routine is the same. "Sometimes she would bring home a girl for the night, in which case they took more time in the bathroom than I approved of," the narrator broods.

Apart from her sexual preferences, there was little to distinguish the woman from Mickey or, for that matter, from the throngs of other nameless, penniless young transplants who came to New York in the late 1920s with only their improbable, crazy dreams. Those who stayed exchanged failed ambitions for a subway ride to the life-sapping routines of big-city life: get up at the same time each morning, work, eat, play, and then fall into bed at the same time each night. Mickey was determined to avoid that fate. "I always found regular hours horrible," she said. "I did it my first year out of college [in St. Louis]. Nine in the morning until five in the afternoon. I vowed never again."[11]

Initially, the narrator of Mickey's story is in awe of her housemate, who seems to have a solid grasp on life. Appearances are deceiving, though, for it gradually becomes clear that the woman is going through life on automatic, never pausing long enough to contemplate what she is doing or why. Mickey found it depressing (and a little frightening) to contemplate that she, too, could end up this way. "I wonder how many people are living in New York and not using it?" the narrator muses. "You would think that the city would burst from so many people. You would think that all the houses would bulge with the thoughts in them about church bazaars and Christmas presents."

What also becomes clear to the narrator is that it is the housemate who is really the stranger in the city. Her life is pointless and shallow, a fate to which she has resigned herself; it is *she* who envies the narrator. The conversation between the two women ends abruptly when the telephone rings. "'You answer,' she said in her flat voice. 'It's for you. It's always for you.'"[12]

Intrigued by what he had read, *New Yorker* editor Harold Ross telephoned Mickey and asked her to drop by his office so they could meet. Although she knew nothing about Ross other than the fact that his magazine had become a raging success, Mickey was terrified at the prospect of meeting him.

In the summer of 1929, the *New Yorker*'s offices were in their original home: on the sixth floor of a tatty old office building at 25 West 45th Street. The structure was partly owned by Raoul Fleischmann's older brother Charles. The extended family had made its fortune in the yeast business, but Raoul Fleischmann, who bankrolled the magazine, made a handsome living from Fleischmann's Yeast corporate stock, which he owned, and by managing his immediate family's big East Side bakery. Almost every dollar that Fleischmann pumped into the *New Yorker* in the early days paid the bills for publishing the weekly magazine. Initially there was little left over for frills or for secretarial and office staff.

Like most visitors, Mickey was greeted at the *New Yorker* by the smiling face of no one. The entry to the offices, a plain wooden door with a pane of frosted glass, was at the end of a long corridor. In the wall to the right was a small receptionist's window. A sign taped to the wall beside it read, "If no attendant is present please ring bell." Seeing no one in the booth, Mickey did as instructed. Presently, the noise attracted the attention of Harold Ross's secretary. She opened the door and ushered Mickey into the editor's office, which like everything else at the *New Yorker*, had a makeshift quality to it that was more by design than accident.

As Ross's colleague and friend James Thurber once noted, "He himself liked a plain newspaper-type office—'I don't want to look like the editor of *Vanity Fair*.' "[13] Ross, in a display of reverse snobbery, disdained that glittery magazine, which was the bible of New York's smart set at the time and the *New Yorker*'s main competitor. *Vanity Fair*'s celebrated art deco hauteur and effete intellectualism were not for Ross. He insisted his magazine's offices be furnished with secondhand stuff. Doing so not only saved money; it signaled to the world that he and the *New Yorker* were different.

Of that there was *never* any doubt.

From the moment Mickey laid eyes on him, she knew Harold Ross was one of a kind. In the years to come, her initial impression would only be reinforced. Ross became Mickey Hahn's mentor, employer, and one of her dearest friends.

What struck her—and most other people—upon meeting Ross for the first time was what his biographer Thomas Kunkel has described as his "ill-proportioned, Lincolnesque body," with gangling limbs and outsize hands and feet.[14] Despite a permanent slouch, Ross was literally a head of hair over six feet tall. He had taken to wearing his hair in a spiky pompadour that added at least three inches to his height and gave him the look of a frenetic porcupine. Frank Case, the owner of the Algonquin Hotel, Ross's favorite luncheon venue, once recalled in his memoirs that he was having lunch with the actress Ina Clare one day when they spied the *New Yorker* editor at his favorite booth. Clare kept staring over at Ross's hair and sighing. " 'My,' she said, finally. 'What wouldn't I give to take off my shoes and stockings and go wading in that?' "[15]

Ross's features were no less distinctive. He had a rubbery, expressive face with a gap-toothed smile. A cigarette perpetually dangled from "a huge Hapsburg lip," a deadly habit that would eventually kill him. Then there were Ross's eyes; Ralph Ingersoll said that "under heavy eyebrows, [they] are fierce, shifty, restless."[16]

When conversing, Ross had a habit of craning his head forward, as if he was perpetually struggling to grasp the essence of what was being said. He laughed often, sometimes leaving others to wonder whether he was amused or merely venting his insecurities, which were legion. Although he would marry three times, Ross was notoriously nervous around women. However, if he felt any apprehensions about meeting Mickey, these surely paled in comparison to the uncertainties *she* felt. "I shook at the knees, but I needn't have," she recalls. "Ross was actually rather sweet to me."[17]

Mickey perched on the edge of her chair as she and the *New Yorker* editor discussed her writing. He told her that he liked what he had read. "Young woman, you have a great talent," he said with a knowing nod. "You can be cattier than anyone I know, except maybe Rebecca West. Keep it up!"

The comparison with her English friend, heady praise indeed, brought a smile to Mickey's face. She was euphoric as she left the *New Yorker* office that day. Mickey would later recall how short-lived was that high. "After that, Ross rejected the next three articles that I submitted," she said.[18]

9

Selling three articles to the *New Yorker* was enough to convince Mickey Hahn that she might have a future as a writer. Her self-confidence received a further boost when she met Dorothy Parker one evening at a party at the Algonquin Hotel. Mickey and Dorothy—whom Mickey affectionately referred to as "Dottie"—discovered they had a lot in common. They began meeting occasionally for lunch and dinner. They gossiped. They giggled. They also talked about life. "We were sitting in the Ladies' Room, as one often did with Dottie, crying alcoholically," Mickey recalled. "I was telling her about my poor little sister who elected out of a sense of duty to live at home with my parents and never had any fun—Dauphine must have been on my conscience at that time.

"Well, Dauph came to New York soon afterwards, and she went to a party somewhere. She was amazed when a strange woman grabbed her by the wrist. You came!' she said intensely. Then the woman—Dorothy—burst into tears and added, 'We must have fun! We must have lots of fun!' Dauphine was terrified."[1]

Mickey and Dorothy also discussed writing. Like Mickey's brother-in-law Herbert Asbury, Dorothy had a keen sense of life's absurdities; she encouraged Mickey, who was flattered to receive words of encouragement and advice from such a celebrated writer. "I like her a lot," she told her mother in a letter.[2]

Mickey's good fortune continued when she received word that the New York publisher Brewer and Warren had finally set a date to publish her satirical guide to seduction. "I was tickled to hear about the book, also the *New Yorker*," Mitchell told Mickey in a letter. "Well, anyway, I guess I knew you *when*—I did, didn't I? And I had faith in you, didn't I? I knew you'd turn out to be a good geologist someday."[3]

Despite all these positive developments, Mickey's self-confidence nosedived with the economy in the fall of 1929.

The significance of the Great Crash of October 23 was lost on Mickey and on millions of other ordinary Americans. "I hardly knew anything about the great crash in Wall Street," she admitted, "and if I hadn't been told the connection later I would never have known that it caused the scarcity of jobs that gave me and my friends so much leisure. Stock market panics happened to the sort of people I had no contact with. . . . I felt merely that life was sad, and this sadness was something . . . I seemed always to have known about."[4]

Following her break with Davey Loth, Mickey had moved into a room in a rooming house. Then she found space in a small apartment on Sixth Avenue in Greenwich Village. Her new housemate was Kathy, a young drama student from the Midwest. Kathy was as poor as Mickey, but at least her classes gave her somewhere to go during the days. With no such focus in her life, time became Mickey's enemy.

When Kathy got involved in an unhappy romance, Mickey found herself listening empathetically as her housemate poured out her troubles. During sleepless nights and endless, desultory days, Mickey pondered what Kathy told her, and she brooded about her own emotional travails. In her mind, life was a dead-end street. Mickey often said that somewhere deep within the Hahns was a gene that periodically triggered depression. She may have been right, for there was a history of suicide and melancholia in the extended family, and now and at other times in her own life Mickey's mood sank dangerously low.

Her unhappiness was exacerbated by the unremittingly dark, cool weather that autumn. Even when she left the apartment for a walk, as she did each day, the long lines of ragged men, women, and children outside the city's soup kitchens were a reminder of the misery that was everywhere. At dusk, Mickey watched the homeless gather under the ornamental bridges in Central Park, preparing to bed down for the night. It was all too much for her to bear.

One day Mickey dropped in on a photographer friend, who commented on how tired Mickey looked. As she was leaving, the woman pressed a bottle of sleeping pills into Mickey's hand. Try them, the woman suggested. Mickey did, and she was still sleeping soundly when the cleaning lady knocked on the apartment door at eleven o'clock the next morning.

Mickey's introduction to sedatives proved significant. Not long afterward, Kathy delivered some devastating news: she was pregnant. Being unmarried and penniless, she and her boyfriend decided there was no choice but abortion. Together, they raised enough money for the operation. Afterward, Kathy moped about the apartment for several days, sobbing and filled with guilt. When she could take it no more, she packed her bags and left for home, leaving Mickey alone in the apartment. "I grieved accordingly, and the more I did, the less I wanted any part of life. Life had let me down. I knew how to get out of it, too," Mickey wrote.[5]

The solution to all her woes, she decided, was an overdose of sleeping pills. Over dinner one evening, Mickey outlined a suicide plan to a boyfriend. Afterward, the young man puffed his pipe as he calmly argued against Mickey killing herself; he suggested that she see a psychiatrist. The idea struck Mickey as absurd, and she returned to her apartment feeling even more confused and frustrated than ever.

No sooner was she in the door than the telephone rang. It was a friend who was also depressed. Then came a call from another friend who was drunk. When the phone rang a third time, Mickey snapped. She began sobbing uncontrollably as she tore the phone cord from the wall. What happened next was a blur. Mickey would only remember grabbing the bottle of sleeping pills and stuffing a handful into her mouth. The next thing she knew, her cleaning lady's voice was speaking to her in a dream, telling her not to cry because she loved her. Somewhere a telephone rang, and her boyfriend was calling out to her. Then Mickey's sister Helen appeared out of nowhere in the dream. She was with a doctor, who stuck a tube down Mickey's throat and pumped her stomach. Mickey's dream had become a nightmare that ended in spasms of retching, tears, and shame.

She awoke the next day on the sofa at Helen's apartment. The sun was shining in the window and the trees looked incredibly green. The world suddenly seemed wondrous and new. When Helen asked Mickey why she had swallowed the sleeping pills, she had no answer. It was not until later, when her boyfriend came by offering to pay the bill if she agreed to see an analyst, that she shook off her daze. "What happened next was a click in my mind, and then it was as if a window blew open, letting anger flow in," Mickey wrote. "I knew all about that anger, although I hadn't felt it for a long time."[6]

Mickey got up, threw her belongings into her suitcase, and stormed out the door. It was with a fresh sense of resolve that she plunged anew into her writing. Despite the objections of several friends, she seized the opportunity when Davey Loth asked her to go with him on another overseas research trip; Mickey was by now willing to forgive and forget Davey's failure to acknowledge her contribution to his book. She hoped to leave her troubles and self-doubts behind as she sailed with him for England one cold day in mid-December. Mickey wrote to her mother from London on December 21, 1929, proudly announcing she had completed a novel about her New Mexico experiences and that she and Davey had rented a flat just steps from the British Museum.

• • •

Armed with letters of introduction, Mickey went calling in London. One of these letters, from her friend the African-American opera singer Taylor Gordon, introduced her to a society photographer named Olivia Wyndham. She was on holiday when Mickey dropped by her King's Road studio; however, Wyndham's young assistant was there, living in a tiny room at the back of the building. Barbara Rhodes (later Ker-Seymer) liked the way Mickey "breezed in," and the two became instant friends. They would remain so for more than sixty years, until Barbara's death in 1992.

Barbara, who knew nothing about photography when Wyndham left her in charge of the studio, began inviting friends to pose so that she could practice using a camera. One of these friends was a ballet dancer. When he began bringing other young dancers in to be photographed, the studio became a hangout for a lot of young people who had no money to socialize in pubs or other night spots. "My new friends were all gay," Barbara recalled many years later. "They were mostly art students and ballet dancers. They were very jolly, and Mickey was this strange, very 'normal,' American girl who came into our midst. We were very cliquey, insular, and up-tight. English people are, you know."[7]

Barbara's "special friend" was a bright young Ecuadorian-born ballet dancer named Frederick Ashton. "Freddie" would go on to a distinguished career as a dancer, choreographer, and the director of the famous Covent Garden company. However, in 1930, the future Sir Frederick was a twenty-six-year-old unknown.[8] Mickey dropped by the studio for tea with Barbara and Freddie most afternoons. She recalls walking in one day just as Freddie was mimicking her. "'Oh, my dear, I think he's just *wooonderful*!' he was saying. They thought I liked everybody, and they made fun of that. Anyway, I came in right in the middle of Freddie's impersonation of me, and he was abashed. I wasn't."[9]

Mickey became one of the Wyndham Studio regulars. In answer to the obvious question, she replied, "No, I didn't experiment sexually. They would introduce me by saying, 'This is Mickey from New York. She's STRAIGHT.' Then they would stare at me. But yes, I suppose you might have called me a Fag Hag."[10] She was not a lesbian, but Mickey's "typically American" lack of pretension and her crackling wit earned her a place in the circle. Barbara would always remember how, despite an outgoing personality and her relative worldliness, Mickey was very much "a loner." She also remembered Mickey's pleasing looks, which shone through even though she was putting on weight and seemed indifferent about her appearance. "[Mickey] wore the most dreadful clothes. We were terrible to her because she used things called 'dress preservers.' These went under your arms to protect against perspiration stains. You don't need them now because of deodorants. But poor Mickey, she got terribly mocked. She didn't appear to mind," Barbara said.[11]

When Mickey needed pampering, she visited Rebecca West, and sometimes Rebecca invited her to dinner. After one such meal, Mickey told her mother, "There was a political economist and his wife and [Rebecca's son] Anthony. Because I'm American, they all talked a good deal about Omaha, in which they have all given lectures at one time or another. I finally confessed that I had never been there. I confessed with shame and blushes, and Rebecca patted my head and promised they'd all take me there some day."[12]

Mickey spent a lot of time during her first few weeks in London in the reading room of the British Museum. She was researching the life of King Charles II, the subject of Davey's next biography. Mickey's heart was not in the job. She told Hannah in a letter that she had skipped going to the museum that morning. Instead she had lounged around the flat in her dressing gown, eating apples, reading, and musing about writing. "I'm having lunch with Rebecca on Monday, and I'll ask her if essays are much better to write. Anyway, I think in essays, not novels," she explained.[13]

Mickey was reconsidering her dedication to the art of fiction writing after having struggled through Thomas Mann's ponderous 1901 novel *Buddenbrooks.* While reading that book, she had found herself "wondering how on earth north German women get through life without dislocating their jaws yawning." While that comment was tongue-in-cheek, Mickey was perfectly serious when she added, "I suppose the U.S. will never have any literature until we develop a calm, stagnant homelife to write triple-volume novels about."[14]

Mickey did not report Rebecca West's opinions of *Buddenbrooks* or of essay writing. What she did relate in her next letter home was how she and Rebecca had met "the dumpy little woman who is [writer] Hilaire Belloc's sister and her friend." Rebecca had told them Mickey was writing a biography of Nell Gwyn [the mistress of Charles II]. "She knows it isn't true, but she likes to make people jump. I notice it because I do the same thing," Mickey confided.[15]

Such introspection reflected a renewed restlessness on Mickey's part. In mid-January, she traveled to Uccle, a suburb of Brussels, to visit a footloose young man she had met at a party in New York. Patrick Putnam, lean, bearded, and possessed of a boyish charm, was the scion of a well-to-do New England family. "A wild shock of hair and a luxuriant beard of flaming red made him seem even taller than his six foot, one inch," his widow would write of him many years later.[16]

Patrick had studied anthropology at Harvard. While on a research expedition in the Belgian Congo (now Zaire), he was gored in the back, buttocks, and thigh by an elephant. Too injured to be moved, Patrick stayed behind when his colleagues went home, leaving him in the care of native women. The experience affected him profoundly. He fell in love with one of his nurses, a Mangbetu woman known as Abanzima. "The Mangbetu make their heads long by binding the babies' heads," Mickey explained. "The tribe is interesting, too, because they claim kinship with Egyptians, and they do come from North Africa."[17] The intriguing origins of the Mangbetu tribe were immaterial in Boston. All that mattered was that Abanzima was black. Because miscegenation was such a powerful social taboo, it was unthinkable for a white, Harvard-educated Bostonian to fall in love with such a woman. When Patrick revealed his feelings for Abanzima, his parents reacted angrily. Mrs. Putnam promptly fired the family's black maid and announced that she would *never* have another black servant in the house. "If Abanzima had been white, we'd have got married," Patrick told Mickey. "She could have come home with me. She'd have been right here now, staying with my family."[18]

The reaction of Belgian colonial officials was no more empathetic. When Patrick requested permission to return to the Congo, they were suspicious of his motives. "Oh, they don't mind my living with [the woman]," Patrick explained. "They wouldn't understand my wanting to stay with her, that's it. Most of the white men there, if their wives aren't with them, have black mistresses—they call them *ménagères.*"[19]

Patrick volunteered to become a medical worker with the Croix Rouge du Congo—the Red Cross of the Belgian Congo. Such people were urgently needed, and Putnam knew that volunteering would afford him an opportunity to live among the locals, and ostensibly to study the native culture.

All of this intrigued Mickey. In her eyes, Patrick Putnam was a hopeless romantic who had been tragically separated from his true love by forces beyond his control. With her curiosity heightened by a few drinks, Mickey asked Patrick about African life. The more she learned, the more excited she got. "This, I felt, was a most fortunate encounter," she later wrote.[20] Six years earlier, during her student days at Wisconsin, Mickey and her friend Dorothy Raper had hatched a plan to travel to Lake Kivu in central Africa; now it seemed fate was offering her the chance to fulfill those dreams. Patrick was amenable when Mickey asked to visit him when he returned to the Congo. However, he cautioned that before he could go there himself he had to complete a Red Cross medical training program and become an *adjunct sanitaire*—a doctor's assistant.

After Brussels, Mickey's life in London seemed insufferably dull. She found herself daydreaming of jungles, palm trees, and languid rivers glittering in the African sun. As Mickey pondered her future, she rushed to complete the research Davey Loth had hired her to do. Africa, wondrous Africa beckoned, but traveling there remained uncertain, and her family and friends were urging her to return to the States. Mickey was not keen to do so. She could not face the prospect of going back to New York, the scene of so much of her unhappiness recently. Besides, with the Great Depression deepening, economic conditions there were bleak. "I get more and more afraid of coming home," she told her mother. "Word comes across the wire that the world has just fired 250,000 people on account of the stock market disaster; that's a helluva bright outlook."[21]

Although the *New Yorker* had bought several more of her articles, Mickey realized that she could not earn a living by writing about the vagaries of life as a single, unemployed woman; the world was too full of them. Besides, such one-note introspection seemed tedious and counterproductive as she struggled to hone her literary skills.

Davey Loth offered another alternative. He urged Mickey to travel with him to Vienna, where he planned to stay until his money ran out. Doing so would have been easy for Mickey because John Gunther and his wife Frances were about to relocate to the Austrian capital; they invited Mickey to stay with them. For now, she declined all offers. Instead, she stayed in London. She continued to dream of Africa and to work on a new novel and on a book about the history of the Royal Society, a subject she had become fascinated with while researching the life of Charles II.

As the weeks passed and her money dwindled, Mickey's spirits flagged. Africa seemed farther and farther away. She continued her daily visits to the reading room of the British Museum, where she felt an odd sense of contentment and belonging, one she had not felt before. This magnificent library, built in 1857, was the place where Karl Marx had sat while writing the *Communist Manifesto* and where generations of visiting scholars and assorted eccentrics—the "regulars," as they dubbed themselves—came to do research, write, and muse. The reading room of the British Museum was always one of Mickey's favorite places, for she felt truly at peace there. "I always sit in Aisle K unless it's full when I arrive," she once wrote. "It is no use asking me why I prefer it. I don't know, because there is absolutely no difference between Aisles J and K and any other; they all radiate like spokes from the hub, a circular counter in the center of the great circular room, surrounded by a dome inset with grimy glass."[22]

When Mickey was not doing research, she wrote feverishly. She had not lost her sense of humor. In late February, Mickey sent her mother a letter with two bits of good news: Davey Loth's latest book, a D. H. Lawrence biography entitled *Lorenzo,* had been published in England, and her own first book was among those listed in the spring catalogue of Brewer and Warren Publishing. Reading the promotional blurb brought into focus the realization that she really was about to become a published author. The prospect excited her. "I was speechless and bemused and almost got run over in the Haymarket," Mickey said. "The full title is *Seductio Ad Absurdum: The Principles and Practices of Seduction; A Beginner's Handbook.* There was my name in print, just like anybody's."[23]

Anticipation does not pay the rent, and Mickey was forced to vacate her flat on March 10, when Davey left for Vienna. Mickey lugged her meager possessions and the portable typewriter she had rented over to a bed-sitting room on Torrington Square. Although her address changed, Mickey's routine did not. By day, she worked at the British Museum or tapped away at the typewriter in her flat; by night, she socialized with friends, including Rebecca West, whom she had by now decided was "quite mad."[24]

People in the London literary community had begun treating Mickey as a colleague, although she was still wrestling with self-doubts about her abilities as a writer. It dismayed her that although the *New Yorker* had bought several more of her articles, her byline still appeared irregularly in the magazine. She was unaware that as the *New Yorker* became more successful, Harold Ross had started stockpiling articles and stories as a hedge against the possibility he might one day again be short of editorial material.

As a result, Mickey's spirits took another downturn in early 1930. She could now think only of Africa. The possibilities filled her mind as she brooded about the future and tried to work on another novel, which by "inertia"—as she put it—soon had grown to thirty thousand words. Her mother's letters did nothing to ease Mickey's growing restlessness. As always, Hannah urged her daughter to return home, to settle down, marry, and raise a family—the way "most girls" of twenty-five did. By now, this had become a familiar refrain. Mickey's fondness for drinking, smoking, and swearing continued to be sore points with her parents, as did her willingness to flout conventional sexual mores. Mickey rejected her parents' concerns, arguing that her life was her own. "Some generations drink more than others, maybe," she explained to Hannah. "On the other hand, some generations drink less than others. I don't worry about it . . . except when I'm home. You shouldn't worry about us when we're away either. Isn't it true that I trouble you more in the flesh, when you can hear me swear and all that?"[25]

For all her bravado, Mickey's self-doubt smoldered. Despite her accomplishments—which were considerable for someone her age—her ambitions remained vague and unfulfilled. Mickey lay awake nights, grappling with fears of her own mortality. "Nasty watching your body wear out. Gold teeth and scars, one after the other, coming to stay," she wrote in her diary in the wee hours of a particularly restless night. "I thought I was gay under grim circumstances, not to mention game and possessed of guts. But just now I spent a week being broke in a foreign land, and I don't hold with adventure. I keep telling myself that every gambler has to have a system, something which he calls a judgment. I've been looking at myself and saying unkind things about the Spirit of Adventure as such. Of course, it won't last; I read too much."[26]

Mickey's confusion was reflected in letters she wrote to her sister Helen and to Rose and Mitchell, in whom she continued to confide. Mitchell sent a playful response to what must have been an especially pessimistic missive. He joked about Mickey becoming famous. "You asked me how I felt about selling things," he wrote. "It is very pleasant to get a cheque for doing something you do even without it. The effect on other people is nice, too. They take it as a manifesto of your intentions and make due allowances in future."[27]

Mickey received advance copies of *Seductio Ad Absurdum* from the publisher on March 21, 1930. As she perused the book, she marveled at the sight of her own name. There it was, prominently displayed on the dust jacket, right next to the $2 price tag. Mickey told Hannah, "The funniest thing is to see it at odd moments—Emily Hahn—and then think, 'Why that's me!'"[28]

On Mitchell's urging, Mickey inquired about having *Seductio Ad Absurdum* reprinted in London. There was some interest, but potential publishers ultimately rejected the idea after concluding that Mickey's humor was too distinctively "American" to appeal to British readers. Reaction was more favorable on her own side of the Atlantic, where initial sales were brisk despite tepid reviews. As Mickey had anticipated, the subject matter alone ensured that the media would pay heed; *Seductio* was widely reviewed in American newspapers. Unfortunately, in 1930 most reviewers were men. Few saw the humor in a book that poked fun at male sexuality. "It is not exactly exciting, and it lacks even the flavor of conversations one might overhear on a Coney Island boat," commented the reviewer for the New York literary magazine *Books.* "And on a Coney Island boat you would at least be getting the stuff first-hand and not warmed over."[29]

Book page editor Harry Hansen of the *New York World* was only slightly more receptive. Being an old friend of John Gunther's, and having occasionally dated Mickey's sister Helen when they both lived in Chicago in the early 1920s, Hansen felt obliged to spotlight the book. "Miss Hahn's method is by no means perfect, but it has points," he wrote. "Her first pages reveal her bent, but some of the episodes that follow are more obvious than subtle."[30]

Poet Carl Sandburg, Mitchell's friend, was one of the few American critics to respond favorably to *Seductio Ad Absurdum.* Unfortunately, his brief, three-paragraph review in the *Chicago Daily News* focused as much on Mickey's family ties as on the merits of her writing. Sandburg noted that Mickey's in-laws included Herbert Asbury, "a direct descendant of Bishop Asbury of the Methodist Church," and Mitchell, whom Sandburg described as "one of the few measurably honest people in Chicago." He continued, "Mitchell Dawson, who unravels tangles of law for readers of the *Daily News*, he who married Rose, sister of Emily, is also known to have assisted in this book. . . . [*Seductio Ad Absurdum*] is recommended with no hesitations. At first, we thought [Miss Hahn] was just one smart kid who enjoyed being smart, but she is a lot more than that."[31]

• • •

Another critic who shared Sandburg's critical assessment of Mickey—although for markedly different reasons—was William (Bill) Benét, the older brother of American poet Stephen Vincent Benét. The elder Benét, forty-four at the time, was working as an editor at Brewer and Warren. He was a friend of Herbert's and had met Mickey at a party in New York. Benét become infatuated with her.

"I'd always loved his poem 'The Falconer of God,'" Mickey explained. "It's a long poem, but I recited the whole thing to him at the party, and, of course, he fell in love with me on the spot. I've an incredible memory for poetry, but he didn't know that, poor guy."[32]

On a March trip to London, Benét had delivered the advance copies of *Seductio Ad Absurdum.* He was keen to make an impression. Although twenty years Mickey's senior, Benét was recently widowed from his second wife and hoped to convince Mickey to marry him and return to New York. They had "a civilized and dressy" dinner at the posh Carleton Hotel. Then Mickey showed Benét her novel, which he praised with appropriate enthusiasm. Although they had a pleasant evening, she rejected his proposal; Mickey had no interest in marrying Benét. She had other plans.

Mickey had written Hannah in late March reporting that she was down to her last £20 and was losing enthusiasm for the Royal Society book. With each passing day she was growing increasingly anxious to leave London. "When I'm with people I get bored no matter who they are. I don't know what's the matter. But it will pass," she said.[33] *It* did not. When Mickey received word that Patrick Putnam had sailed for the Congo, all her uncertainties faded. She knew the time had come to fulfill her dream of going to Africa. However, first there was the question of saving enough money for the trip and of tending to a few other matters.

Mickey sailed for New York in mid-April at her publisher's urging to promote *Seductio Ad Absurdum.* The book was already into its third printing after going on sale April 1, and so the media were clamoring for interviews with its attractive female author. The *New York World* arranged for Mickey to debate gender issues over lunch with novelist-playwright Floyd Dell, whose latest book was titled *Love in the Machine Age.* The question they discussed was whether the notion of romantic love was absurd amidst the glass and concrete towers of Manhattan. The resulting article by reporter Gladys Oaks was headlined "Two Authors Discuss the Fate of Marriage." The accompanying photo showed Mickey elegantly dressed and looking svelte in a flowered cotton dress, her hair in a flapper bob. She was leaning back in her chair, one arm resting on the table and her hands folded in front of her. She scowled at Dell, who was leaning on the table, glaring at her. Oaks wrote that Dell was "an artistic-looking man, with sensitive face and fingers" whereas "Emily Hahn looked, despite the small excited quaver in her voice, like a cool-dark, disdainful stranger who had wandered rather casually down from Olympus for an hour's call."[34]

If *World* editors hoped Mickey would be provocative and play the role of the radical feminist, they were not disappointed. The opportunity to pronounce from a soapbox was irresistible. Mickey played to the audience, arguing that romance was the bait of the trap known as marriage; women marry for love, but are quickly caught up in what she termed a "mill of mature realism"—babies and diapers and bovine domestic servitude. "I don't mean that there should be no relationship between the sexes. But let there be various relationships," Mickey was quoted as saying. "And never have a love affair with a man whose friendship you value. Because there's nothing like sex to make people hate and misunderstand one another."[35]

The tone of other interviews with Mickey that appeared in the Chicago *Evening Post* and the *Daily Times* during a May visit home was less theatrical. Louise Dejung of the *Daily Times* commented that Mickey looked like "a high school student, rosy cheeked, and refreshing; with dark eyes and a crinkly brown bob."[36] The *Evening Post* reporter took a similar approach, alluding to Mickey's younger days in the Windy City. "She may be remembered as the Senn High School girl who was nearly expelled . . . for appearing in school in such unladylike garments as knickers."[37]

Mickey's family, while dismayed at her insistence on going to Africa, made only a token effort to dissuade her. Hannah and Isaac knew that once their daughter set her mind on something, arguing only heightened both her resolve and the possibility of a serious rift between parents and daughter. The Hahns could only kiss Mickey good-bye and wish her well as she caught the train back to New York.

Mickey spent the first week of June visiting with Helen and Herbert, meeting with her publisher and a literary agent who had agreed to represent her, and fending off yet another marriage proposal from Bill Benét. Mickey left for London on June 11 aboard the S.S. *Majestic.*

• • •

Back in London, Mickey lived a barebones lifestyle while struggling to save money for the trip to Africa. She spent her days at the British Museum researching the Royal Society book and her spare time working on a novel she was calling *Gin and It.* Each day's mail brought yet another letter from Bill Benét. Whatever he may have lacked in persuasiveness, he more than made up for in persistence. "Well, I must be crazy, but since your ship left I have hardly been able to think of anything, . . ." he said in a rambling thirteen-page letter. "Do you really suppose she will marry me? I really seem to be groping in the dark."[38]

Benét addressed that uncertainty directly on June 30, when he cabled Mickey: "Can't live without you. No promises, except have excellent plan. Let us be married London early August."[39] Mickey said no; she still had no intention of marrying anyone. The problem was that Benét refused to believe her. He was determined to make his third trip to the altar with Mickey Hahn as his bride. He wrote again on July 12 taking a new approach. "I don't blame you, and I don't blame myself," he said. "God bless and keep you! Our ages and the amount of life each has lived are what make the difference. I knew that all along. But love is something that takes you by the scruff of the neck and shakes all the sense out of you."[40]

Two days later, Benét sent a fresh proposal. While admitting that he was opposed to Mickey's planned Africa trip, he pledged that if she agreed to marry him, he would let her travel whenever and wherever she wanted; in effect, Mr. and Mrs. William Benét would continue to lead separate lives. When Mickey rejected that idea too, Benét sent her a thirty-four-page opus, complete with newspaper clippings, and a poem dedicated to "Mickey Mouse," his pet name for her.

Mickey, though flattered and bemused by Benét's dogged pursuit, wrote a wickedly witty satirical poem, which appeared in the *New Yorker:*

Poets lead such simple lives;
Straight and true as blue steel knives.
They use words like 'love' and 'death';
They never even stop for breath.
They fall in love and never doubt it,
That's all there is about it.
And when their lives have passed them by,
Poets beautifully die.[41]

Mickey, herself, had no intention of allowing life to pass her by. Her weekly letters to her mother back in Chicago made that clear. She was now as preoccupied with other people's writing as her own. She read voraciously. "I see by the paper that Conrad Aiken has pocketed the Pulitzer Prize and gone to England with it, saying America does not provide adequately for her poets. Sometimes I get annoyed with poets," she told Hannah. "I don't think it is patriotism—I don't want to live in America myself, God knows—but in the same paper is a declaration by [journalist] Heywood Broun about running for Congress, and I'm getting very skeptical about the literati and their powers. Take me, for instance, I will be a literati if I can possibly make it, but will I have any common sense? No. Can I manage a government? No. Could I ever manage a business office? Ask Papa.

"I think the literati are getting very greedy. They have money and a vast admiration which is proportional to the degree of ignorance among the admirers. . . . Imagine John Gunther in Congress; and yet could anyone write a better account of Congress? It's one thing or the other. If you are inarticulate, you don't think, you talk. If you can't write you probably turn to the development of common sense as a substitute. Look at this paragraph of generalizations.

Did you ever read such unscientific nonsense? I'm getting awfully good with a typewriter."[42]

Mickey enjoyed some success selling her freelance articles during this period. Herbert had helped her find a literary agent in New York, a man named Lieber. The agent badgered her to write longer stories, which, of course, would earn more and increase the size of his commissions. "[He] wrote me that he hopes the editors won't go on insisting that I be 'smart.' It's true, I can't sell the other stuff yet, but he doesn't know that it's not the editors. I LIKE being smart. I AM smart," Mickey wrote to her mother.[43]

New Yorker editor Harold Ross, a friend of Herbert's, evidently agreed. He continued buying Mickey's "smart" submissions, and Bill Benét used his connections to help her sell one entitled "Lunch" to *Harper's*, which at the time was one of America's leading magazines. "Lunch" poked fun at what the English referred to as "Americanism." In it, Mickey related an amusing lunchtime conversation that she had with a young Englishman. He had asked of her, "Now, tell me why it is that the Americans are so eager for the history of another country. Why do they come here to see relics of English history?"

Mickey responded, "We want some history . . . and we haven't much of our own, so far. We need some traditions, so we come over here to look for them."[44] She was, of course, laughing at herself, and at the boatloads of American tourists, journalists, writers, and academics who flocked to London each year, even in the depths of the Great Depression. The city's hotels were full of Americans. Once she had completed her new novel and sent it off to her publisher, Mickey was no longer content to be among them. She was unable to concentrate on her writing or anything else. To occupy herself, Mickey enrolled in a course on "tropical hygiene" and set about learning the basics of survival in Africa, where conditions were harsh and diseases rampant. Mickey joked that if she took all the recommended medical supplies with her to Africa she would have "about two tons" of luggage.

By autumn, Mickey became anxious about the trip. She had saved only a few hundred dollars and was going nowhere fast. Patrick Putnam wrote to suggest that Mickey contact a Paris businessman who was traveling to Africa and might pay her way if she accompanied him as his secretary. Mickey rejected the idea. She had an alternative plan. Mickey had calculated that she needed about $1,500 a year to live in London; the amount for Africa would presumably be less. "Don't worry about me getting deeply into debt. I hate it as much as you do," she told Hannah. "What I'm going to do, if possible, is borrow about $500. That isn't very much, is it? Especially since I plan to split it up and borrow $250 from two people, if I can, and I probably can."[45]

The key question was whom to ask for a loan. She rejected the idea of asking Bill Benét for the money. Her old friend John Gunther might have offered her a loan when he visited London the first week of September, but she decided not to ask him, even after he propositioned her. "About John, he has written a good short novel which I read, but as for myself, he is so remarkably disagreeable and messy that I herewith announce that I will never see him again. If I do, I might kill him," Mickey told Hannah. "Something about his big fat hands and his nasty little nature and his nasty big body drives me crazy, especially when he tries to make love. He is such a poor liar, too."[46]

Mickey borrowed $250 from a journalist friend and various smaller amounts from other people. She also received a check from her parents and an unexpected windfall payment of $175 from the *New Yorker,* along with a request that she submit more articles as soon as possible. With this money Mickey purchased a third-class ticket from the French port of Bordeaux to the town of Avakubi. Patrick Putnam's medical mission was at the village of Wamba, in the Ituri Forest, about fifteen hundred miles up the Congo River. The ticket agents for the freighter on which Mickey booked passage were distressed that a woman would even think of making such a trip on her own, let alone doing so in third class; it simply was not done, they insisted. But Mickey was adamant, and so they sold her the ticket—at a mere £21—about $102 (U.S.). The fare was about half the price of second class.

With Mickey's departure confirmed for Christmas Day, and $800 in the bank, she set about making last-minute preparations for the trip. Mickey resisted a provisioner's suggestions that she buy a portable bathtub, tents, assorted folding furniture, shotguns, and a pith helmet, which he insisted that "everyone" who traveled in Africa needed. Mickey had neither the money nor the need for such paraphernalia; she planned to travel light in the Dark Continent.

Instead, Mickey purchased a supply of medicine, several reference books (an *Oxford Book of English Verse*, some Shakespeare, and a Bible "to be at my heart when I'm found dead," she joked[47]), and reams of typing paper, because she had told her literary agent in New York that she intended to write "two books, a play, and lots of articles in Africa."[48] The one extravagance she allowed herself was "a stylish elephant hunting suit," as she called it. The dark brown flannel outfit, white cotton blouse, and matching silk scarf made her look suitably jaunty when she had her photograph taken in it, but it was otherwise totally impractical.

On a much more serious note, Mickey visited a doctor to get the necessary inoculations and a required medical certificate stating that she was free of syphilis, tuberculosis, scrofula, and other communicable diseases. As a single woman traveling alone, even as a "mining engineer," the occupation listed on her passport, she was also obliged to obtain a notarized affidavit attesting to her "high moral character." Mickey reported in a letter home, "Arthur Mann is going with me to a notary public to swear out an affidavit that I have morals. The [Belgian] consul demands this. Arthur says he's used to lying; he's a newspaper man and won't go to Heaven anyway."[49]

Having settled her travel plans, Mickey was buoyant. It was with a renewed sense of urgency that she set about completing research for the Royal Society book and wired Joe Brewer at Brewer and Warren in New York for an assessment of her novel. "Please cable whether book accepted. Losing sleep, appetite, and beauty," she implored. Brewer replied promptly: "Darling, keep sleeping, eating, and beautiful," he said.[50] He followed up a few days later with a letter explaining in detail exactly what changes were needed before the book could be published. Mickey locked herself in her room, working nonstop on the revisions as she gobbled aspirins to ward off a cold.

A few days before Thanksgiving, Mickey dispatched the revised manuscript, now called *Beginner's Luck*. She then cabled Patrick Putnam informing him that the way was at last clear for her to leave London. An ominous and unnerving silence followed. Mickey passed several anxious weeks waiting to hear from him. Why had he not answered? Was something wrong?

Mickey, uncertain and fearful after a tearful Christmas Eve on her own, decided to press ahead with her plans no matter what. She had dreamed of Africa for too long to turn back now.

III

Traveling Light in the Dark Continent

10

"Africa was an unusual hobby for a young woman in the late 1920s," Mickey recalled in her memoir *Times and Places,* "and, as I had learned by painful experience, most men didn't understand my ambition to go there."[1] Her family, friends, and even the ticket officials of the company in London on whose ship she booked passage were dismayed by her eagerness to visit "Darkest Africa," let alone to save £20 by traveling third class rather than second. After all, there was nothing in Africa but heat, disease, wild beasts, and "uncivilized native hordes," as the wife of one intrepid traveler writing in *National Geographic* magazine put it.

But it was precisely because of all these dangers and because it was *not* "a proper thing" for a lady to do that Mickey was determined to travel to Africa on her own. Those who had known her at university would have understood as much. They might also have understood that in the beginning, at least, even Mickey must have had second thoughts about the course she had charted for herself. Her doubts were never stronger than on Christmas Day 1930 as her ship steamed out of cool, foggy London bound for the French port of Bordeaux, just across the Channel. Despite the festive mood on board, Mickey was a forlorn figure. Tears rolled down her cheeks as she watched the lights of the great city fade from view. Soon there was only the rumbling of the ship's engines and the plaintive moan of its foghorn to intrude upon thoughts of family, friends, and home half a world away.

While Mickey passed two days waiting for the departure of the ship to Africa, Bordeaux's glum weather did nothing to lift her spirits. Nor did the surly porters who chided her for the weight of her tin trunks, each of which was to carry no more than thirty pounds—the approved weight for an African bearer. Her outlook improved on the evening of December 28, when she boarded the *Brazza*, a French passenger ship, to discover that, despite the fears of the ticket agents, third class was "perfectly clean and comfortable." She was surprised to discover that there was also a fourth-class area. It was packed with African troops and chickens.

Third class was filled with noncommissioned French army officers on their way to the French Congo. They were "swarthy, undersized men from Marseille and Corsica, with deep voices and five-o'clock shadows," as Mickey wrote. "They were polite to me but often quarreled with each other, and most nights were noisy after I had gone to bed."[2]

Mickey was put in a sparsely furnished four-bunk cabin so far down in the ship that the hull sloped in to meet the floor, and condensation dripped constantly from the bulkheads. Mercifully, there were no bugs, and Mickey was on her own for the three-week voyage. That was just as well; during the first two days at sea she was deathly seasick. She lay in her bunk unable to eat and barely able to function. It was not until December 30 that she recovered enough to go to the ship's galley, where she sat and wrote a letter to her mother. "I have been SICK. For two days I lay moaning (I think, but I don't remember)," she said.[3]

Within a few days, Mickey's spirit returned. So did her charm. A little sergeant began taking a special interest in her, offering her lemonade when she was ill and appearing at her cabin door on New Year's Eve with a phonograph and some records. A crowd gathered when the music started. Another young woman with a baby appeared, as did a cheerful older woman, a pimply youth, and a baleful soldier. All of them began dancing and singing with great enthusiasm.

Life aboard the *Brazza* settled into a lazy routine. Days began with morning coffee in pajamas at seven-thirty. Mickey found that the food served in the two meals each day was plentiful and better than she had eaten in second class aboard British ships. Mickey passed her days reading, writing, or up on deck. She leaned on the railing staring at the waves for long hours and watching a lone shark that had trailed the ship. If she wanted conversation, Mickey tried

Mickey posing with French soldiers aboard the Brazza, *en route to Africa, January 1930.*
Courtesy Emily Hahn Estate

talking to the little sergeant or his colleagues, who flirted ceaselessly with her. They were hard put to restrain their curiosity about this attractive, single American woman. Because she was traveling to Africa solo, and in third class, some assumed she was a prostitute, others that she was on her way to join her husband who was obviously in Africa already. After all, why else would any woman go to such a place? Mickey's French being limited, she did not tell them.

On January 5, after nine days at sea, the ship arrived at Dakar, capital of the West African nation of Senegal. Although it was midnight, Mickey and a couple of the soldiers disembarked. They did some sightseeing, checked out the night spots, and had a few drinks. They arrived back at the ship several hours later feeling contented, but tired after having walked for miles. It had felt good to be back on dry land.

Giddy at finally being in Africa, Mickey went ashore again the next day with a Corsican adjutant named Martini. When he suggested they have a drink, Mickey agreed, on condition that she buy. Martini was aghast. "If anyone should see, they would think that you were a woman who . . ." he insisted, his voice trailing off.

"Oh, hell!" Mickey responded, motioning to him to sit down.

The Corsican shrugged. As they sat down and began talking the conversation got around to the other women on the ship. They had been sleeping with the sergeants, Mickey's companion informed her in a hushed voice. When she asked how he knew, Martini smiled knowingly as he explained he had seen one of them coming out of a soldier's cabin early one morning. Mickey laughed; she suggested that perhaps the woman and her friend had simply been talking. Martini was exasperated. They could have talked on deck, he insisted. Mickey countered by charging he had "bad thoughts." When she announced she was bored by this talk, the Corsican became indignant.

"Then I should not make love to you?" he said.

"I wouldn't consider it an insult if you *didn't*," Mickey snapped.[4]

Back at the ship, they shook hands. Mickey had made her point, while Martini, sadder but wiser, had learned a lesson about women—or at least about this headstrong young American. His attitude toward her changed after that. He grudgingly conceded they were just friends. The following evening, Mickey was the special at a party in honor of Napoleon, that most famous Corsican. Martini and five other Corsicans celebrated in the ship's galley with champagne, cake, and gramophone music. Mickey whirled about the floor, dancing polkas with each of them in turn.

Seeing that Mickey loved to party and could hold her liquor with the best of them, one of the soldiers jokingly challenged her to a drinking contest. He was taken aback when she accepted. The spectacle occurred a few days later, before a crowd in the galley. Mickey and her challenger downed drink after drink, Pernods being the weapon of choice. They each had five before the liqueur ran out. When it did, they switched to cocktails of champagne, cognac, and "God knows what else," as Mickey recalled. Afterward, she made her way to bed feeling bleary eyed but victorious. Although there was no shortage of volunteers to accompany her, Mickey insisted on being left alone to sleep it off, and they reluctantly agreed. Looking back on the experience, and on the entire voyage, Mickey later told Hannah, "In a funny way, I enjoyed every minute of it."[5]

· · ·

The ocean portion of Mickey's journey ended January 19, 1931, when the ship arrived at Boma, the port near the mouth of the Congo River. A Belgian customs official perused Mickey's travel papers and curtly announced, "You haven't enough money to get in." The law was that a traveler needed at least 50,000 Belgian francs in the bank or 10,000 in hand to be admitted to the colony. Although Mickey had neither, she had been assured by shipping company officials in London that this requirement was only a formality. In a fit of exasperation, Mickey pointed to her travel documents.

An argument ensued. It ended with the official agreeing to wire his superior for instructions. When there was no immediate response, Mickey was obliged to stay aboard the ship when it arrived upriver in Matadi later that day. There was a good deal of what Mickey termed "the usual Latin confusion" as she was "waited upon by a committee of fat Belgians with badges."[6] While the other passengers disembarked, she spent several anxious hours waiting for the situation to be resolved. Mickey sweated and worried that customs officials would search her belongings, where they would find a handgun one of the Corsicans had given her for protection. She knew this would cause trouble. Belgian colonial customs officers in the Congo were notoriously fastidious.

Fortunately, they bothered Mickey no further. The impasse was resolved unexpectedly and amicably when an official from a multinational trading company intervened on her behalf. The man, whom Patrick Putnam had asked to watch out for her, vouched for Mickey. It was fortunate that he did. Officials in Boma had already issued orders that Mickey was not to be allowed to purchase a train ticket to Kinshasa, the jumping-off point for boats that took passengers and cargo upriver.

Mickey was thrilled, but suddenly fearful of the dangers involved in such a journey. Even before it could begin, she faced a fourteen-hour overnight train ride that was the only way to get to Kinshasa, 225 miles away. The narrow-gauge railway, poorly maintained and subject to frequent derailments, had been built in 1900 on orders from King Leopold of Belgium. The line skirted rapids at the mouth of the Congo River, just one of a series of natural obstacles that rendered the river unnavigable in places. The French writer André Gide, who rode the Matadi–Kinshasa railway in 1929, observed that "The Congo would be a natural outlet for the riches of the interior if it were not that the river traverses a mountainous region not far from the coast and ceases to be navigable at Matadi."[7]

In Kinshasa, Mickey found haven in a steamy, but comfortable, hotel room. Kinshasa was a bustling port and trade center with a European population of about 2,500 and at least five times as many natives. Mickey wrote to her mother to say that it was unlikely anyone at home would hear from her for several weeks, postal service to the interior being slow. "This place is fascinating, but not pleasant," she said.[8]

Mickey kept busy for four days while she waited for the departure of the boat to Stanleyville. She did her laundry, toured the town with the wife of a local businessman, an English-speaking woman who befriended her, and wrote in her room. "I feel smug and virtuous today because I finished another long story and got it off in the mail this morning, although I had to be rude all day yesterday and say to people who stopped at the door, 'Do you mind going away? I'm awfully busy.' "[9]

Mickey also went out dancing with three young American men she met. "The music was listless," she reported, "and when I danced I had a horrible vision of rows and rows of fat glistening faces staring . . . out of bulging pale blue eyes . . . at me and the few other white women dancing round and round and pretending not to know what the men were thinking about. And how civilized and polite they all look in their white suits. . . . I'm not in the least terrified, but I'm impatient to get away from here."[10]

She did so on January 28. The boat for Stanleyville, the *Micheline*, reminded her of the steamboats she had seen plying the Mississippi River during her childhood in St. Louis. Several of the stern-wheelers operating on the Congo at the time had actually been transplanted from the Mississippi. Their new owners had disassembled them and shipped them to Africa, where their shallow drafts made them ideal for shuttling goods and cargo to the scattered settlements along the Congo and its tributaries. With few roads and only limited air service, these boats were the principal means of transporting goods and passengers.

The *Micheline* left Kinshasa on its two-week trip to Stanleyville carrying a load of priests, nuns, and medical aid workers—what Mickey irreverently termed "new mosquito-fodder from Belgium."[11] Despite the crowded conditions, she again had a cabin all to herself. For this, she could thank a woman she had met in Kinshasa, who had bribed a ticket agent on Mickey's behalf. Mickey welcomed the privacy because tsetse flies, mosquitoes, and other biting insects drove her to distraction. It was also as hot and humid as a sauna, particularly after dark. The engine was shut off when the boat dropped anchor to avoid the hazards of nighttime river navigation and to take on wood for fuel. Without the engine, the electric lights and ceiling fans went dead. "Last night . . . it was so hot that I thought I would rather die than lie there any longer," Mickey wrote, "but even my desire for death was languid and unpassionate. It's the first time in my life that I grew slippery with perspiration just lying in bed."[12]

In daylight, the tropical sun beat down incessantly. Progress against the river current was slow—seventy miles on a good day—and the hours passed in slow motion. Mickey tried to sleep or she sat around worrying about the hideous tropical diseases and infections she was sure she would catch. Sometimes she escaped the heat by sitting with the captain up in the wheelhouse, where it was breezy. The man, a gruff but good-natured Belgian named Roger Baillon, welcomed the company of an attractive young white woman. "I'm learning a lot about navigation because I spend a good deal of time up ahead with the captain," Mickey reported to her mother. "Whenever he starts to make love I ask him an intelligent question about the boat—he can never resist answering in full detail, which saves me a good deal of trouble."[13]

Mickey's fear of illnesses was valid. A native woman on board died one evening from an undiagnosed illness, and Mickey spent the next day trying to figure out which of her fellow passengers was now missing. Afterward, she became obsessed with scouring her cabin for tsetse flies. She knew the tiny insects carried sleeping sickness, an often fatal affliction that causes insomnia, lethargy, headache, convulsions, and coma. Death always seemed perilously close in this cruel place, and Mickey's nights were filled with bizarre, fearsome nightmares, which left her trembling in a cold sweat. In one, she dreamed of awakening to find her intestines spewing out onto the pillow beside her.

Each evening as the boat dropped anchor it was besieged by locals who made their living from fishing or trading. They came with fish or palm oil to sell. Sometimes, if the *Micheline* was close enough to the riverbank, in the blackness Mickey could make out the inhabitants of the settlements. They gathered in the jungle clearings, like ghostly shadows around their campfires. The sight of them stirred in Mickey a curiosity that was tempered by primal fear; these were rooted in a youth filled with tales of the dangers of African jungles. Her imagination had been fired by Edgar Rice Burroughs's *Tarzan* books, British explorer Mary Kingsley's 1897 best-seller *Travels in West Africa*, Joseph Conrad's classic novel *Heart of Darkness* (1902), and by thrilling popular accounts of the adventures of Sir Henry Morton Stanley, the former St. Louis newspaperman who had achieved worldwide fame in 1871 by finding the Scottish missionary and explorer—David Livingstone. "I knew as much as I could read about Stanley," Mickey recalls, "and of course, Conrad—'Mistah Kurtz, he dead.'"[14]

Like most young Americans of the time, Mickey was profoundly influenced by a simplistic and highly romanticized image of Africa. Such mythology was an inescapable part of the intellectual baggage that she, and many others, carried to Africa. The scenes of everyday life that Mickey witnessed from her van tage point at the ship's railing did nothing to dispel the stereotypes.

Many of the local women were bare breasted and had elaborately curled hair; the men were naked but for tiny loincloths. Wrote Mickey, "At night, with their eyes shining and the ridges of tattooing on their foreheads standing out strongly and their brown bodies almost glistening in the lamplight from the boat, they make me wonder uneasily why we're all intruding in this country anyway. What do they think about? It shouldn't be so hard to tell." Mickey's words, hopelessly racist by today's standards, spoke volumes about the prevailing white attitude toward African blacks in 1931. "They are animals, but articulate animals," Mickey continued. "And their eyes—I never noticed their eyes till yesterday. Some of them are narrow and bloodshot, startlingly intelligent and fierce, especially when they are quarreling."[15]

Mickey felt uneasy about her fears and about engaging in this sort of racial stereotyping, but it came so shamelessly and naturally in this place that it was difficult to avoid or debate it. Being new to Africa, she reasoned, she did not understand "the system." Nonetheless, in her own mind Mickey struggled to draw a distinction between the African Americans she knew back home and those she now encountered in the Congo. The attitude among whites in the African colony was that the natives were lazy at best, downright stupid at worst. Observing the treatment afforded blacks by Europeans had moved André Gide to write, "The less intelligent the white man is, the more stupid he thinks the blacks."[16]

Mickey would have agreed with Gide's observation. It was not unusual to see a white man whipping black workers, although it was generally riverboat captains—Captain Baillon being an exception—or the Belgian colonial district commissioners who attempted to beat enlightenment into the savages. "It shocked me gravely; I never got used to it," Mickey said.[17]

For now, she watched and listened. She did not yet dare to object to what she saw, for she realized that by implication she was now part of the "system." The captain usually acted as an ersatz judge in disputes between his crew and the locals. However, when these quarrels did not occur on board, Baillon refused to get involved, and the natives began asking Mickey to do so. For a twenty-five-year-old, the sense of power was intoxicating and more than a little intimidating. In the eyes of the natives, her skin color and the fact that she sometimes sat in the wheelhouse with the captain conferred upon her "official" status.

• • •

The *Micheline* docked on February 10 at Stanleyville (now known as Kisangani) a bustling trade and administrative center established a half century earlier by Henry Stanley. Mickey was the guest of the local Belgian consul. Like other colonial officials, he believed that she was an American journalist on her way to interview Patrick Putnam. The consul informed Mickey that the Belgian Red Cross had transferred Patrick from Wamba, Mickey's original destination, to the even more remote settlement of Penge. Located on a Congo tributary known as the Aruwimi River, about two hundred miles northeast of Stanleyville, Penge had once been an important trading post. No longer. As the only white person in that area, Putnam lived in a redbrick house originally built for the district administrator. An adjacent two-room schoolhouse served as the Red Cross hospital and clinic.

Mickey considered buying either a motorcycle or car to drive to Penge. She abandoned those ideas upon learning that the settlement, deep within the Ituri Forest, was accessible only by river. Mickey hitched a ride to a place called Avakubi on a supply truck run by SEDEC, the Belgian arm of the multinational corporation Lever Brothers. The company had a monopoly at the time on trading posts and on much of the river transit in the Congo.

En route to Avakubi, the SEDEC truck stopped at an elephant farm, where the animals were domesticated and trained to do work. Mickey took notes for an article that her literary agent in New York eventually sold to *Travel* magazine.[18] The piece was a precursor of the sort of investigative stories—by "our far-flung correspondents"—that later would become Mickey's bread and butter in the pages of the *New Yorker*.

The SEDEC driver, a randy Englishman named Barlow, dropped Mickey off at the dock in Avakubi, but not before making a clumsy pass at her. She rebuffed him disdainfully. Barlow, embarrassed and angry, drove off muttering to himself that he would not forget the slight. He did not—as Mickey would eventually discover. However, for now, she had a far more pressing concern: the final leg of the journey to Penge.

She had just missed Patrick, who had been in town for supplies a few days earlier. He had made arrangements for Mickey to travel to Penge with a Belgian elephant hunter named Smet, several native men, and two native women. The night before they were to depart, Mickey received bad news: the truck carrying her luggage from Stanleyville to Avakubi had been involved in an accident. It was feared her typewriter, notes, medical supplies, clothing, and all of her belongings had been lost. That meant she was left with just the clothes on her back and the few personal items in her satchel. "I received the tidings with a surprising apathy," Mickey wrote. "Hell, I'll never get home at this rate, yet I don't seem to care. What's the matter with me. Am I crazy?"[19] Mickey found solace in a bottle of Pernod that she split with Smet. They sat drinking and talking until one o'clock in the morning.

Bright and early the next day, March 3, 1931, Mickey and her party set out for Penge in a pirogue, a native canoe made from a hollowed-out tree trunk. Mickey escaped the scorching sun by sitting under a canvas awning spread over a wicker frame. The makeshift shelter was tied to the bow of the pirogue. Because the locals did not speak English and because Smet spent most of his time at the stern tinkering with a small outboard motor, the only sounds for hours on end were those of waves slapping against the hull and the rhythmic singsong of the paddlers. They glistened with sweat as they stroked the reddish brown water and tapped the side of the pirogue in time to their music. The jungle on both sides of the river, lush, dark, and mysterious, was a green wall at the water's edge. Mickey stared in fascination. This was the untamed Africa of myth and storybook, the Africa of every child's imagination.

They traveled all that day before stopping at a village to bathe, eat, and make plans to haul the pirogue past some rapids. It was now just a few hours' paddling to Penge. To celebrate this fact and the news that her missing trunks had turned up, Mickey donned her best dress. Her bare arms attracted swarms of voracious insects and the curious gaze of the locals, who gathered to stare at the first white woman many of them had ever seen. Mickey's every movement was followed with rapt attention, particularly when she brushed her teeth and spat out the toothpaste. When the crowd buzzed with sotto voce remarks, Mickey decided it was just as well she did not understand any of what was being said.

Even without most of the native paddlers, who stayed behind after being paid off, the next day's travel was relatively easy. As they neared Penge, it was dusk. Mickey noticed that all along the riverbanks groups of people had gathered in the clearings. Some stared in silence; others shouted and waved. Word of her arrival had spread, and the curious were out in full force. Several pirogues appeared. In one of them was Patrick Putnam. À la Stanley, Mickey stood up and called out across the water: "Dr. Putnam, I presume?" Patrick waved. "I never thought you'd get here, not once in a thousand years!" he said with a laugh.

11

Night comes with the speed of an arrow in equatorial Africa, and there were only a precious few minutes of daylight left as Mickey and Patrick unloaded the pirogue for the hike to Penge, high on a bluff overlooking the river. As she stepped ashore, Mickey was greeted by Chimpo, the same chimpanzee Patrick had kept in Brussels, and by Abanzima, his native love. Mickey was taken aback by the sight of her. "Though it was dark on the beach I could see that my Undine, my maiden of classic tragedy, was no beauty. Why, she was an old woman!" Mickey wrote.[1] The teeth in Abanzima's giggly welcoming smile had been filed to points, as was the custom in the Mangbetu tribe; her bare breasts were shriveled and droopy, and her bald head was as shiny as a bowling ball.

Mickey mused on this as she, Patrick, and the welcoming party made their way up the bluff, marching the hundred yards to Penge in single file. Mickey's tin boxes were skillfully balanced on African heads. They bore the boxes up the front steps of Patrick's bungalow, across the big veranda, and inside the front door. Mickey saw that the grounds were littered with piles of junk. There were discarded boots, pieces of old machinery, empty bottles, and bits of rag—the badges of civilization.

Mickey's boxes were deposited in the main living room of the single-story dwelling. It was cluttered with piles of books, a wooden table covered with decaying insect and worm specimens, a couple of folding camp chairs, and a cot with sheets and a mosquito net. The entire scene was washed with the soft yellow light of an oil lantern. Patrick informed Mickey this would be her quarters until his "boys" could build her a proper hut. "A house for me? But I'm only visiting, not staying here," she reminded him.

Patrick smiled as he explained there was not much work involved in erecting a hut; wood was plentiful, and labor was cheap in Penge. Besides, he noted, the settlement needed a guest house, since those who visited usually stayed a long time. This suited Patrick, for he already had devised plans to lure well-heeled white tourists and big-game hunters to the area and to turn the settlement into a kind of African dude ranch. In the fall of 1930, prior to Mickey's arrival at Penge, someone had sent him a *New Yorker* cartoon, which depicted a couple of cameramen trying to get a group of African pygmies to pose. The caption had the pygmies quipping, "Nothing doing! We can do better with the Paramount-Mayer-Goldwyn people."

In response Patrick wrote a letter to the *New Yorker* poking fun at the frequency with which photos of African pygmies—"the mysterious little people of the forest," as he called them—appeared in the Sunday rotogravure sections of American and British newspapers. According to Patrick's "Report from the Field," the reality in the Belgian Congo was closer to that of the cartoon than the newspaper stories. The pygmies had become so used to meeting intrepid white "explorers" that posing for photographs at a few Belgian francs per session was now a thriving cottage industry. Patrick pointed out that a French film company recently had hired some pygmies to act as primitive tree people, who for dramatic purposes pretended to be coaxed down from their leafy perches with proffered bananas.[2]

Putnam's biographer, Harvard anthropologist Joan Mark, speculates that he wrote his report for two reasons: to establish himself as an expert on pygmies and to remind friends and colleagues back home of where he was and what he was doing there.[3] Patrick also may have had his business plans in the back of his mind. Within two years, he would be dismissed from the Red Cross after his superiors learned he had been smoking *bangi,* the native version of marijuana, which was illegal under Belgian law. Unemployed, Patrick moved to a camp on the Epulu River, one hundred miles east of Penge. Here he petitioned the colonial administration for a tract of land on which to farm and build a hotel with the financial backing of his family in Boston. Government officials leased him the land after he played host to Crown Prince Leopold and Princess Astrid of Belgium on a visit to "Camp Putnam" in early 1933. A pamphlet jointly written by Putnam and his wife Mary, a white American whom he had married in May of that year, describes their Epulu camp in quaint terms that make it sound like a rustic New England inn.[4]

Mickey's own discussion with Patrick about accommodations ended abruptly when he left the room with Chimpo, who had been making a nuisance of herself by poking into the crates of supplies. At this point Mickey realized with a start that she was not alone. Her every move was being watched by a large crowd of locals who were on the veranda, peering in the window. The darkened faces, with their white eyes and gleaming teeth, were barely discernible in the lantern's golden glow. "The audience was quiet, but I could hear some sounds—heavy breathing, a soft whisper, an occasional inadvertent squeal of wonder," Mickey wrote.[5]

Being watched was something Mickey got used to. The only white woman in Penge—and for many miles around—was the object of intense curiosity. When Abanzima and two other young native women arrived with dinner trays, Mickey caught the three of them studying her. Abanzima burst into laughter as she covered her mouth, and began rocking back and forth in embarrassment; Abanzima liked her, Patrick explained. Mickey smiled and began examining her new friend more carefully. As she did so, she realized Abanzima was not as old as her initial impressions had led her to believe.

What Mickey had assumed were deep, leathery wrinkles on the woman's face and chest were actually cicatrization—scarring caused when the skin of the face, torso, or limbs is cut in decorative and highly distinctive patterns. Pronounced wheals, or keloids, are then created by rubbing irritants into the wound; the effect is akin to embossing a piece of leather. The Mangbetu, like many other African people, regard cicatrization and the filing of teeth (which many whites wrongly suspected was synonymous with cannibalism) to be beautifying processes, much the way people in North America regard cosmetic surgery or body piercing.

Even more striking than Abanzima's scars and shaved pate was the peculiar elongated shape of the head of Abanzima's cousin Nambedru, who had helped to serve the food. At birth, her mother had tightly wrapped Nambedru's head with bandages to make her skull grow melon shaped. With her beautiful, wide-set eyes and high cheekbones, Nambedru's features were striking. Now it was Mickey who could not help but stare in amazement.

She inquired about the identity of the third server, a diminutive girl named Sissy. Mickey noted that while she, too, was cicatrized and had filed teeth, her features were different from those of her companions. The reason, Mickey learned, was that Sissy's mother was a pygmy. That accounted for her distinctive turned-out lips and the lighter color of her hair. Beyond that, Patrick confided that he knew little about the girl. "I just *got* her last week," he said.

While this latter remark struck Mickey as an odd turn of phrase, she thought nothing more of it at the time. Weary from her travels, she was ready for bed. Patrick obligingly departed so she could undress, taking the lantern with him. Outside in the inky blackness, Mickey could hear the shuffling of dozens of feet on the veranda and the disappointed murmurs as the audience dispersed. The curtain had come down on the evening's "entertainment."

• • •

The spectators were back at the window next morning, shortly after the bugle call that signaled dawn at Penge. They returned for several more mornings, until the novelty of studying Mickey waned. Nonetheless, she remained a local curiosity for several weeks. "Mickey-mania" was rekindled when she moved into the new guest hut, and again when she began accompanying Patrick to the hospital.

At first, Mickey sat and watched. Then she got involved in the medical care. Patrick gave her a crash course in how to give injections, wrap bandages, take blood, do Red Cross paperwork, and remove chigoes, or "jiggers"—small fleas that burrow painfully under the victim's toenails, where they lay eggs. The first Swahili words Mickey learned were medical terms and how to swear. There being no other female medical workers in the region, perhaps in the colony, there were no native words to describe her; locals referred to her as "the doctor's sister." Mickey explained, "It was probably because they couldn't figure out why I was there otherwise; they knew I didn't sleep with Pat, so I must be a relative. He may even have told them I was his sister."[6]

Outside the clinic, Mickey found there was also much to learn, mostly about everyday life among the Ituri people, the area's dominant tribe, and about the Ituri Forest, which teemed with wild creatures and mysterious plants. Some of the skills Mickey acquired were mundane—such as learning to speak Kingwana, the local dialect of Swahili. Others were matters of survival: she learned how to sit inert in a pirogue when there were crocodiles in the river, how to avoid leopards and other predators when making a noctural visit to the outhouse, how to track an elephant in the forest, and how to keep Chimpo from stealing things.

As the weeks passed, Mickey slowly pieced together the character of her host; what she learned was disquieting. Mickey got a hint while shopping with Patrick one Sunday morning at the local marketplace. A casual observation he made stopped her cold. "It's a funny thing how much three wives can cost a man, even in the Congo," he said as he paid for a dress length of printed cotton.

The comment hit Mickey like a kick in the stomach. She was speechless. She could think of no polite way to raise the issue of Patrick's relationship with the women in his house—and with her. It was evident that Patrick relished Mickey's company and her "civilized" conversation. Now she could not help wondering if that was the limit of his interest in her. Did he consider her, too, a kept woman, a wife in training? Such thoughts angered her, as did the realization that Patrick's supposedly beautiful, pure love for Abanzima was not the fairy-tale romance Mickey had imagined. When she had read fairy tales as a girl, she often identified with the prince, but no prince she knew of had practiced polygamy. That was not a topic with which a young woman from the American Midwest had much familiarity, and for all her liberalism it was one that she did not feel at ease discussing. It felt odd to be a prude.

Polygamy and miscegenation were open secrets in the Belgian Congo, although official policy was for colonial officials to frown on the practices. Banning them would have proved difficult. Many European men were cohabiting with native women. "Openly and without restraint the white man lives with his black women or those of his friend, frequently exchanging the same," British adventurer Douglas Fraser had written a few years earlier.[7]

For their part, many native women were eager to live with a white man. Doing so afforded an elevated social status and guaranteed a relatively easy lifestyle. There was no social stigma to bearing children out of wedlock, and the mulatto offspring of such relationships were not treated differently than other children in the community.

After several weeks of musing about this situation and of observing daily life in Penge, Mickey's concerns abated. She noted that the local chief had half a dozen wives, and every man seemed to have an extra wife or two, if he could afford the goats, spears, or money, which custom dictated had to be paid to the bride's parents. No one seemed at all concerned about the practice. So Mickey concluded that here in Penge, at least, it was *she* who was out of step. "Whenever I made some new male acquaintance in the villages round about, he invariably would ask me severely, 'Where is your master?,' or, in another version, 'Where is your husband?,' for both ideas were expressed by the same word in the vernacular."[8]

Mickey did not acquire a husband in Penge; however, she did become a foster mother. One day at the clinic, she inoculated an orphan. He appeared to be about three or four years old. He was naked, hungry, and hobbled by foot sores caused by jiggers. Since no one knew his name, he was dubbed Matope, which Mickey later learned means "mud" in Kingwana. "His tribe? Well, most of the villagers, descendants as they were of slaves brought in by the Arab traders, were simply called 'Arabisées.' Only the Mangbetu and a few other imports laid claim to [being] a special tribe," Mickey explained.[9]

Matope shrieked with pain and fright as Mickey cleaned and dressed his

Emily Hahn with the orphan boy Matope, Penge, 1931.
Courtesy Emily Hahn Estate

wounds. Afterward, he was not supposed to walk on his bandaged feet, so she volunteered to care for him at her own hut. Mickey dressed the tiny lad in a woolen undershirt that fit him like a nightgown. Some Red Cross blankets piled on the floor became his bed, and Mickey began teaching him the alphabet. Her friendship with Matope was cemented when she bought him a tiny kaftan and a fez. Grateful Matope became Mickey's "shadow," trailing her wherever she went. He also joined Patrick's extended "family," becoming every bit as much at home in Patrick's house as were his three wives, the household staff, and Chimpo and the various other critters that hopped, crawled, and flew in and out the open door.

As time passed, one season slipped imperceptibly into another, for the climate in Penge, almost three thousand feet above sea level, was far more moderate than that of Stanleyville and other river towns. As 1931 became 1932, Mickey realized that she had found a home there. While sitting in the shade of the porch at Patrick's house one hot afternoon, as she often did, it dawned on her that Abanzima was no longer bald; her head was covered with jet-black plaits. This realization set Mickey musing about her own situation. Several times, she had announced vague plans to leave. Each time she did, Patrick had offered compelling reasons why she should stay a bit longer. Adding an air of logic to his words was Mickey's lack of money. The $750 she had carried in her trunks from London was mostly gone. Even more significantly, the value of the pound had plummeted when England abandoned the gold standard on September 20, 1931. This in turn led to a lengthy delay in the arrival of additional traveling money, not that this mattered.

There was little reason to go home. Economic conditions remained grim there; more than twelve million workers were unemployed. Conditions were no better in England. As a result, the letters that Mickey periodically received from family and friends no longer stirred her to be on her way. She replied when she felt the urge, sometimes not at all. With no job and little chance of finding one, Mickey had no reason to leave Penge, even if she'd had the money to do so. Despite the shortcomings of life there, the constant threats of disease and of quick death in the jaws of wild beasts, she was relatively content. Here, at least, there were no bread lines. Mickey had enough to eat, a place to sleep, work to do, few expenses, friends, ample time to read, and peace to write her articles and short stories.

Meanwhile, Mickey's publisher in New York had released her novel in mid-August 1931. *Beginner's Luck*, which Mickey dedicated to her brother-in-law, Mitchell Dawson, told the story of three young Americans who run away to Mexico after becoming disillusioned by the emptiness of life in the artists' colony at Sante Fe. At almost three hundred pages, *Beginner's Luck* was Mickey's first successful attempt to write "something longer," as her agent was continually urging her. The dust jacket hype announced that "Miss Hahn here captures movingly the bewilderment of youth." It went on to proclaim, "As her short stories have placed her among the most important of the younger American writers, so this novel brings her definitely into the front ranks of that company which has already proved its strength and its significance."[10]

Unfortunately, it was easier said than done to sustain over the long haul the sort of wry wit and lightness of touch that had become Mickey's literary calling card; the critics did not like *Beginner's Luck*. "The novel leaves one with the feeling that there has been made a worthy attempt toward an end which lacks a little of having been quite successfully achieved," wrote a *New York Times* reviewer.[11] Even less encouraging was the assessment of the *Saturday Review of Literature*—coincidentally the same publication Bill Benét edited. An anonymous reviewer dismissed the characters in *Beginner's Luck* as "trivial" and concluded that "the material and the people both fall short of justifying their claim to having a whole novel devoted to them."[12] Whether or not Benét, the spurned suitor, wrote these words is uncertain; what is not is that at the very least he read and edited them.

An incident that occurred one day in November 1932 finally snapped Mickey out of the lethargy into which she had fallen. She learned that Patrick had shaved off Nambedru's hair after overhearing her argue with Sissy about how to plait it. This was Patrick's way of punishing a woman he regarded as a naughty child. Nambedru was reduced to tears; Abanzima and the other women in the household were incensed. Mickey was puzzled, even more so when she sought out Patrick to ask him about the incident. She immediately

Patrick Putnam's passport photo, 1933.
Courtesy of the Houghton Library, Harvard University

sensed his impatience with the topic. Patrick ended the conversation abruptly when he shouted for his dinner to be brought to him.

That night, Mickey tossed and turned in her bed as she reflected on her host's hostility and on his attitude toward his wives and the other natives. Once, Mickey had seen Patrick in a rage throw a paddle at one of his workers. On other occasions, he had drilled Penge's inhabitants and made them stand at military-like attention in the hot sun. Patrick justified his behavior by arguing it was natural that "the strong should dominate the weak." That was the law of the jungle. The only time that was wrong, he added, was when white missionaries and colonial officials couched their motives in altruistic or moralistic terms. Patrick justified his own presence in the Belgian Congo on the grounds that he was an anthropologist and medical aid worker. The more Mickey thought about this, the more convinced she became that he was really nothing more than an opportunist in an altruist's clothing.

Mickey fell asleep that night only after having once more convinced herself that she was overreacting if she allowed her own cultural and moral biases to color her interpretation of events in Penge. Yet she could not shuck a niggling sense that her attitude toward Patrick had changed. Not long afterward, that notion was reinforced when Mickey overheard him expounding something to the members of his household; "the sound of his voice, heavily authoritative, made the skin on the back of my neck prickle unpleasantly," she later wrote.[13]

Spurred by a gnawing sense of unease, Mickey decided that she needed to get away for a few days. Her opportunity came when a visiting Belgian official

The view of Penge from the river, circa 1932.
Courtesy Emily Hahn Estate

invited her to accompany him on an elephant hunt in the bush. When Mickey did so, she was thoroughly digusted by the spectacle of the bloody slaughter. She returned to Penge with a renewed willingness to resume her life there. These feelings of rapprochement did not last long.

No one was there to meet her when Mickey's pirogue arrived at the landing. The reason for this unusual situation quickly became evident upon her arrival at the settlement. Mickey found a tearful Abanzima sitting under a tree on the lawn in front of Patrick's house. A collar, like the one sometimes used to restrain Chimpo, was padlocked around her neck, and she was tethered to a tree by a length of chain. Abanzima was not talking, and the other native members of the household had made themselves scarce, so Mickey sought out Patrick. She found him sitting in his office doing paperwork. He looked tired and worn, having been hit with one of the periodic attacks of malaria from which he suffered because he spurned quinine. Otherwise, all seemed normal. It was only when she inquired about Abanzima that Patrick discarded his mask of tranquility.

He explained how he had caught Abanzima in flagrante delicto with one of the local men. As punishment, Patrick had beaten her and made her carry her bed through the village. Then he had decreed that she should be chained to a tree each day for a week from sunrise to sunset. Furthermore, Patrick had sent Nambedru home to her native village because she had known about Abanzima's affair, but had kept it secret. Mickey listened to all of this in silence. She knew it was pointless to argue. Instead, she retreated to her hut, where she mused anew about Patrick and about his treatment of the women of his household. Once again, Mickey rationalized her own complacency by concluding that none of this was any of her business. After all, she did not really understand the underlying cultural imperatives at work here. Or did she?

Life gradually returned to normal. Abanzima, freed after her week in chains, reacted as though nothing had happened. For Mickey, though, things could never be the same. One evening in mid-November, she casually asked Patrick to help her trim her hair. He curtly told her that she must either let it grow or *he* would shave it off entirely. Mickey, taken aback, said that she would have one of the women help her. "No they won't!" Patrick snapped. "No member of my family is going to use halfway measures on her head anymore. And that goes for you as well as the *other girls* . . . clippers or nothing!"[14]

Bright and early the next morning, after a twenty-month stay, Mickey Hahn left Penge forever.

12

The hazards and hardships of travel in Equatorial Africa were not to be taken lightly in the early decades of this century. Few nonnatives dared set out on a trip without a lot of careful planning. For example, when French writer André Gide visited the Congo in 1927 and 1928, he and his party moved about the country with an army of porters lugging thirty-four packing cases, enough baggage to fill two small trucks.

When Mickey Hahn decided to leave Penge bound for Lake Kivu, and eventually the port of Dar es Salaam on the east coast of Africa, she did so on the spur of the moment, with minimal luggage and no clear sense of how to get where she wanted to go—or *if* she could even get there. Although Mickey had talked of leaving for several months, doing so proved more difficult than she ever imagined.

In part, this was due to the impromptu nature of her decision. In part, it was due to a lethargy that had seized her after almost two years of living at Penge; her life there had been elemental and uncomplicated, and there was little need to make pressing decisions of lasting importance. Mickey long ago had lost track of the number of days she had simply sat in the shade on her porch, reading books from Patrick's library, writing, or staring vacantly into the distance.

When Mickey visited the local chief to ask about the availability of a guide and a dozen porters to accompany her on the initial leg of the journey, a three-hundred-mile trek to the border of Uganda, the man shook his head. He then muttered the Ituri equivalent of "You can't get there from here." According to Patrick's *Encyclopaedia Britannica*, he was wrong. Once she reached the border, Mickey expected to find a road. She would hitch a ride south to Lake Kivu, and from there she would make her way to the coast. If she'd had a map, Mickey *might* have reconsidered her plans. Ahead of her lay a grueling and dangerous eight-hundred-mile journey.

The chief explained that no one ever went northeast from Penge to Lake Kivu: The area was swampy and there was no "road." What he meant by "road" was one of the footpaths, about six inches wide, that traversed the otherwise impenetrable forest. It would be necessary instead to follow the spider's web of meandering elephant trails that ran in the general direction Mickey wanted to go. Apart from the dangers of getting lost or being attacked by wild beasts, there was always the possibility that the natives whom Mickey met would be cannibals, that she would be captured by Arab slave traders, or that her porters would simply tire of the ordeal and abandon her.

"All this I ignored because in the Congo in those days, if you listened to local warnings you never got anything done," Mickey wrote. "You had to possess a strong conceit. . . . With my usual sublime self-confidence, therefore, I rode roughshod over the objections."[1] She did accept one of the chief's suggestions, however: she hired a pygmy guide. Everyone knew a pygmy never got lost in the forest. "We spoke Swahili, or rather Kingwana, a sort of bush Swahili," Mickey said. "Swahili is a kind of trade language used by Arab traders, not hard to learn. Anyway, that's what I used. Pygmies had their own language, which sounded like birds talking, but they spoke Kingwana when necessary. They had a definite accent when they did; we called it a 'pygmy brogue.'"[2]

Another initial problem for Mickey was gathering enough supplies and equipment to get her to her destination and to allow her porters to return home. Mickey had no sugar, butter, or cooking fat. These valuable commodities were scarce, and the only place to obtain them in Penge was from Patrick's stores; Mickey did not want to ask him for fear of being refused, or of touching off a row. For the same reasons, she did not seek to borrow a tent, cot, or a portable bathtub, all of which were standard gear for any white person traveling in Equatorial Africa.

The "classic" Belgian pattern of safari was to rise in the predawn darkness, walk until midday, when the sun became unendurable—only "mad dogs and Englishmen went out in the noonday sun," as Noel Coward so aptly put it—and then to rest until late afternoon, when walking resumed. At twilight, tents were pitched for the night. Lacking the usual "necessities" of travel, Mickey decided to make do by going from village to village and buying whatever food she could afford or find, as colonial officials often did when they traveled to remote areas.

The logistical questions aside, Mickey agonized about what to do with Matope. She had always imagined he would go home with her. Doing so would enable him to escape the compulsory two years' labor that all young men were obliged to do in the government mines. The work there was dirty and hazardous there; accidents were common. The European mine owners regarded native laborers as expendable. Mickey envisioned Matope living with her and attending school like any American boy, but the difficulties to be overcome before this could happen were suddenly and painfully apparent to her.

For one, there was an immediate financial concern. To control the export of labor, the colonial government demanded a bond of $250 for each native emigrant. Mickey did not have the money, nor did she know if she could get Matope into the United States. She feared what would happen if he became ill or if immigration officials in New York refused to let him enter the country. What would become of him then?

Mickey had sorted out none of these concerns by the time she marched out of Penge in the predawn darkness on November 23, 1932. She was accompanied by her pygmy guide, Matope, her cook Sabani, her pet baboon Angélique, and a dozen native porters bearing luggage and food.

Progress was frustratingly slow that first day. The pygmy guide led them on a desultory course through endless miles of swamp; the elephant trails they followed ran along what little solid ground there was to be found. In this part of the forest, the trees grew to more than one hundred feet, and the thick canopy of vegetation blocked out the sun. Mostly they traveled in the arboreal shadows. Mickey was dripping with perspiration, spattered with mud, and bedeviled by biting insects. After walking in a similar forest for only a brief time, André Gide had observed that "the absence of any ray of sunlight gives it a look of being sunk in sleep—in hopeless sadness."[3] Mickey experienced this same sense of despair. The only thing that buoyed her spirits was the singing of the porters as they marched. Hour after hour they sang an improvised tune about how hard Mickey made them work.

By dark, they had reached higher ground, but with no village nearby, they had to spend the night in the forest. The men built Mickey a lean-to out of tree branches, and Sabani cooked her a meal of chicken and boiled rice. Afterward, as she lay on her bamboo mat listening to the strange noises of the night and watching the men eat their meal around the campfire, Mickey fell asleep. She was tired and fearful, but content. Being on her own again felt good.

The next day, Mickey and her party emerged from the swamp. The landscape was less thickly forested, and Mickey was relieved to find that in the first village they came to the people were friendly and keen to sell food. Mickey discovered there was a definite protocol to be followed here and at each subsequent community they visited. The local chief, dressed in an Arab robe as a sign that he was a "civilized" man, lead a welcoming delegation of elders. After shaking hands and recovering from the initial shock of realizing that beneath the baggy clothing the white visitor was a woman and not a young man, the chief usually agreed to provide Mickey and her party with accommodation for the night. At this first village, at least, the chief also had a request of Mickey: he asked her to preside at a *baraza*. The word, which literally means "front porch," referred to a practice by which Belgian colonial officials would sit on their front porches, listening to disputes and dispensing judicial rulings. Since no colonial official had visited this village for several months, there was a backlog of cases.

Mickey sensed this was a more formal procedure than the dispute resolution she had seen aboard the riverboat that carried her to Penge. Her protests that she was not a government official fell on deaf ears, as did excuses that her Swahili was not good enough to understand the subtleties of the arguments. The entire village had gathered in a semicircle before the chief's hut to await the start of proceedings. With no option, Mickey took her assigned seat on the porch and nodded. With that, the chief waved his hand, and a man emerged from the throng to begin making his argument in the day's first "case." He spoke eloquently and passionately about how his wife had run off with another man, and so he was demanding that she either return to him or else that he receive compensation from the philanderer or the woman's family. When finally the plaintiff had finished speaking, the other man came forward to offer contrary arguments. He claimed the woman really had never been the first man's wife because he had not fully paid the parents for their daughter's hand.

When the men had finished their arguments, the crowd grew hushed. All eyes were on Mickey as the chief asked, "What do you say, Bwana?"

Mickey paused a few moments. Then, clearing her throat, she surprised everyone by calling for the woman herself to speak. A murmur ran through the crowd as the woman stepped forward to begin relating her version of events. She confirmed what the second man had said: her husband had not paid her parents enough for her hand. Equally significant in Mickey's mind, at least, was the woman's revelation that the first man had beaten her.

Having heard from all parties in the dispute, Mickey rendered her decision. It was a prudent compromise. What she decreed was this: It would do the aggrieved husband no good to have a wife who did not love him and who was likely to run away again. The man and his in-laws should negotiate a deal whereby he would get a refund on most of what he had paid them. The woman could then stay with the second man, and he could pay the parents a fair sum, which they could work out. All of this seemed simple enough, and heads nodded throughout the audience. With that, arguments began in the next case, Judge Mickey Hahn presiding. "As time wore on, I gathered confidence, and by the end of the proceedings was laying down the law like a veteran," Mickey wrote. "Nevertheless, it was a relief when everything was over and I could go to bed."[4]

Apart from the monotony of a diet of chicken and rice, things went surprisingly well the next day and on the others that followed. There were a few notable exceptions. On one occasion, a surly porter refused to carry the chickens because Mickey had purchased two additional ones. However, the man relented, becoming almost tearful when Mickey announced that she was "fining" him. She agreed to forgive him, providing there was no repeat of the incident. There was not. "All of this still seems audacious to me," Mickey wrote. "I can't get it through my head that a large lumbering crew of males are really so cowed that I can get bossy with impunity."[5]

On another occasion, Mickey's party came upon an intolerably officious native government clerk who had been abandoned by both his porters and his pygmy guide. The man, his sister, and two small girls were making do as best they could, which was not very well. Mickey understood why. The clerk, she decided, was a blubbering idiot. When she asked him about traveling conditions ahead, he offered information that she knew was wrong. To her astonishment, Mickey snapped at him, calling him a liar. Nonetheless, she could not let the man or his party go hungry; she gave them food and some Epsom salts they asked for. Mickey then said good-bye, leaving them with a local man, who had come along with Mickey's party just for a day to carry fresh food.

Then Mickey herself got lost. She and her party wandered for several hours in a torrential rain after the pygmy guide discovered that a village they had walked to was abandoned. They also had a terrifying and painful encounter with a migrating stream of red army ants.

One day Mickey was crossing a log bridge over a creek after a long, tiring march. A waiting delegation of village elders looked on in amazement as Mickey slipped off the log into the muddy water. Her pet baboon Angélique, who was riding on her shoulder at the time, shrieked in terror. Fortunately, the only thing that Mickey hurt was her pride, for Sabani the cook shouted to the spectators not to laugh. It was an ignominious entrance that Mickey was not keen to repeat.

Such incidents faded from memory as walking conditions improved. The landscape through which they marched became more hospitable with each passing day. The trees became shrubs, and the swampy ground grew rocky and dry. With the sky now visible all around them, they felt the wind on their faces. This terrified the porters. They were uncomfortable being out in the open, and they complained of being cold, even though the sun was beating down on them. Mickey empathized. "It had been a long time since I'd heard the wind so close to my ears," she wrote. "In the forest, it was visible, moving the tops of the trees, but, except on the river you never felt it. I, too, was cold, and lay shivering all night."[6]

Mickey's trembling may also have been in anticipation—or perhaps fear—that the initial portion of her journey was almost over. A village chief she met told her a group of Europeans were camped along a nearby road. This meant there would be trucks and cars. Government regulations forbade traveling on foot with porters if any other mode of transport was available, and so Mickey would be obliged to make alternative arrangements. Besides, she knew the homesick porters were eager to begin their return trip. It was time for her to go on alone. "I dreaded the change. I shrank from the thought of living in a white world again, where I would have to talk to people," Mickey wrote. "For months I hadn't had to make conversation, and I felt that I'd lost the knack. It was all too much effort—problems to grapple with, uncomfortable clothes, and practical arrangements to make."[7]

All of Mickey's concerns and fears crystallized on the afternoon of December 11, 1932. She and her party had walked for eighteen days. During that entire time they had encountered no other whites. Now, as they reached the crest of a bluff, Mickey spied a group of gray buildings in the valley below. Nearby were a rusty truck and some narrow-gauge railway tracks that led off into the distance. Mickey could see native workers carrying baskets filled with dirt. She had stumbled onto Motokolia, a rude mining camp in the rolling hill country just southwest of Lake Kivu.

As Mickey's party approached, a white man emerged from one of the buildings to watch them. At first, he seemed puzzled by what he was seeing. Then his body language revealed anger. "Where is your husband, Madame?" he shouted as soon as Mickey was within earshot.

She shrugged. After explaining that she was traveling alone, on her way to Lake Kivu, Mickey asked for directions. The man, a Belgian mining company official, muttered something unintelligible as he inspected Mickey and her porters. As he did so, the reason for the chilly reception became clear; the man had assumed Mickey was a big-game poacher. Even after noting that the porters were not carrying skins, ivory, or hunting rifles, the man was still suspicious. He instructed Mickey to come into the building with him.

There, in the mining company office, they met another Belgian. He was younger than his colleague, bespectacled, and puzzled by what was happening. It was not every day that a white woman, let alone one traveling solo, marched into Motokolia. As the three of them sat down, the first man shouted to an African clerk to bring tea. He then asked Mickey for her passport, which he studied. Then he slapped the document down and glared across the desk at Mickey. "I thought so! Here it is in black and white," he shouted. "You can't deny it, Mademoiselle!" He pointed to a space where Mickey had written her occupation: mining engineer.

The man's anger abated only when Mickey convinced him that she was not an American spy looking for uranium. Still suspicious, however, the man produced a map and explained to Mickey that she and her party had been walking on the Belgian mining company's concession for several days. Her reaction must have been convincing. Mickey did not deny that she had been walking on the company's land—which she could not have known because she had no idea where in Africa she was!—but she marveled at the distance that she and her party had traveled. As the birds fly, they were now about 250 miles from Penge; they had obviously walked a lot farther.

The Belgian man informed Mickey that she would have to stay there and he would hold onto her passport until her story had been verified by the American consul. When it was, the man assured her, she would be free to go. He would arrange a ride out for her on a supply truck. Mickey agreed that this was fine, especially after she saw the spacious tent that had been set up for her. A rug covered the dirt floor. There was a comfortable cot to sleep on, a chair, and even a dressing table. While Mickey unpacked her belongings, Sabani admired the furnishings. "Nice," he repeated over and over, as he ran his admiring hand over everything.

It was at this point that Mickey realized how downcast Matope was. She sat in the chair in her tent while he climbed up onto her lap to talk. Mickey grew tearful as she explained how the time had come for her to go away. However, she assured Matope he could leave, too, and could live with her and her family. To her surprise, Matope began sobbing when she said this. He explained that while he would miss Mickey very much, he did *not* want to leave Penge to go to the white man's world so far away. There he might be chained up, as Abanzima had been, or as Angélique was whenever there were other whites around. Besides, Matope added, the porters had explained to him that if he went to the white man's land they might cut him into little pieces, put the pieces into tin cans, and sell them for meat. Mickey did not attempt to explain or argue with Matope. Instead, she dried his tears and told him that he could go back to Penge and could take Angélique with him. Matope hugged her. Then he jumped down and ran to tell the others the good news. He was not going to end up as canned meat after all.

That night, as Mickey donned her only dress and dined with the Belgians, in the distance she heard her porters singing and beating their dance drums. They were celebrating the trip home. Mickey was much less certain of her own next move, although a dessert covered in thick meringue momentarily eased her concerns. She gobbled down a huge slab of the pie, and then eyed the rest greedily. Her host, the Belgian who had been so surly earlier that day, grinned as he put the pie plate down on the table in front of Mickey and motioned with his hand that it was all hers. She did not need a second prompt.

• • •

When the American consulate verified Mickey's story, she was free to go. It was just a few days before Christmas when she paid her porters and bid Matope a tearful farewell. He and the others marched southwest, back the way they had come. Mickey watched until they were just specks in the distance. Then she hitched a ride to the nearest village, where she stayed at a government rest house while impatiently waiting for a bus to Lake Kivu. After two days of sitting on the porch, she finally decided that no bus was coming, and so, despite her unpleasant experience with the randy Englishman in Avakubi, when the next SEDEC truck came along she bought the driver a bottle of beer and begged a lift.

The countryside through which they drove that day was scenic, the air was fresh, and Mickey felt a renewed sense of purpose. "The old euphoria of the traveler, a sensation I'd almost forgotten in the forest, was stealing over me—that keen expectation of something happening soon, something fascinating," Mickey wrote.[8]

En route, the SEDEC truck called at a coffee plantation in the foothills of the Mitumba Mountains. It was incredibly beautiful there. Mickey would never forget the grandeur of the setting: the reddish soil, the brilliant blue African sky, and the sweetness of the air. Danish writer Karen Blixen, who was intimately familiar with the same landscape, wrote, "Looking back on a sojourn in the African highlands, you are struck by your feeling of having lived for a time up in the air."[9] Mickey felt this same sense of celestial euphoria as the truck pulled up to the front door of a sprawling wooden and stone bungalow.

The stop was as much social as it was commercial. The driver was a friend of the middle-aged British couple who owned the plantation. Peggy Walker, the lady of the house, greeted them cheerfully and explained that her husband Ronald would soon be home from hunting. They awaited his return in the parlor, a room filled with mounted animal heads and hide rugs that bore glassy-eyed testimony to Ronald Walker's marksmanship. Mrs. Walker served tea, shortbread, and iced cakes.

Ronald Walker appeared presently. He was lean and middle aged, with a white military-style moustache. Mickey surmised that he was a big-game hunter turned coffee farmer. His marksmanship was evidently still good, for he had shot an antelope. The felled beast had been carried home by native helpers, one of whom stood just inside the door, ramrod straight, a fez atop his head. He was as silent as the distant snow-capped mountains that Mickey could see behind him out the window, shimmering in the afternoon heat. The African was not introduced, nor did any of the whites so much as acknowledge his presence. Mickey reflected on how different things were in this place, just a few hundred miles from Penge. "Here, without conscious intent or malice, Africa seemed to be kept out-of-doors, at far more than arm's length," she wrote.[10]

Despite this, Mickey enjoyed the Walkers' company. She accepted gratefully when they invited her to spend Christmas with them and to attend the annual party they threw for their British neighbors. There were many, for the area was close to the border with Uganda, a British protectorate. Peggy Walker took Mickey to the local marketplace, where they bought cloth to make some new clothes. The two women spent several afternoons together sewing and talking.

Christmas came and went. It was a merry two days filled with lots of British people with names like Poppet, Tiny Tim, and Bunty. Someone brought along a phonograph, and there was music and dancing, drinking, and good food. Mickey finally managed to satisfy her sweet tooth, something she regarded as a milestone in her return to "civilization." Feeling sated, she was eager to resume her journey home. Mickey had written to the SEDEC district office in Stanleyville asking that a supply truck drop by the Walker farm to pick her up. The negative reply was written by Mr. Barlow, the would-be Lothario whom Mickey had spurned on the road to Avakubi. Under no conditions, Barlow announced, would any SEDEC truck *ever* offer Mickey a ride. He had issued orders to that effect. Mickey was livid, as were the Walkers when she told them the reasons for Barlow's antipathy.

When the SEDEC truck pulled into the Walker's yard that evening, over drinks Mickey told the driver the story of her encounter with Barlow. While the driver was sympathetic, he said orders were orders; to disobey would cost him his job. It was Ronald Walker who hit upon a solution. He asked the driver if he would be willing to cart a large, empty wooden packing crate that had once contained a truck axle. Mickey could hide inside until after the driver had checked in at the local SEDEC depot. Once they were on the road, Mickey could reemerge. The driver agreed to the plan.

When the truck drove off early the next morning, it did so with Mickey peering out from the packing crate as the Walkers stood on their veranda in their dressing gowns, waving good-bye. "I felt the truck's engine start up, and there was a jolt. My blind, voiceless body was carried cautiously, slowly to the bottom of the drive," Mickey wrote, "bumpety-bump across the cattle drive, grindingly around the bend, and on toward [Lake] Kivu."[11]

Mickey's long-anticipated visit to the lake was a disappointment. It was "as dull as the ditchwater it did not resemble," Mickey said. "I didn't stay any longer than it took to send a cable to Dot (Raper)."[12]

Mickey traveled by riverboat from Lake Kivu to the town of Ujiji (now Kigoma) on the eastern shore of Lake Tanganyika. There she caught a train for the six-hundred-mile ride to Dar es Salaam, on the Indian Ocean. Mickey was obliged to spend precious dollars on a first-class ticket; whites were not permitted to travel in a lower class. Money was tight, and Mickey still did not have a steamship ticket for home. This troubled her, as did the realization that her great African adventure was drawing to such an inglorious close. Her future was no less cloudy now than it had been when she had left London two years earlier.

13

LONDON ON A COOL, GRAY DAY in late January 1933 from the deck of her ship looked no different to Mickey than it had the day she sailed for Africa two years earlier. However, initial impressions were deceiving. The Great Depression had deepened; with millions more now unemployed, the streets of the British capital were full of unrest, hardship, and pain. On January 30 the street-corner newspaper vendors sang out the ominous news that Nazi leader Adolf Hitler had become chancellor of the German Reich. The diminutive Austrian promised to restore his Germany's pride, ease its economic woes, and deal with what he termed "the Jewish problem."

There was considerable interest in Hitler and his politics in the drawing rooms and salons of fashionable Mayfair. Der Führer even had admirers at Westminster, for in 1932 Sir Oswald Mosley, a former junior cabinet minister in Ramsay MacDonald's Labor government (1929–1931), had established a British fascist party. Mickey could not fail to notice how trendy fascism had become in the West End. Ladies had taken to wearing swastika charms on their bracelets, and young men combed their hair down across their foreheads in emulation of Hitler.

None of this troubled Mickey; what was happening in Germany as yet seemed to have little relevance to her life. Besides, she was far more concerned with scraping together enough money to get back to the United States and completing work on a book about her African adventures. Mickey's agent in New York had sold the manuscript to the Bobbs-Merrill publishing company. The editor, one of Mickey's old boyfriends, was enthusiastic about the book's sales potential, both because of its literary merit and because the economic situation in America was looking up. Franklin D. Roosevelt's victory over Herbert Hoover in the 1932 presidential election had rekindled hope. Many Americans wanted to believe FDR when he proclaimed in his inaugural address on March 4, 1933, that "the only thing we have to fear is fear itself."

Mickey, who watched all of these developments from afar, shared in the hope that the economic crisis was finally over. Despite her own lack of prospects, Mickey's spirits soared when she found money waiting for her in her London bank account: book royalties and payment for articles and short stories that the *New Yorker* and other magazines had published while she was in Africa. "I arrived back in London . . . broke and practically without any wardrobe," she later wrote. "But material needs didn't matter. I felt I had come out ahead of the game because I had learned a lot. For one thing, I could speak Swahili pretty fluently, not the elegant kind they used on the coast, but the dialect called Kingwana. Say what you would, I was the only gal in the crowd who spoke Swahili."[1]

Mickey's facility with the language led to a memorable encounter one evening in a Soho café that was popular with Africans. She and one of Barbara Ker-Seymer's gay male friends were having fun eavesdropping on conversations. As they did so, Mickey overheard two African men at an adjacent table talking about lesbians; at her companion's urging, she interjected with a few words of Swahili. Of course, that stopped the conversation cold. "The men almost blushed," Mickey recalled with a laugh.[2] After the initial shock of hearing a white woman in London speak Swahili, the Africans invited Mickey and her companion to join them at their table. One of the men was an anthropology student at the London School of Economics. He introduced himself as Jomo Kenyatta. A member of the Kikuyu, the largest and most progressive of Kenya's tribes, he had been born near Nairobi in 1891 and educated at a Church of Scotland mission school. In 1928, Kenyatta became general secretary of an organization called the Kikuyu Central Association (KCA), which advocated the return of "whites-only" land being farmed by British settlers. He journeyed to London in 1931 to petition the Colonial Office on behalf of the KCA, and, with time out for several "educational" trips to Moscow, Kenyatta remained in England the next fifteen years. By the time he returned home in 1946 with an English wife and son, Kenyatta was one of the leaders of the burgeoning nationalist movement that reshaped the face of Africa in the postwar era.

When Mickey and Kenyatta met in early 1933, he was sharing an apartment with the noted black American singer Paul Robeson, who was performing in London. Unfortunately, Mickey never learned this bit of news, which would have interested her, for although she did not know Robeson personally, she certainly knew *of* him. They had mutual friends in Harlem, where Mickey knew many prominent black musicians, writers, and artists.

Even without discovering Kenyatta's Harlem ties, Mickey sensed she had just met someone destined for greatness; the admiration was mutual. Kenyatta was impressed by Mickey's knowledge of Africa and her ability to speak Swahili. Neither of them forgot that chance encounter in Soho. In fact, when they next met, more than thirty years later, each would recall the incident fondly. By that time, Mickey had become a well-known writer and Kenyatta was an important political leader. When his Kenya African Nationalist Union (KANU) party was elected to power in 1963, Kenyatta became Kenya's first prime minister. The following year, he became president of the Republic of Kenya, a position he held until his death in 1978.

Being attractive, outgoing, and female, not to mention an exhibitionist—a trait she had inherited from her father—Mickey had a knack for meeting people in public places. "I thought she was very brave to walk in and start talking to perfect strangers," said Barbara Ker-Seymer.[3] This kind of openness was a distinctly American behavior that befuddled the acutely class-conscious British, especially when it led to "awkward situations," as it inevitably did.

One day Mickey and a friend were having lunch in a London restaurant. Mickey's exuberance attracted the attention of a nattily dressed American man at a nearby table. His dark hair was combed back high off his forehead, and he gazed at Mickey through wire-rimmed glasses. A lazy left eyelid that drooped and a full, thick mouth were his most prominent features. Mickey remembered him as "a big man and running to fat. Of course, he drank a lot and I suppose that showed."[4] She ignored him when he stared at her, and even when he called out her sister Helen's name. The man watched for Mickey's response. She pretended not to hear, already having sensed he was someone who had pursued her sister "and probably caught her," as Mickey later quipped.[5]

A few weeks later, after Mickey had returned to New York, she recounted her story to Helen, who confirmed that she knew the man Mickey described. He was Edwin ("Eddie") Mayer, a playwright and Hollywood screenwriter whom Helen had once dated. Mayer had called recently to ask Helen if she had a sister in London; he said he had spotted a young woman in a restaurant there who bore a stunning resemblance to Helen. When Mayer found out that Mickey was in New York, he sought her out.

Eddie Mayer had a rough-hewn charm. He was a thirty-seven-year-old native New Yorker. Although he had only a grade-school education, Eddie had a burning desire to succeed as a writer, and he did. He was dapper, outgoing, and loved the high life. He also drank too much and was estranged from his wife of five years. She had stayed in Hollywood when Eddie traveled to London and New York. He was candid about his marital status when asking Mickey out. Initially, she wanted nothing to do with him. However, when he persisted, she finally agreed to have dinner with him. What harm could it do? Eddie seemed nice enough, and, besides, a brief flirtation with him promised Mickey some relief from the tedium of scratching out a living. Her enthusiasm for being back in New York was already waning. Despite all of the promises and the best efforts of President Roosevelt, the depression was still getting worse.

Mickey wrote of the plight of single women like herself in an article that appeared in the May 31, 1933, issue of the *New Republic* magazine. "Women Without Work" delved into why there were so few females in New York's breadlines. Most such women, perhaps as many as one hundred thousand of them, had worked as factory workers, secretaries, receptionists, sales clerks, and teachers before being laid off. Now they were the nameless, faceless poor—shadows drifting from boardinghouse to boardinghouse with despair as their only possession. Mickey described how these women lived together, four or five to a candle-lit room, surviving on meals of coffee, bread, and bananas. Some had fallen so low that they made "the supreme sacrifice," turning to prostitution. Even this was futile, for with so many desperate women on the streets, there was no money to be made. The situation was so grim that one middle-aged woman told Mickey, "I had $60, but I spent it. I didn't even try to save it. I thought perhaps God would be good to me and let me die."[6]

Mickey was more fortunate than most, for she had the emotional support of family in town and the ability to earn money as a freelance writer. Despite this, she, too, was becoming disillusioned. These frustrations and uncertainties were at play in Mickey's mind when she agreed to go out with Eddie Mayer. What she intended was "merely innocent flirtation," or, as the poet Byron had once put it, "not quite adultery, but adulteration."

Eddie was a willing participant. He craved the company of good-looking young women and life in the fast lane almost as much as he enjoyed the celebrity that came of being a Hollywood screenwriter. Eddie took Mickey out on the town and lavished money on her. He bought her gifts. They danced, dined, and drank in the speakeasies. Inevitably, they became lovers. Mayer was out for the proverbial "good time." Mickey knew that, yet she found herself falling in love with him. "God knows what I saw in Eddie," Mickey admitted many years later. "It was probably vanity—he did make a determined play for me. Also he knew a lot about the stage and had read a lot, which my usual friends . . . did not. And he told funny stories."[7]

Mickey and Eddie parted company in early May 1933, when he returned to Los Angeles. Mickey retreated to the sleepy town of Woodstock in Upstate New York, where she had found a summer job as secretary to J. B. ("Mac") MacAvoy, who wrote the text for a popular newspaper comic strip called "Dixie." "He was in the drama crowd I knew in New York," Mickey explained.[8] The work was not difficult, and it paid $50 a month plus room and board. Woodstock at that time was the site of a small colony of writers and artists. It reminded Mickey of Santa Fe, and she spent a quiet summer there collecting her thoughts, working on a novel about the Belgian Congo, and musing about her future.

Meanwhile, *Congo Solo: Misadventures Two Degrees North*, Mickey's journal of her African adventures, was published in June 1933—but not until she had done some quick rewriting. Fearing a libel suit, Harry Block, Mickey's editor at Bobbs-Merrill, asked Mickey to obtain Patrick's written permission before going ahead with publication. Patrick had already assured Mickey that he did not care what she wrote because he was not ashamed of anything he had done. Patrick's parents in Boston were of a different mind. Charles and Angelica Putnam, being prominent socially, were aghast at Mickey's matter-of-fact account of their son's life at Penge. It was one thing that he was "living in sin" with three black wives; it was quite another to have the sordid details of this relationship recounted in a book. Charles Putnam warned that if *Congo Solo* was published as written, the embarrassment would be such that *his* life "might not be worth living."

In the face of this thinly veiled suicide threat, Patrick cabled Mickey asking her to amend the manuscript to obscure his identity. She agreed to do so, altering key details of her narrative. Patrick became Den Murray. The name of the settlement was changed from Penge to Sanga; the nature of his relationship with his three wives was obscured, and parts of Mickey's story were attributed to "an Englishman from South Africa" who had traveled through the Belgian Congo. While these changes had the desired effect, Mickey's story now contained some puzzling loose ends.

If the critics noticed the seams in Mickey's 1933 version, they did not make an issue of it. *Congo Solo* was entertaining and informative reading, and the reviews were mostly favorable. A couple of things set *Congo Solo* apart from other contemporary travel books: its casual, personal style and the gender of its author. Some people were aghast that any woman would travel to Africa on her own, much less have the temerity to write about her experiences in such an offhand manner. Walter White of the NAACP, a reviewer in the literary journal *Books*, commented, "The uniqueness of Miss Hahn's book is in Miss Hahn herself. She went to Africa and saw Africans neither as funny nor different people. . . . Instead she saw them as human beings, completely identified herself with them, entered into their lives and joys and sorrows and tribulations with the same understanding objectivity with which she might have written of her own friends in the United States."[9]

Other reviewers were uneasy with the realization that Mickey was neither a "lady" traveler in the grand Victorian tradition, nor was she an academic in pursuit of knowledge or higher truth. She did not fit the usual stereotypes, and that made people uncomfortable. She was simply a woman who had gone to Africa because she wanted to. That was difficult for many people—male and female—to accept or understand. Reviewer E. H. Walton of the *New York Times* praised *Congo Solo* for being "impressionistic, informal, vivid." He also allowed that "it probably gives one a better notion of the . . . atmosphere than one could get from a more conscientious and conventional writer." Nonetheless, Walton chided Mickey for her "attitude" and for forgetting that she was "a Bright Young Person."[10] A reviewer for the magazine *Forum* voiced similar criticism, commenting that *Congo Solo* was "slightly marred by Miss Hahn's tendency to strike a gallant, offhand pose and to wisecrack where wisecracks are not quite appropriate."[11]

Despite all of the media attention for the book, *Congo Solo* sold poorly. That was unfortunate because, in many ways, it was a remarkable book, years ahead of its time. The colonial Africa that Mickey described is long gone, yet many of the themes about which she wrote—racism, sexism, and cultural bias—are as timely today as they were in 1933. In that sense, *Congo Solo* is a neglected literary treasure waiting to be rediscovered by some enterprising publisher and a whole new generation of readers.

• • •

Many of the same progressive themes Mickey touched upon in *Congo Solo* echo through the novel she had been writing in Woodstock. She was determined to vent her indignation and to expose the systemic exploitation in black-white and male-female relationships in colonial Africa. "It was a situation in the Congo [that] I wanted to describe and get off my chest," Mickey explained. A work of fiction seemed the ideal way to do so. The resulting book, *With Naked Foot*, told the story of a black African concubine named Mawa and her relationships with various white "masters." The last of them, an American schoolteacher, though gentle and well intentioned, wounded her most of all. It is clear that the book, which Mickey always felt was the best of her novels, was based on her own experiences. The story has an undeniable ring of truth, yet it moves briskly, the themes are deftly handled, and the characters are skillfully drawn; Mawa was a thinly disguised Abanzima, and the teacher was obviously Patrick Putnam.

Ironically, at the same time Mickey was writing *With Naked Foot*, she was falling ever deeper into her own ill-advised feelings for Eddie Mayer. When Mickey wrote to him professing her love, Eddie replied with a long letter in which he reiterated how unhappy and lonely he was living in the house he had once shared with his wife. Eddie confessed that there was a good chance his wandering eye soon would settle upon some young, aspiring Hollywood starlet.[12] Eddie's subsequent letters hint at his own emotional turmoil. He was flattered by Mickey's infatuation with him and surprised by the intensity of his own feelings for her. When Mickey wrote to let him know she was working in Woodstock for the summer, Eddie replied, "I received your letter and am a little amazed with myself (*little* being a synonym with me for *immensely*) at my promptly replying: not to speak of my amazement at my keeping up any correspondence at all—even with you. I must like something about you."[13] That being so, he offered some fatherly advice: Mickey should try to keep her relationship with J. B. MacAvoy on a business basis. "From what I've been told about him, that will be just as difficult as it would be with me,"[14] he noted.

Eddie reported he had "shopped around here discreetly" without success for a job for Mickey. However, he assured her that if she came to Hollywood he was certain he could find work for her. At the same time, he cautioned, "I

City Girl Feels Safer Alone in Gorilla Wilds

Emily Hahn, 27, graduate mining engineer, believes an American woman can go anywhere in the world alone without molestation, if she conducts herself properly. Miss Hahn is just back in New York from a long stay in the pygmy country in Africa, where she was the only white woman; and is now preparing to go to the wilds of Indo-China. Some of her African impressions are pictured.

A composite Emily Hahn cartoon that appeared in a New York newspaper, August 14, 1933.

Courtesy Emily Hahn Estate

am absolutely unbearable under present circumstances. I'm having great trouble with my [current screenplay project]."[15]

Mickey, sensing the trouble she was getting herself into with Eddie, tried unsuccessfully to forget him. She began dating a young Canadian newspaperman who worked at the Canadian Press office in New York City, but promptly stopped seeing him when his intentions became serious. Mickey escaped when she returned home to Chicago that fall in response to her mother's requests. Mickey's father Isaac, gravely ill with diabetes for several years, was near death. Sores on his limbs had turned gangrenous, and he was suffering terribly. "Daddy wanted to die, but his doctor wouldn't help him. Mannel couldn't do it," Mickey recalled. Mickey, who had learned to give injections in Africa, gave Isaac an overdose of morphine. "I did it. I killed daddy," she admitted.[16] She was there at his bedside, holding his hand as he slipped away that cold, bleak day in January 1934. He was seventy-six years old.

Mickey had seen men, women, and children die in Africa, but this was different; watching her own father die left Mickey feeling empty and emphasized the aimlessness of her own life. She was twenty-eight, well traveled, university educated, and had written three books, yet while her sisters and most of her girlfriends were married—Helen twice already—and had settled down to raise families, Mickey was still struggling to decide what to do in life. She was loathe to admit how much this troubled her.

Following Isaac's death, Mickey's mother gave up her apartment. Hannah moved into a room in the large house that Mickey's sister Rose and her husband Mitchell had bought in 1929 in Winnetka, an affluent lakeside suburb just north of the city. "Daddy died, and it seemed natural that the rest of the Hahns still in Chicago should move out to Winnetka so they wouldn't have to drive so far to get together," Mickey later wrote. "They all moved. Dauphine married, and she and her husband bought a house in Winnetka. Mannel had long since bought a house in Winnetka."[17]

Mickey stayed with her family for a few weeks. She spent the time working on a new novel, this one about a love affair between two young people on the mean streets of New York City. She also did her best to play the role of dutiful daughter. This latter task proved impossible, given Hannah's strong personality. At age sixty-six, she remained as vigorous and opinionated as ever, continually urging Mickey to settle down. When Mickey confided her feelings for Eddie Mayer, Hannah was dismayed. She disapproved of the relationship, but knew better than to voice her concerns. Mickey's younger sister Dauphine recalled, "By that time (1934), we knew that you didn't say anything to Mickey about what you thought she should do. Daddy was dead . . . and mother said it was the first time she was glad [that he was]. What would Daddy have thought?"[18]

Mickey continued to correspond with Eddie all through this period, and in the spring of 1934 she went to Los Angeles to be with him. Mickey's mother, having decided to make the best of what she regarded as a "bad situation," took the train to Los Angeles to visit and meet the man she had heard so much about. "Eddie got me a job working on the dialogue of what must be the worst movie ever made," Mickey recalled. "Dr. Freud could tell you why I've forgotten, [but] I can't even remember the title."[19]

Mickey did not enjoy her Hollywood interlude, brief though it was, so when Eddie left for England that fall on business, she went with him. Being there gave Mickey the opportunity to enroll in a graduate-level diploma program in anthropology at Oxford University; her experiences among the people of the Belgian Congo had kindled her interest in the discipline. Mickey and Eddie rented a small house in the town of Oxford, hired a housekeeper, and even bought a pet Airedale terrier. Mickey attended classes while Eddie worked on a movie script and a stage play. Hannah came over from Chicago to visit and stayed for several weeks. For now, at least, Mickey and Eddie were the picture of bliss.

Oxford being just an hour's train ride from London, they often spent weekends in the city. When Mickey introduced Eddie to her friends, she discovered they had little in common. Barbara Ker-Seymer remembered visiting Mickey and Eddie at a "very grand hotel" where they stayed. The women giggled as Mickey showed Barbara some silk underwear and a diamond-studded watch Eddie had given her. "He bought her nice things," Barbara said. "Eddie Mayer was from a different world. He was much 'grander' than us. I don't think he was putting on airs; that was just the way he was. . . . I couldn't think why Mickey liked him."[20]

Barbara kept her misgivings to herself. Mickey and Eddie seemed to be very much in love, and having read Mickey's recent stories in the *New Yorker* and her new novel, Barbara decided that Mickey's literary career was thriving, so the relationship must be good for her.

With Naked Foot was published in the fall of 1934. Most critics praised the power and vigor of Mickey's prose, but some were uneasy with the book's explosive sexual and racial themes. "There it is—a tale that might offend if it were not for the vitality and deftness of the telling," wrote M. C. Hubbard in the literary publication *Books*. "That is the way those affairs go in Africa, and Emily Hahn has made you understand that the natives, too, are human."[21] The reviewer for the *Boston Transcript* voiced distressingly similar sentiments when he noted, "One may seriously doubt whether any American or European can get successfully inside the heart of a woman such as Mawa [the book's central female character] any more than they can portray the feelings of a dog."[22] Such comments, shocking and offensive as they are today, were nothing unusual in

1934. That much was underscored that fall by the way her fellow students at Oxford treated Mickey.

As had been the case at Wisconsin, she was the only woman in her class. She derived a certain satisfaction from this, for although she had an American tutor, she found Oxford to be "a pretty stuffy place." Said Mickey, "I became friendly with an African student. Because no one would speak to either of us, we always walked together. We were referred to around campus as 'the woman and the nigger.'"[23]

By the time Mickey and Eddie returned to the United States in early 1935, their relationship was strained. It had become clear they were too much alike to ever be happy together. What is more, Mickey and Eddie were quarreling about money. Eddie, deeply in debt as a result of his free-spending lifestyle, had borrowed money from Hannah Hahn on the understanding he would repay it to Mickey. When it became clear he had neither the means nor the intention of doing so, Mickey's patience with him ended. She gave Eddie an ultimatum: choose between her and his wife. Mickey returned to New York, while Eddie went back to Los Angeles to think things over.

The final break between them came in late February, when Mickey flew out to L.A. to see him. That was a mistake. When they got into a heated quarrel in the car on the way home from the airport, Eddie announced he was going back to his wife. In her heart, Mickey had known this day would come. She spent several tearful days sorting out her emotions. "I was so upset that it took even

Mickey had a torrid love affair with Hollywood screenwriter and playwright Eddie Mayer in 1933. Years later, she wondered, "What did I ever see in him?"
Courtesy Margaret Herrick Library, Academy of Motion Picture Arts and Sciences

me by surprise, and I was not able for some months to understand this reaction. I mean, I'd never really *adored* [Eddie]. . . . Anyway, I soon figured it out. What hurt me was my pride."[24]

Eddie wrote Mickey again on March 6, 1935, after an apparent change of heart. He, too, had been taking a long, hard look at his life. What he saw depressed him. "Although I believe I am a naturally creative person, I have done almost nothing to date—one or two things scarcely worth recording," he wrote. Eddie asked Mickey to take him back, "if you will still have me."[25]

She would not. The Eddie Mayer chapter in Mickey's life was closed. She had already made other plans. Mickey had resolved to run away, maybe even to marry the first decent man who came along. Had she been male, she reflected, she would have joined the French Foreign Legion. That option being closed, Mickey resolved to return to Africa. Her sister Helen, whose own marriage with Herbert was foundering, suggested that she and Mickey visit the Far East together. From there, Mickey could continue on to the Belgian Congo. Patrick had written with news that Mickey's pet baboon Angélique had been killed by a leopard, but otherwise life at Penge was unchanged; Matope still cried for her. That was all she needed to hear. Mickey realized her place was in the Congo. She was needed there, and it was as far away from Eddie Mayer as it was possible to get.[26]

IV

China

14

IF MISERY TRULY DOES love company, it was fitting that Mickey and Helen sailed for China together the first week of March 1935. Both sisters were downcast as their ship steamed out of San Francisco. It was not until they were at sea that the Japanese captain announced that the ship was not going to Shanghai, the Hahn sisters' destination; the *Cichibu Maru* was instead bound for Yokohama, where they could make connections. Mickey and Helen were not much concerned by this unexpected change of plans. They were happy just to be going somewhere, anywhere.

Mickey's affair with Eddie Mayer had come crashing to an inglorious end; Helen was dejected after a big argument with Herbert. It was because of this and because Helen was on her first trip abroad that the women traveled first class. The change was one Mickey enjoyed, especially when she and Helen met a Japanese-American businessman who introduced them around the ship and then entertained them royally in Japan.

Everyone Mickey and Helen met during the three-week stopover in Japan was friendly and cordial, and so the sisters were truly sad that they could not stay longer in Japan. But they had to go; a family friend was waiting for them in Shanghai. Mickey planned to stay there a few weeks before traveling on to Africa on her own. Helen had booked passage home to New York on a ship that was due to sail June 12. It was in late April when the Hahn sisters left Yokohoma for China aboard a "dirty little tub" of a mail ship, as Mickey termed it.

"The mind of a traveler has only one spotlight, and it is always trained on the present scene," she later wrote.[1] As a result, Japan seemed much less benign from their new vantage point. There was a good reason: in the spring of 1935, long-simmering hostilities between Tokyo and Peking had boiled over into war. Mickey and Helen were astounded that the Japanese they had met were the same people whose army had invaded the northern Chinese province of Manchuria, where soldiers were engaging in an orgy of raping and pillaging. Mickey could only agree with Helen who said, "Over there [in Japan], we saw everything in a misty light. Here, [Japan] is all much more harsh."[2]

Her disillusionment was nurtured by the seductive charms of Shanghai. The city, then known as "the Paris of the Far East," is situated midway up China's coast. It is thirteen miles inland, on a tributary of the mighty Yangtze River then called the Whangpoo. Shanghai, the world's fifth largest city in 1935, was a bustling port and commercial center. In the minds of westerners, the very name Shanghai conjured up images of mystery, adventure, and romance. "Life there was a highly charged affair, what the Chinese called '*jenao*,' a perpetual 'hot din' of the senses," British historian Harriet Sargeant wrote.[3] The writer Aldous Huxley summarized the essence of Shanghai as "Life itself . . . dense, rank, richly clotted . . . nothing more intensely living can be imagined."[4]

Shanghai was trendy in the mid-1930s. It was *the* place to visit if you had the time and money. No world cruise was complete without a stop in Shanghai. It was said that Wallis Simpson, clad only in a life preserver, had posed there for a series of dirty postcards. Charlie Chaplin and Paulette Goddard, his wife to be, had holidayed in Shanghai in 1936. Mussolini's son-in-law, Count Galeazzo Ciano, went there to chase women in the city's legendary dance halls and nightclubs. Even Hollywood jumped on the Shanghai bandwagon, setting several popular films against the city's backdrop; among them were a Busby Berkeley musical and the 1932 melodrama *Shanghai Express*, starring Marlene Dietrich. ("It took more zan vun man to change my name to Shanghai Lily.")

Shanghai's superheated economy made it the Hong Kong of the early 1930s. American journalist Vincent (Jimmy) Sheean wrote that Shanghai was the place par excellence for two things: money and the fear of losing it. This suited the foreigners who were there for the proverbial "good time, not a long time." Rice was cheap, so cheap that as far as westerners were concerned, it was almost free. Cheap rice meant cheap labor, and that meant cheap prices. With the exchange rate at three Shanghai dollars to one American dollar, the cost of most consumer goods and services was staggeringly low, even by depression-era standards in the West. Mickey Hahn, like everyone with foreign currency to spend, lived a lifestyle that she could only have dreamed of back home. The material for a tailored suit sold for about $1 (U.S.); dinner in a good supper club was the same price, with the floor show an extra $1.50. Westerners living in Shanghai raised hedonism and conspicuous consumption to gaudy art forms.

There were no taxes of any kind, and foreigners came or went freely, because passports were not needed. As a result, Shanghai was a mecca for refugees, adventurers, arms dealers, entrepreneurs, missionaries, spies, and tourists. Many who came also stayed, and so by the late 1930s, there were 60,000 foreigners among Shanghai's four million residents. "One never asked why someone had come to Shanghai," one British observer noted. "It was assumed everybody had something to hide."[5]

Joining the British, French, and German businessmen—the taipans—were the Japanese, who arrived in the 1890s. They set up industries that took advantage of the abundant supply of cheap labor. Next came thousands of White Russians, the royalists who fled the 1917 Bolshevik revolution. Then came boatloads of German and Austrian Jews, the victims of Nazi persecution. The White Russians and Jews were stateless, meaning that they were legal nonentities. As such, they were subject to Chinese law, courts, and prisons.

It was the British who set the tone in Shanghai's foreign community, both morally and socially. Sinophobia was rampant, although Mickey noted, "Not since I left the U.S. have I heard [Chinese] referred to as 'Chinks.'"[6] The British condescendingly considered that word a crass Americanism. In the British vernacular Chinese males of all ages were routinely referred to as "boys"—in the same derogatory way that whites in the U.S. South used the word when talking about blacks; Chinese women were seldom referred to at all. Mickey recalled a story one Englishman told her about his visit to San Francisco, where he had encountered a Chinese "boy" who did not get out of the way as he walked along the street. "Why, in a civilized country I'd have flayed the bastard!" the Englishman sputtered.[7]

Despite such unabashed racial discrimination, Chinese people flocked to Shanghai. Rich and poor alike were drawn by the lure of jobs, fast money, and contact with Western culture; Shanghai was where the action was. In the late 1920s and early 1930s, the city briefly displaced Peking as the epicenter of China's cultural and intellectual life. Although China's rulers, army leaders, and conservative intellectuals frowned, there was little they could do about it or about "the white men behind the desks" who ran Shanghai. To make the best of a bad situation, Chinese authorities granted control of areas of the city—called "concessions"—to each of the intruding nationalities. In total, foreigners ruled more than 60 percent of Shanghai's twenty square miles of territory. This area, the International Settlement, was governed by an elected council representing foreigners in each concession. Peking appointed a mayor to run the Chinese sections of the city, which were bustling, squalid, and poor.

This was the backdrop into which Mickey and her sister Helen stepped when they arrived in Shanghai from Japan that spring day in late April 1935. Their ship anchored in the harbor, among passenger liners, freighters, and naval ships from twenty nations. A steam launch ferried passengers the two miles into the city because the mouths of the Whangpoo and Yangtze Rivers were too clogged with brownish yellow silt to allow the big oceangoing ships any closer. Miles out in the blue Pacific, beyond the horizon, the mud that was discharged by the Yangtze announced the proximity of land.

The Whangpoo River at Shanghai was jammed with Chinese junks and houseboats that anchored just off the Bund, the city's bustling main street and promenade. Here Mickey and Helen saw long blocks of shops, Western-style apartment buildings, and commercial towers that housed the air-conditioned offices of the city's taipans. As they stepped ashore, the Hahn sisters were assailed by a dizzying kaleidoscope of sights, sounds, and smells.

"On the Bund at midday human beings became insects again," British writer Harold Acton once observed.[8] "Stand [here] any day . . . and watch the variety of traffic that passes under the signals of a tall, bearded Sikh traffic policeman," advised another contemporary account. "Electric tramcars, loaded buses, and trackless trams, filled to all available standing room; motor cars and trucks . . . wheelbarrows that trundle along with tremendous loads: coolies turned beasts of burden, bearing bales and baskets of incredible weight: great two-wheeled trucking carts, with as many as six or eight perspiring coolies straining at the pull ropes; rickshaws . . . bicycles, carriages, pedestrians—the whole contrasting procession passes."[9]

• • •

Bernadine Szold-Fritz, an old friend of their sister Rose's from Chicago, met Mickey and Helen on the pier in Shanghai. A divorcée, Bernadine later married a wealthy American stockbroker named Chester Fritz and in 1935 was one of the leading *tai-tais* (taipan wives) in Shanghai society. There were few prominent American visitors who did not have a letter of introduction to Bernadine or who did not seek her out. Not only was she herself a renowned hostess; she was a regular at the constant whirl of parties, balls, club meetings, and other events that made up the local "social scene" in Shanghai's tightly knit foreign community.

British influences dominated, and there was no shortage of snobbery, but a "colonial" atmosphere prevailed, meaning that people socialized in Shanghai who would never have spoken two words to each other in polite London society. "Occasionally an enterprising tai-tai would attempt to introduce a new note into Shanghai's social life," one observer noted. "Some American ladies pioneered, although not too successfully, in inviting both Chinese and foreigners to their homes. One of them, [Bernadine] Fritz, who gave parties every Sunday night, prided herself on presiding over Shanghai's only 'salon.' Foreigners mingled with prominent Chinese. . . . But the hostess was too extravagant (she always wore a turban) to be taken seriously."[10]

Bernadine Fritz welcomed Mickey and Helen to Shanghai, then immediately whisked them off to one of her famous dinner parties. The other guests at the table that evening included a French count and his Italian wife, a Pole who was a naturalized French citizen, and a Chinese customs inspector. Mickey and Helen were quizzed about what was happening in the United States and about their views on China's "troubles" with Japan. The Hahn sisters became prizes in a social tug-of-war. "There were feuds between the cliques, and I was soon mixed up in them," Mickey recalled. "The arty group battled for my scalp with the plain moneyed class as long as I was a novelty, and in the end nobody won at all, or cared."[11]

In New York, Mickey had been an unemployed writer with no money, a broken heart, and a vague future. It was different in Shanghai. There she was a somebody, and it felt good. Mickey's free spirit and lively wit became the talk of the foreign community. With the money she carried and with the kindness of strangers, Mickey realized that she could live a lifestyle that back home she could only dream about. The company she kept was certainly better.

While attending one of Bernadine's amateur theater nights, Mickey and Helen met Sir Ellice Victor Sassoon, the most powerful of Shanghai's taipans and one of the wealthiest men in all of the British Empire. "I thought him unusually quick and witty, *especially* for a businessman," Mickey said.[12]

"Eve," as his family knew him (because of his initials, E.V.), had been born in Baghdad to a prosperous Jewish family who claimed descendence from King David himself. The Sassoons—the "Rothschilds of the East"—were unique in other ways. As Sassoon family biographer Stanley Jackson noted, other merchant families amassed larger fortunes, "but none . . . more dramatically spanned two worlds, oriental and Western, or generated so many virtuoso talents outside the commercial sphere."[13]

Sir Victor—as Mickey affectionately knew him—was a renowned ladies' man. He was tall and athletic, with handsome dark eyes. Sir Victor sometimes sported a monocle in his weak left eye, but there was nothing foppish about him; he was handy with his fists. A strong swimmer, Sir Victor also excelled at tennis and golf and loved dancing, the theater, and horses. His "Mr. Eve" stable was one of the world's largest and most successful in the 1930s.

Another of his great loves was photography. He was an avid amateur shutterbug. Sir Victor invited the Hahn sisters to visit his private studio. There he showed them a big album in which he kept the nude photos he had taken of many of Shanghai's most beautiful women. When Sir Victor asked Mickey to pose for him, she readily agreed. Mickey was flattered that he had asked *her* and not Helen; deep in Mickey's subconscious there simmered the rivalry between the sisters that had its roots in the resentment Mickey had felt over Helen stealing her boyfriends. "Sir Victor didn't ask to photograph Helen, and she kept saying, 'I wish I had a good figure.'" Mickey recalls. "Sir Victor just smiled. 'But you have such a nice *nature*,' he said."[14]

It was not long before more than photos had developed; Mickey and Sir Victor became intimate friends, who each got something out of the relationship. For Mickey, it was material "favors," one of which was a shiny new blue Chevrolet coupé that she began using on weekend trips. For Sir Victor, a committed bachelor, it was the ego boost of having the companionship of one of the few attractive, intelligent, and single American women in Shanghai. Money and ego aside, there was also an element of genuine affection between Mickey and Sir Victor, two kindred spirits in a faraway place. It did not hurt that the Hahns also had Jewish blood.

Everyone in the foreign community scrambled to curry favor with Sir Victor and wrangle invitations to the lavish parties he threw in the penthouse of his Cathay Hotel or at his home. A photographer from the *North-China Daily News,* the city's British-owned English-language daily newspaper, would invariably appear. The next day's paper would be filled with photos of those who had attended.

Despite his social standing, Sir Victor was regarded with haughty disdain by many in the foreign community. The prevailing sentiments were voiced by British writer Sir Harold Acton, who dismissed Sir Victor as "a very agreeable fellow if rather a Philistine."[15] Some people resented his money, some his power or his well-deserved reputation as a "lady chaser." Some disapproved of the fact he had moved his business from Bombay to Shanghai in 1931 to escape British taxes. Still others disliked Sir Victor because he was Jewish, or because he dared to socialize with Chinese. As Mickey recalled, "[He] . . . was not well liked by most young men. They'd set up a chant when he appeared in a bar: 'Back to Baghdad! Back to Baghdad!'"[16]

He was well aware of how people regarded him, so Sir Victor delighted in delivering occasional reminders to his "friends" of the power that he wielded over them. At one of his parties, he poured a bottle of crème de menthe down the back of a distinguished British visitor's suit. Another time, he held a costume ball at which guests were invited to dress as circus animals. When they did, Sir Victor made a grand entrance dressed in a ring master's costume.

Given her relationship with Sir Victor and the many other ties she had developed, Mickey decided to remain in Shanghai longer than planned. "Helen

Sir Victor Sassoon's portrait of the Hahn sisters, Helen and Mickey, in profile, Shanghai, 1935.
Courtesy Emily Hahn Estate

left early this morning," Mickey told her mother in a letter dated June 12, 1935. "I felt slightly dismayed as she disappeared in the distance and more so when I discovered that she had left her white coat, which I'll send over with somebody else on the next boat."[17]

Mickey went on to report she was being "whirled around in the usual senseless (pardon me) activity" of Bernadine's amateur theater group. "Tonight is a charity ball, and I am dancing in the American part of the entertainment; a barn dance in tennis shoes and checked gingham with hair ribbon."[18]

Following Helen's departure, Mickey rented a two-room flat on the ground floor of a Chinese bank building. The living-sleeping area was painted dark green. Over three of the walls, some artistic person had erected a silver metallic grillwork that was meant to resemble bamboo trees. Stars and a crescent-shaped moon were painted on the ceiling. Through the grimy windows, Mickey looked out on busy Kiangse Road, in the city's red-light district. Whatever the flat lacked in elegance it more than made up for in affordability, especially because Mickey now had a job. She found temporary work as a reporter with the *North-China Daily News.* She was hired to fill in for a woman who was away on her honeymoon. By the terms of the Land Regulations laid down by the Chinese government, all white females who worked in Shanghai's International Settlement were supposed to be signed on "at home." This meant they were hired on contract and came to China under the sponsorship of the firms that had hired them. There were exceptions, of course, particularly

The very photogenic Sinmay Zau, circa 1935.
Courtesy Dr. Xiaohong Shao

if one knew the "right person." Mickey had no trouble obtaining the necessary permission.

Her job at the *Daily News* was busy, although not terribly challenging. Mickey's assignments provided her with lots of opportunities to meet and socialize with a cross section of people. She was still seeing Sir Victor, but she also fell in with a circle that included a half-dozen single men from various foreign consulates and legations. Her social life never lacked for excitement or variety. At one of the group's dinner parties, she met an inquisitive Englishman named McHugh. Mickey knew he was an intelligence agent, and so when McHugh began questioning her about her friends, she spun him an elaborate tale about her meetings with "bearded Russians and communist plotters." McHugh listened intently, and after he had gone home to write it all down, Mickey and her friends had a good laugh at his expense. When she next encountered McHugh a few weeks later, he grabbed her by the lapels and shook her. When he had reported his conversation with Mickey, his superior had scolded him; British intelligence had a thick file on one Emily ("Mickey") Hahn, and across the front of it someone had written the words, "Disregard Miss Hahn's entire story."[19]

Bernadine and other wagging tongues in the foreign community applied no such caveat to tales of Mickey's escapades. "Shanghai gossip was fuller, richer and less truthful than any I had ever before encountered," Mickey later wrote.[20]

As it looks today: the building at 348–349 Kiangse Road, Shanghai, where Emily Hahn lived from June 1935 to the fall of 1937.
Gulbahar Huxur

The more people talked about her, the more outlandish her behavior became. Mickey's relationship with Sir Victor provided ample grist for the gossip mill, but it was her love affair with a well-to-do Chinese gentleman poet and publisher that scandalized the foreign community. Even her most tolerant friends warned Mickey that she was "crossing the line" by taking a Chinese lover. In Mickey's mind, that only made it all the more deliciously wicked—and therefore appealing.

15

MICKEY'S RELATIONSHIP with the Chinese intellectual and publisher Sinmay Zau began as casually as it did unexpectedly when they fell into conversation at one of Bernadine Szold-Fritz's "integrated" dinner parties at a restaurant in the Chinese section of Shanghai. Mickey and Helen had first noticed Sinmay at an International Arts Theatre event a few weeks earlier. Like most women, their eyes were drawn to him, a slight figure almost feminine in his brown *ishang*, the traditional silk gown worn by Chinese gentlemen. Describing a Sinmay character a few years later in one of her novels, Mickey wrote: "When he was not laughing or talking his ivory-colored face was perfectly oval, but one did not think of perfection, one looked at his eyes. In their oblique and startling beauty they were full of light and life. . . . His soft carved mouth [he] had decorated with mustaches like those of his ancestors, marking sharply the corners of his lips. His tiny beard, no more than a brush of whiskers at the end of his chin, was a sly joke at his youth. In repose his face was impossibly pure, but it was rarely in repose."[1]

Sinmay's beauty did not escape the notice of other Western women in Shanghai. Later, when word got around that Mickey and Sinmay had become friends, women began approaching Mickey to hint, sometimes none too subtly, that they would relish a discreet introduction to him. One woman, an accomplished amateur painter, begged Mickey for help in convincing Sinmay to sit for a portrait.

However, there was more to Sinmay than just physical beauty. He was soft spoken and cultured and possessed an enchanting curiosity about life. A born raconteur, he had a puckish wit and loved epigrams, limericks, and wordplay. Mickey delighted in the lighthearted—and sometimes naughty—epitaphs that he composed for well-known personalities. Sinmay devised some lines for the imaginary headstone of Pearl Buck, the American writer whose novels and short stories about China earned her the Nobel Prize for literature in 1938. Buck's writings, enormously popular in the West, were scorned by many Chinese. Noting that the pastoral quiet of Western-style cemeteries in China made them popular places for the nocturnal trysts of Chinese lovers, the epitaph Sinmay had fashioned implored: "Villagers, please don't fuck. Here lies Pearl Buck."

Such irreverence was something that few Chinese had the self-confidence to reveal in public. "[He] was an intellectual, and so funny. I'd never met anyone quite like him," Mickey recalled. "And I'd never even seen anybody in a Chinese gown before."[2]

Sinmay came by his exotic persona genuinely. He had been born to a wealthy and distinguished mandarin family—mandarins being the civil servants who had run China for thousands of years in the name of the celestial emperor. In the late nineteenth century, Sinmay's grandfather served as the Qing dynasty's ambassador to the court of the Russian tsar. Sinmay's father is said to have been governor of Formosa—now known as Taiwan—for a time, before being appointed mayor of Shanghai.[3] In her writings, Mickey painted a somewhat less exalted picture of Sinmay's father as a "die-hard rake" who lost large sums of money speculating and smoking opium.[4]

Sinmay himself was born in Shanghai in 1906. As the favored son, he enjoyed a comfortable upbringing; in Mickey's words, he "[ran] as wild as he liked."[5] By age seventeen, Sinmay had discovered the wicked pleasures of Shanghai's nightlife. Dressed in a purple tweed suit, he was a familiar figure racing around town in his red sports car. The Chinese press delighted in reporting his 1923 affair with a beautiful Chinese actress. The resulting publicity and the fact that Sinmay's family were well-to-do attracted the attention of Chinese gangsters, of whom there was no shortage in Shanghai. Sinmay was imprisoned on a trumped-up charge and was released only after his parents paid the necessary "fines." Afterward, Sinmay boasted of having "learned four ways to commit a murder" during his stay in jail. At this point his elders decided a change in his lifestyle was advisable.

Sinmay was shipped off to Paris, where he fell in with café society and came under the spell of an expatriate poet named Hsu Tse-Mo, one of the leaders of the movement to modernize classical Chinese poetry. Together, Sinmay and Hsu edited an influential literary journal they called the *Crescent Monthly*. At his parents' insistence, Sinmay reluctantly left Paris in 1924 to enroll at Cambridge. There he was supposed to study political economy. Instead, he spent two years perfecting his English and immersing himself in progressive trends in Western literature and culture.

When he returned home to China in 1926, Sinmay was married to one of his cousins in an arranged ceremony. By the time Mickey met Sinmay in the spring of 1935, five of the couple's nine children had been born, and Sinmay's wife was pregnant again.

Although he was cash-poor and in debt up to his pigtail, Sinmay lived the good life on his family's fortune plus the income he made from publishing. He had spent most of his legacy on a press. Sinmay's business, the Modern Book Publishing Company, specialized in Chinese-language editions of pirated Western novels and popular nonfiction books—including the *Inside* books written by Mickey's friend John Gunther. Modern Book also published volumes of poetry by Sinmay and his friends, as well as a bilingual Chinese-English literary journal, a humor magazine, and even some pornography. Sinmay's eclectic interests in business and the arts and his frenetic lifestyle gave him a wide circle of acquaintances in both the Chinese and the foreign communities.

The more Mickey talked with Sinmay that first evening over dinner, the more intrigued she was. Afterward, when Mickey was waiting for a taxi, Sinmay invited her to go home with him and a group of his friends. Bernadine and other whites looked on in amazement when Mickey accepted the invitation. She and Sinmay piled into his brown Nash automobile with several other Chinese people. They then sped off into the night in the direction of Sinmay's house in the Yangtzepoo Road district of the city's east end. That no "respectable" white woman would dare do such a thing either never occurred to Mickey, or she simply chose to flout the racial taboo. This was not the first time she had chosen to do so, nor would it be the last.

• • •

From the outside, Mickey saw that Sinmay's home looked like the Victorian redbrick houses that were so common back home in Chicago. The interior was a different matter. "It was bare, as one could see at a glance because the doors stood open between rooms—no carpets, no wallpaper, very little furniture," Mickey wrote. "Yet the house wasn't deserted."[6] Several young children, who had been playing under the watchful eyes of two servant women, stopped to gawk at her. Mickey would have been embarrassed had her curiosity not gotten the better of her. She noticed several Chinese adults sleeping in various rooms.

Presently, a short Chinese woman appeared. This was Sinmay's wife Zoa. She smiled and followed along as Sinmay led his guests upstairs to the Zau family's living quarters. The rooms here were furnished, papered, and more cozy. Sinmay and his guests made themselves comfortable in a bedroom where there were a couple of flat sofas, some chairs, and big pillows piled on the floor. Mickey noticed a silver tray sitting in the middle of one of the sofas. On the tray were a small silver oil lamp, some tiny boxes, and other assorted paraphernalia that Mickey did not yet recognize.

Sinmay set the tray on the floor. Then he laid down beside it and lit the lamp. One of his friends lay down opposite him while they talked in Chinese. Mickey saw Sinmay doing something with what she took to be knitting needles. Leaning closer, she realized he was manipulating a tiny lump of sticky brown taffy over the lamp's flame. When he stopped, Sinmay placed the molten material in a covered cup, where he allowed it to cool for a few moments. He then dropped the smoking lump into the bowl of a bamboo pipe. Mickey watched with rapt attention as Sinmay put his lips to the silver mouthpiece and inhaled the blue smoke. As he exhaled, the air was perfumed with a strange caramel-like odor, one which Mickey had often smelled in the streets of Shanghai. In that instant, it dawned on her what was happening. "You're smoking opium!" she blurted.

Sinmay nodded slowly. He offered the pipe to Mickey, who accepted it even though she knew smoking opium was illegal under Chinese law. Only a few days before, a story in the *North-China Daily News* had reported that from 1932 to 1935, the Chinese government had executed 655 drug traffickers. What is more, the authorities claimed to be forcing almost a quarter million opium addicts to take a "compulsory cure."[7] Mickey—like most foreigners—was not subject to Chinese law, and so this knowledge only added to the intrigue of the moment for her. She was keen to experiment. To her, smoking opium seemed exotic, daring, and romantic, even if most young, Westernized Chinese considered the practice hopelessly old-fashioned; it was something their grandparents did.

None of this mattered to Mickey. She had never been able to inhale cigarette smoke, but she was determined to give this a try. "When I breathed in, I felt *almost* sick, but my throat didn't close, and after a moment I was fine," she later wrote. Mickey was convinced that the sweet lingering taste of opium had no effect on her, until she tried to stand. She was so dizzy she nearly fell over. Sinmay motioned for her to sit down and join in the group's discussion, which was about books and politics. When she did so, Mickey became totally absorbed. "I listened to everything the others had to say in English," she later wrote, "and when they branched off into Chinese I didn't mind. It left me to my thoughts. I wouldn't have minded anything. The world was fascinating and benevolent as I lay there against the cushions, watching [Sinmay] rolling pipes for himself."[8]

At one point, Sinmay asked Mickey how she felt. Apart from the dizziness, which had now worn off, she felt fine. Sinmay smiled. He suggested she check her watch. When Mickey did so, she was astonished to realize it was now 3 A.M. She had remained in one position without moving a muscle for several hours. "That's opium," Sinmay explained. "We call it *Ta Yen*, the Big Smoke."[9]

Before long, a few pipes of opium had become as much a part of her daily routine as coffee. British writer Graham Greene, writing in his autobiography *Ways of Escape* (1981), observed that of the four winters he spent in the Far East, it was opium that "left the happiest memory." Mickey shared that same sense of utter contentment. "I had learned what was so pleasant about opium," Mickey wrote. "Gone were the old romantic notions of wild drug orgies and heavily flavored dreams, but I didn't regret them, because the truth was much better. To lie in a quiet room talking and smoking—or to put things into their proper order, smoking and talking—was delightfully restful and pleasant. I wasn't addicted, I told myself, but you had to have a bit of a habit to appreciate the thing. One used a good deal of time smoking, but, after all, one *had* a good deal of time."[10]

Mickey's days were pretty much her own, which was the way she liked it. Her mornings began with a late breakfast served by her houseboy. Afterward, she would make her way to the office of the *North-China Daily News*. Here she churned out feature articles and columns for the news pages and reviews for the Tuesday book page. Once her day's work was over, Mickey did as she pleased. Since she had embraced Sinmay's carefree ways, the clock no longer had any meaning to her; Mickey was as apt to be an hour late as an hour early for meetings and social engagements.

Sometimes she ate lunch with Sir Victor or Bernadine. Other times she met a girlfriend for drinks at the lounge in Sir Victor's Cathay Hotel, where they went to flirt and be wined and dined by the European and American men who ate lunch there. Afterward, usually late in the afternoon, Mickey returned to her flat, where she spent several hours at her typewriter. "[Shanghai] is honestly a good place to work," she told her mother in one of her letters.[11] Mickey was writing a stage play and articles for the *New Yorker* and other American publications. She was also editing and writing several magazines for Sinmay, including the English-language newspaper called *Candid Comment* (Sinmay edited a Chinese edition) and a literary magazine called *T'ien Hsia*. The title of the latter, which translates as "everything under the sky," was aptly chosen, for the publication's contents were as wide-ranging as the discussions during the smoke-filled evenings Mickey and many of the *T'ien Hsia* contributors spent at Sinmay's house.

As Mickey became more attuned to Chinese, she found herself taking an interest in politics and current affairs. She used to pride herself on being a dedicated "artiste," disdaining both partisan politics and politicians. Back home, she boasted that she had never voted. Now, in Shanghai, where politics was a life-and-death affair—especially where her Chinese friends were concerned—it was not quite so easy to remain aloof.

In the wake of the 1911 collapse of the imperial dynasty, Dr. Sun Yat-sen, the founder of the republican People's Revolutionary Party—popularly known as the Kuomintang—became China's first president. His reign was short, however, and the country quickly descended into chaos when he died of cancer in early 1925. Sun Yat-sen was succeeded as Kuomintang leader by Chiang Kai-shek, who struggled to regain control of China. There followed a period of near civil war during which various warlords vied for power. Only the two strongest survived: Chiang and his communist arch rival Mao Tse-tung, neither of whom was yet strong enough to deliver a knockout blow to the other.

The political equation was complicated by the presence of foreign troops on Chinese soil. The Japanese invaded Manchuria in 1931 and seized as much land as they could. When the Japanese moved south and captured Peking in June of 1935, Chinese nationalists, guerillas, and spies of all stripes in Shanghai retaliated against Japanese interests in Shanghai. When the Japanese began to reciprocate, the violence grew ever more bloody.

Even Mickey could not ignore what was happening. "My letters home show a sudden change after Helen went away," she later wrote. "No longer did I bubble for pages about seeing the races from Sir Victor's box at the club."[12] What Mickey was alluding to was her growing social and political consciousness. Although she still shunned partisan politics and "isms," for the first time in her life she was paying attention to the political events that were going on around her.

American news reports about the "civil war" in Shanghai worried Mickey's mother. In letter after letter, Hannah pleaded with her daughter to come home and "settle down." Mickey turned a deaf ear. When she did respond, her letters displayed her impatience with those who dared offer advice, no matter how well-intentioned it was. "I want to see you too, very much. But darling, that isn't the only thing we have to think about, is it?" she chided Hannah at one point in early 1936. "I know you would rather . . . that I get a job and stay in Chicago, or better still marry someone and 'settle down' somewhere not too far away. But jobs aren't simple anymore; anyway, I'm set in my work, which is writing, and as for marriage . . . well, it just hasn't happened."[13]

Later, as conditions in Shanghai continued to deteriorate, Mickey adopted a new approach, downplaying the dangers. "We see nothing of the civil war you read about in the papers," she said. "All our news is about how it's going to start tomorrow or else . . . anyway, it's a long way from Shanghai."[14]

• • •

Mickey's heightened awareness of China and of all things Chinese was reflected in the short stories and articles she was writing for the *New Yorker.* Editor Harold Ross dubbed her the magazine's "China coast correspondent" when she began a series of witty and elegantly written vignettes about a footloose Chinese gentleman named Pan Heh-ven. The character, a thinly disguised Sinmay, was almost childlike in his approach to life. But there was also a beguiling complexity to him. "Unlike those fiction writers who imagine they know the Chinese soul once they have crossed Shanghai's Golden Bridge in a rickshaw, Miss Hahn tactfully and cautiously refrains from generalizations," critic Marianne Hauser of the *New York Times* observed. "She merely relates what she has been able to observe, and having such a perfect eye for people and such obvious pleasure in writing about them, she can teach us a great many things."[15]

Mickey's relationship with Sinmay yielded a wealth of compelling and exotic experiences to write about. She was seeing Shanghai in a way few other foreigners did—from a Chinese perspective. For that reason, Mickey was no longer repelled by polygamy, a part of Chinese culture for centuries. In fact, the practice now had a certain odd appeal to her. While she maintained her relationship with Sir Victor, and dated various men in the foreign community, Mickey spent time each day with the Zaus; she had become a member of the extended family and even had a Chinese nickname: Hsiang Mei-li, which means "fragrant beauty," or so Sinmay told her. "But Chinese names can always be punned into less polite translations, and I never trusted it," Mickey said with a knowing smile.

Hsiang Mei-li was included in Zau family gatherings. She went on weekend trips into the interior of the country with them. She played with the children, who referred to her affectionately as "Mickeymama," and Sinmay's wife Zoa even bought her small gifts. What belonged to the Zaus was Mickey's, and vice versa. "Now I think it's one of the most fascinating things about the Chinese the way they look at marriage, almost the same as the French do," says a character in one of Mickey's 1935 short stories, who was voicing the author's own views. "So utilitarian, so sensible. The Chinese are *practical.*"[16]

As a result of Mickey's relationship with Sinmay, her flat on Kiangse Road became a popular gathering spot for the Zaus. "[They] come in bunches, like bananas," Mickey told Helen.[17] Sinmay, his brother (who was involved in the guerilla underground), and assorted cousins, nieces, nephews, aunts, and uncles dropped by whenever they were downtown. This was usually in the early evening. Whenever Sinmay appeared, he was usually with friends. They used Mickey's telephone. They lounged around. They drank Mickey's liquor. They smoked opium in her living room. Or they met there before a night on the town. A group, Mickey among them, regularly went to Chinese operas, or they hung out in the cabarets and restaurants.

Many of Sinmay's friends who hung out at Mickey's flat were poets, artists, teachers, and intellectuals. Most had lived or studied in the West; some were involved in the murky, cutthroat world of Chinese politics. Occasional visitors included the Communist guerilla leader Mao Tse-tung and his spokesman, a very cultured and elegant Chinese man named Chou En-lai, who eventually became the first premier of the People's Republic of China. Also among the Chinese visitors to Mickey's flat in those days was a young man named Tao, who possessed a decidedly dramatic flair in everything he did; when Mickey asked Sinmay who he was, she learned that Tao was Chiang Kai-shek's chief "hit man"—a paid assassin who arranged executions of the Kuomintang party's political enemies.

Mickey wrote stories "thick and fast," as she put it,[18] about many of these characters. When people in Shanghai read these pieces in the *New Yorker* and asked Mickey if she felt this was "nice," she merely shrugged and echoed the sentiments of the English writer Somerset Maugham. "I use everything I find in my brain—experiences, impressions, memories, reading matter by other writers—everything, including the people who surround me and impinge on my awareness," Mickey explained. "It isn't a question in my mind of being nice or not nice. I can't help it any more than I can help breathing. I am not apologizing or defending myself: there it is. I do it and I will always do it as long as I write. . . . People who mind should stay away from writers."[19]

Sinmay enjoyed the celebrity that resulted from the Pan stories Mickey wrote for the *New Yorker*. Only occasionally did he complain that she made him seem "like an idiot." For the most part, neither he nor his friends cared what Mickey wrote. It was the income from her writing that supported Mickey's opium habit and paid many of her day-to-day expenses. Although the cost of living in Shanghai remained low by Western standards, her expenses were high. She had developed a taste for the finer things in life—tailored clothing, expensive jewelry, exquisite jade carvings, and Chinese massages. "In placid ignorance, I sat on top of a heap of underfed coolies. I didn't run into debt," Mickey later wrote. "On the contrary. I was living easily, just within my means."[20]

• • •

British historian Harriet Sergeant wrote that when she began researching the 1930s for her book on Shanghai, she discovered that "nearly everyone I interviewed had an anecdote about Emily Hahn. Men recalled her wistfully; women with vitriol."[21] Although Shanghai's foreign community, about 60,000 people in the mid-1930s, had no shortage of larger-than-life characters, Mickey Hahn had emerged as one of the best known and most visible. In fact, when film director Josef von Sternberg—an acquaintance of Herbert Asbury's—visited Shanghai, he sent Mickey a huge bouquet of flowers and took her and Sinmay to lunch. Such was the extent and nature of Mickey's celebrity.

She was relentless in her pursuit of the limelight. Typically, Mickey outraged some of the more fusty people in the foreign community with her vampish acting in an International Arts Theatre production of *Lysistrata*. In that ancient Greek play, a group of wives refuse to sleep with their husbands until they stop waging war. Some of the audience stormed out in protest, feeling that Aristophanes' satire was inappropriate in a city racked by violence among various ethnic and political factions. "It seems I was very good," Mickey informed her mother. "I never knew I could act, but this part didn't call for much moving about. Mostly I stood in one place looking noble and intoning 'Women of Athens!' Since the scandal [of Mickey's involvement with Sinmay] I am very much in demand, and in case you haven't read all of the clippings by this time let me tell you that the editor of the paper is very much in love with me and keeps sending me notes."[22]

Mickey also attracted attention because of the pet she kept. One day in September 1935 she was passing a downtown shop when she spotted a baby-sized ape tethered in the window by a "too-short string." The proprietor told Mickey the animal was a wauwau, a type of monkey from Malaya. It reminded her of Angélique, her pet baboon in the Congo, and so when Mickey left the shop she did so with the wauwau clinging to her arm. It had cost her $120 Shanghai dollars—less than $40 (U.S.) Although that would have been a decent weekly wage for many of her unemployed friends back home and she could not afford it, Mickey did not hesitate to pay the asking price.

"It was a man from Malaya, a Mr. Mills, who recognized the species and told me that what I had was a gibbon, so I named the wauwau after him," Mickey later wrote. "Soon I learned that gibbons are mentioned, as shing-shing, in classical Chinese poetry. There is a line about them singing at dawn, but the poem dates back to the days when Chinese territory included Indo-China and Malaya as far down as Malacca."[23]

Mickey's "Mr. Mills" was about eighteen inches tall, with beige fur, a black face, and a deliciously mischievous disposition. "He has a pretty face and walks upright, waving his long arms, and is very affectionate and not too naughty to be possible," Mickey reported in a letter home.[24]

The gibbon proved to be almost as much trouble as a baby, but a lot more fun. In fact, when Mickey realized just how much attention her new companion attracted, she began taking him everywhere. She took him with her to the bar of the Cathay Hotel, and sometimes when she ate lunch at the deli counter of a bakery called the Chocolate Shop, a popular hangout with Americans. A group that included writers Harold Isaacs, Agnes Smedley, and Edgar Snow dropped by each day to drink sodas, gossip, and debate China's future. The

The mischievous Mr. Mills.
Courtesy Emily Hahn Estate

first time Mickey strolled in with Mr. Mills perched on her shoulder, a legend was born.

Not everyone was as amused by the gibbon's presence as the Chocolate Shop crowd. Mickey's neighbor complained to police that Mr. Mills was "a dangerous animal" when he ventured into the woman's garden and ate the flowers. To Mickey's dismay, a policeman with a Gallic accent came calling. Mr. Mills, who often bit strangers, was the model of deportment and even gave the man a hug. "How could anyone, I still ask myself, object to a gibbon with his black pansey-shaped face, his enormous round eyes, and his incredible grace," Mickey wrote. "I'm happy to say that [they] saw things my way."[25] Mickey was forced to make one concession: she agreed to do what she could to keep Mr. Mills out of the neighbor's yard. To keep him company, she bought a pair of young Chinese macaque monkeys. "Mills showed me my mistake as soon as I put them together with him: the monkeys hated him on sight, and he was terrified of them," Mickey wrote. "Like a ballet-dancer threatened by Neanderthal thugs he curled up in the corner of the room, all arms, and cried, while they romped around him making faces and pulling his hair. I extricated him and called a carpenter, who built a cage out in the garden for the macaques."[26]

Mr. Mills preferred human company, but not everyone preferred his. Some hostesses complained when Mickey began bringing Mr. Mills along to dinner parties. Not wishing to offend anyone, she dressed him in his diaper and a tailored outfit made of trimmings from her sable fur coat. Mickey later recalled, "I received one nervous little invitation from an Englishwoman with a penciled note on the back: 'Sorry we cannot extend invitation to Mr. Mills.' I was unreasonably angry and didn't go to the party at all."[27]

Mr. Mills, like his owner, lived life on his own terms. He snarled jealously at anyone who dared to look at Mickey the wrong way; Sinmay and other visitors, among them Tiger Kanai, felt the pain of a Mr. Mills bite. Mickey loved it. She and her pet gibbon became inseparable—some would say insufferable.

A few months after Mr. Mills's arrival, Mickey bought a female gibbon to keep him company. "Auntie," who was older and in failing health, had none of her mate's playfulness. She spent her days peering down at the world from a perch atop the curtain rods in the parlor. When Auntie died, Mickey bought a young black gibbon she called Junior. At one point, she was keeping five of the animals, which drove Mickey's Chinese cook and houseboy crazy because the gibbons had the run of her place. "I must have been a pathetic picture of a spinsterish woman at the time," Mickey later wrote.[28]

In addition to the stories about her primate family and the constant swirl of rumors about her, Mickey's journalism kept her in the public eye. She was prolific. Mickey wrote for Sinmay's English-language publications. She did feature articles, reviews, and columns in the *North-China Daily News*. She wrote for the *New Yorker*, and her latest book—her fifth, a novella entitled *Affair*—had been published in the States in early June. Unlike Mickey's two Congo books, this one received an enthusiastic promotional push from her publisher. Unfortunately, although the notices were generally favorable, the book was not widely reviewed. Many of the critics who did read *Affair* were unsure of what to make of it. The book's dark themes—the abortion issue and the emptiness at the core of the lives of unemployed young women in New York—were not ones often discussed in 1935, particularly in the pages of family newspapers. Writing the novella had been a cathartic experience for Mickey, who admitted that even she did not much enjoy reading the final product.

Affair had an undeniably autobiographical flavor to it. Like some of the stories Mickey had sold to the *New Yorker* early in her writing career, the book's plot was based on her experiences in the fall of 1929. That year, she had shared a flat on Sixth Avenue in Greenwich Village with the starving drama student named Kathy. In fact, *Affair* is really a *New Yorker* sketch that had been fleshed out to 30,000 words. It tells the story of Kay Carter, a young woman living in a Village flat with two other "unattached and jobless girls." The three of them struggle to scratch out a living. As Kay says at one point, "We can just manage to get along, and it isn't any use trying harder because we've all tried and there's nothing in it. So we get along. Do you think I feel good about it?"[29]

The only time Kay is not preoccupied with finding money to pay the rent or to buy her next meal is when she is with her boyfriend Jimmy, her first true love. When Kay becomes pregnant and Jimmy loses his job in a real estate office, their relationship unravels like an old sweater. Kay's pregnancy ends quickly and traumatically. So does her relationship with Jimmy. In the midst of this melodrama, Mickey tosses in a subplot about a suicide attempt by Kay's favorite flatmate. All of this has a palpable echo of reality to it; *Affair* is grimly realistic and uncompromising. Its wry, cynical tone and implicit proletarian political message disturbed some critics.

Reviewer Herschel Brickell of the *New York Post* praised the novella for its "considerable social significance," and observed that "[Miss Hahn] writes with taste and terseness, and her novel belongs strictly to us and our times."[30] Leane Zugsmith of the *New York Times Book Review* also praised the book's lean structure and style and what she termed its "air of verisimilitude." Even so, she had no sympathy for the characters Mickey portrayed. Zugsmith's criticisms suggest her reasons were as much moral and political as literary. She rejected the book's central premise: that Kay and Jimmy, like millions of other young people, were innocent victims of fate and the caprices of a cruel economic system. "Kay and Jimmy did not want to marry, they did not want to marry each other," Zugsmith wrote. "They wanted an affair and had it. It was not a happy affair; but the failure was determined by their emotions far more than their pocketbooks."[31]

Despite the readability of Mickey's prose and the fact that the book was one of the few to deal honestly with women's concerns during the Great Depression, *Affair* was not a hit with the book-buying public. Its message was too glum, too full of real-life pain. Sales were sluggish. Mickey's literary agent did her best to put a positive spin on the news, reporting that the book had sold better than most other recent Bobbs-Merrill fiction. That was small comfort to Mickey, who was now seriously reconsidering her future as a writer. "My feelings are mixed," she confided in a letter to Helen. "I don't like *Affair* much, and if it had been a raving success I would have mistrusted my judgment, . . . but on the other hand, when the devil am I going to be successful? And is it worth going on? Maybe I just haven't enough something or other to make a go of writing. And still, I go on getting scads of publicity and glad hands from the critics."[32]

In the face of this latest setback, Mickey's spirits sagged. She began to fantasize about striking out in entirely new directions: marrying and settling down, or maybe even trying her hand at business; she mused about opening a shop to sell Chinese silk lingerie "that really fits." Despite all of the activity in her life, Mickey was achingly lonely. In her flat at night, she often cried herself to sleep. Her friends and fair-weather acquaintances knew none of this, of course. When she wanted to be, Mickey was a master at masking her emotions. Most people assumed she was the same blithe bon vivant whose smiling face regularly showed up in photos on the *North-China Daily News* society pages. One week, readers could spot Mickey attending a luncheon for the famous Chinese actor Mei Lan-fang. The next week, there she was cruising the river on Sir Victor's houseboat, *Vera*, or attending one of the foreign community's lavish social events. On June 16, 1935, the *Daily News* published a typical picture of Mickey, Bernadine, and two companions sharing a table at the annual Military Camp Gardening Competition garden party. Mickey was seated in a wicker chair in a sunlit garden, looking for all the world as though she had just stepped out of a Monet watercolor.

This was hardly the face of someone plagued by self-doubts and wracked by opium addiction. This was the face of a beautiful, self-confident woman. She was attired in a stylish cotton dress and peered smugly at the camera from beneath the brim of a jaunty sun hat. To Mickey's right, resting on the arm of her chair, was Doris Chen, a petite young Chinese woman in a sleeveless silk gown. Beside Mickey, to her right and sideways to the camera, sat Bernadine, instantly recognizable in her silk turban and trademark oversize earrings. To Mickey's left sat a middle-aged couple identified as Mr. and Mrs. Eric Nerholm. The group was the personification of carefree affluence and gentility.

Appearances were deceiving. Mickey's enthusiasm for such gatherings ebbed as *Ta Yen* increasingly became the focus of her life. Her social circle shrank, and her closest companions became Sinmay and other opium smokers, with whom she felt a keen bond of kinship. This was all too much for Bernadine, who began talking about Mickey everywhere she went and then called her to report she was being "talked about all over town." Bernadine cautioned Mickey that she was spending far too much time with Sinmay. Mickey responded angrily. "Diplomatic relations have practically ceased between us," she reported to Helen.[33] Undeterred, Bernadine wrote a note to Sir Victor, who had evidently grown somewhat jealous of Mickey's relationship with Sinmay.

"I remember there was an Austrian or German Jewish refugee who had a dress shop, and Sir Victor steered people there sometimes," Mickey said. "The man's name was Gamaling, and once I called him 'May-ling.' Sir Victor slammed his hand down and shouted, 'His name is *Gamaling*! You're getting too damned Chinese!'"

Sir Victor mentioned Bernadine's note to Mickey one day over lunch. She fumed while Sir Victor nodded knowingly. He remained silent as she cautioned him "not to dare to speak to me about anything, as I don't take kindly to correction."[34]

Mickey (in hat, seated at center) at a June 16, 1935, Military Camp Gardening Competition gardening party, Shanghai. With her are Bernadine Szold-Fritz (seated at left), Doris Chen, and friends Mr. and Mrs. Eric Nerholm (seated at right).
North China Daily News

At the time, Mickey refused to believe anything was amiss in her life, despite her constant sneezing, watery eyes, and runny nose—the classic symptoms of opium addiction. Even when Sinmay's wife Zoa expressed concern that Mickey had developed a drug "problem," she was incredulous. "When you're smoking opium you don't stop to think," Mickey explained. "The strange thing is that you're so cheerful and euphoric you think, 'So I'm an addict. Big deal. I can stop any time.' . . . You don't care about paying your bills. In fact, you don't really care much about anything. Whoopee!"[35]

In the midst of all of the uncertainties in her life, and despite her aversion to any kind of regular routine, Mickey quit the *Daily News* in the fall of 1935 to take a job teaching English at Customs College. She may have told her family and friends she intended to concentrate on her freelance writing, but her actions suggested otherwise. Even Mickey could not explain why she had quit, other than to muse that perhaps her ego could not stand having a boss; Mickey always found it much easier to give orders than take them. "I had my first morning of teaching and felt the old intoxicating sense of power rising within me when I saw sixty-four hapless youths in the chairs before the desk," she reported to Helen. "Now I am teaching dispatch writing, English composition, modern poetry, and Shakespeare, all in one term—and me with a Bachelor of Science in Mining Engineering!"[36]

Mickey loved teaching. She was a natural; the classroom was a productive outlet for her exhibitionism. It also provided her with a route to avoid confronting her opium addiction. Occasionally, Mickey found her concentration

Sir Victor Sassoon with some "admirers," Shanghai, 1936.
North China Daily News

drifting off during a lesson. When it did, she would stop talking and stare blankly into space. Sometimes this went on for a few moments; other times, it went on for several minutes. The Chinese students, who grasped what was happening, waited patiently for these spells to end. Then Mickey would continue as though nothing had happened.

Despite these incidents, Mickey was a popular and effective teacher. In fact, when a friend who taught at another college fell ill, Mickey was invited to take on his class as well. She was teaching nine hours a day, yet even this schedule did not deter her from her opium habit. Nothing did.

16

MICKEY'S LIFE GREW more and more uncertain as what she termed "the blood-red blossom of war" began unfolding in China. A workaday routine, normally anathema to Mickey, now provided a welcome structure to her days but made it difficult to find time to write. She began to instruct her houseboy Chin Lien to tell people she was not home. The British soldiers who dropped by her flat to play the radio and drink her whisky, Sinmay's friends and family, even the sad-eyed Pole who confided the secrets of his love life to Mickey would have to find someplace else to hang out. During the long, hot Shanghai summer afternoons, Mickey drew the window shades of her flat to escape the heat and find privacy.

Despite her reclusiveness, Mickey kept up a social life. On Mondays, she took part in a "gourmet dinner club" with half a dozen single men from the staffs of various consulates and legations. On weekends, she visited nearby cities, especially the traditional Chinese southern capital of Nanking, two hundred miles inland from Shanghai. "I would like to live [there]," Mickey told her mother Hannah after one particularly enjoyable motor trip with Sinmay. "Everyone was very nice to me, and the whole four days was an Anglo-Chinese mixture . . . of walks, horseback rides, and dinners."[1]

On one memorable occasion, Mickey and a housemate named Mary took the train to Nanking for a fall weekend. Doing so meant crossing the front lines during a furious battle between attacking Japanese troops and the Chinese who were defending Shanghai. Mickey and Mary each carried a hatbox with their party clothes, and Mary had a wicker basket containing a pet baby duck named Sweetie Pie. Later, when asked why she had risked her life for a weekend in Nanking, Mickey explained that "even now it doesn't seem such a damn-fool thing to have done. . . . There were young men, dinner parties, and dancing in Nanking." Besides, as if to clinch the argument, she noted, "Nobody said *not* to go."[2]

At other times, Mickey and a girlfriend accompanied Sir Victor and his uncle Nunkie on junkets to Hong Kong. They shopped, savored the legendary hospitality of the Hong Kong Hotel—known affectionately to patrons as "the Grips"—and watched the Sassoon horses race. "Once in a while Sir Victor, who is the nicest man in the world, finds some way to make me a present. I take it without blushing, everybody does, because he's the richest man in the world," Mickey explained. "And unlike Mr. Rockefeller, he seems to like to waste his money like that. So long as I never let myself slip into the habit of *expecting* him to help me, I think it's safe."[3]

Mickey's relationship with Sir Victor remained amicable and open. Sir Victor sometimes became impatient, but it was really Sinmay who became jealous and was upset by Mickey's "emotional complications"—as she described them. These *affaires de coueur* seemed to come and go with the regularity of the seasons. For a time in the spring of 1936, Mickey was madly in love with a Polish diplomat named Jan. ("A nice big hunk, but an opium addict," Mickey noted. "Avoid addicts."[4]) This upset Sinmay as much as it did Hannah, who became distressed when Mickey mused in her letters about marrying Jan, or perhaps just having a baby by him. "I wish Helen were here," she said wistfully.[5]

It would not have mattered if she had been. The romance ended abruptly when Mickey's diplomat boyfriend was transferred to Peking. Afterward, Mickey tried to soothe Hannah's concerns. "One of your recent letters, Mother, sounds very agitated about my idea of having a baby," Mickey wrote. "Calm yourself; I hereby promise not to, until I can Give It A Name. All right. All right. I wasn't really serious, you know. Where would I put a baby?"[6]

Hannah could hardly have found such flippancy reassuring; she knew how impulsive her daughter could be. Almost as troubling to her was the "hopeless crush" Mickey developed on an earnest young British naval officer named Robert. Because he had a fiancée back home, Robert's interest in Mickey was not as serious as she would have preferred. Mickey was intent on changing that. Several times she flew to towns along the Yangtze River where Robert's naval gunboat had dropped anchor. That's how Mickey came to be dining in Nanking with Robert and his fellow Royal Navy officers on December 12, 1936. Two days earlier, King Edward VIII had announced he would abdicate and marry American-born divorcée Wallis Warfield Simpson. As Mickey rose to offer a toast, the half-dozen Brits in the wardroom scrambled to their feet, their glasses raised in anticipation of the customary salute to the King. "Gentlemen, I give you . . ." Mickey said with a mischievous smile, "Mrs. Simpson!" There was no response as the navy men slumped into their chairs. "Please pass the potatoes," the captain muttered.

Mickey's clumsy attempt at humor fell as flat as a tombstone, and the rest of the meal was eaten in silence. Afterward, a tearful Robert "gave her hell," as Mickey put it. At that point, it must have been apparent even to her that the British did not regard the King's abdication as lightly as she did. "As an American I didn't quite understand the way they felt," Mickey admitted. "To me it was an exciting and humorous incident, intensely interesting but not really near the heart. Of course, I was secretly tickled, anyway, that it was an American woman who had so ruffled the dignity of our cousins across the Atlantic."[7]

The Simpson faux pas was one more reminder of why Mickey remained the talk of Shanghai's foreign community; her escapades continued to titillate some people and outrage others. This was how Mickey liked it. Her delight in defying convention was boundless. The one constant throughout her life was her dogged insistence on taking the uncertain path, in doing the unexpected. "I have deliberately chosen the uncertain path whenever I had the chance," Mickey once told an interviewer.[8] If that caused a stir, so much the better.

This same irreverence sparked Mickey's adventure as a taxi dancer—dancing with men for money. After a few drinks one evening, she and a girlfriend named Betty devised a plan to investigate the "mysteries and techniques" of the taxi-dancing trade. The experience would be a bit of naughty fun, they decided, and at the very least would make for interesting conversation at their next dinner party.

Shanghai was famous for its dance halls, each of which specialized in women of a different color or nationality. Missionaries and other "respectable" foreigners regarded dance halls as disreputable and taxi dancers as whores in fancy shoes. Not Mickey, of course. Her curiosity was piqued by what went on in those smoke-filled establishments. She and Betty arranged to spend a night working as taxi dancers at a place called the Frisco. The hall was popular with soldiers from local garrisons and with visiting sailors. Here, for just a few cents per turn, the men could dance with white women of any nationality.

Taxi dancing was not the lark that Mickey anticipated. For one thing, the moment she and Betty entered the dance hall in their party gowns, they realized they were "hopelessly overdressed." The dresses worn by the regular taxi dancers were frayed and "sweated out under the arms," as Mickey noted. This shopworn look was an occupational hazard, the product of a few thousand too many turns on the dance floor and a few too many spilled drinks. For another thing, when Betty's boyfriend appeared, the pair got into a noisy argument.

Mickey gamely ignored what was happening. She had no shortage of customers lining up with dance tickets in hand. But it was evident even to the drunken sailors and soldiers with whom she whirled about the dance floor that she did not belong there. "What are *you* doing here?" her customers asked one by one. Mickey responded with a tearful yarn about hardships and evil stepmothers. One drunken Scottish engineer was so concerned that he announced his intention to take Mickey "out of all this." Her would-be savior passed out before he could attempt a rescue.

Betty eventually settled her argument, and by the end of a long and wearisome night, she and Mickey had each collected a handful of dance tickets, worth a few precious American dollars. Rather than cash the tickets, they gave them to the regular taxi dancers. This helped soothe the resentment their presence had caused. Later, Betty's boyfriend drove her and Mickey home. The chilly silence in the car lasted until they began rehashing the evening's events over a pot of coffee. Their conclusion: the life of a taxi dancer was not much fun, nor was it an option for either of them. Still, Mickey's curiosity about Shanghai's flesh trade was not quite satisfied. Not long afterward, she ventured into one of the most infamous brothels in the city's red-light district.

Mickey had rented a spare room in her flat to a mysterious young woman named Jean, who had once worked as a prostitute. In response to Mickey's questions, Jean suggested they visit a brothel; she promised it would be an adventure. Ever curious, Mickey agreed. She put on a slinky black dress, donned a large hat, and dabbed on plenty of eye makeup. Then she tagged along as Jean went to tea with a woman named Louise, who was one of Shanghai's most successful madams. Louise's, as her establishment was known, was popular with Japanese bankers and businessmen. "I was amazed by [her] . . . personality," Mickey later wrote. "I don't know what I had expected: the sort of madam you read about, I suppose. Louise was just a comfortable, chatty fat woman."[9] What is more, she deplored bad language and dirty jokes. As they sipped tea and ate chocolate cake, Jean told Louise a wondrous story about her friend: Mickey's name, Jean said, was "Mrs. Wong." She was the American wife of a Chinese student who had run off, leaving her penniless. Louise listened and nodded sympathetically as Mickey tried her best to look the part. As she later put it, she "lived to regret that silly prank."[10] Louise, always looking for "new girls," began calling Jean to plead with her to invite "Mrs. Wong" to return to the brothel to meet some of her "gentlemen friends." Jean thought Louise's interest in her flatmate was great fun, but the humor of the situation was lost on Mickey. Taxi dancing was one thing, prostitution was quite another.

If nothing else, such experiences provided Mickey with material for her writing and some welcome diversion. By 1937, events half a world away were irrevocably changing her life in "the Paris of the East." Millions of European Jews were fleeing Nazi persecution. Shanghai was one of the few safe havens that remained open to Jewish refugees. As the trickle of emigrants became a flood, those who arrived were poorer and poorer. These were hungry, desperate and frightened people. A local relief committee, which Sir Victor helped to organize, set up a Jewish relief camp on the outskirts of the city.

The presence of so many refugees was impossible to ignore; white beggars and peddlers, once a rarity, were now common on Shanghai's bustling streets. Being Jewish herself, Mickey found the refugees' presence unsettling. For a time, she tried to help with the relief work. When she could cope no more, she withdrew in horror; the immensity of the suffering depressed and terrified her. "I had been feeling livery, impatient, restless," she wrote. "I didn't like anyone: I didn't like anyone, except perhaps Sinmay. It was time for a change. In the happy prewar days I would have settled the matter by purchasing a ticket for somewhere; now, surrounded by Japs, I could not run away."[11]

The Sino-Japanese conflict was savage and bloody, but sporadic. Chiang Kai-shek's army was outgunned and poorly trained, so the Generalissimo was reluctant to engage the enemy in all-out battle. What developed was the classic invasion scenario: the Chinese guerillas retained control of large sections of the countryside, while the Japanese were under siege in the cities they occupied when their army swept down from the north. Chiang, whose forces still held the area around Shanghai in early 1937, had committed a quarter-million troops to defending the city. Chiang's initial plan was to hold off the Japanese advance for six weeks and to inflict as many casualties as possible on his enemy before retreating. When that strategy worked better than expected, Chiang extended the defense in hopes the U.S., British, and French governments would be forced to intervene to save their nationals trapped by the fighting. Even when many foreigners were killed in the fighting and by a cholera outbreak, the Western powers maintained a steadfast neutrality.

The battle for Shanghai raged from August to early November 1937. As it did, Chiang's guerilla fighters slipped into the Japanese-controlled sections of the city each night to carry out acts of spying, hit-and-run killings, and sabotage. Other guerillas hid out in Shanghai's foreign settlements. The Japanese, as yet unwilling to provoke the Western powers by overrunning these areas, were content to have their agents do their dirty work. Shanghai became a hotbed of intrigue as the two sides played a deadly game of cat and mouse. At dawn each morning, city workers cruised the streets in trucks to pick up the bodies of victims on both sides who had been killed overnight. "The guerillas were our chief topic of conversation during that period," Mickey later wrote.[12]

She found it impossible to carry on with her life in the midst of such mayhem. In late 1935, she had moved to a larger flat upstairs in the bank building. But finally it became apparent that life in Shanghai's downtown had become too risky; political violence, nightly gun battles, and rampant crime had become features of life in the Chinese sections of the city. The deteriorating situation in Shanghai attracted the attention of the Western media. A steady parade of "vultures," as Mickey called them, came to report on the situation. In the time-honored tradition of journalists everywhere, most passed their evenings in a bar, particularly in the Tower, a nightclub atop Sir Victor's Cathay Hotel. Mickey took to joining the crowd there as they drank and watched the war in comfort. From there, the fighting seemed remote and unreal, like watching fish fighting in an aquarium. "People liked the Tower as well as any place in town for the view it afforded of dogfights and general shooting and excitement," Mickey explained.[13]

Far more hazardous and unsettling than the fighting, which ebbed and flowed with the political situation, was the Japanese habit of indiscriminately bombing or shelling buildings in the Chinese neighborhoods where guerillas were thought to be hiding. During the day, the Japanese attacked these locations. Dive-bombers swooped down from the skies, or else the big guns on the Japanese battleship *Izuma*, anchored in the harbor, bombarded selected targets. The Nationalists replied with artillery fired from the streets or with bombs dropped from planes. Predictably, shells fired by both sides went astray. The consequences were disastrous. In one particularly horrific incident, bombs from Nationalist aircraft overshot the *Izuma* and slammed into a crowded hotel and an adjacent department store. More than 3,500 people died in the explosions, ensuing fire, and panic; blood literally ran in the gutters.

The randomness of the carnage was unnerving, not to mention unsettling. When the foreign-controlled banks closed their offices during the worst of the fighting and moved to the relative safety of the French Settlement, life for Mickey and other foreigners who lived downtown became intolerable. Mickey ignored the risks as long as she could. She once drove through the deserted downtown streets during a Japanese artillery barrage in order to visit a dentist to have a broken tooth fixed—she had broken it returning a bite from Mr. Mills—so that she could attend a dinner party that evening. "Hissing, spitting tracer bullets and shells fell around us; the deep blue air was like water in which swam glowing fish, always in parabolic curves," Mickey later wrote.[14]

When such risks finally became too great, Mickey rented a house on Yuyuen Road in the city's International Settlement.

• • •

On November 8, 1937, a pall descended on the foreign settlement in Shanghai. That day, the Chinese army withdrew, abandoning the city to the victorious Japanese who were now free to do as they pleased. Five weeks later, on December 12, the Emperor's warplanes touched off an international crisis when they sank the American gunboat *Panay* in the Yangtze River. The next day, the Japanese army swarmed over the Nationalist capital of Nanking. The troops looted the city, slaughtering more than 200,000 Chinese in a drunken frenzy of rape and murder. Reports of the "rape of Nanking" raised fears about what lay in store for other Chinese cities, possibly even Shanghai, should a full-scale war break out.

With most of the city now under Japanese control, and the harbor blockaded, Shanghai's economy began to falter. The Shanghai dollar dropped like a stone. As a result, many Chinese were devastated financially; Sinmay tottered on the verge of bankruptcy "four times a month," as Mickey put it.[15]

The cost of living became even cheaper for those with foreign currency to spend. Since Mickey's pay from the *New Yorker* had recently been increased to several hundred dollars per story, she was flush. On occasion, she lent money to Sinmay to stave off his creditors, and when a Japanese bomber flew so low over her house that it knocked over the chimney, Mickey did not hesitate to move. She found a comfortable cottage at 1826 Avenue Joffree, a busy thoroughfare in the city's French Settlement. The dwelling was spacious, with a garden and even a spare bedroom that Mickey rented out for the needed income.

She was joined in the French Settlement by the Zaus. They fled their home in the Japanese-controlled Yangtzepoo Road district under cover of darkness, taking with them what they could carry by car. They abandoned everything else to the roving gangs of looters who now ruled the streets. "Poor Sinmay, having lost everything, he moved to . . . a slummy house where a dozen people are crowded into one room," Mickey told her mother.[16] Fortunately, the Zaus soon were able to rent their own cottage, not far from Mickey's place.

Despite rising tensions over a variety of domestic concerns, Mickey remained close to the family. With the Japanese military strictly enforcing a nightly curfew, going out had become difficult and dangerous. Mickey spent most evenings with the Zaus. She ate meals with them, took part in family activities, smoked opium, and played with the children. Mickey relished the opportunity to be part of a family again, for she was feeling lonely and vulnerable. Recent events in Shanghai had heightened her growing fatalism. Mickey was convinced that everything was about to come crashing down around her. "You ask if I am putting down roots," she told Helen in one of her letters home. "No, you can't get rooted in Shanghai, but I still love China. I haven't any desire to go anywhere else—well, not much—and I couldn't afford to anyway."[17]

Mickey's uneasiness was fueled by the knowledge that Sir Victor Sassoon was liquidating assets prior to moving his business interests back to the relative safety of Bombay. In the meantime, Sir Victor bought time by cultivating amicable relations with top Japanese officials and military officers. But Shanghai's notorious criminal gangs had stepped up their trade in extortion, kidnapping, and murder under the compliant eyes of their Japanese protectors. Sir Victor knew he was a marked man. His avowed pro-British sentiments, and his efforts on behalf of Jewish refugees had singled him out as a target.

The more time he spent abroad (ostensibly for treatment of an ailing hip), the more obvious it was to Mickey that he was about to move. As rumors to that effect swirled, resentment spread through the city's foreign community. In their clubs and offices, many taipans sneered that Sir Victor was "running away," all the while wishing they could do the same. Many wealthy Chinese had no such hesitation. Some quietly began moving money out of Shanghai; others left for Hong Kong on the ships carrying the wives and children of uneasy British citizens. Hong Kong, a thousand miles south, was considered safe.

The Japanese might be eager to tackle a weak and divided China, conventional wisdom had it, but they were no match for the British Empire and would never attack a British colony.

Among those who fled were Mickey's Chinese friends who feared their names were on the Japanese "blacklist"—a secret police hit list of prominent Chinese journalists, intellectuals, civic leaders, and politicians. Mickey naïvely scoffed at the idea of such a list, but she knew Japanese spies were everywhere; they had even tailed her sometimes. Mickey maintained a pretense of neutrality, although her relationship with the Zaus left no doubts where her sympathies lay. Nevertheless, her friendships with people of various nationalities, including some Japanese, puzzled some friends and angered others. Despite the rising chorus of hatred, Mickey continued to treat people as individuals. Occasionally this trait landed her in awkward situations.

For example, one day a Japanese friend invited her to a lunch where he introduced her to an "associate." The man proposed a tempting business deal: if Mickey agreed to adopt a more pro-Japanese editorial stand in a newsletter she edited, the man vowed to purchase enough advertising to pay for the printing of the entire issue. Mickey declined, claiming that she did not have responsibility for the publication's editorial content.

Another time, Mickey overheard some Chinese guerillas plotting to kill one of her Japanese journalist friends. Mickey risked her own life when she discreetly contacted the man, advising him it would be "wise" to stay home the evening of the planned assassination attempt. He did so.

Mickey also continued to earn part of her living by offering English lessons. One of her customers was a Japanese man named Kanai—"the tiger," as he called himself. Mickey and everyone else in town knew that Kanai was a spy, but as long as he was willing to pay for English lessons, Mickey was happy to take his money. Besides, she hoped to gather from him information that she could pass along to friends in the Chinese underground.

These guerillas sometimes met in Mickey's parlor. For a time, Sinmay's brother Huan set up a radio transmitter in the upstairs spare bedroom at her house. The transmitter's existence was a poorly guarded secret, and Mickey was fortunate that it was moved by the time the Japanese military came calling.

The Japanese had put a bounty on Huan's head, and Sinmay was suspect by implication. He refused to flee, despite the cautions from his friends. Shanghai was his home, Sinmay said, and Hong Kong was too stuffy, too crowded, and too expensive. Even so, Sinmay invested some money in a Hong Kong edition of *T'ien Hsia*, taking as his business partner a man named Sun Fo, the son of Kuomintang founder Sun Yat-sen. The move had an unexpected benefit from Mickey's perspective; Sun Fo's involvement raised the magazine's profile in Hong Kong and helped make Mickey's name known there.

• • • •

For a time in late 1937 and early 1938, Mickey toyed with the idea of going home for a visit. At one point, she asked Helen to "make job inquiries" at Harvard University on Sinmay's behalf. Mickey and Sinmay gave up the idea when the news from home was not encouraging. Unemployment remained high in the United States. Labor violence was rising, and a conservative backlash was threatening to destroy many of the economic gains of the New Deal's first three years. Most Americans remained preoccupied with their own problems, and isolationism was growing. Grim though the situation was, Mickey's literary agent urged her to return to New York.

The news from Helen and Hannah was no less glum. Helen wrote of the ongoing frustrations of trying to recover from Eddie Mayer the money that Hannah had loaned him in 1934. Eddie was drinking heavily and had separated from his wife for good.

From the Congo, Mickey received occasional missives from Mary Linder, an American woman who had married Patrick Putnam in 1933, a few months after Mickey's departure. Linder kept Mickey informed about events at Penge, where the big news was that Matope had been circumcised, and another of Mickey's favorite baboons had died. Then came a letter from Patrick bearing the sad news that Mary herself had succumbed after contracting pneumonia. Patrick begged Mickey to return to Africa to live with him once more, preferably as his wife. Mickey declined.[18]

Such dispiriting reports from abroad were vivid reminders that despite her best efforts to make a life for herself in Shanghai, her own future was as cloudy as it was limited. Mickey remained ambivalent about her relationship with Sinmay. Whenever she felt vulnerable and lonely, she was content to think she could spend the rest of her life there with him. Other times, she dreamed of meeting a handsome, rich man and running off with him. For a time in mid-1937, Sinmay had "grown wild and chattered about divorcing Zoa" in order to marry Mickey.[19] The prospect of being forced to make a long-term commitment terrified her, and she told Sinmay as much. Then she went away for a holiday on her own.

Sinmay was distraught. When Mickey returned, he repaid some of the money he had borrowed and vowed to stay away from her until he had sorted out his life. Mickey decided that the time had come to break with Sinmay. "I'm terribly sad about it, but feel for once I was right; it was getting absolutely impossible and there was no prospect of improvement," Mickey wrote Helen. "I do love that little bastard, but it's like playing marbles with quicksilver."[20]

But Mickey could not stay away. The Zaus listened sympathetically one evening as Mickey poured out her woes—omitting the parts about her relationship with Sinmay. Zoa offered quiet reassurance, while Sinmay stroked his beard pensively. Then he proposed a plan; it was one he said would benefit everyone. Polygamy being legal under Chinese law, Sinmay suggested that he and Mickey visit a Chinese lawyer to sign a document stating that they were husband and wife. This idea, more a matter of legal procedure than substance, appealed to Mickey. While it would make her a member of the Zau family in Chinese law, she knew such a "marriage" would be null and void under American law. In becoming Sinmay's wife, Mickey was entitled to special status. Zoa presented her with a pair of jade bracelets, the traditional gift for a new concubine. Sinmay promised Mickey a plot in the Zau family graveyard, so that if she should die there in Shanghai, she would not be alone, as she had feared. What's more, Mickey was entitled to certain legal rights under Chinese law. From Sinmay's standpoint, these were the real benefits of the plan.

It was now easy to prepare documents purporting to show that Mickey had bought Sinmay's printing press from him a couple of years earlier. Otherwise, the equipment would be confiscated by the Japanese, who regarded Sinmay as an enemy. As an American citizen, Mickey was still officially neutral. This status entitled her to apply to the Japanese authorities for a permit to recover "her property" from the Zaus' house. She was granted permission to go there with a truck and a crew of Russian workers. (The Japanese forbade whites to hire Orientals for manual labor.) Mickey and her crew of Russians rescued some of Sinmay's priceless library of Ming classics and other Zau family heirlooms.

Mickey was accompanied on her salvage expedition by a Japanese marine, who was assigned to act as her guide and protector. While the man was in the Zaus' house, he picked up some copies of "vaguely pornographic" magazines that Sinmay had printed. The rules set by the Japanese stipulated that Mickey's truck could not be driven right up to the door of the house. As she and her soldier escort were carrying armloads of goods to the vehicle, he nodded toward the magazines. "What do you call this?" he asked.

Mickey smiled. "Fuck," she said sarcastically.

The soldier looked puzzled. "Puck?" he repeated.

"No, no. This is English. FUCK!" said Mickey.

As they walked, the exchange continued in a similar vein. The soldier repeated the unfamiliar four-letter word, with Mickey correcting him each time.

"He was getting a little better by the time we got back to the truck," she recalled. "I suspect I did him a favor because at some point in his soldiering career I'm sure he would have needed that word again, or else somebody would have handed him a hockey puck."[21]

Another right that Mickey enjoyed as Sinmay's wife was being entitled to "adopt" one or more of the Zau children. Still haunted by her experience in the Congo with Matope, Mickey resisted the temptation to become a "parent" again. At age thirty-two, she was convinced she would never bear her own children. In quiet moments, this idea troubled her deeply. The feelings of uncertainty and inadequacy she experienced were heightened by two things. One was the news from home that her sister Helen had undergone a hysterectomy. The other was the effects of Mickey's own opium smoking. Her addiction went untreated, largely because she still continued to deny she had a problem. Mickey was living in a world of pipe dreams, convinced she could quit smoking any time she wanted. Proof positive was that she had gone "on the wagon" several times, when her stomach bothered her. Of course, such periods of abstinence ended the moment she felt better.

At the time of her arrival in Shanghai, Mickey had been preoccupied with her problems with Eddie Mayer. Her weight had ballooned; she wore a size sixteen dress. As Mickey's opium consumption increased, and her appetite fell, so did her dress size. This posed no problem at first. All that changed as she became run-down. Her fondness for smoking cigars, another of her bad habits, added to the problem. Mickey suffered from jaundice and stomach cramps. She also gradually stopped menstruating. It was a mixed blessing to be free of "the curse," as she called it, yet the psychological effects of this development were profound. Mickey experienced a sense of fear and loss. The former she could live with for now, the latter she could not.

• • •

News of Mickey's love affair with Sinmay had spread far beyond Shanghai's foreign community. In distant Hong Kong and Singapore, many Europeans clucked their tongues at the scandal of the American woman who had taken a Chinese lover. Of course, a few romantic souls saw the relationship differently. Among them was Charles Boxer, a British army officer stationed in Hong Kong. Being fluent in Japanese, Boxer was involved in military intelligence work. However, his heart lay elsewhere. In his spare time, Boxer was an avid amateur historian. His articles about eighteenth-century Dutch and Portuguese mercantilism occasionally appeared in the Hong Kong edition of *T'ien Hsai*. Because of this, Boxer read Mickey's writings, and he became curious about her. "I like this woman's mind," Boxer told a *T'ien Hsia* editor. "Who is she? Where does she live?"

The editor, a friend of Sinmay's, provided Boxer with Mickey's address and a caveat: Emily Hahn was "madly in love" with Sinmay. Boxer shrugged. He was just curious, he said. He was going to Shanghai on business, so he would call on Miss Hahn for tea.

That is how Captain Charles Boxer came to be standing in Mickey's parlor late one afternoon reading the spines of the books on her shelves. Hearing someone coming down the stairs, Boxer turned to offer his hand. There, staring him in the eye, was Mr. Mills, clad in a bright red fez. Boxer and the gibbon eyed each other suspiciously. Both were greatly relieved when Mickey and her flatmate Jean breezed into the room. After hasty introductions, they sat down to talk. Their conversation and drinks were interrupted when Sinmay joined them. Then several other visitors arrived, and meaningful conversation became impossible. A disappointed Charles Boxer headed toward the door. He had decided Miss Emily Hahn and her Shanghai friends were all quite mad. As she saw him to the door, Mickey felt sorry that they had not had the opportunity to talk longer. Something about Captain Boxer had caught her fancy, in a vague, undefinable way. "I remember . . . that just for a fleeting second that afternoon I . . . felt a certain regret," Mickey would later recall. "'What a pity,' I thought."[22]

17

IN THE SPRING OF 1938, Mickey's old friend John Gunther was well on his way to becoming (as a writer for the *New Yorker* would describe him) "one of the half dozen or so international celebrities" of the day—as famous as such luminaries as Roosevelt or Lindbergh.[1] Two years earlier he had written *Inside Europe*, a book that warned of the dangers posed by Hitler, Mussolini, and Stalin. In the wake of that success, Gunther quit his job as the London correspondent for the *Chicago Daily News* and became a full-time author. His next book was another "Inside," this one dealing with Asia and the threat of Japanese militarism. Gunther and his wife Frances were on a research trip when they stopped in Shanghai in April 1938.

The Gunthers called on Mickey, whom John had not seen for nearly ten years. Mickey still had not forgiven him for the fanciful stories he had invented about their friendship; her scorn was reflected in letters in which she mocked Gunther's ability to become an instant expert on nearly anything. "The Gunthers are horribly almost here, stopping for a time in Hankow," Mickey told her mother, "where John can learn all about China and how to end this war, with his usual speed and precision."[2]

Despite her pique, Mickey enjoyed the visit. The Gunthers, in turn, were concerned about Mickey, particularly by her appearance, which was gaunt and sallow as a result of her opium use. Instead of chiding her, Gunther took a different tack: he suggested that Mickey quit her teaching job and, like him, write full-time. Mickey rejected the idea. Her most recent novel, *Affair*, had flopped, she explained, and publishers had rejected her latest effort, about a love affair between an American woman and a Chinese gentleman. Although Mickey wrote "like a streak," her agent complained that it was difficult to sell her work; nobody in New York was interested in her stories about China.[3] (Mickey wrote for the *New Yorker* under a contract, meaning that her agent did not get a commission for that material.)

Gunther refused to take Mickey's no for an answer. The Sino-Japanese War had awakened America to the growing threat of Japanese expansionism, he argued; the key to writing successfully about China was to focus on personalities, not the arcane world of Chinese politics. With that in mind, he suggested that Mickey write a book about the Soong sisters. The timing was perfect.

Gunther's suggestion flattered Mickey. She knew that other far more well-known journalists had failed in efforts to write about the Soongs. Although all three sisters were Western-educated and spoke excellent English, they were notoriously inaccessible to the press. This distancing was very much a function of the powerful men they had married, and it was what made them so beguiling to the Western media.

Ai-ling Soong, the eldest Soong daughter, had wed Dr. H. H. Kung, the wealthy Shanghai banker who became China's prime minister in the late 1930s. Kung boasted an impressive lineage, tracing his descendants back to Confucius.

Ching-ling, the middle Soong daughter, married her father's friend Sun Yat-sen, founder of the nationalist Kuomintang Party. It was a 1912 Kuomintang-led rebellion that forced the abdication of the child emperor Pu-Yi, thus toppling the Manchu dynasty after almost three centuries of absolute rule.

Mei-ling, the youngest, prettiest, and brightest of the Soong sisters, was thoroughly Westernized. She had studied at Wellesley College in Massachusetts. In 1927, she became China's most influential woman when she married Generalissimo Chiang Kai-shek, who succeeded Sun Yat-sen in 1925 as leader of the Kuomintang. As such, he became the linchpin of American foreign policy in the Far East. It mattered little to Washington that he had once been a staunch supporter of the Soviet Union, or that he was one of the kingpins of the Shanghai Triad organized crime gang. To American politicians, whose grasp of Chinese affairs was fuzzy at best, the Generalissimo's devout Methodism (there was "Methodism to his madness," as Frances Gunther quipped[4] when she learned that Chiang had converted to marry Mei-ling Soong) and his antipathy to Mao Tse-tung's Chinese communists were enough to recommend him.

"[Chiang] was first and last a military man," Mickey explained.[5] He could not have cared less about foreign public opinion, *unless* it affected the U.S. military and financial aid he received. That was the only reason the Generalissimo heeded his wife's counsel when she urged him to meet with Gunther. A cabled account of the interview appeared in the *New York Times* on April 6, 1938.[6] Gunther later wrote in more depth about the Generalissimo, Madame Chiang, and the Soongs in his book *Inside Asia*, which appeared the following spring. As Gunther predicted, the book's timing was perfect; like *Inside Europe*, it became an international best-seller. For that reason, New York publishers took notice when Gunther announced that his friend Emily Hahn in Shanghai was writing the "inside" story of the Soong sisters. Mickey was surprised one day in the fall of 1938 to receive a letter from her agent informing her that Doubleday, Doran and Company had offered her a contract and a $500 advance if she would write the Soong book; the British publisher Macmillan was even more keen and had also promised Mickey a cash advance along with an unusually attractive royalty rate. Mickey initially had dismissed Gunther's idea, but the more she thought about it, the more attractive it seemed, especially after Sinmay teased her about being lazy.

In her heart, Mickey knew he was right. She was just putting in time in Shanghai. Her writing, like her life, lacked purpose; her recent failures had eroded her self-confidence. The easiest thing in the world would have been for Mickey to stay put and do nothing; it was awfully tempting. "If I had a chance to take a full-time job I think I would do it," she told her mother in one of her letters, "but just for discipline and to threaten my muse."[7] Even her social life was adrift. Sir Victor was not in town much anymore, and Bernadine had gone back to the United States. From Chicago, Hannah Hahn sent letter after letter urging her daughter to do likewise. Hannah had begun her latest campaign in the spring of 1938.

Mrs. Hahn was distressed by news reports about the Jewish refugee situation in Shanghai and about the war between Chiang and the Japanese; she worried her daughter was "in the midst of it all." Mickey scoffed at the notion. "The Midst of it All has traveled away from Shanghai long since and far, far away," Mickey explained. "And when the midst was here, Mother, it was not thrilling except to see some half-witted male adventurer who might have galloped over for a job. Air raids are not thrilling; war is not thrilling; dead bodies are not thrilling. They are exasperating, and terrifying, and wicked, and anything in the world but desirable and thrilling. . . . I want very much to see you and the others, but that is the only reason I would come home. I haven't any desire to see Hollywood, or to hang around New York autographing books and going to cocktail log-rollings. I should very much like to go to England, but not until the trip is necessary. I can't afford it."[8]

Even with the falling Shanghai dollar, it was difficult for Mickey to make ends meet. She was she paying to maintain her own house and lending money to the Zaus. Sinmay was trying to earn a living by writing as many as three pulp detective novels a month for a Chinese publisher, but that did not feed his family or support his spendthrift lifestyle. It fell to Zoa to keep the Zaus going by selling her jade and diamond jewelry.

Mickey's own financial situation became critical when her income from teaching and private English lessons dried up. She economized by heating only one or two rooms of her house and by taking in female boarders. Her financial situation was not helped when her temper got her into trouble with her New York contacts, upon whom she depended. Mickey had been "on strike" because of a petulant dispute with her editor at the *New Yorker*. What is more, she had chastened her agent Carl Brandt for complaining about the stories and other material she sent him. At one point in the fall of 1938, Brandt was trying unsuccessfully to find publishers for two novels, a collection of short stories, and a play about Mickey's university days in Wisconsin. He was finding no takers, and he told Mickey it was because her work was no longer saleable. He may have been right. Mickey had written a novel called *Ching*, about a Shanghai prostitute who was a thinly disguised version of her former flatmate. Brandt feared the book was libelous and far too risqué for the American market. Its publication, he warned, might generate the sort of critical comments that would ruin Mickey's literary reputation. Mickey refused to believe this and reacted angrily to Brandt's advice, however well intentioned it may have been. "I really think a lot of people are interested in what goes on in brothels," she told Brandt. "As for criticism, I'm a long way off from that, and I'd face worse to see my name in print again."[9]

In letters to her mother, Mickey's bitterness and rage bubbled over. "Those agents always act as if every writer worth his paper lives in New York, . . . but what they really want is for me to do their work for them, meeting and pampering editors into buying my stuff," she complained. "And as for being out of touch, what sort of jungle does [Brandt] think I live in? I read everything he does, and I talk to as many Americans every day. I wrote him to go ahead and peddle [the novel] and never mind babying me. When will I find an agent who knows what an agent's job is, which is to sell what a writer writes, and not to tell him what to write?"[10]

For all her bluster, Mickey knew she would be lost without the income from her *New Yorker* stories and the few other articles her agent managed to sell. That made the possibility of being paid American dollars and British pounds for a book about the Soongs appealing. The big problem, of course, was to succeed where others had failed, namely in convincing the Soong sisters to cooperate.

The sisters were the subject of endless gossip, and Mickey, like most foreigners in China, had heard the stories. Beyond that, she knew little about them. Mickey had seen Madame Chiang only once, and that was from a distance. She had once attended a reception at the Kung home with Bernadine Szold-Fritz, and her only contact with Madame Sun was even more distant: she had met Agnes Smedley, the American leftist and author, who was doing secretarial work for Madame Sun.

Mickey and Sinmay discussed the difficulties of writing about the Soongs. He advised her that the key to doing so was to secure the cooperation of Madame Kung, the eldest Soong sister. If she agreed to go along, her younger sisters would, too. Sinmay stroked his beard and announced that he could help in that regard. His "favorite auntie" happened to be a childhood playmate of Madame Kung's. Sinmay promised to ask her to broach the subject of the proposed book with her friend. When Sinmay rang his aunt, she was away in Hong Kong. Mickey made use of the two months until her return to do some research.

When Sinmay finally took Mickey to see his aunt, she was doubtful that Madame Kung would cooperate on a book. Nevertheless, she vowed to speak to Madame Kung on Mickey's behalf and suggested it would do no harm for Mickey to write each of the Soong sisters a letter.

Mickey did so. As expected, she got no reply from Madame Sun. She got a delayed response from Madame Chiang, who was with her husband in Chungking, beyond Japanese reach. Madame Chiang's note to Mickey was cordial, but she explained she was too busy just then to bother with a book. Mickey's lone positive response came from Madame Kung, who was intrigued by Mickey's pledge to write "a truthful book." Madame Kung had read John Gunther's book, *Inside Asia,* and, like her sisters, she was angry at how he had portrayed the Soongs. She suggested Mickey come to see her in Hong Kong.

• • •

When Mickey and Sinmay arrived in Hong Kong in June of 1939, they took rooms at the Hong Kong Hotel, startling the staff and other guests, who gawked at Sinmay. In those days, the few Chinese who stayed there were thoroughly Westernized. Chinese gentlemen in Hong Kong had shorn their long hair and discarded their gowns in the wake of the 1912 downfall of the Manchu dynasty; European-style suits and hats had become de rigueur. Only intellectuals and others who were "hopelessly old-fashioned" wore traditional garb. People stared at Sinmay, who was an exotic sight, drifting through the hotel lobby in his robes and pigtail.

At first, Sinmay seemed not to mind. He and Mickey went about their business. They visited the offices of *T'ien Hsia*, and Sinmay looked up many old friends, some of whom had found sanctuary there from kidnappers and Shanghai's death squads. Mickey also knew a lot of people in Hong Kong, most of whom were British. She was invited to several cocktail parties and socials, which gave her an idea of how different life in Hong Kong's foreign community was from Shanghai's. The pace was infinitely slower, more genteel, and expensive. It was also much stuffier; the British in Hong Kong did not socialize with Chinese. The foreigners kept to themselves, and for amusement they golfed, played bridge, sailed, staged amateur theatricals, and drank. It was all terribly lazy, benumbing, and ultimately pointless. People in Hong Kong had heard the rumors about Mickey's affair with Sinmay, and she was as much a curiosity as when she had arrived in China four years earlier. "I was a symbol of that delightfully attractive and wicked metropolis of Shanghai. They grabbed at me eagerly," Mickey wrote. "I spent one or two evenings of sheer social boredom and I loved all of it, the rapid, gay, empty chatter, the drinks, the slow-sipping hours above the harbor, looking down at the beautiful stage setting of lights and mountains. This was the other side of Hong Kong which the

Chinese didn't know. I wouldn't be able to stand it much of the time, I said to myself, but for a change how nice it was!"[11]

Mickey was surprised when Sinmay began sulking over her "defection." His mood brightened only when a note arrived from Captain Charles Boxer, the British army officer-turned-historian who had called on Mickey in Shanghai. Boxer invited both Mickey and Sinmay to attend a racially mixed luncheon that he and his new wife, Ursula, were hosting at a Chinese restaurant. "Now *there* is a gentleman," Sinmay said of Boxer. "He knows his manners."

An eclectic crowd of British, Europeans, and Chinese guests attended the party. They filled all the chairs at two large tables. Ursula Boxer was there. She struck Mickey as being an attractive and proper young British woman, especially after she told Mickey above the din that she read and enjoyed her articles in *T'ien Hsia*. Ursula, troubled by the heavy drinking, abruptly informed her husband that she was going home and "taking the car with her." Boxer kissed her good-bye and then resumed his partying without missing a beat. He was bouncing from table to table, urging his guests to *kenpei* their wine glasses. *Kenpei* is "bottoms up" in Chinese, and by tradition a good host keeps pace with his guests, drink for drink. Boxer had no difficulty doing so. When Mickey joined in, she retained only a fuzzy memory of her host as "a brilliant, amusing, mad man." At one point, she congratulated Boxer on his recent marriage. "It always happens when one lives in Hong Kong, you know, more than four years," he said with a shrug. "One either becomes a hopeless drunkard, or one marries. I did both."[12]

• • •

Mickey was overcome by nerves the afternoon of her appointment with Madame Kung. Sinmay found her sitting on the bed of her hotel room, shaking and fighting off tears. Mickey sensed the importance of this interview; if Madame Kung agreed to cooperate, Mickey knew she was going to have to start working seriously again. Her agent, Carl Brandt, had high hopes for the book. It had become the panacea for all of Mickey's troubles. "Everything, of course, depends on [it]. If the book goes well, I needn't worry . . . people will fall over themselves to buy my every word," Mickey joked in a letter home. "If the book goes well, there won't be a war in Europe, the war in China will stop. Nobody will say what will happen if the book *doesn't* go well, however."[13]

From the moment the meeting with Madame Kung began, Mickey knew she had nothing to fear. The atmosphere inside the Kung home was formal but not intimidating. Mickey was reassured by the presence of Sinmay, his aunt, and Madame's secretary, Alice Chow, whom Mickey had known in Shanghai. Then there was Ai-ling Kung herself. She was petite and elegant with tiny hands, darting black eyes, and coal-black hair piled atop her head in an attempt to compensate for her diminutive size.

At first, the conversation was stiff, and the book proposal was not mentioned. When finally it was, Mickey understood why Madame Kung had summoned her. Madame explained that although she normally shunned publicity, she felt compelled to speak out after the way John Gunther had portrayed her in *Inside Asia*. She had never met him, Madame fumed, yet Gunther had painted her as a corrupt schemer who paced like a caged tiger when she didn't get her own way. Gunther also hinted about dark secrets: vast sums of money the Kungs and Chiangs had supposedly squirreled away in foreign bank accounts, about indiscretions in Dr. Kung's private life, and about his fondness for "the squeeze"—the age-old Chinese version of political graft. Madame Kung's voice trembled when she spoke of all these things. She also noted that her sister, Madame Chiang, was even more angry at how Gunther had portrayed her and the Generalissimo. As Mickey listened, she decided John Gunther, in New York, was fortunate to be out of Madame Kung's reach.

Mickey wanted no such trouble for herself. Again she promised Madame Kung that she would write "a truthful book." If she didn't, she vowed, she would not submit it for publication. Madame nodded. The only question lingering in her mind, she confided, related to Mickey's judgment: could a foreigner truly understand Chinese affairs? Madame remained unconvinced by her guest's assurances. When Mickey left the Kung home that day, she still had no firm agreement that her hostess would cooperate on the book. Madame Kung promised she would "consider" the idea further and her secretary would contact Mickey with her answer. Sinmay was sure that Madame Kung had already made her decision. In the backseat of Madame Kung's car on the way back to the hotel, he smiled as he whispered in Mickey's ear. Madame Kung would cooperate, he said.

Sinmay was right. When Alice Chow came calling on Mickey at the hotel a few days later, it was to announce that her employer had agreed to provide Mickey with whatever information she needed for the book.

• • •

Having made all of the necessary arrangements with Madame Kung, Mickey and Sinmay sailed for home one hot day in mid-July 1939. They returned to find that life in Shanghai was becoming ever more constricted as the Japanese tightened their control over the city. "First, we couldn't go outside the town limits, and then some of my friends were shot at while riding, and we had to give up hacking [horseback riding] even in the Settlement," Mickey wrote. "The shops ran short of things. Chinese acquaintances quietly disappeared, and there came a time when the staff of my college, with the exception of me, moved to Hong Kong."[14]

All of these developments were related to events in Europe. Everyone knew war was inevitable; it was now only a matter of time. When the shooting began, the Japanese would be ready. With each bold new step that Hitler took, Britain and France seemed more and more tentative. The Japanese decided they had a free hand in the Far East. The thousands of Jewish refugees from Europe who crowded into Shanghai's relief camps felt the same way. They had jumped from the proverbial frying pan into the fire.

Mickey agonized over developments in Europe and over the falling value of the British pound and U.S. dollar. She and everyone else in Shanghai's foreign community wondered what would happen when war broke out in Europe. Would the Japanese jump in? If so, would they seize control of Shanghai, intern all the foreigners, and settle accounts with their enemies? Or would they bide their time? No one knew for sure.

The optimists in Shanghai expressed doubts that the Japanese would do anything rash; after all, the argument went, the Japanese virtually controlled the city now and had too much to lose in the court of world opinion by a repeat of the rape of Nanking. Mickey wanted to believe this; her instincts told her otherwise. All she knew for certain was that whatever happened in Shanghai would not be pleasant. Life had become a race against time. "Nobody stopped working," Mickey wrote. "With one eye on. . . the news from Europe, we worked feverishly . . . packing trunks, counting money, [and] telephoning the newspaper offices for the latest bulletins."[15]

Mickey hurried to gather additional information about the Soongs and to tidy up all of the loose ends in her own life. She attended a round of farewell parties for Sir Victor, who had confirmed that he was moving back to India. When Mickey outlined her plans for a book on the Soongs, Sir Victor was enthusiastic, at least until he read a draft of the first chapters. "This is dull," he told Mickey. "It bored me to death. If I hadn't been in bed already, I would have fallen asleep in my chair, reading it."[16] Mickey tore up what she had done and started all over again.

She was serious about the Soong book. She knew the growing threat of war and other recent developments heralded big changes ahead. It wasn't just that Sir Victor was leaving town; there was more to it than that. When Mickey's female gibbon, Mrs. Mills, died of pneumonia, Mr. Mills was forlorn. Mickey had lots of time to commiserate with him; she was no longer going out in the evenings. The fighting between the Japanese and Chinese had moved off to the northwest part of China, but Shanghai's streets were as dangerous as ever. Japanese sentries were in the middle of "a slapping epidemic." Foreigners were smacked across the face for even the slightest violation of the arcane Japanese rules and regulations; no one was immune. The situation was even riskier after dark. A ten o'clock curfew was strictly enforced, and violators who evaded the roving gangs of thugs and political guerillas risked being shot on sight by police or soldiers.

Mickey was now spending most of her spare time with the Zaus, talking and smoking opium. She was still jaundiced from her drug habit and now sometimes vomited after smoking. In addition, she was still tortured by terrible stomach cramps and an irregular menstrual cycle. Mickey still refused to accept that her opium addiction might be responsible for any of these symptoms, but she listened to a friend who urged her to see a doctor. She recalled being more concerned that she might "grow a mustache" than with the possibility that she was seriously ill.[17] Mickey also recalled how on the day she told Sir Victor she couldn't have lunch with him because she had a doctor's appointment, he asked, "Yes, what's this about you having twins?" Even without Bernadine, the Shanghai rumor mill continued to churn.[18]

The American doctor Mickey went to see didn't need to ask about the rumors. He took one look at Mickey and shook his head. Then he quizzed her about her opium use and about how many pipes a day she smoked. "I was startled because I hardly knew him," Mickey recalls. "I said, 'Oh, about twelve.' "[19] The doctor suggested that she check into a clinic where she could break her addiction. For now, he gave her some medicine for her jaundice and informed her that it was unlikely she would ever be able to have a baby. Mickey resented that the doctor had "stuck his foot in the door of my exclusive domain," as she put it.[20] She remained adamant that she was not an opium addict. "I can stop any time," she continued to insist.

In reality, Mickey was not as carefree as she pretended. She knew that she could not travel to do the research needed for the Soong book unless she kicked her opium habit.[21] Compounding the risks was a Kuomintang edict that called for the beheading of all opium addicts. It was assumed that foreigners were still exempt from such punishments, although there was no way of knowing for sure. Mickey doubted that her doctor had reported her to the police, as he was required by law to do, but she felt vulnerable knowing that a stranger shared her secret. Until now, she had cared little about who knew what about her; Shanghai was filled with rumors. Until now, Mickey had blithely assumed most foreigners had no idea that she used opium. Had she been wrong? If so, she now realized she was open to blackmail or much worse. Such thoughts troubled her. So did the persistent reports she heard about the fate of opium addicts who had been taken away by the police. For the first time, Mickey was afraid.

She discussed her fears with a French couple who dropped by the Zaus' house to smoke. They told her about a German doctor who claimed he could cure opium addiction using hypnosis. Mickey was intrigued. She was also ready to clean up her life. When she told Sinmay about the German doctor, he urged her to go to make an appointment. Mickey did.

She checked herself into his clinic one day in the late summer of 1939. Any doubts she had about the extent of her problem were quickly erased. The next week was living hell. Mickey was in agony with a variety of withdrawal symptoms. She could not sleep and her legs were knotted with severe cramps. "[The latter] are a well-known withdrawal symptom," Mickey wrote. "They make themselves felt everywhere in the addict's body, but most people get them in the arms—they feel as if all the bones have been broken. I had mine in the legs, all the way up to the hips, and at four in the morning I figured out that this was because I'd had to wear braces on my legs as a baby."[22]

When Sinmay came calling one afternoon late in the week, Mickey was shocked by his appearance. She realized for the first time how cloudy his eyes had become and how stained and dirty opium smoking had made his teeth. She was repulsed. When they went out for tea, Mickey noticed something even more startling: for the first time in three years, she could taste and smell her food. Sinmay listened with interest when Mickey explained this; he too had been trying to break his opium addiction. Doing so on his own was harder than he had anticipated. Sinmay's latest abstinence had lasted just thirty-six hours. Most of all, he had missed the opium lamp's comforting glow. "Just light it and lie there," Mickey advised. They laughed to hide the pain.

At that point, Mickey realized that she had regained her sense of perspective; she could now joke about her addiction. No longer fearful of traveling, Mickey left on a research trip a few days after checking out of the clinic. She planned to stay a few days in Hong Kong before flying on to Chungking, where Chiang Kai-shek had set up his wartime capital.

With money tight, Mickey was determined to live within her budget. She traveled second class to Hong Kong and took a room in a noisy, inexpensive hostelry. "I'll be back in three months at the most," she shouted as she waved good-bye to her driver Chin Lien on the wharf. Mickey had no way of knowing that would be the last time she would ever see Chin Lien or Shanghai. That chapter of her life was forever closed. It would be several long, dangerous, and painful years before Mickey Hahn saw Sinmay again. Then it would be far away and under vastly different circumstances.

18

MADAME KUNG HAD arranged for Mickey to interview Madame Chiang in Chungking, so Mickey presumed her wait for a flight would be brief. How wrong she was! The list of people eager to travel to China's wartime capital was a long one, and journalists got no special treatment. Much of the six-hundred-mile journey was over Japanese-controlled airspace, so it could only be made under cover of darkness. The Douglas DC-3 passenger planes flew one-way each night, and their departures were varied to confuse the enemy. Given the unpredictability of the weather and the vigilance of the Japanese air force, the journey was still dangerous. The risk of being shot down was very real.

Mickey knew that she would be terrified if she stopped to think about what she was doing. She occupied herself by visiting friends and socializing with an elderly American professor she had met on one of her trips to Peking. Bob Winter, who had once taught Romance languages in Evanston, Illinois, had spent the last eighteen years working in Peking with the Rockefeller Institute. Then life under Japanese occupation became too dangerous, and he sought refuge in Hong Kong. Winter dabbled in espionage, keeping a radio transmitter in his house and passing on secret messages to Kuomintang agents. For Winter, as for Mickey and many other foreigners in China, the thrill of being involved in clandestine activities was as important as any ideological principles. Mickey, too, had dabbled in "the game." She allowed Sinmay's brother to keep a radio transmitter in her house in Shanghai and sometimes acted as a courier for the guerillas. It all seemed innocent and harmless, and Mickey received "favors" from the Chinese government in the form of small cash payments or courtesies where her passport was concerned.

Mickey knew the Japanese were not quite as blasé about all of this. Bob Winter discovered it, too. His quixotic lifestyle in Peking became problematic. He and his retinue, which included several Chinese friends and a pock-faced, middle-aged Tibetan man known as the Living Buddha, sought refuge in Hong Kong. "We are apt to think there is only one Living Buddha, the Dalai Lama," Mickey explained. "There are, however, at least seven of them. The Dalai Lama just happens to be more publicized than the others."[1]

Mickey wasn't sure how much she should believe of what Winter told her. "Like myself, Bob is an exhibitionist and would sell his grandmother if the transaction would make a good story," Mickey explained. "Or rather, he wouldn't *bother* to sell her; he would merely say he had done it and make a better story than the truth out of the old lady."[2]

Winter planned to take the Living Buddha to Chungking, where he could lend spiritual support to the Chinese war effort. British military intelligence officers were suspicious, however, and they detained and questioned both men in Hong Kong. Winter was convinced Mickey's friend Colonel Charles Boxer was behind this because the questioning began the day after Mickey, Winter, and the Living Buddha had lunch at the Boxers' flat. Everyone except the holy man drank too much, then Winter insisted Charles had "squinted at him suspiciously."[3] The episode alerted Mickey to Boxer's duties as the head of British army intelligence in Hong Kong. That in itself explained a lot about his activities. However, Mickey continued to defend Boxer to the suspicious Winter; Charles was too perceptive and subtle to behave in such a heavy-handed and transparent way, she said. Mickey may have been right, although she allowed, "He was very careful not to talk [with me] about his work."[4]

The more Mickey saw of Boxer, the better she liked him. Charles confided after a few drinks one day how bored he was with his life. He longed to be where the "real war" was happening and had applied for a transfer home to England. Mickey's interest in Boxer did not escape Sinmay, whose jealousy showed in the pleading tone of his letters. "Couldn't you love me as much as I do you and write me a little more?" he complained. "It makes me worried because your letters sound rather absent minded. Sick? Or what? It makes me a cynic, too. How could a human being forget a human being so easily and quickly?" Even if Mickey no longer cared for him, Sinmay moaned, how could she forsake her dear Mr. Mills? The poor gibbon's movements "look slower owing to stretching out his hand too much for nothing," Sinmay wrote. "[Mr. Mills] has some trouble with his throat. . . . He is crying day and night" for his owner's return.[5]

Mickey's delay in writing was due in part to how busy she was and in part to a decision she knew she had to make. Now that she had recovered from her opium addiction, she had a fresh perspective. Mickey knew the time had come to break up with Sinmay. The question was how. Her work on the Soong book and the trip to Chungking gave her the opportunity she needed.

Mickey knew Sinmay's talent for melodrama, but it was still painful to ignore his pleas. Fortunately, she had no time to get depressed. Mickey received this cryptic message from a Chinese government official one day in the second week of December 1939: "The airline ticket for Mrs. Wang is ready." Mrs. Wang was the pseudonym that Mickey had been given to travel incognito to "Free China." Why she needed an alias was never explained, and Mickey didn't ask. It was just another part of "the game."

Mickey was escorted to the Kai Tak Airport in Kowloon for her late-night flight by one of Mrs. Kung's menacing-looking bodyguards. The man went everywhere Mickey went, standing with arms folded, his eyes watchful. The

Chinese people Mickey encountered stopped and stared. Mickey could not decide if they were looking at her protector or at her.

There were strict limits on the amount of luggage passengers could take on the flight to Chungking, but there were none on body weight. As a result, passengers donned as many clothes as possible, and crammed their pockets with sundry items. This led to some bizarre scenes. When Mickey clambered into her seat on the plane, she tipped the scales at 180 pounds—fifty pounds above her normal weight. She was doing a "small favor" for some friends in Shanghai, who had asked her to take an overcoat to their son in Chungking. The coat's pockets were stuffed with extra pairs of socks, tins of toothpaste, bond certificates, and "God knows what else that was contraband," Mickey said.[6] On top of this coat, she wore extra layers of her own clothing. She had heard stories about how cold the Chungking winter was. Over a heavy woolen dress and jacket, Mickey wore a cloth coat, a fur coat of Chinese mink, and a padded Chinese gown of plum-colored silk. A pair of sheepskin boots muffled her feet. Had there been an emergency, Mickey could never have scrambled out of the plane. "I looked like a deep-sea diver," she said. "I walked like one, too."[7]

The starlit Kowloon skies were clear and cool on the December night that Mickey's plane left for Chungking. The Japanese air force pilots must have been sleeping that night, for the DC-3 touched down at its destination about eight o'clock that morning after an uneventful flight. As she peered out the window of the aircraft into a dreary, overcast day, Mickey saw that the Chungking airstrip was located on a sand spit that jutted out into the Yangtze River. Planes took off and landed in the shadow of cliffs crowded with rude wooden shacks, most of which had been propped up by poles and stilts.

This first view of Chungking was memorable. The city, built on a peninsula and surrounded by protective walls, was like a great feudal village—overcrowded, smoky, and dirty. For six months of the year, Szechuan Province, where Chungking is located, is rainy and glum. "[The] sun appears only at long intervals as a watery pale-yellow blob through the fog," Mickey wrote.[8] The rest of the year, the city's weather is hot and humid. However, it was not for fair weather that Chiang Kai-shek chose Chungking as the site of his wartime capital.[9] The city's wintertime fog discouraged attacks by Japanese bombers, and the cliffs provided ready-made natural air-raid shelters. Chiang Kai-shek knew this; he also understood why Chinese warlords had pitched their tents there for thousands of years. As the eighth-century Chinese poet Li Bo once observed, "It is more difficult to go to Szechuan than to get into heaven."

Most foreigners who visited wartime Chungking shared the locals' disaffection; they hated the place. There were few automobiles, gasoline was scarce, and liquor was more valuable than gold. None of this bothered Mickey, who cheerfully accepted the deprivations of life there. She had lived with the Zaus long enough that nothing much in China bothered her anymore. It was a good thing, because her introduction to Chungking was trying. The guide who was to meet Mickey at the airport failed to show up, and she had difficulty communicating with the coolie chair porters she hired to take her to a hotel; they assumed she was another missionary come to save Chinese souls. "There's nothing [here] but the war and the people," they cautioned her. Soon enough she learned that they were right. The Chinese government expected Chungking to be blitzed by Japanese bombers, so little money had been spent on the municipal infrastructure or new public buildings to accommodate all the new residents.

The jerry-built nature of many structures was evident from the condition of the Chungking Hostel, where Mickey stayed. The building, originally for use by the American pilots who flew between Hong Kong and Chungking, was a rickety frame building that the government had commandeered for the use of visiting foreign businesspeople. The toilets were primitive, and the favorite pastime of regular guests was complaining about the plumbing and the noise. However, there was running water, a restaurant, and charcoal braziers in each room for the cool winter nights. Conditions in the hostel were better than in many of the city's other lodgings, including the hostel where the foreign press corps stayed. Mickey was not considered a "working journalist," so she was not eligible to stay there; those who were assured her that she was fortunate.

Whatever the Chungking Hostel lacked in amenities, it more than made up for with the friendliness of the other guests. Within just a few hours of her arrival, Mickey was befriended by a young Englishwoman named Corin Bernfelt, who introduced Mickey to the other foreign women staying at the hotel. Then her own talent for making friends took over. By the evening of her first day in Chungking, Mickey had received a dinner invitation from a group of Chinese government workers and had met Tilman Durdin, the *New York Times* correspondent, and Teddy White of *Time* magazine. White, who would go on to win a Pulitzer Prize in the 1960s for his popular *Making of the President* series of books, was a twenty-four-year-old graduate of Harvard when Mickey met him in 1939. Chungking was White's first overseas journalism posting. "He was very young and cocky, and simply knew everything," Mickey noted.[10] She disliked him at first, but they gradually became good friends and talked almost every day of Mickey's stay in Chungking.

· · ·

When news of Mickey's arrival in town spread, she was invited to tea at the home of William Henry (W.H.) Donald, the elderly, bespectacled Australian journalist who was the closest foreign advisor to the Chiangs. "Don," as he was known, was a rarity among government officials in China; he said what he meant and deplored dishonesty with an almost messianic zeal. Donald had been in China since 1904 but had never bothered to learn Chinese. Nevertheless, he developed an affection for the country that, as Mickey observed, "mingles the watchful censoriousness of a schoolmaster with the proprietary pride of an old family doctor."[11] Donald told Mickey he would arrange an interview for her with Madame Chiang, and a car arrived at the Chungking Hostel early the next morning to take Mickey to the meeting.

The Chiangs lived in a ten-room Edwardian house owned by the Kungs. It was one of the buildings in town that had been built by foreign businesspeople early in the century. The grounds were surrounded by a stone wall and the gates were patrolled by armed guards. The setting was appropriate, for Mei-ling Chiang was well guarded in everything she did.

Mickey was struck by Madame Chiang's beauty. Like her older sister Madame Kung, Mei-ling was a petite woman with enormous eyes and the delicacy of an exquisite jade carving. She dressed simply, yet with great style. Mickey also sensed Madame Chiang's legendary sangfroid. Here was a woman, Mickey reflected, whose "heart is kept cool."[12] On W. H. Donald's instructions, every word that Madame Chiang uttered in the presence of foreigners—journalists particularly—was carefully scripted. Nothing was left to chance.

Maintaining this icy reserve proved difficult for Madame Chiang as she and Mickey discussed John Gunther's book *Inside Asia.* As her sister had explained, Gunther had angered the Chiangs. His observations about Madame Chiang were a way of "getting at my husband," she insisted. Mickey and her hostess were chatting about this when they were unexpectedly interrupted. The Generalissimo ambled into the room, unaware that his wife had company. Mickey jumped to attention. Chiang stopped short. He was embarrassed that Mickey had seen him in his house slippers. Chiang nodded deferentially as his wife introduced Mickey. Then he bowed and backed out of the room. "*Hao, hao, hao,*" he apologized. "Good, good, good."

Madame smiled. "He didn't have his teeth in," she explained. "Sit *down*, Miss Hahn."[13]

That toothless encounter with China's most powerful warlord broke the ice. Mickey and Madame Chiang soon were chatting like long lost sisters. By the time she left the Chiang house that day, Mickey and her hostess had agreed on the ground rules for the Soong book: Madame Chiang would cooperate as long as the book was not "a gush" about her. She also agreed to read the manuscript for facts, nothing more; that was all she had time for, she insisted. These arrangements suited Mickey, as did Madame's suggestion that Mickey stay in town for Christmas, attend some government functions, see the sights, and interview Madame Chiang at her leisure.

The British presence in town was strong, and because the Chiangs were Methodists, the Chinese government observed a Christmas holiday. Mickey arrived back at her hostel to find a stack of social invitations awaiting her. After reading them, Mickey decided there was more yuletide spirit in Chungking than in Shanghai. Would she take part in the local Christmas radio broadcast? Would she visit the Chungking war orphans' home when Madame Chiang gave out gifts to the children? Would she attend the hostel Christmas party? Would she have a Christmas Eve dinner with Bob Winter, who was now in Chungking, too? Would she attend a New Year's Eve party that was being thrown by Dr. H. H. Kung at a downtown hotel? Of course. Mickey was glad she had brought along her sheepskin boots and winter clothing. It was becoming evident that she would be away from Shanghai much longer than expected.

· · ·

Mickey's "long weekend" in Chungking eventually stretched into ten weeks. As the Chungking weather cleared and the rains stopped, spring came. So did Japanese bombers, ferocious oversized mosquitoes that rained death and destruction. The Chinese authorities had ringed the city with a primitive early warning system that consisted of a network of watchtowers equipped with metal gongs. When enemy planes were sighted entering Szechuan Province, the watchmen hurriedly beat the gongs in double time—one, two; one two; one, two. As the sound eventually reached the city, air-raid sirens wailed, and people had only a few minutes to rush to the air-raid shelters. Mickey never forgot her first air raid.

She was in her room at the hostel typing one bright spring morning when her thoughts were interrupted by a distant moaning sound. She realized it was an air-raid siren. "*Waooooo, waooooo, waooooo.*" As Mickey noted, no one who has gone through the drill of an air raid can ever again hear that sound without an involuntary tightening of the heart muscles. "After a long, steady blast the siren lowers its voice, then heightens it again, then lowers it, then heightens it, in a mad sine-cosine pattern of sound," she explained.[14]

Mickey's friend Corin led her downstairs to the basement. Seeing the facility for the first time reminded her why most visitors sooner or later referred to Chungking as "the city built on rock." Mickey sat there for two hours that day with a dry mouth and sweaty palms, her mind filled with awful images of cave-ins. She dreaded being buried alive under tons of earth and rock and dying in this godforsaken place. Mickey shut her eyes so tightly that she saw stars. With only flashlights to illuminate the shelter, there was nothing to do but sit and wait and talk. Mostly the people listened to the sound of water dripping down the cave's walls and waited for the explosions that mercifully never came. On this occasion, the planes attacked a nearby military airfield.

After the first few raids, the routine became second nature to Mickey. She would scoop up her typewriter and whatever other possessions she could carry and race downstairs to the shelter. The Japanese planes came almost every afternoon or in the early evening during the warm weather. Four waves, consisting of about 150 planes in total, would swoop down from the clouds to attack the city. Chungking was virtually defenseless, apart from some antique anti-aircraft guns that chattered away ineffectively.

The authorities had ordered everyone who had no compelling reason to be there to get out of Chungking. In theory, at least, there was space for everyone in an air-raid shelter. Each resident was assigned a dugout close to home. However, in practice there was no way of controlling who came and went in a bustling city such as Chungking, and there were far more people than spaces in the shelters. Those who found refuge from the raids hunkered down during the raids to pray for themselves and for those poor souls who had been left outside to bang on the locked doors. These people and anyone who chanced to be away from home when a raid began were at the mercy of the Japanese planes. The town's flimsy homes and public buildings offered no protection, and so the carnage among the Chinese workers and peasants was horrifying. Within the old city's walls there was utter devastation. There were entire blocks where not a single building had a roof. On one occasion, when Chungking's alarm system failed, thousands of people were slaughtered when they were trapped in the streets in the air raid and ensuing fires. There would have been even more casualties had it not been for the inexperience of the Japanese pilots. These dangers and the predictability of the raids prompted Mickey to travel across the Yangtze River in the afternoons, despite the dangerous two-hour ride on a crude ferry that battled the swift-flowing currents every inch of the crossing. Mickey had been befriended by a Canadian missionary named James Endicott and his wife Mary. Mickey met them through Madame Chiang, who no doubt hoped the couple's Christian proselytizing might change Mickey's "wicked ways." There was no chance of that. Like her father, Mickey felt all missionaries should go home and "mind their own business." But she liked the Endicotts, and they liked her.

James Endicott was headstrong and opinionated. He was forthright in his views, which were usually too far to the Left for Madame Chiang. Mickey sometimes overheard Madame Chiang and her "missionary advisor" argue politics. Mickey, too, had disagreements with Endicott, who seemed to relish these verbal sparring sessions. Their differences of opinion did not deter Mickey from accepting invitations to dine and work in the Endicott's home, in a quiet village a few miles downriver from Chungking. The Endicotts ran the village school, and Mary Endicott preferred to live there rather than in Chungking, which she considered far too dangerous and dirty. Mickey's visits were a welcome diversion from the hardship and isolation the Endicotts often endured. "Emily Hahn was very sociable, and my parents were very sociable," recalls Stephen Endicott, one of the Endicott's four children. "She was gung-ho and willing to talk about her experiences and opinions in an open sort of way. That was one of the things my parents liked about her."[15]

Mickey sometimes took meals with them and sometimes made use of the attic work space in their home. There was a heater there, a typewriter, and a big stack of copy paper. Some days as Mickey worked there, the peace and quiet was broken by distant explosions and gunfire when Japanese warplanes attacked Chungking. She could imagine the terrible scenes. She and some friends had once witnessed an air raid from the relative safety of the south bank of the Yangtze, where European, British, and American diplomats and friends lived in an area of Western-style housing. There was an "understanding" that the Japanese wouldn't bomb this "diplomatic zone." Instead they pounded nearby Chinese military targets or government buildings two miles across the river in Chungking. Mickey described the air raid that she saw. "The first lot of planes came over from upstream—a shoal of silver fish swimming in the blue," she wrote in one of her many *New Yorker* articles about Chungking. "A load of bombs fell between us and the city, in the water. Several more fell on the shore, in the city. There were sickening detonations; there were red flashes in the suddenly appearing flowers of smoke and debris."[16]

• • •

Mickey's Chungking sojourn ended as unexpectedly as it had begun. W. H. Donald telephoned one day in mid-February 1940 to report that Madame Chiang was returning to Hong Kong; he suggested Mickey do likewise. As she got ready, Mickey realized her bags were a lot lighter than when she had arrived. There was an "unwritten law" that when one left Chungking, whatever others could use was left behind. So Mickey boarded the plane to Hong Kong carrying only an empty suitcase, her portable typewriter, an old hatbox she had lugged everywhere on her travels for the past twelve years, and a few personal toiletries. Everything else she gave away: all her perfumes, toothpaste, stockings, hats, dresses, and winter coats. Mickey's English friend Corin, who had helped her so much by retyping and proofreading the Soong manuscript, took Mickey's old Chinese mink coat, even though it was now so tattered that it was literally falling apart. Mickey threw nothing away. A Chinese friend even snapped up one of her old toothbrushes, explaining that he would boil and reuse it; foreign-made toothbrushes were precious items in wartime Chungking.

The contrast between life in that beleaguered city and in the British colony of Hong Kong was breathtaking. Mickey, who sat up with the pilot for most of the return flight and even took over the controls for a while, was reminded of that as they approached Hong Kong at dusk. The city was ablaze with lights, and the waterfront throbbed with pulsating red, white, blue, and gold neon signs. There had been no blackouts at Chungking, yet the city seemed dark by comparison. The warm glow of Hong Kong's lights was inviting.

Mickey had arranged to stay at the flat of a Chinese woman named Little Billie Lee, the secretary at *T'ien Hsia*. Billie's place was near the Happy Valley Racetrack. She shared the flat with a Eurasian woman named Mavis, who worked as a stenographer. The pair were keen to have Mickey stay with them as long as she could because the room and board she paid helped them with their expenses. It was not cheap to live in Hong Kong.

The arrangements suited Mickey fine, for her flatmates brought home a steady supply of news and gossip gleaned from workplace conversations with their peers. When Billie and Mavis went off to work in the morning, Mickey stayed home to write. Her work on the Soong book was going well, despite the fact that she was bored and was impatient to be done with it. Mickey was also feeling lonely; she missed the Zaus, especially when she received a five-page letter in which Sinmay went on at length about how selfish and spitefully jealous he had been. As she read, Mickey felt bad about all of the nasty thoughts she had been having about him. Perhaps she had been too critical after all. Then she read the last paragraph of Sinmay's letter. He asked her for $500. "If you want to know why this letter is as it is," he added in a postscript, "it is because I have been reading, Dale Carnegie's book *How to Win Friends and Influence People*."[17] Mickey did not send him the money.

She had resolved to return to Shanghai as soon as possible to explain everything to Sinmay face-to-face. She felt she owed him that. Then she would break off their relationship and wind up her affairs there. Her old restlessness had returned with a vengeance. Mickey could not explain or understand it. "Why should I now feel that I must undo everything, smash the edifice I had built, throw myself out on the road again?" she mused. "I didn't exactly know. I had never before stayed in one place so long, and the familiar routine of starting out fresh did not seem so familiar any more."[18]

Mickey's uncertainties were underscored by the air of fatalism in Hong Kong. Many people had fled, and the Boxers were among the few foreigners Mickey still knew in town. When she rang them, they invited her to dinner. There she encountered a dashing Royal Air Force officer named Alf Bennett, whom she had met two years earlier in Shanghai. Like Charles Boxer, Bennett had come calling one day when he was in town. He told Mickey that he had met Charles in London in 1934 and now worked with him in Hong Kong.

Bennett had a real presence. He sported an incredible handlebar mustache, growled like a tiger, loved to recite poetry, danced divinely, and drank like a funnel. Women were intrigued by him; men sought his company. Everyone liked Alf Bennett. He and Charles were inseparable drinking buddies. When Mickey began joining them in their revelries, she and Alf hit it off, too. "Mickey was very, very outgoing and warm. . . . I don't mean she was aggressive, just go-go," Bennett recalled. "She was very different from the British women we knew in Hong Kong. She was on the ball. She was a New Yorker." Then, breaking into song, he added, "My girl's a corker; she's a New Yorker."[19]

Mickey was the fourth whenever Alf and the Boxers went out. Mickey listened with interest one evening as Charles, his tongue loosened by gin, expounded on the end of the British Empire and on the death of capitalism in the Far East. "Don't you agree, Emily Hahn, that the day of the white man is done out here? Russia or no Russia, we're finished out here and we don't know it!" Charles bellowed. "It's a nice party, too! Have another [drink], Emily Hahn."[20]

19

FOLLOWING HER RETURN to Hong Kong in late February, Mickey awaited further word from the Soongs. She had been working on the book for almost a year, and the manuscript was complete except for a last chapter and some final rewriting. Mickey was eager to be done with it; she did not much like Hong Kong. "[This] is still the crossroads of the world," Mickey told her mother in a letter home, "and I run into all sorts of people I have known here and there when I go downtown. I've had a haircut and a manicure and a few good meals; I've seen a movie; I've danced furiously to make up for lost time."[1]

Mickey savored these luxuries after the deprivations of life in Chungking, but she was distressed at how quickly her money was disappearing. Her anxiety mounted when she heard nothing from the Soongs for several weeks. Then one day Madame Kung called to report that she and her sisters planned to dine together that evening at the Grips. Rumors were sweeping the colony that the Soongs were feuding and no longer on speaking terms, so this meeting was newsworthy. It was also highly political; Mickey knew she was a pawn in the Soong's public relations game, but she did not care. She was making progress on the book again.

Mickey, escorted by Alf Bennett, appeared at the hotel dining room as Madame Kung had suggested. There she saw all three Soong sisters eating with W. H. Donald and several other people. Mickey and Alf took a table and watched until it became apparent that the only thing noteworthy about the Soongs getting together was how ordinary they looked having dinner. Mickey and Alf had their own meal and drinks and then kicked up their heels on the dance floor. As they whirled about, Madame Sun watched with disapproval. She still had not warmed to the idea of the book or to its author. "There's Mickey Hahn," she hissed to Madame Kung, "I suppose that's Mickey Mouse she's with?"[2]

This latest "non-encounter" with the Soongs confirmed in Mickey's mind that she was wasting her time in Hong Kong. She felt self-conscious and out of place there gathering crumbs of information as she spent the last of the advance money her publisher had provided. The rest of her research could be done by mail, she decided. Mickey booked passage to Shanghai the last week of March. That is where she undoubtedly would have gone had Madame Kung's secretary Alice not appeared at the dock breathlessly asking Mickey to come at once to "an important meeting." She reluctantly agreed, leaving her bags partially unpacked in the stateroom of her ship while she and Alice sped off to the Kung home. They arrived just as the Soong sisters were finishing a meeting with some foreign journalists.

Madame Kung got straight to the point: she did not want Mickey to leave town. Madame implored her not to return to Shanghai, where she had no family and would be all alone if "trouble" began. That development seemed likely; most people knew it was only a matter of time until the Japanese entered the war on the side of the Axis powers. Madame Kung told Mickey that she had chatted with Sinmay's aunt, who had arrived in town from Shanghai that very morning. She reported that the Zaus were well. Mickey's house was still rented. Her gibbons were fine, and Sinmay was still broke and desperate for money. In short, nothing had changed in Shanghai. Madame Kung said she feared if Mickey went there, the Japanese would punish her for her involvement with the Soongs, and Sinmay would "take advantage" of her. In either case, Mickey would end up hating all Chinese people. In an odd way, Madame Kung made sense.

What Mickey did not reveal was that although she had boarded her ship, she too had been having second thoughts about her travel plans. She was touched by Madame Kung's concern, which seemed genuine, even if it was misplaced. "[It] was characteristically Chinese, I reflected: I could never have explained to her that I was alone in China because I had *run away* from my family," Mickey later wrote.[3]

Now that Mickey's curiosity was aroused, Madame Kung revealed the "secret" she had to share: she and her sisters were traveling to Chungking together the next day in a show of unity in the war against Japan. Madame Kung suggested this might provide the perfect ending for the book. Mickey agreed, as her hostess smiled knowingly. Madame Kung said that she would make all the arrangements so Mickey could travel to Chungking and be near the Soongs.

Mickey passed a couple of anxious weeks waiting in Hong Kong. Many foreign civilians, including the wives and children of the soldiers of the British garrison, had been evacuated to Australia, out of harm's way in case of war with Japan. Mickey attended a noisy dinner at a Chinese restaurant in mid-April, two days before she was due to fly to Chungking. Everyone there drank too much, and Charles put his arm around Mickey as they talked. With the evening wearing on and the party growing ever louder, Ursula Boxer rose from the table and announced to Charles that she was going home. "Yes," Charles said, and so she did. The drinking and merriment continued.

The next evening, Mickey had dinner once again at the Boxers' flat. There Ursula took her aside to confide a secret: she had decided to go to Australia. She planned to rest and recover her health, which had been poor in recent months. What Ursula did not reveal, but which was readily apparent, was that all was not well in her marriage. "You take care of him, Mickey," Ursula said. "Do. I wouldn't trust a blonde."[4]

Mickey agreed, but she pointed out that first she had important business to tend to in Chungking.

• • •

Mickey was delighted to find Teddy White waiting at Chungking Airport when she arrived. It was another cool, wet, and overcast morning, and she badly needed a friend. As they made their way to the hostel, White told Mickey the latest gossip and news. The city was abuzz over the Soong sisters' reconciliation and their return. The rumor mill was in overdrive as people speculated about the meaning of this development. The Japanese, angry at their failure to drive a wedge into the Chinese leadership, began a spring bombing offensive three days after the Soongs' arrival in Chungking. There were a few "warning" raids before the attacks began in earnest. When they did they were fearsome. Each day brought two or three waves of planes, and the bombers came even on moonlit nights. With Chungking more crowded than ever with refugees, these latest raids were devastating.

Despite the destruction and the gloomy weather, Mickey remained buoyant. Now that she had easy access to the Soongs, there was no shortage of material to write about. Madame Kung invited Mickey to attend official functions, as did Madame Chiang, especially after the air raids became too intense and her older sisters returned to Hong Kong in early May. Mickey had decided to remain in Chungking until she finished the book. She would then follow Madame Kung's advice: she would build a new life for herself. Somewhere.

Work on the book was taking longer than Mickey expected—so long that her publisher had to give her a six-month extension on her deadline—and she was almost broke. To make ends meet, she took a part-time job working for a Belgian journalist named Jacques Marcuse, the Chungking correspondent for the Havas news agency. Mickey covered for him when he was busy, which was much of the time because he was in a heated romance with Mickey's English friend Corin.

Having access to the Havas cables and radio messages allowed Mickey to follow the progress of the war in Europe. The Allies were being pounded. Hitler's blitzkrieg had smashed the Dutch and Belgian armies. The British and French had been sent reeling. On May 26, 1940, more than 388,000 retreating Allied soldiers facing annihilation were plucked from the beach at the French port of Dunkirk by a ragtag armada of British military and civilian ships.

Soon after, Paris fell to the advancing German army, and the following week the French government capitulated. In far-off Chungking, the mood was glum. Teddy White, Jacques Marcuse, and many of Mickey's other male friends in the foreign press corps felt the time had come to stop "playing around" in the Far East. They talked of going to fight in the war. Mickey felt guilty and angry that America was not yet involved. Her despair and confusion were understandable given the situation in Chungking.

The Japanese air force did its utmost to add to the sense of impending doom; the daily air raids reached unprecedented levels. Japanese spies had pinpointed where the Chiangs were staying, and their house became a bombing target. Unfortunately, the dwelling was next door to the Chungking Hostel, and so both buildings were badly damaged. Mickey emerged from the air-raid shelter one day to find much of the hostel destroyed. She spent several hours angrily picking through the rubble for her belongings. Mickey had suffered losses before, but nothing like this. Among her missing possessions was a suitcase containing the Soong manuscript, her research notes, and photographs for the book. All that she managed to save was the chapter she was writing. Mickey was lucky to find another room at a nearby hotel, and there she spent an anxious week waiting for the Chinese workers picking through the rubble of the hostel to find her missing bag. When finally they did, it was battered and covered with green mold, but the contents were miraculously intact.

Now that the Japanese had a fix on the Kung home, their bombers made up for lost time. The building was completely leveled. So too were most of the nearby buildings. The Chungking Hostel was reduced to a pile of smoking rubble. When the Chiangs fled to the south bank of the Yangtze River, Mickey followed. Friends there had invited her to stay with them in a big house owned by the Asiatic Petroleum Corporation (APC). "From the moment I set foot on the South Bank I knew I was in a different atmosphere," she later wrote. "I had left the new China and stepped into the old. I was in a safety zone, the magic circle drawn by the once omnipotent Europeans."[5]

Mickey bathed in a real bathtub again and found bandages for a knee she had cut while running to an air-raid shelter. In the evenings at the APC House, she sipped gin cocktails on the screened-in porch as she and her companions sat looking across the river at Chungking and waiting for the planes to come, as they inevitably did. The Japanese were relentless in that summer of 1940, bombing Chungking with murderous regularity. The only respite came when, as an RAF officer explained to Mickey, the enemy planes were on the ground being serviced at their base in Hankow, four hundred miles to the northeast.

Mickey was now spending most of her time on the south bank. It had become too dangerous in Chungking, and there was little reason to go there; most everyone she knew had moved to the south bank. On one of the few times she did make the crossing, Mickey discovered how foolish she had been. The air-raid sirens suddenly began to warble. The Japanese planes were coming! On her own in a strange neighborhood with no dugout in which to hide, Mickey felt totally helpless. She joined a frantic crowd that was racing toward the ferry dock. She was swept along by the surge of people cascading down the steep stairs to the docks at the water's edge. Suddenly Mickey felt herself falling.

Her hand instinctively reached out for a handrail; however, she realized in that megasecond that there was none. Nothing separated her from a 100-foot drop to the rocks below. An image flashed through her mind: her bloody, broken body was lying among the rocks below, on the banks of the Yangtze River. She had died alone and far from family and home. If Mickey had not believed in guardian angels, she did at that moment. "A coolie grabbed my arm," Mickey recalled. "[He] pulled me back on the step—I can still feel the iron grip of his skinny fingers—and was away down the steps before I could thank him."[6]

Although she was dazed and disoriented, Mickey somehow made her way to the bottom of the stairs and pushed her way onto the ferry. The barge was so crowded that Mickey realized it might capsize in midstream. If that happened, everyone on board would die. Those who were not swept away by the

Mickey joins the Soongs on an "official tour" of the Friends of the Wounded Hospital, Chungking, May 1940. Shown are (l–r) Generalissimo Chiang Kai-shek, Madame Sun, Madame Kung, unidentified aide, Mickey, Colonel J. L. Huang, and Madame Chiang.
Courtesy Emily Hahn Estate

river would be sitting ducks for the Japanese planes. Luck really was with Mickey that day, for the ferry chugged across the river without incident. Its anxious passengers were scrambling to safety just as the first enemy planes arrived. At the APC house, Mickey found Teddy White and several other friends waiting on the porch with celebratory bottles of beer in hand. They had been watching the ferry through binoculars.

After this incident, Mickey was reluctant to make further crossings to Chungking. She mostly stayed on the south bank reading, writing poetry, and working on the Soong book. The shady screened porch became her study. She sat there in the sweltering heat of the afternoons, tapping at her portable Hermes typewriter. The daily air raids now helped her to write, for even the routine of becoming deathly afraid had grown mundane. Mickey did much of her best writing in the quiet time between the initial alarm and the second "Urgent" alarm, when only the foolhardy or the fearless did not take shelter. Mickey loved this "calm before the storm" since the usual bustle of activity around the APC house stopped, and it was then possible to concentrate.

Mickey and her housemates escaped all this excitement on weekends. They would load the servants, food, and liquor onto a company boat and travel downriver a few miles to an old summer house at one of the APC pumping stations. A British gunboat was anchored there, safely hidden away from the enemy planes. The atmosphere downriver was leisurely and unhurried, because there was nowhere else to go. Many of the British and Europeans played bridge. Mickey socialized with the non-cardplayers or found a quiet spot in which to work. On Sundays, they all ate lunch aboard the gunboat. Chungking weekends, Mickey observed, would have been "a much less pleasant experience."[7]

She also spent many afternoons in the summer of 1940 visiting with Madame Chiang. The Kuomintang first lady and her husband were living in a large old south-bank house that was tucked away on a tree-covered hillside. One of Mickey's friends at the APC house had his own sedan chair. His Chinese bearers were bored sitting around day after day and welcomed the opportunity to run Mickey over to visit the Chiangs. She looked for all the world like a princess on these outings, in her cotton summer dress, wide-brimmed straw hat, and dark glasses. Mickey sat in her chair reading a copy of the *Oxford Book of English Verse* that she had borrowed from Madame Chiang or else she chatted with the coolies as they padded their way along the clay pathways between the rice fields. In marked contrast to chaotic, dirty Chungking, the scene here was green and pastoral. This was the China of picture books: timeless and serene. Sometimes Mickey just sat amidst this sunlit splendor breathing in the earthy aromas or contemplating the grandeur of the nearby mountains and the sky, which were mirrored in the waters of the rice paddies.

Mickey found the Chiangs' house cool and comfortable even in the heat of the Szechuan summer. In that relaxed atmosphere, Mickey and Madame Chiang became friends. Madame suffered from migraine headaches and hives that summer. She was bored, and welcomed Mickey's company. The two sat for hours chatting like schoolgirls. There was no talk of politics or war. They discussed books and writing. They gossiped about mutual acquaintances, or sampled the marmalades that Madame Chiang made from citrus fruits from the nearby groves. By now, Madame Chiang had read portions of Mickey's manuscript and decided that she trusted this strange American woman after all.

With Madame Chiang's encouragement, Mickey finished the Soong book. She did so early one morning in late July. Mickey shook with excitement as she typed the words "The End" and pulled the last page from her typewriter. "Done!" she shouted as she leapt to her feet and ran through the house sharing her good news. No one much cared. The presence of a writer in a house full of businesspeople was nothing more than an occasional diversion for them. Her housemates' indifference underscored the profound sense of isolation that Mickey felt. "This book was not only another book, it was my life," she explained. "That sounds melodramatic, but it was literally true. Because of the book I had left my home, broken up my house, deserted the gibbons and Sinmay, and lived under conditions of acute discomfort. . . . The manuscript had done that, leading me around by the nose for eighteen months."[8]

Mickey mused about where her obsession had gotten her. She had no place of her own, nowhere to call home. She was an unemployed thirty-five-year-old writer with few belongings and little money. Her shoes were worn out. Her teeth were in need of repairs. She felt unloved and unwanted. Apart from Sinmay, with whom she knew her relationship was over, she believed the only one who hadn't forgotten her was Patrick Putnam.

He had sent a cable a month before, suggesting that Mickey and her gibbons return home to the United States. Patrick proposed they meet up in Los Angeles, where he had been working as a script advisor at the Metro-Goldwyn-Mayer Studios. Among the film projects Patrick worked on were some Tarzan movies, which were to be shot in the jungles of central Africa. One of these was a proposed film version of Mickey's 1934 novel *With Naked Foot*. According to Putnam's biographer, Joan Mark, "It must . . . have occurred to [him] that he could play the young American teacher, a version of himself in a film based on [the book]."[9] When the war ended any possibility of filming in Africa, Patrick's contract was not renewed. Like Mickey, his plans were vague, his future uncertain beyond the drive back East; if Mickey joined him on the trip, he would drop her off in Chicago, he promised. Mickey knew none of this until much later. Patrick had sent his cable to Shanghai, and it had taken a month to reach Mickey in Chungking. By the time it did, Patrick had already left for his family's summer home at Martha's Vineyard. He and his second white American wife (his first had died in December 1937) spent the latter half of 1940 there, while Patrick contemplated their prospects.

Mickey had no interest in reentering Patrick Putnam's troubled life. The Congo was behind her now, so were Shanghai and Chungking. Mickey knew she would not be coming back when she left this time. The Soong book was finished, and many of her friends were planning to go or had already gone. Mickey decided to fly back to Hong Kong. There she could catch a ship home. She planned to visit her family in Chicago on the way back to New York. Her agent was urging her to come home as soon as possible to do media interviews for her latest book. The Shanghai novel she had written four years earlier about an affair between a young American woman and her Chinese lover had finally been published that fall. The reviews for *Steps of the Sun*[10] were disappointing. M. L. Rossbach of the *New York Times* dismissed it as "slow moving" and emotionally flat.[11] Reviewer Olga Owens of the *Boston Transcript* voiced another criticism that said more about the racial attitudes in American society in 1940 than it did about the merits of Mickey's book. Although she conceded that *Steps of the Sun* was "written beautifully," Owen complained that she found the notion of an interracial marriage "extremely distasteful."[12]

Mickey was too savvy to be hurt or surprised by such comments. She knew that many things about America were unchanged—her other novel about a Shanghai prostitute remained unpublished—even if she herself was a changed woman after seven years in China. "I am not at all enamored of the individuality I lost," she wrote. "I was a crass young person, overeducated and underexperienced, like most Americans. I was a smart aleck. It wasn't a bad thing at all, leaving that young woman at the bottom of the Whangpoo [River] or wherever I had dropped her."[13]

V

Hong Kong: Sunset on the Empire

20

"AS AN EXPERIENCED observer of myself," Mickey once said, she should have realized that she was "set for mischief" in the summer of 1940. After all, she had arrived back in Hong Kong full of uncertainty about her future. "That feeling has always been responsible for my more outlandish decisions," she reflected. "It was as if I had to plunge into things, take steps which I couldn't retrace, just to get myself settled."[1]

Mickey treated herself. She splurged on some new clothes, had her hair done, and rented a comfortable room at the Gloucester Hotel, one with a private bath and endless supplies of hot water and towels. It was glorious. The cost of such grand lodgings was a drain on her bank account, but why not? She had mailed the last chapters of the Soong book to New York, and as soon as she fetched her gibbons in Shanghai, she was going home. To paraphrase the poet T. S. Eliot, Mickey's five years of self-imposed exile in China were about to come to an end with a whimper, not a bang. That was just fine with her.

Mickey dined with Charles Boxer and his friend Max Oxford the evening of her return to Hong Kong. As the three of them chatted, it dawned on Mickey how much she had come to enjoy Charles's company. He had a real depth to him, she decided. The more time they spent together, the more apparent it became that they had a lot in common.

Charles was thirty-six years old and, like Mickey, was still drifting through life, despite his army career. He was bright, congenial, possessed of a wonderfully wry wit and was keenly interested in writing and in things literary. What's more, Charles cut a dashing figure and had an air of mystery about him. Mickey noted how scrupulously he avoided talking about his military duties. However, it was obvious just by the company he kept that Charles was someone important. Mickey was curious. What exactly did he do, she wondered? Since Charles was reluctant to talk about himself, it took some initiative for Mickey to piece together the details of his life. The effort proved worthwhile, for Charles's story was an intriguing one.

What Mickey learned was that the Boxers were one of Britain's distinguished military families. At least four generations of Charles's male ancestors had served their country as officers; as often as not, they had died in the process. The late British historian Miles Clark chronicled the Boxer family's military history in a 1991 book entitled *High Endeavours*. Ironically, it is a biography of Beryl Boxer, Charles's only sister. In the early years of the twentieth century, a career at arms was impossible for a woman, of course. Beryl found adventure and fame in other ways; she and her second husband, Miles Smeeton, were world-renowned mariners and travelers.

Hugh Boxer, Charles's father, was commissioned into the Lincolnshire Regiment in 1892 at age twenty-one. While on leave and visiting his mother on the Isle of Wight in the summer of 1896, he met a dark-haired, twenty-one-year-old Australian girl named Jane Patterson. Jeannie, as her family called her, was a spirited young woman with a strong, vibrant character. The Pattersons had been prosperous sheep farmers before moving back to England with their three daughters.

Hugh and Jeannie were married in September 1897. After a brief honeymoon, they settled in Cairo, where the 1st Battalion of the Lincolnshire Regiment was stationed. Jeannie was pregnant when Hugh's unit was sent up the Nile a few months later as part of an Anglo-Egyptian army under Lord Kitchener. Their mission was to quell an uprising in the Sudan by Dervish rebels, a fierce army of Muslim warriors who had taken Khartoum in 1885 after a long siege and slaughtered General Charles Gordon (a battle that was re-created in a 1966 Hollywood epic film called *Khartoum).*

When Hugh returned to Cairo in May 1898 after the successful campaign, he did so aboard a hospital boat. His ankle had been shattered by an enemy bullet, and he would never again walk without the aid of a walking stick. Hugh and Jeannie, now seven months pregnant, sailed home to England. Hugh planned to convalesce there, Jeannie to give birth to their child. The baby, who arrived in July, was a boy they named Myles. He would be the first of four children born to the Boxers in and around Hugh's other postings in the seven years between 1898 and 1905. The next arrival was a boy named Edward, who was born in India in October of 1902. Sadly, he contracted meningitis on the ocean voyage to England. He died at six weeks of age, shortly after Hugh and Jeannie arrived at Thorpe Lodge, his paternal grandmother's home on the Isle of Wight.

Next came Charles, born March 8, 1904, at Sandown, Isle of Wight, and finally a daughter named Beryl arrived in December 1905. According to Miles Clark, being just two years apart, Charles and Beryl grew up together. Theirs was one of those distinctly British upper-class childhoods: while older brother Myles was away at boarding school, Charles and Beryl were raised by a nanny. For the most part, they were "seen and heard" only when summoned to the drawing room by their parents. Hugh and Jeannie were devoted parents, although Hugh was a strict disciplinarian who refused to tolerate tears or any other sign of "weakness" on the part of his sons. For that reason, his favorite of the two younger children was the tomboy Beryl. Charles was a sensitive lad who grew up fearing his father and being devoted to his mother.

By all accounts, Charles was bright and inquisitive. When it came time to begin his formal education, his mother puzzled over her choices: a Protestant school for the sons of lower-class enlisted men, or a Catholic convent school for the daughters of the well-to-do. In the end, she opted for the latter. "Class snobbery overcame theological scruples," explains British historian James Cummins, one of Charles's closest friends.[2] The choice proved to be a sound one, for Charles received an excellent education under the nuns' tutelage. Nevertheless, his attendance at the school was not without complications. When the little girls encountered a nun in the cloister, they curtsied. Being the only boy, Charles presented "something of an etiquette problem," Cummins notes.[3] The solution was to have him salute, just like a soldier. The training stood him in good stead for the military career his father had mapped out for him.

What struck people most about young Charles Boxer was his memory, which was exceptional. This served him well, since he shared his uncle Edward's passion for ideas and words. Hugh Boxer's older brother had invented an improved entrenching tool and a new type of shrapnel, was fluent in Arabic, Hindustani, and Persian, and wrote books on linguistics. Charles was also interested in literature and by an early age had read most of the family's library. Among his favorites were collections of poetry by Shakespeare, Alexander Pope, and A. E. Housman, as well as a set of weighty tomes entitled the *Harmsworth's Encyclopedia;* the latter occupied him for countless happy hours. Charles was also intrigued by languages and taught himself Portuguese at an early age. But what most fascinated him were stories of the Orient. Charles' great-uncle reportedly had been a captain in the Opium Fleet, and the Boxer family owned a collection of books about China, Japan, and the Far East. Charles shared his father's enthusiasm for stories of Japanese samurai and their stoic code of honor known as *bushido*—literally, "the way of the warrior." When he played soldiers as a boy, Charles sometimes pretended to be a fearless samurai. Later, his interests in these ancient knights became more scholarly. By age seventeen he was intent on learning Japanese and already had read his first paper on Japanese history to the Royal Asiatic Society.

Charles was eleven in June 1915, when his father was declared "presumed wounded and missing" while fighting with the Lincolnshire Regiment in France. Hugh Boxer was last seen leading his lads "over the top" in an attack on the German lines. Bullets were whizzing. Shells were crashing all around, and the air was filled with the shrieks of the wounded and dying. Major Boxer pressed ahead through the smoke and flames, walking with an arm over his batman's shoulder, the ground being too muddy to use his walking stick. The image is a haunting one. "[Hugh Boxer and his batman] were both killed, and they probably knew they both would be," says Boxer's granddaughter Clio Smeeton.[4]

Miles Clark provides a vivid description of the day the War Office telegram bearing news of Hugh's disappearance arrived at Thorpe Lodge. Understandably, Jeannie Boxer was inconsolable. After attempting to comfort her for a time, Charles and Beryl went out onto the terrace. As they talked, Beryl asked her brother which of their parents he loved most. "Mummy, I think," he said.[5]

Jeannie Boxer at first refused to accept that her husband was dead. After all, he had survived his wounding in the Sudan, and then in November 1914 he had been decorated for his bravery with the British Expeditionary Force. In Jeannie's mind it seemed impossible that her Hugh could die in battle. She clung to the hope he had been taken prisoner. But he had not. Final confirmation of Major Hugh Boxer's death came from German military authorities several months later: his body had been buried on the battlefield, not far from where he and twenty of his men had fallen. That grim news forever changed life for Jeannie Boxer and her children. Fifteen years later, to the week, Jeannie took her own life, throwing herself from the upper window of a nursing home in Weymouth, England. She was just fifty-three years old.

All that was in the future. For now, Jeannie was determined that her children should be raised properly. In the summer of 1917, Charles began studying at Wellington College in Berkshire on a War Exhibition—a form of scholarship awarded to the sons of "Old Wellingtonians" who had died in the Great War. Charles's teachers were impressed by his academic potential, and they urged him to go on to university. He did not, because Hugh Boxer had decreed both of his sons should follow in his footsteps and serve in the military. Because his older brother Myles chose to join the army, Charles was keen to see the world as a member of the Royal Navy. Those plans changed when it was discovered that he was too nearsighted for the senior service.

Charles instead enrolled at the Royal Military Academy at Sandhurst, where British army officers are trained. He graduated in the fall of 1923 with a commission as a Second Lieutenant and was promptly posted to Northern Ireland with the Lincolnshire Regiment, his father's old unit. Six years of peacetime service on the home front left Charles bored and frustrated. In 1930, he applied for a posting to Japan as part of an Anglo-Japanese officer exchange program. After taking what he described as a "farcical" introductory course in Japanese, Charles traveled to Tokyo for a year of language training. This was all in preparation for a two-year stint (1931–1933) with a Japanese army unit: the 38th Infantry Regiment stationed in Nara.[6] The experience gave Charles an opportunity to practice his language skills and develop a thorough understanding of Japanese culture. He spoke Japanese like a gentleman and became skilled in kendo, an ancient martial art derived from the techniques of Japanese sword fighting. Combatants wield a *shinai*—a bamboo sword that is bound with leather and held with two hands.

Following his stint in Japan, Charles's duties took him to Indonesia and Macao, where he visited the grave of his great-uncle, the opium trader. During this time, Charles honed his abilities in Portuguese and Dutch, two languages he had been studying on his own for several years. (He also dabbled in French, Spanish, German, and Italian.) When Charles's Far East tour of duty ended, he joined the staff of the intelligence department at the War Office in London, chiefly on the strength of his superb linguistic skills. To Charles, anything was preferable to returning to the mind-numbing workaday routine of the British army in peacetime. Being in London also gave him the opportunity to pursue his scholarly interests. By now Charles was presenting papers and lecturing on various aspects of Far Eastern history. It was at one such occasion—a 1934 appearance before the Japan Society—that he met and became friends with Alf Bennett, who would later work alongside him in the British intelligence office in Hong Kong. Many years later, Bennett still recalled the indelible first impression Charles created. "I went to a lecture [in London] which this immaculate, but immaculate, young officer gave," said Bennett. "He had a gold watch chain, which he twirled as he spoke."[7]

Charles was posted to Hong Kong in January 1936. As a major, he became a senior army officer in the British intelligence office there. Charles used his linguistic skills in serving as the liaison between British commanders in Hong Kong and their Japanese counterparts across the frontier in occupied China. Charles also traveled extensively in Korea, Manchuria, Siberia, the Philippines, and China during the prewar years, doing reconnaissance via a regional network of contacts. This is how he had come to visit Mickey in Shanghai in the fall of 1937.

Intelligence work soon became mundane. Charles grew bored. He may have looked, talked, acted, and drank like the archetypal British army officer, but beneath that cool patina of professionalism and gentlemanly aplomb Major Charles Boxer was a dyed-in-the-wool cynic. "Hong Kong is a dumping ground for the duds," he was fond of telling anyone who would listen, "including me."

These feelings of discontent smoldered in the dark days following the September 1939 outbreak of war in Europe. Many of the British military's best men and their equipment were summoned from the far-flung outposts of the Empire to defend Britain against an anticipated German invasion. To those left behind, it seemed as if they had been forsaken and forgotten. Life in Hong Kong continued as before—the cocktail parties, the dancing, the drinking, and the indolence. The absurdity of it all only added to the air of pessimism that pervaded the colony. "The day of the white man is done out here," Charles told Mickey. "All of this is exactly like the merriment of Rome before the great fall."[8]

Charles stayed put only because he had no choice; this was where the Army had sent him. That was that. In actual fact, he was not so badly off. Charles lived comfortably on his officer's salary and perks. The pace of life in Hong Kong was languid and desultory, so Charles had ample opportunity to indulge both his scholarly interests and his fondness for more hedonistic pleasures. Ironically, despite his intellectualism, he had developed a reputation as a playboy and an eccentric. Charles was an anomaly in the officers' mess. Here was a man who caroused as hard as any of his colleagues, yet afterward in the wee hours of the morning and on his days off, he could usually be found at his desk. He was an intellectual trapped in khaki clothing. Charles read, translated original source documents about Dutch or Portuguese colonial history in the Far East, or wrote articles for *Tien H'sia*, the journal that Sinmay and his friends published. By 1940, Charles already had three scholarly books to his credit.[9]

His eccentricities and his affinity for solitary pursuits were sources of trouble during his brief marriage to Ursula Tulloh, a beautiful young kindergarten teacher he had met in Hong Kong. Ursula, orphaned at the age of ten, was an independent-minded young woman. She had traveled extensively throughout India, China, Burma, and Ceylon in the 1930s and taught at schools in Singapore and Hong Kong, where she was purportedly "the most beautiful woman in [the colony]." As the writer of her 1996 obituary in the *Times of London* put it, "Her striking appearance combined with her spirited manner brought her many admirers."[10] Among them was Charles Boxer, whom Ursula married in late 1939 despite the fact she "was never remotely a match for Charles's intellect," as she confided to Miles Clark.[11]

Mickey knew about the discord between the Boxers. How could she not? The Hong Kong rumor mill, like Shanghai's, worked nonstop, and what little Ursula had not hinted at in her conversations with Mickey was painfully evident. Although they had been married only a few months, the Boxers argued often. They were totally unsuited for a life together. Ursula, like the wives of many other British officers, finally left the colony. She went to Australia, ostensibly to recover from a bout with dysentery and to escape the dangers of war. It was the war of the sexes that Mrs. Boxer was fleeing, as much as any imminent conflict with Japan. Ursula and Charles continued to spar via the mails. He insisted their marriage was over, but she was not so sure.

Mickey was aware of all this her first night back in Hong Kong, as she, Charles, and Max Oxford finished off their evening out with nightcaps at a geisha parlor in a downtown hotel. Max lay back on the floor, where he fell asleep. Mickey and Charles sat with the elderly Japanese proprietor. Charles explained to the madame that Mickey had just come back from Chungking, where Japanese warplanes were on the attack. As Mickey told stories of the air raids, Charles nodded approvingly and observed that she had "guts." The more he said it, the more Mickey liked it. As Charles spoke, Mickey felt herself falling in love with him. She could not help it.

Mickey and Charles saw a lot of one another in her first weeks back in Hong Kong. Charles liked Mickey's audacity and lack of inhibition. She was exciting. She was passionate. She was witty and fun. She was full of life. In short, in Charles's mind, Mickey was everything that Ursula and all of the other prim and proper British women he had known were not and never could be.

Of course, Mickey's footloose ways occasionally landed her in trouble. That was so one splendid weekend in the fall of 1940, when she and Charles attended a wild party thrown by a rich Hong Kong taipan named J. J. Patterson. Mickey recalled that everyone went swimming at a nearby beach. Afterward they drank too much and did gymnastics on the lawn of their host's country home. As night approached, the party grew wild. Mickey went walking in the garden with a very drunk British army captain. When he suddenly grabbed her and became "violently amorous," Mickey pushed him away. This made him even more insistent. In the ensuing struggle, Mickey fell backward down an incline, twisting her ankle. The gentleman officer pounced on the opportunity, attempting to carry Mickey into a nearby clump of bushes. It was apparent that he was not interested in further conversation. Scratching and kicking madly, Mickey managed to escape. She hobbled across the lawn toward the house with her drunken attacker in hot pursuit. Despite Mickey's protests, neither Charles nor anyone else in the crowd standing around the drawing room with drinks in hand paid much attention to her injuries or to her attacker. It was only later as Mickey and Charles were climbing into the car for the drive home that Charles took note of Mickey's swollen ankle. "What *have* you been doing out there in the moonlight?" he asked.

Mickey saw a doctor the next morning. The diagnosis was a badly sprained ankle. When the bandaged joint still hurt ten days later, the doctor ordered X rays. It was then discovered that Mickey had broken the ankle in her fall. She was fitted with a plaster walking cast, in which she clomped around uncomfortably for the next month.

Despite the pain and inconvenience, Mickey's stay in Hong Kong was mostly happy. After all, she was in love. As the weeks stretched into months, she mused about her options. Patrick Putnam had written again urging her to return to Africa,[12] but she was no longer interested in doing so. Meanwhile, the Endicotts, her Canadian missionary friends from Chungking, suggested she join them in Free China, where she could teach in a missionary university there. "[This] idea appeals to my sense of what's fitting. I should like to have it carved on my tombstone or the jar that holds my ashes that I taught in a mission school," Mickey told her mother, with tongue firmly in cheek. "But I don't like to leave the coast."[13]

Mickey hoped to stay in Hong Kong with Charles as long as possible. With that in mind, she contacted her brother-in-law, Mitchell Dawson, an attorney in Chicago, asking him for advice on the chances she would be allowed to return to the British colony after a visit to the States. Mitchell made some inquiries and reported back that with the political tensions in the Pacific, it was unlikely Mickey would be allowed to return to Hong Kong. That settled it. She informed her mother she was delaying her return home yet again. On December 1, 1940, Mickey rented a flat in the Tregunter Mansions on Hong Kong's fashionable May Road. The building was halfway up the Peak, right next door to where Charles lived.

Hong Kong social etiquette required that Mickey retain at least three servants: a cook-houseboy, a coolie helper, and a wash amah (a female servant or nursemaid) to do laundry. Fortunately for Mickey, the cook-houseboy she retained was a Cantonese man who had spent the past quarter century in Hong Kong in the employ of Charles and other British army officers. "Ah King was an old man, as they count age in China, where people age fast," Mickey wrote in one of her *New Yorker* articles. "He must have been nearing fifty, but he didn't look it. He carried himself straight, conscious that he had served British Army officers for the better part of his life, and though his manner towards those he considered his inferiors was not exactly bullying, he was certainly majestic with them."[14]

Ah King was efficient and loyal to his employers and acted more like a faithful old family retainer than a cook-houseboy. Mickey's decision to hire him would prove crucial to her very survival in the dangerous months ahead; at the time, of course, she had no way of knowing this. She knew only that having three servants in her house was expensive, even with a financial contribution from Charles. However, it was a price she was willing to pay. For now. Mickey was intent on continuing her relationship with Charles. "I don't know why I have always had so little conscience about married men," she later wrote. "It can't be Mother's fault; she brought us up very carefully."[15]

If forced to explain her actions, Mickey would do so using the typical lines uttered by sexually liberated women in the 1920s, when she herself was coming of age: being married doesn't mean one becomes a possession. When a man wants to be unfaithful to his wife the damage is already done; or a woman who can't hold her man doesn't deserve to keep him. Such thinking was the product of simpler times, when a man was the sexual pursuer and a woman the innocent—although sometimes *not* entirely innocent—pursued.

Gender politics had been a parlor game in the Hahn household when Mickey was a girl, one played with no holds barred. Anytime one of the three younger Hahn sisters had brought a promising suitor home to meet the family, he was immediately assessed. Then the scramble for his affections began.

As often as not, it was Helen who won out in this sibling rivalry. Being older and more mature, she used her physical charms to full advantage. While that may have been how things usually ended, it did not mean Mickey acquiesced. Later, when she left home, Mickey took this same competitive spirit away with her. In the larger world, many people found it disturbing, even threatening.

During her time in the Belgian Congo, Mickey had been shocked to discover that Patrick Putnam, like many other white men, had "gone native" and adopted the practice of taking multiple wives. Despite the best efforts of well-meaning white Christian missionaries, polygamy was a part of everyday life in many tribes. Mickey had come to accept this; the propriety of it, she finally decided, depended on circumstances and on one's viewpoint. In Shanghai, Mickey, too, had "gone native" when she began her relationship with Sinmay. She did so because it was easy, socially acceptable (at least in Chinese culture), attracted attention in the foreign community, and filled a void in her life at a time when Mickey was in dire need of emotional support and reassurance of her femininity.

Hong Kong was different. After all, Hong Kong was a British colony. Here polygamy was taboo, and although life was insular and people sometimes got bored or drunk and played around on their spouses, there were still strong moral strictures against adultery.

Mickey knew this. She also knew that many people frowned on her relationship with Charles. Mickey was regarded by many Brits in the colony as a shameless hussy—like that other "dreadful American woman" Wallace Warfield Simpson, who'd brought about Edward VIII's abdication four years earlier. In Mickey's mind, she was doing nothing improper in dating Charles. "I didn't feel particularly aware of his marriage. He said that it was over," Mickey later wrote. "If [he] had been ordinarily married and contented, if he had only wanted to indulge in an extramarital affair because his wife wasn't around, I would have run away. I wouldn't have been satisfied. I was serious about Charles from the beginning, and that was a completely new departure for me. I told him so. We never talked seriously, but I told him so just the same when I had fortified myself with whisky."[16]

Once Mickey revealed her feelings, Charles admitted the attraction was mutual. He proposed a bold plan: rather than going to Shanghai and then home to the States, Mickey should send for her gibbons and stay with him in Hong Kong. He suggested they have a child. When his divorce came through, Charles said, they could even get married, if they wanted. Crazy as it seems, the idea made sense to Mickey at the time. She had been talking in a lighthearted way for several years about having a baby, and now at age thirty-five her biological clock was ticking loudly. She was not even sure she could become pregnant, and recently Mickey had been feeling downcast. With the Soong book done, her relationship with Sinmay finished, and her plans uncertain, she felt her own life had become bleak and pointless. It was a relief to be in Hong Kong, where Mickey was distracted from her woes by Charles and by the colony's tenuous situation.

Most people in the British community who were in a position to know would have agreed with a June 1940 secret report written by the director of Japanese military intelligence. It concluded, "There is nothing to stop Japan from seizing French Indo-China, the Netherlands Indies, or Hong Kong."[17] To anyone who cared or dared to consider the matter, it was clear the colony was teetering on the brink of something profound, even cataclysmic. A few blithe souls remained happily oblivious to the whole situation; they adopted a kind of "it can't happen here" attitude. Such sentiments were fueled by old hands like Major-General Edward Grasett, a Canadian who commanded the British troops in China for three years until he was replaced in September 1941 by acting Major-General Christopher M. Maltby. The new commander, a fifty-year-old career soldier, had a reputation as a tough, fearless soldier. He had served many years in the Indian army. During the First World War, he had been wounded three times, mentioned in dispatches, and received the Military Cross for bravery. Grasett told Maltby the Japanese were bluffing and would not dare attack; remaining neutral was Japan's wisest course of action, he argued.

"General Maltby, fresh from the more astringent atmosphere of India's turbulent North West Frontier, did not agree," wrote British historian Tim Carew in his book *The Fall of Hong Kong*. "General Grasett resembled a nanny who, on handing over her charge with assurances of perfect cleanliness, lands her successor with a baby that wets its bed three times nightly and steadfastly refuses to mount the pot."[18]

Whether Grasett's bravado was genuine or merely for appearance is uncertain. In the latter regard, at least, some people wanted to believe Grasett's words. Charles's friend and colleague Alf Bennett recalled, "There were many civilians making lots and lots of money, and they didn't want to believe anything bad was about to happen. [Those of us in Intelligence] didn't really want to believe it either, but we saw it was clearly hopeless. Hong Kong could be taken overnight."[19]

Bill Wiseman, a former British officer who was posted to Hong Kong in September 1940, said looking back on his experiences he has fond memories of the months leading up to the Japanese attack. "It was a marvelous year of peacetime soldiering," he said. "I was twenty-two and lived the life of Riley for a bit more than a year. The Hong Kong dollar bought the earth, and although I was on the equivalent of less than £300 a year, I had a share in a sailing boat. I was a member of four clubs, and spent most weekends at parties. By the end of the first year [in Hong Kong] I knew the form locally, and I knew a lot of people in the garrison. I didn't know Charles then, but he was fairly notorious. He was living with this American woman who had come down from Shanghai. . . . To use our colloquial expression, they were 'shacked up.' This, in a regular army garrison, was regarded as a great scandal."[20]

Mickey was not at all bothered that tongues were wagging throughout the colony. She was far more concerned by all the speculation about a coming war with Japan and about the possible impact on her own life. Having seen the might of Japanese firepower in Shanghai and Chungking, she was not eager to experience it again. Yet as an outsider, Mickey could be relatively detached, even analytical, about the situation. "We all sit here and wait, and we are not quite sure what we are waiting for," she mused in a letter to her mother. "When does that feeling of hopelessness begin? Or is it boredom? If it is, perhaps I inherited immunity from you."[21]

Being very much in love with Charles, Mickey decided she was ready to accept his proposal and to bear a child, who would be Charles's heir if he should die in the coming war. When Mickey told Charles this and revealed that a doctor in Shanghai had informed her that she probably could not become pregnant, Charles snorted indignantly. The doctor must be wrong, he insisted. He and Mickey then set about disproving that diagnosis. By early 1941, they had succeeded in doing so.

21

AT FIRST, MICKEY AND CHARLES told almost no one that she was pregnant. However, when a rumor began that they had secretly married, news of the baby leaked out. When Ernest Hemingway and his wife Martha Gellhorn visited Hong Kong in the spring of 1941, Mickey met them in the bar of the Repulse Bay Hotel, where the Hemingways were staying. "When Hemingway found out that I was pregnant, he told me he'd claim to be the child's father if I wanted him to," Mickey recalled. "I declined. I said Charles wouldn't like that."[1]

Not long afterward, Mickey received a letter of congratulations from a girlfriend in Australia, and Ursula wrote to Charles demanding to know what was happening. As news of Mickey's pregnancy spread, the confusion about her relationship with Charles grew. Mickey had taken up residence in Hong Kong, and she and Charles seemed to be a couple. They attended social events and were together out on the town. As always, Mickey delighted in being the center of attention.

Charles ignored the whispers and icy stares whenever he and Mickey went out. She reveled in the notoriety, for she seldom missed an opportunity to tweak the noses of the fusty members of the British community. Eyebrows were raised in the dining room of the august Hong Kong Hotel one evening when Mickey pulled out and lit a huge cigar. If the men were smoking, she could too, she argued. "I like you and would like to know you better," one love struck American navy officer wrote her after witnessing the scene. "Any girl that has the temerity to smoke cigars in the Hong Kong Hotel in front of all the limey colonels has my respect and admiration."[2]

Charles's friend Bill Wiseman recalled, "Hong Kong was a peacetime garrison, with all the peacetime bullshit. The King's Birthday parade was followed by the General's cocktail party, to which Charles took Mickey. That caused a tremendous raising of eyebrows and 'tut-tuts,' particularly from the handful of senior service wives who'd managed to stay behind [in Hong Kong] on one excuse or another. I think Charles introduced Mickey to the General as 'my mistress.' But Charles is the sort of bloke about whom so many tales have been told, many of them apocryphal, that unless you've seen or heard it for yourself, you can't say it was actually so. Anyway, it was regarded as a great scandal."[3]

Charles's intelligence duties kept him busy six days a week, and many evenings he was busy with his reading and scholarly writing. That was his routine; in some ways, his life was compartmentalized and structured with an eye to military precision. Mickey understood, and she did not mind. She was deeply in love with Charles and lived for the precious time they had together, limited though it was. On Wednesday afternoons and Saturdays, they swam at the beach, spent quiet hours together, or attended social events. "Viewed on the surface, I had made a bad bargain," Mickey wrote. "But we didn't exist on the surface. I took surprisingly well to the stuffy routine of Hong Kong, and talked gently and patiently and contentedly with the wealthy bourgeoisie."[4]

Having so much time to herself gave Mickey an opportunity to pursue her own interests. One project she undertook was to learn Mandarin Chinese—now known as *Kuo Yu*. This was problematic, for it was difficult to find anyone in Hong Kong who spoke the dialect well enough to teach it. Although 90 percent of Chinese use Mandarin as their everyday language, the most common of China's seven major dialects, *Yue*—also called Cantonese—is dominant in Hong Kong. When a Chinese friend introduced Mickey to a woman named Ying Ping, who agreed to tutor her, Mickey began her lessons. At times this proved awkward, given the woman's occupation: a "hostess" in a downtown "escort bureau" (brothels being illegal in Hong Kong). Mickey practiced her Mandarin by paying the woman to sit and talk. She could do so only in the early afternoon when the escort business was slow. On one occasion, when Mickey made the mistake of dropping by at night, a male patron offered to "buy her a drink." Ying Ping and her suspicious coworkers were distressed, not so much because of the impropriety of the situation but because of the potential threat of lost business.

When she was not studying Mandarin or spending time with Charles, Mickey worked at her writing. Carl Brandt, Mickey's agent in New York, wanted her to do another book. He hoped to follow up on the success of *The Soong Sisters*, which was published in the spring of 1941. The book received excellent reviews in the national press and sold well. It was Mickey's first big commercial success. Katherine Woods, a writer for the *New York Times*, praised the Soongs' story as being "as absorbing as any novel's and much more important." She went on to laud Mickey's easy style and what she termed her "self-effacing intimacy."[5] W. H. Chamberlain of the *Atlantic Monthly* pronounced *The Soong Sisters* to be "a spirited, well-informed book."[6]

Even those critics who chided Mickey for not passing judgment on the Soongs' politics found a lot to like in the book. Despite a growing Western fascination with China and the Soongs, the sisters' inaccessibility meant that Mickey's biography was just the second to appear; the other had been a 1939 book called *Three Sisters* by Cornelia Spencer, the sister of Pulitzer Prize–winning novelist Pearl S. Buck.

Clifton Fadiman, writing in the *New Yorker*, noted that Mickey's "readable book fills its niche most acceptably."[7] Reviewer Nym Wales of the Left-leaning publication the *Nation* described Mickey as "the clever American novelist" and observed, "[She] is eminently qualified to have done a much better study had she not been obliged to pussyfoot in order to secure the necessary cooperation." Even so, Wales went on to concede that "*The Soong Sisters* is a delightful and well-written book, and the author has handled a delicate subject with much skill."[8]

Mickey was ecstatic with such reviews. They were vindication for all the misery and sacrifice she had gone through to write the book and avoid the ideological pitfalls of Chinese politics. She always felt *The Soong Sisters* was one of the best things she ever wrote. "I did what I think was a reasonably good job, considering the difficulties of [Chinese] politics then," she said.[9]

The favorable reviews were a boost to her self-confidence, especially after the disappointing public reception for her novel *Steps of the Sun* the previous year. The only sour note for Mickey was that when she received an advance copy of *The Soong Sisters*, the first thing she saw was that an embossed Soong character on the front cover was printed upside down. This was considered bad luck to the Chinese. Fortunately, a frantic cable to her publisher in New York corrected the problem.

The book's success helped Mickey convince Carl Brandt that she really was not "out of touch" with the American literary market. There was a growing interest in the United States just then in Singapore, which was seen as a bulwark against Japanese expansionism in the Pacific, so at Brandt's urging, Mickey began researching a biography of Sir Thomas Stamford Raffles. "Raffles of Singapore," as he was popularly known, had played a key role in the founding of the British Empire in the Far East in the nineteenth century. Mickey took on the project for three reasons. One was that it gave her an opportunity to work with Charles, who translated some Dutch historical documents for her. Another was that Mickey felt an affinity for Raffles, who, like her, had kept a pet gibbon. Finally, and most importantly, she needed the publisher's advance money. Life in Hong Kong was expensive, especially with Mickey's spending habits.

The articles and short stories she sold to the *New Yorker* continued to pay most of her living expenses. Bylined submissions by the magazine's "China coast correspondent" appeared regularly, sometimes twice or three times a month in the early 1940s. The extraordinary thing about these writings is their breadth and variety. Everything in Mickey's life was grist for her literary mill; in the hands of a lesser writer, such material could have been banal, even tedious. Mickey had an uncanny eye for intriguing detail and a refreshingly casual perspective on life. Her short stories about the Chinese character named Pan Heh-ven—a thinly disguised Sinmay—were among the most popular to appear in the *New Yorker* at that time. As well, Mickey attracted a large and loyal readership with her articles about everyday life in Hong Kong and Chungking, about the eccentricities and foibles of her colorful friends and neighbors, and even about her mischievous gibbons.

A friend in Shanghai had shipped many of Mickey's personal possessions down to Hong Kong. Mr. Mills and the two other apes Sinmay had bought while Mickey was in Chungking came too. Having herself purchased two more young gibbons in Hong Kong, Mickey had acquired a small zoo. Much to the dismay of the household staff and neighbors, the five animals made themselves at home in the fresh air and sunshine on Hong Kong's peak. When Ah King had enough of the gibbons' hijinks, he erected a makeshift chicken-wire cage on the balcony of Mickey's fashionable May Road flat. This proved of limited value, since Mr. Mills had a Houdini-like ability to escape. When he did so, his curiosity invariably got him into trouble. "He usually scales some likely wall and enters an open window," Mickey explained in a *New Yorker* article. "After a horrible pause there comes a shriek or a crash or both, and shortly afterward he climbs out the window, saying thoughtfully to himself, 'Oop, oop,' as he climbs higher towards another open window."[10] Mr. Mills's penchant for dropping in unannounced caused no end of trouble and led to strained relations between Mickey and her neighbors.

The same problems had occurred in Shanghai. This had never bothered Mickey in the past. Now, as her "condition" became apparent, it began to worry her. She and Charles had still not announced that Mickey was expecting. They had agreed that it was better if she kept a lower profile until after the baby was born in the fall of 1941, but that proved difficult. Mickey had taken a temporary job teaching school. She continued to socialize and confided her secret to only a few trusted friends. One was Hilda Selwyn-Clarke, the wife of Hong Kong's director of medical services and the "highest ranking" wife still in town. Hilda was a red-haired, headstrong woman who was a staunch socialist; she was called "Red Hilda." She made no moral judgments about Mickey's pregnancy. Hilda maintained that marriage was nothing more than a "bourgeois nicety." If a woman chose to become pregnant, that was her business alone. Such unorthodox views were not all that set Hilda apart from the crowd.

She was legendary in Hong Kong's British community because, unlike most British people, she got involved in the muck of Chinese politics. Hilda was the secretary of an organization called the China Defense League, headed by Madame Sun. Even after publication of *The Soong Sisters*, Madame Chiang's older sister remained suspicious of Mickey. Madame Sun had refused to be interviewed for the book or to have anything to do with its author. Now she cautioned Hilda that Mickey was a spy. Another of Mickey's leftist friends vouched for her, convincing Hilda that she could be trusted.

That friend was Agnes Smedley, the well-known American leftist. Smedley, who traveled for a time with Mao Tse-tung's guerilla army as an "unofficial" Red Cross worker, was a dour, quarrelsome, and moody woman. Mickey was one of the few people with whom Agnes got along well, although they would have a serious falling out after Agnes read the Soong sisters biography and Mickey's memoirs of her years in China. Mickey and Agnes had met in Shanghai in the late 1930s, when Agnes sometimes stayed at Mickey's house. Their paths crossed again in Chungking. "Smedley appreciated [Emily Hahn] as a fellow writer and as a lively conversationalist with a fondness for the well-placed four-letter word," one of Smedley's biographers explained.[11]

When Mickey heard Agnes was in the hospital with a gall bladder problem, Mickey visited her. Had Agnes not been a friend of Hilda Selwyn-Clarke, she would have been kicked out of the colony. Agnes Smedley was a notorious radical, whom the British regarded as "dangerous," in a vague, undefined sort of way. Hilda had spoken up for Agnes, who nevertheless was allowed to enter a Hong Kong hospital for treatment only after promising not to give any speeches or to otherwise disrupt the peace. Hilda also became Mickey's patron, arranging for her medical care during her pregnancy and generally taking her under her wing.

• • •

Charles left Mickey alone in Hong Kong in May, when he went on an intelligence-gathering trip. Among the stops on his monthlong tour of the region was Singapore, where Ursula was now staying. Charles planned to meet her and to tell her the details of his affair with Mickey. He and Ursula would then iron out the details of a divorce, Charles assured Mickey. Ursula had been trying to return to Hong Kong, but was prevented from doing so by a compulsory evacuation order issued by the colonial government; the wives and children of all British citizens were ordered to leave. As an American and an "essential worker"—because she had volunteered for nursing duty—Mickey was not obliged to join them. Ironically, it was Charles who had recommended the evacuation to Hong Kong's governor.

During his absence, Charles arranged for a friend to rent the spare bedroom in Mickey's flat. Art Cooper, a free-spirited young army intelligence officer with a passion for literature, was in Hong Kong awaiting a posting. Mickey welcomed both the rental income and the company; Cooper was a would-be poet. "[Art] was about twenty-five," Mickey wrote. "He had a long, sorrowful face and a deep Irish voice, and he really didn't give much of a damn about anything but words."[12] Mickey and Art became good friends, a development that proved all-important when Charles returned with the news that he had settled nothing with Ursula.

Mickey was distraught. Charles was now evasive and noncommittal about their future together. It was Art Cooper who forced the issue. He initiated a discussion one evening over drinks. It came out in the course of this "shotgun interview," as Mickey termed it, that Ursula still had no idea Mickey was pregnant or that Charles had promised to marry her. For that reason, Ursula refused to agree to a divorce. Cooper got angry when he heard this. He accused Charles of being immoral and selfish. When Charles denied it, the discussion grew heated. Finally, in exasperation, Cooper looked at Mickey and asked, "Will you marry me?" She smiled. "Yes," she said.

There followed a long, uncertain pause as the three of them sat looking at one another. Suddenly they all broke into laughter at the absurdity of the situation. Charles pledged to tell Ursula everything and do the "honorable" thing by Mickey: he would marry her as soon as his divorce was final. He would also rewrite his will so Mickey and the baby were "taken care of" should anything happen to him.[13] Charles's initial strategy was to ask his sister Beryl, who planned to visit Singapore the first week of July, to meet with Ursula and convince her to grant him a divorce. By the time of Beryl's arrival, Ursula had already heard from friends that Mickey was pregnant, and she was eager to end the marriage. "Poor thing, she's had a rotten time with [Charles] and it's not going to be easy for her now," Beryl's biographer Miles Clark quoted her as writing in her diary. "She's awfully nice . . . and in such a beastly position. It's too late for me to do anything, much as I should like to."[14]

Mickey had Art Cooper to thank for forcing Charles's hand. Had Art not done so, the relationship between Mickey and Charles might well have turned out differently. Mickey was deeply grateful to him. Not long afterward, when Alf Bennett came back and Art returned to Singapore, Cooper did so bearing a precious gift from Mickey: one of her favorite gibbons.

. . .

With everything between them settled, Mickey and Charles began sharing news about the baby with friends. Mickey told Madame Kung one day as they were out driving. "Her reaction was typical," Mickey wrote. "There was a little silence, while I held onto her hand firmly, possibly for fear she would slap me, and she stared straight ahead at the back of the chauffeur's head. Suddenly she giggled. I dropped her hand and turned around to look at her. She giggled like a little girl."[15] Madame Kung, a devout Methodist, then proceeded to scold Mickey.

When few others in the colony noticed Mickey's "condition"—or, she wondered, was it that no one dared inquire about the unmentionable?—Mickey and Charles made a game of it. They decided to reward the first person who asked if Mickey was pregnant. The prize would be cigars for a man, chocolate for a woman. The contest winner, in late July, turned out to be Hal Sweet, a devil-may-care American airline pilot. Sweet's reaction to Mickey's news provided some insight into the nationalistic antipathies that were bubbling away just beneath the colony's placid veneer of civility. "All right, but Mickey—Why a limey?" Sweet asked. An elderly American woman friend of Mickey's reacted the same way to Mickey's news. "Some women will stop at nothing to bring discredit to our nation!" she sputtered.[16]

Such comments reminded Mickey there was reason to be fearful about the reaction of Charles's superiors when they learned about the baby. Keeping an American mistress when one's wife had been forcibly evacuated was one thing; it was quite another to have a child with that woman. That simply was not the sort of thing a British officer did. Mickey's fears of a backlash lessened after a chat with Archibald Clark-Kerr, the British ambassador to Chungking. He came calling when he was visiting Hong Kong. Over drinks at the Grips, Mickey confided in Clarke-Kerr. He assured her that Charles would probably not get into "bad trouble" because his superiors needed him just then; war with Japan was virtually certain. The only real question was, how soon would the shooting start?

War hysteria pushed up the cost of living in Hong Kong during the summer of 1941. Mickey, five months pregnant, struggled to cope with the heat and humidity and to pay her bills. She reported in a July 28 letter home, "I am working as fast as I can on the Raffles book, but it is hot weather for heavy reading and I neglect it sometimes in favor of lighter stuff for the *New Yorker*. . . . I have not collected any [advance] money as yet since the first statement hasn't come in and I am in danger of going broke in the midst of plenty!"[17]

Mickey realized how difficult it would be for her to travel to Singapore and Java to research the Raffles book. Tensions were high in the region as the slow, inexorable drift to war continued. Japanese spies were busy everywhere, especially in Hong Kong. "The waiters, barmen, hairdressers and *masseurs* watched, listened, and reported assiduously," wrote British historian Tim Carew.[18] The staff of the Japanese consulate noted all military movements in and around the colony, dutifully sending daily intelligence reports to Tokyo. The real "star" of Japanese spying operations in Hong Kong was an army officer named Suzuki. Everybody knew Colonel Suzuki and why he was in town, yet few people took him or his mission seriously. When he left "on holidays" at the end of November 1941, he did so with the "details of the British defence plan down to the last strand of barbed wire," according to Tim Carew.[19] Suzuki's information proved invaluable to Japanese commanders a week later when they began their assault on Hong Kong.

The colony was rife with rumors that crack units of the Japanese army were massing to the northwest, on the Chinese side of the frontier. Charles and other intelligence officers dutifully reported these developments to their superiors, who remained skeptical. Most senior British military planners felt that if the Japanese tiger pounced on Hong Kong, the attack would come by sea; an "impregnable" defense line of pillboxes, gun emplacements, and troops strung across the hills of the New Territory would deter any landward assault. How wrong this thinking was became apparent the moment fighting began.

For now, life in Hong Kong's insular British community continued, even after the departure of many of the wives and children. The war, as described in radio reports and newspaper wire stories, seemed distant and unreal. Even more unreal was the continuing success of Hitler and his allies. On June 22, a German army three million strong launched Operation Barbarossa—the invasion of the Soviet Union. On July 24, France's Vichy government yielded to a Japanese ultimatum, surrendering French colonies throughout Indochina. The news was equally glum elsewhere.

Despite these developments, Mickey and other residents of Hong Kong carried on with the routine of their lives. They did so despite an influx of hundreds of thousands of Chinese refugees "fleeing the bomb and bayonet of China's invaders," as one contemporary account noted.[20] Most British citizens in Hong Kong still had little social contact with Chinese; Charles was an exception. He and Mickey had many Chinese friends. They sensed the anti-British sentiment among well-to-do Chinese, and Mickey was "homesick" for the China she had known in Shanghai. "My servants were Hong Kong servants," she wrote, "May Road style, respectful and distant."[21] Ah King was uneasy whenever Mickey's Chinese friends dropped by the flat. Once, when she invited a visiting Sikh policeman to tea, both men were acutely embarrassed. The Sikh friend confided that the people he was staying with had warned that if the Hong Kong police spotted him on the Peak he would be sent away.

Such blatant racism angered Mickey, who did not hesitate to speak her mind on the subject. Not that it did any good. No one listened to her; after all, she was a "foreign neutral" with no real involvement in the colony or in the turmoil that was raging around her. The only thing that really made her different was that unlike most of her friends, Mickey had not joined the exodus of women and children. In July, she received a visit from James and Mary Endicott and their four children, who reluctantly had decided to return home to Canada. Stephen Endicott, the eldest son, recalled meeting Mickey and Charles in Hong Kong. What struck him most was that Charles seemed "ill at ease." This was understandable, given James Endicott's occupation and his evangelical fervor. "I gathered [Charles] was married," Stephen Endicott said, "but my parents didn't discuss with Mickey the fact she was having his child."[22]

The Endicotts stayed several weeks in Hong Kong, waiting for their ship. In the interval, one of the Endicott boys fell ill with measles. He and his father stayed behind when the rest of the family departed on a Norwegian freighter. James Endicott and his son left in mid-August, sailing via Shanghai, where they visited some of Mickey's friends, including Sinmay and Corin Bernfelt, the young Englishwoman Mickey had chummed with in Chungking. "Met with Corin and Sinmay. He had shaved and didn't look quite so dignified, but more youthful," Endicott reported in a letter to Mickey. "He had a slight paralytic stroke to the left side of his face, which spoiled the symmetry . . . but I could see the beauty of it. It is certainly a remarkable face. There is a naïve and child-like quality to his makeup. We talked a bit about your novel [*Steps of the Sun*], which [Sinmay] said had been ruined by the publisher. He claims it originally had a philosophy and real depth to it, but the U.S. publisher had made it 'cheap.' That was the word he used. Only the adventures of an American girl in the Orient."[23]

Mickey smiled at that latter phrase, for her "adventures" were continuing at a bewildering pace. She was increasingly anxious as her baby's projected early October due date drew nearer. Charles, fearing a Japanese attack and a bloody uprising against the British by embittered Sikh and Chinese dissidents, suggested Mickey go somewhere "safe" to give birth. She refused. Her place was at Charles's side, she argued. That decision was not easy. Often in the dead of night, when the heat and her aching back kept her awake, a million questions ran through Mickey's mind. How would she know when it was time to have the baby? What would happen to it if she died in childbirth? What would happen to her and to the baby if Charles was killed in the coming war? Where would she go? What would she do? What would her family back home say about all of this? Suddenly it was all overwhelming and bewildering.

Mickey's angst heightened in the wake of Agnes Smedley's departure. Agnes had agreed to visit the Hahns in Chicago to alert them to developments in Mickey's life. The only American woman Mickey knew who was still in town was Charlotte Gower, an anthropology professor at Ling Nan University. Dr. Gower, bespectacled and scholarly, was surprisingly empathetic when Mickey told her about the baby. When Charles asked Gower to move in with Mickey during the last six weeks of her pregnancy, she agreed. Mickey was grateful for the female company, especially after she fell and sprained an ankle while getting out of a taxi.

It turned out that Gower was not Mickey's only houseguest that fall. When Ah King's wife and daughter, who lived across the bay in Kowloon, fell ill with typhoid fever, Mickey got them admitted to a hospital. They recovered, and Mickey paid the bill, "which was very low; about twelve Hong Kong dollars altogether, as I remember," she recalled.[24] Afterward, Mickey invited the women to stay at her flat despite a landlord's edict that forbade the families of servants from living with them. "I said to hell with the landlord," Mickey explained. "It wasn't a legal ruling anyway."[25]

That act of kindness was returned in spades and helped save Mickey's life, for it bought her Ah King's undying gratitude and loyalty. Both proved invaluable in the difficult and dangerous days that lay ahead.

22

A FIRST BABY—like the proverbial check that's "in the mail"—arrives when it's least expected, so for five days after entering the hospital, Mickey waited. Her contractions began several times, only to stop each time as unexpectedly as they had begun. "I would just halfway get there and then have to start all over again," Mickey wrote in a letter to Helen.[1] Finally, two weeks past her anticipated due date, Mickey's doctor, a British missionary named Gordon King, tried to induce labor. When that failed, he performed a cesarean section.

"How much of this do you want to feel, before we help you?" he asked.

Mickey was taken aback. "Did you think I was doing all this to write a book about it?" she replied.

King shrugged. "Why yes," he said. "Isn't that the idea?"[2]

The cynicism of King's remark angered her; however, the more she thought about it, the more Mickey felt that maybe he had a good idea. She resolved to make the best of the situation. "I thoroughly enjoyed the operation," she quipped. "It was my ideal of an experience: something happened to you that you can watch without feeling it."[3]

All went smoothly, and the baby arrived late on the evening of October 17, 1941. The child was a tiny five-and-a-half-pound girl whom Mickey and Charles named Carola Militia Boxer. When the nurses took the baby away to clean and dress her, Mickey remained on the operating table while her doctor removed a large fibroid tumor from her uterus. While such lumps are common and usually benign, they can cause severe pain, abort a pregnancy, or even pose a risk during a delivery. "You're lucky," the doctor told Mickey. "We'd have had to have that out within a month anyway, and the child couldn't have survived a normal birth."[4]

Afterward, as Mickey lay in her hospital bed surrounded by baskets of flowers sent by Charles and various friends, she drifted in and out of consciousness. Her abdomen ached, and her sleep was troubled by horrible recurring nightmares. One moment, Mickey dreamed she was back in Chungking in an air raid. The next, she dreamed of Carola's face floating in the clouds. The baby was dying of starvation, her withered body shrinking ever smaller, until finally all that was left was a huge pair of eyes. Babies died every day in China; Mickey had watched them. She was determined that hers would not suffer the same fate.

Mickey's month-long hospital stay was sheer torture. She quickly tired of being "bullied" by her nurses and of adhering to the hospital routine. Mickey worried that if war with Japan broke out, Charles might be posted elsewhere. If he was, she knew she might never see him again. The thought was unbearable. Mickey announced she was going home. She ignored her doctor's advice, packed up Carola on November 15 and left. Despite a sore abdomen and a host of worries, life suddenly didn't seem too bad. Mickey had decided everything might turn out all right after all. She found a part-time teaching job, partly because she needed the money and partly because working was a boost to her self-esteem. Teaching, she observed, "is a cheap form of maintaining a superiority complex."[5] Carola stayed home in the care of her Chinese amah, while Mickey resumed her career. She was late for her first afternoon of classes when she drank too much at a celebratory lunch and got lost on the way to the school.

Having a job again was just one reason Mickey's mood brightened. There was another: the renewed air of optimism in the colony. A new British governor, Sir Mark Young, had arrived in Hong Kong, as had reinforcements for the garrison, a regiment of brash young Canadian troops. Mickey began to relax. Perhaps she *could* feed and look after a child on her own. Most people in the colony were preoccupied with their own problems, so Mickey did not even face the social ostracism she had anticipated. Nevertheless, Mickey herself was having sober second thoughts about becoming a mother. In a letter to Sir Victor Sassoon in Bombay, Mickey explained that she was already agonizing over how to one day tell Carola the circumstances of her birth. Sir Victor advised Mickey never to do so. "We look at it from different angles," he explained in a

Mickey with the newborn Carola, Hong Kong, October 1941.
Courtesy Emily Hahn Estate

letter of congratulations. "No one has the right to handicap the child from the start deliberately. I cannot see the child will think it better when she grows up to know that the action was deliberate, but you seem to [disagree]. Maybe you think she will be so superior to others of her generation that she shall not complain at being handicapped; all I hope is that she will be conceited enough to think so. You see, you look on it from the selfish personal point of view. I, with all the *advantages* possible of an unhappy childhood, and cannot forget it."[6]

As Mickey puzzled over her situation, other aspects of her life were clearer. For one, the uncertainties between her and Charles were resolved. He received a letter from Singapore a few days after the baby's birth announcing in "lady-like tones" that Ursula had filed for divorce. Mickey's Chinese marriage to Sinmay was not recognized by British law, so the only remaining obstacle to Mickey and Charles's marriage was a legal requirement that they wait six months. "I suppose we'll marry," Mickey told her friend Vera Armstrong. "It doesn't seem to matter any more."[7]

Those words were puzzling and prophetic, for three weeks after Mickey's return home from the hospital, the international situation deteriorated quickly. The governor, Sir Mark Young, ordered the mobilization of all Hong Kong volunteers, and the military garrison was put on alert. Meanwhile, in Washington, what one historian termed "the ponderous diplomatic ballet" that had been going on between the United States and Japan took a dramatic turn. News bulletins reported that two Japanese envoys were meeting with President Roosevelt in a last ditch effort to avert war. Acting on a suggestion by one of the envoys, on December 6, 1941, Roosevelt sent Emperor Hirohito a personal appeal for peace. "The son of man has just sent his final message to the Son of God," Roosevelt told White House dinner guests that evening. The President had written: "Both of us, for the sake of the peoples not only of our own great countries but for the sake of humanity in neighboring territories, have a sacred duty to restore traditional amity and prevent further death and destruction to the world."[8]

There was no indication that the Emperor shared Roosevelt's sentiments or that he even read the conciliatory message. The Japanese fleet had already put to sea en route to its rendezvous with history. Late that same night, as Roosevelt and his commerce secretary Harry Hopkins sat talking in the Oval Study, a courier arrived with some intercepts of decoded Japanese radio messages. Roosevelt learned that Tokyo had rejected his latest peace proposal. It was no longer a case of "if," only of "when" the fighting would begin. Roosevelt also knew from naval intelligence reports that the Japanese fleet had put to sea. The world held its breath and waited, but not for long.

Just a few days earlier, on December 3, Hong Kong's commander Christopher M. Maltby and his staff officers had toured the border area north of the colony. Despite reports from British spies in China that Japanese troops were massing for an attack on Hong Kong, Maltby continued to ignore the warnings. He was confident that the six battalions under his command—two British, two Indian, and two Canadian, totaling about 13,000 men—could ward off any enemy offensive. As late as December 7, dispatches sent from Hong Kong to the War Office in London stated that rumors of a Japanese military buildup were "certainly exaggerated and have the appearance of being deliberately fostered by the Japanese who, judging by their defensive preparations around Canton, appear distinctly nervous of being attacked."[9]

Charles was much less sanguine about the situation. He had spent a lot of time working with and observing the Japanese army—particularly the 38th Infantry Regiment, which happened to be one of the enemy units poised at the border. Charles knew that while some of the Japanese troops appeared to be shabby and ill equipped, appearances were deceiving; this was an enemy not to be underestimated. Charles was filled with a profound sense of foreboding. When he arrived at Mickey's flat for lunch on December 6, a photographer was snapping pictures of Mickey and the baby. Charles posed reluctantly. Later, he told Mickey how he had spent the previous night at a dinner party hosted by Lieutenant General Takashi Sakai, commander of the 23rd Army, the Japanese occupying force in the Canton area of southern China. Everything had seemed "normal," yet Charles had a nagging sense that his hosts were being almost too cordial, too jovial; he could not help but wonder if this was the proverbial calm before the storm.

Mickey invited several friends for drinks on Sunday evening at Charles's flat. They included Colin MacDonald, who was the correspondent for the *London Times,* and Dorothy Jenner, "an amusing Australian newspaperwoman," as Mickey described her.[10] Jenner had been a silent film star before she began writing under the pen name "Andrea." Charles, who was supposed to spend the night at headquarters, ignored the orders and tried his best to be cheerful. The guests stayed for dinner even though it was a subdued gathering. "Charles's uniform and the fact that he sat in front of the radio most of the evening, had a dampening effect upon our spirits," Mickey wrote.[11]

Dorothy Jenner initially declined when the vanilla soufflé came around for seconds. "You'd better take some more. You never know when you'll next be offered vanilla soufflé," Charles had cautioned. Many times over the next three and a half years, Jenner would remember those words and how delicious that extra serving of dessert had tasted; like all Hong Kong civilians who were interned by the Japanese, Jenner starved. By the time of her liberation in the summer of 1945, her once "ample figure" had shrunk to just eighty pounds.[12]

Mickey stayed behind after the guests left Charles's flat about midnight. They listened to a radio broadcast from Tokyo at 4 A.M. on December 8, Hong

Kong time, and an hour later Mickey went home to feed Carola. It had been raining, and the air on the Peak that Monday morning was clear and cool. It was going to be a nice day, Mickey remembered thinking. How wrong she was! In the immortal words of President Franklin D. Roosevelt, it was "a day that shall live forever in infamy."

Mickey was feeding the baby when Charles called at about 6 A.M. After Mickey's departure, he had gone downtown to "the Battle Box," the British military's underground bunker on Queens Road Central. There, thirteen stories below street level, Charles sat down at the radio set to relieve Major "Monkey" Giles of the Royal Marines, the senior naval intelligence staff officer in Hong Kong. Giles had spent the night monitoring Japanese radio broadcasts. At 4:45 A.M., Charles was listening when a voice on Radio Tokyo interrupted some classical music to announce that units of the Japanese Imperial Navy and Air Force were attacking American and British forces in the Pacific. Charles roused Giles, who had just gone to sleep on a camp cot in the radio room. "The war's started. You don't want to miss it, do you?" he shouted. Charles then rang Major General Maltby's aide to alert him to the news: that morning, (Hong Kong, on the other side of the international date line, is a day ahead),

The view from atop the Peak, looking northward across Hong Kong harbor toward Kowloon, circa 1940.
National Archives of Canada, Neg. #PA161884

just before first light on December 7 in Hawaii, 366 Japanese warplanes had taken off from aircraft carriers for a devastating sneak attack on the U.S. naval base at Pearl Harbor. By the time Charles roused the alarm in Hong Kong, the "Battle of Hawaii," as the Japanese media dubbed it, was already over.

The word "battle" was a misnomer, for the American forces at Pearl Harbor had been taken completely by surprise. At five minutes before 8 A.M. on that sunny Sunday morning, most people were still having breakfast or were snuggled in bed. Their peace and quiet was shattered by the angry drone of warplanes, and then the cacophony of falling bombs, explosions, and gunfire. All hell had broken loose. By the time the Japanese pilots returned to their carriers two hours later, the United States naval base was in ruins; 2,330 Americans lay dead or dying amidst the flaming wreckage. Seven battleships had been sunk or badly damaged, and 188 military aircraft had been destroyed. Japanese losses were twenty-nine aircraft and sixty-four crewmen.

Within hours, the Japanese launched a series of surprise attacks on other American bases at Guam, Wake Island, and the Midway Islands, and troops were landed on the Malayan coast near the British colony of Singapore. "The balloon's gone up," Charles told Mickey when he called her at 6 A.M. Hong Kong time. "It's come. War."[13]

• • •

It was two hours before the general alarm sounded throughout Hong Kong on what the British refer to as "Imperial Rescript Day"—the day the Japanese emperor issued a proclamation declaring war on Great Britain. During that time, wild rumors swept the colony. One of the first things that Mickey did after Charles's call was to ring Hilda Selwyn-Clarke. Charles had arranged that if war began Mickey and Carola would move in with Hilda and her husband, Selwyn Selwyn-Clarke, Hong Kong's chief of medical services. Their spacious home was higher up on the Peak than Mickey's flat, and presumably it was safe from any "unpleasantries" that might occur. At 8 A.M., Charles called again to assure himself that Mickey had made plans to move. As they were talking, the peace of the Hong Kong morning was pierced by the wail of air-raid sirens. Then from the direction of the harbor came sounds that Mickey knew all too well from her time in Chungking: the whump of falling bombs and the *tata-tata-tata* of anti-aircraft guns. Mickey raced out onto her terrace. Across the harbor, she saw flames and smoke rising above Kowloon. Japanese warplanes from Canton, 125 miles northwest, were attacking the RAF squadron at Kai Tak Airport. Mickey's neighbor, a British man to whom she had never spoken before, was puffing on his pipe as he surveyed the scene.

"Good morning," Mickey said. "Here it is."

"Yes," he replied, shaking his head in disbelief. "Japan's committed suicide."[14]

Mickey, like Charles, was not quite so sure. Her doubts proved to be well founded, for that initial air strike was one of the keys to the success of what the Japanese had planned. In bombing the runways and hangars at Kai Tak, the Japanese had destroyed five aging RAF planes: two Walrus amphibians and three Vickers Wildebeeste torpedo bombers. All were more than ten years old, slow and useful only for reconnaissance flights. The Chiefs of Staff in London had refused requests for a fighter squadron for Hong Kong because the airport there was considered an easy target. As a result, the outdated planes based there were no match for enemy fighters. The RAF pilots were under orders to fly them only at dawn or dusk when the light was poor, and only if there was "an opportunity" to attack an enemy ship. How the pilots were to know an opportunity existed *unless* they flew is unclear.

Major General Maltby had assumed that Japanese troops posed the main threat to Kai Tak Airport, and the only enemy units in the area being in occupied China, fifteen miles north of the colony, he placed his faith in the Gindrinkers' Line to discourage any attack. Named after a bay, the eleven-mile-long network of slit trenches, barbed wire, and pillboxes was strung out across the rugged, sparsely populated land along the Chinese border. Japanese spies had pinpointed the gaps between the line's defenses, rendering it useless, even

Hong Kong, fall 1941: (l–r) Agnes Smedley, Mickey, Hilda Selwyn-Clarke and daughter Mary, Margaret Watson Sloss.
Courtesy Agnes Smedley Papers, Arizona State University

if the Japanese had chosen to attack Kai Tak Airport by land. No matter, it took the enemy planes just five minutes to destroy the runways, facilities, and most of the planes there. Given the raid's success, Hong Kong's outnumbered defenders were now sitting ducks for enemy aircraft. Triumphant Japanese pilots swooped low over Kowloon after their raid. They dropped bundles of leaflets that warned of bloody consequences unless the colony surrendered.

From her vantage point, Mickey watched as the planes roared off into the northwest sky. She returned to her flat feeling dazed and shaken. Inside, she found her wash amah, Ah Choy, folding laundry in the bedroom. "You scared, missy?" she asked softly.

"Nooooo," said Mickey. "You're not scared, are you, Ah Choy?"

"Yes," the woman admitted. Then she began sobbing.

Mickey walked slowly over to Carola's crib. The baby had remained fast asleep through all the excitement. No, Mickey decided as she stood there, *she* was not yet frightened for herself; she was terrified for her baby. Mickey had seen the ferocity of the Japanese army at Shanghai. She had also witnessed the carnage of the Chungking air raids, and like everyone else in China, she remembered the horrifying fate of Nanking when it had fallen to the Japanese three years earlier; drunken troops had slaughtered 200,000 Chinese.

Even as these thoughts raced through Mickey's mind, the first of what would be the two-act tragedy of the Battle of Hong Kong was unfolding in the hills above Kowloon. British commanders, anticipating an attack from a Japanese naval task force that was lurking just south of Hong Kong Island, had redeployed their forces. Maltby and his staff remained confident that the troops stationed on the Gindrinkers' Line could repel any enemy attack. The Japanese feint worked perfectly. As their planes were attacking Kai Tak Airport, hundreds of their soldiers from the 38th Infantry Regiment crossed the border separating the New Territory from occupied China. These advance units of the 60,000-man Japanese 23rd Army traveled quickly on foot and in armored cars. They encountered no resistance during the first four miles of the attack. This puzzled their field commander, Lieutenant General Sano Tadayoshi. He feared a trap, but ordered his troops to press ahead regardless.

What Tadayoshi soon grasped was that for all the talk of British military prowess, Hong Kong's defenders were ill prepared, poorly armed, and led by officers out of touch with reality. The strength and speed of the Japanese offensive caught the British off guard. Forward elements of the 38th Infantry Regiment had reached the Gindrinkers' Line early on the afternoon of December 8. Guided by detailed maps drafted by the observant Colonel Suzuki and other spies, the Japanese troops made quick work of the defenders. Japanese commandos infiltrated the British positions that night, killing the sentries who patrolled the vital gaps between the gun positions. The Allied soldiers in those positions then did not stand a chance. Most were still in bed early on the morning of December 9 when they were slaughtered by Japanese grenades, bullets, and bayonets. With them died any hope of stemming the enemy advance.

Japanese commanders knew this and were now hell-bent on quick victory. Thousands of battle-hardened troops poured through a widening gap in the British lines. The Japanese chased the defenders down the Kowloon Peninsula and onto Hong Kong Island in just five days—four ahead of the schedule drawn up by military planners in Tokyo. By Friday, December 12, the Japanese army, aided by Chinese fifth-columnist saboteurs in Hong Kong, had overrun Kowloon. Lieutenant General Sakai was poised to begin part two of his battle plan: the siege of Hong Kong Island.

It began early on the morning of Saturday, December 13 when Japanese artillery in Kowloon began a murderous barrage on Victoria. Shells rained down on Victoria Peak and on the town below. At 9:45 A.M. there was an unexpected lull in the firing. A launch bearing a Japanese delegation sped across Hong Kong harbor from Kowloon toward Victoria pier. On board were three high-ranking Japanese officers, a civilian interpreter, two female civilian hostages, and a couple of dachshunds that belonged to one of the hostages. Flying from the boat's stern was a large white flag. Across the bow was a white banner with the words "Peace Mission."

Colonel Tokuchi Tada, the head of the Japanese delegation, stepped ashore and was met by startled British officers. The men saluted smartly as a heavy-set Japanese officer with a portfolio in hand announced in English, "Here is a peace offer from our government. Please send it to your Governor-General, Sir Mark Young." That letter demanded that the colony surrender by 4 P.M. that day or face all-out attack.

"For a few minutes we stood, silent, looking at one another. We were in the middle of the British garrison, yet here were three Jap officers obviously demanding surrender," wrote American journalist Gwen Dew, an acquaintance of Mickey's who was the correspondent for the *Detroit News.* "They were all smaller than I, and I'm five-five. A cordon was flung around the block; and behind British soldiers with fixed bayonets, curious onlookers surged. Someone tried to break through. There were shots."[15]

Presently, a staff car bearing a British flag drove onto the pier. Charles jumped out and saluted the Japanese officers, whom he recognized. They then exchanged some papers and spoke quietly for a few moments in Japanese. With that, Charles bowed, got back into the staff car, and sped off toward Government House. After he had gone, Tada approached Gwen Dew, who was busy snapping photos. Tada asked if Dew would like to take a picture of the Japanese delegation. She did. Afterward, Tada chatted obligingly and volunteered information for a photo caption. "The names were important [to the Japanese officers]," Dew realized, "for they were making history."[16]

As the crowd on the pier awaited Charles's return, the Japanese released one of the female hostages, a pregnant Russian woman. The other, the wife of a British civil servant, reluctantly returned to the launch with one of her captors after leaving her pet dogs with one of the steel-helmeted sentries on the pier. After fifteen minutes, Charles returned from his meeting with the governor. Young's response to the Japanese ultimatum was one word: "No." An official communiqué later announced that Sir Mark had rejected the terms of a proposed surrender. "It can now be revealed that the Japanese who came from Kowloon under cover of a white flag brought a letter inquiring if His Excellency the Governor was willing to negotiate for surrender," the communiqué said. "His Excellency summarily rejected the proposal. This Colony is not only strong enough to resist all attempts at invasion, but all the resources of the British Empire, of the United States of America, and the Republic of China are behind us, and those who have sought peace can rest assured that there will never be any surrender to the Japanese."[17] The Japanese bombardment of Hong Kong resumed with renewed vigor at 4 P.M., as threatened.

Initially, only a handful of Hong Kong residents had grasped how grave the colony's situation was at the onset of the Japanese attack on December 8; an air of unreality continued to prevail. Even after the enemy had seized Kowloon, cut off most of the colony's water supplies and began shelling Victoria, some British commanders continued to insist that the Japanese would not try to invade the island. Some people—civilian and military alike—believed it was only a matter of time before planes and ships from Singapore arrived to chase away the impertinent Japanese. British radio reports told of units of the Chinese army that were supposedly attacking the Japanese from the rear, and there were heartening messages of encouragement and support from the King and military leaders in London.

However, there were also alarming reports that Allied forces elsewhere in Southeast Asia had suffered crushing defeats. On December 10, Japanese torpedo bombers had attacked and sunk the British battleship *Prince of Wales* and her sister ship, *Repulse*, off Singapore, and a Japanese invasion force was sweeping across the Philippines. From Shanghai came word that Japanese troops had seized all of the city; Mickey hoped that Sinmay and her other friends there had fled. If not, they were now in prison or dead. The Allies were on the run all across the South Pacific. The presence of Japanese officers on Victoria pier demanding Hong Kong's surrender brought this reality home with startling clarity. It also dashed any hopes that rescuers would arrive from Singapore.

Sir Mark's terse rejection of the surrender terms enraged Sakai, the Japanese commander. He responded by ordering an all-out two-day blitz. This move was intended to break British morale and soften up the island's defenses for a planned invasion. Unlike Chungking, there were no air-raid shelters in Hong Kong where civilians could seek refuge. Not that it mattered. Artillery shells were far more terrifying and lethal than aerial bombs. "Once a bomb has popped, it has popped, and the plane can't stay in one place pegging away at you," Mickey wrote. "Shells are different. Shells keep coming and hitting the same spot. Shells are the devil."[18]

The next few days were a blur of confusion, fear, and carnage. When she was not tending to Carola, Mickey worked in the War Memorial Hospital helping with an inventory of supplies. That did not take long, because in peacetime the hospital had been a private nursing home, and it was not well equipped. The task of organizing what was there was a welcome diversion for Mickey, who did not see Charles again until Wednesday. When she did, he was downcast. Charles took no satisfaction from seeing that his prediction was about to come true: British rule in the Far East was at an end; Hong Kong was indefensible, and the locals could not be counted on to rally to the British cause.

Charles was determined to do his duty come what may, and he urged Mickey to do likewise. She did, but fear became an enemy that gnawed at the heart and the brain. Hilda Selwyn-Clarke also fell victim, weeping uncontrollably at times. She sobbed about how the children—her own six-year-old daughter Mary, Mickey's baby Carola, and all the other children in Hong Kong—were going to die. Hilda was under enormous strain and guilt, particularly after her husband had ordered nurses at the auxiliary nursing stations on the mainland to remain at their posts even as Japanese troops swarmed over Kowloon. The Selwyn-Clarkes' house was besieged by relatives of these nurses, many demanding to know why the women had been abandoned to their fate, which in some cases had been gang rape and death. "Strictly speaking, I suppose Selwyn was right; I suppose there isn't a question of it," Mickey later wrote. "Nurses must be left to care for the wounded, and in the old days when war was more civilized, the days in which Selwyn was mentally living, doctors and nurses were treated with respect by the enemy. Maybe. I have my doubts."[19]

Mickey's own fears were eased by Ah King, who arrived to supervise the Selwyn-Clarke household when all the other servants fled to escape the shelling and bombing. Mickey joined Hilda and others in the house when they took refuge in the basement. They emerged briefly on Sunday afternoon, when Charles, Alf Bennett, and Max Oxford came calling. The trio were dressed in combat gear. Everyone gathered in the Selwyn-Clarke's drawing room, where Ah King calmly served drinks. It was an eerie, almost surreal, scene.

Inside the house, this small group sipped cocktails and chatted as they had done countless times under happier circumstances; it was all terribly dignified and civil. Outside, there was a constant rumble from the enemy shells raining down on the Peak and the sporadic return fire from the British artillery. As they sat sipping drinks, Mickey and Charles held hands. Charles noticed that she was shaking. "I'm worried about you," Mickey whispered.

He would be all right, he assured her. Charles explained that he and his fellow intelligence officers spent their days in the underground bunker that served as Hong Kong's military headquarters and communications center. If anything did "happen to him," he assured Mickey, she and Carola would be looked after. Charles confided he had sent his will to Mickey's brother-in-law Mitchell Dawson in Chicago. All the money in Charles's bank accounts in England, as well as the title to Conygar, the family estate in Dorset that he had inherited from his maternal aunt, would go to Mickey and Carola.

The discussion of these arrangements was cut short by a volley of incoming shells that shook the windows. As the group raced outside to see what was happening, Charles advised Mickey and Hilda that the women and children should move somewhere safer. He suggested Repulse Bay on the far side of the island. With that, Charles, Alf, and Max marched off to rejoin the battle. Mickey and her companions wiped away tears as they watched the men go. Mickey knew it was impossible for her, Carola, and the others to act on Charles's advice. There was nowhere safe now, and it was too late to leave town. They were trapped.

• • •

The final act of the battle of Hong Kong began on Thursday, December 18. That night, after several failed attempts, Japanese troops landed on the east end of the island. Under cover of darkness, foul weather, and a heavy pall of black smoke from burning oil tanks at North Point, they evaded British flares and searchlights to slip across Lyemun Pass. Just a year earlier, a writer for *National Geographic* magazine had described the formidable British defenses at this strategic 500-yard-wide narrows this way: "Enough barbed wire to fence in all the cattle in Texas stretches and tangles about hilltop searchlight posts, powder magazines, gun emplacements, and across valley trails up which enemy landing parties might try to march."[20] Even this was not enough to hold back the determined enemy. Despite horrendous casualties, the Japanese troops stormed ashore, gaining a beachhead. When they did, wave after wave of reinforcements poured ashore, screaming *Banzai-ai!* as they threw themselves at the outnumbered defenders. The Japanese roped together and bayoneted twenty captured Hong Kong volunteer soldiers, whose bodies were then pitched down the slopes and into the harbor. Miraculously, two of the men survived to give evidence against the killers before the postwar Hong Kong War Crimes Court.

From high up on the Peak, Mickey watched the battle on the morning of Friday, December 19. In the distance, she saw and heard the fighting as the Japanese troops bypassed Victoria and fought their way inland. Japanese commanders had two objectives: split the island's defenses and seize the town's water reservoirs in the surrounding hills. They realized that without drinking water Hong Kong would be forced to surrender quickly. The British, Canadian, and Indian defenders knew this too, and they resisted with grim desperation.

As fighting spread across the thirty-two square miles of island, rumors of Japanese atrocities fueled a growing panic among Hong Kong's civilian population as the inevitability of defeat became clear. Victoria's transportation system crumbled. The power was cut, and the town slid into anarchy. Chinese thugs and pro-Japanese gangs roamed the streets and looted shops and homes. Fearing the worst, Selwyn-Clarke sent word that his wife and the others staying in his house should seek refuge in War Memorial Hospital. There was nowhere else to run.

Mickey was working at the hospital when she saw some of the people who had been staying at the Selwyn-Clarke house trudging toward her along a hallway. They were lugging belongings. Then Mickey spotted Ah Cheung with Carola in her arms. A coolie accompanying them carried Mickey's suitcases. "The Japs were coming!" one of the British men informed Mickey. Terror and resignation were evident in his hushed voice. The words stunned her. Mickey was only vaguely aware of staggering into the dispensary, where she collapsed on a chair and began sobbing. For the first time, she realized that they might all die at the hands of the Japanese—her baby, the Selwyn-Clarkes. Everyone. And she had no idea what had become of Charles. It had been two days since Mickey had heard from him. Perhaps he was already dead. Charles had always been careful never to discuss his work with her, but Mickey had deduced that he was involved in intelligence work. If he was taken prisoner by the Japanese, Charles faced "a rough go of it." Mickey knew how ruthlessly efficient the Japanese were in extracting information from prisoners.

"I wasn't fated to stay long in the War Memorial Hospital, but my impressions of that short interval are vivid," Mickey wrote.[21] The nurses who ran the facility with an iron hand were determined to maintain order. Even when the enemy shelling intensified, they resented the tearful, hungry, dirty, and tired refugees who came knocking on the hospital door. Most were turned away, and Mickey knew if she had not been part of the Selwyn-Clarkes' extended "family," she, too, would have been told to leave. With shells falling all around and looters and fifth-columnist saboteurs in the streets, she had nowhere else to go.

Mickey and Carola slept on the floor of a hospital room they shared with the Selwyn-Clarkes and several other people. Finding enough to eat was a major concern. When the hospital's Chinese kitchen staff fled, Ah King stepped into the breach and began cooking. However, his job became impossible when the members of Hong Kong's Food Control Committee moved into the hospital and assumed responsibility for rationing the limited supplies in the pantry. Mickey noticed that committee members always ate before everyone else. They dined on potted meat and bread, while the others made do with meager servings of rice or cereal.

Mickey cared less about herself than about finding enough food to keep Carola alive. She continued to be haunted by recurring nightmares about her baby starving to death. As Carola's appetite grew and she refused to breastfeed, she cried for powdered milk formula. Even so, Mickey's worries about food and personal safety vanished in a split second on the morning of Saturday, December 20, when Hilda breathlessly reported some news she had just heard from her husband: Charles had been badly wounded on Friday in the Battle of Shouson Hill, on the south side of the island near Repulse Bay. A Japanese bullet had caught Charles high on the left side of his chest. He had lain in a paddy field overnight. The medics who found him had carried him to Queen Mary Hospital in Victoria, where Selwyn-Clarke was on duty. It was he who had sent word that Charles's doctors thought he might survive his wounds.

"I am inclined to gloss over it and say I felt nothing but a very strong impulse to go to Charles," Mickey wrote, "but that wouldn't be true. I remember feeling like a volcano, and then I was mixed up in a ridiculous quarrel, after all those days of self-control, with Hilda. She didn't think I should go to the Queen Mary. She was willing to fight like a lioness to keep me with her."[22]

Mickey refused to listen. After making arrangements to have her friend Vera Armstrong come to fetch Carola and Ah Cheung (Vera had taken refuge in the basement of a friend's house not far from the hospital), Mickey donned a tin helmet and set off down the Peak on foot, accompanied by a young man who was on his way to Happy Valley. He agreed to escort her to the downtown business district. From there she hoped to hitch a ride to Queen Mary Hospital, in the town's west end. That was good enough for Mickey. She had resolved to go to Charles or die trying.

23

IT TOOK MICKEY several hours to travel the five miles to Queen Mary Hospital. Each time Japanese planes flew over, Mickey and her escort ran for their lives. Fortunately, it was quieter downtown, where the two parted company. British troops were still in control there, and the Japanese were not bombing or shelling; they did not want to destroy their prize.

Mickey chanced to run into Gordon King, the doctor who had delivered Carola. King and two medical students were on a supply mission for an emergency clinic at Ling Nan University. Mickey walked to the campus with them, then caught a ride in an ambulance going to Queen Mary Hospital, where she arrived about 3 P.M.

All was quiet in the streets around the hospital, and apart from the fact that the elevators were not working, everything seemed normal. Neither the doctors nor the nurses gave any hint they were concerned about the battle that was raging all around them. Mickey concluded they were calmed by the "serene conviction that they, above all others, were immune" from the carnage that was taking place.[1] She hoped that they were right.

At first Mickey did not recognize Charles, so pale was he from loss of blood. He lay on a camp cot in a room in the maternity ward, which he shared with another wounded British army officer, a fair-haired, twenty-four-year-old captain named Bill Wiseman. He had only one leg, having apparently lost the limb some time earlier, for it was the ankle on his good leg that was bandaged. It did not matter that the bullet had been a British machine-gun bullet—so-called "friendly fire;" Wiseman was in a lot of pain.

But Charles was alert. He looked up in surprise when Mickey took off her tin helmet. She sat down on a chair next to his cot and reached for his hand. "I didn't mean for you to come," Charles said weakly. "I just wanted them to notify you."

"Well, I *wanted* to come," Mickey replied.

As they talked, Charles explained what had happened to him. He and Alf Bennett had driven to the south side of the island, to a residential enclave known as Shouson Hill, where fighting was intense. There they encountered a small group of retreating East Indian troops whose commanding officer, Lieutenant-Colonel Gerald Kidd, had been killed. Charles stepped into the breach and attempted to lead a counterattack. That is when "some bugger got me just as I was climbing out of a nullah. I never even saw him," Charles explained.[2]

Afterward, he lay where he had fallen, and the battle moved on. Flies buzzed, and the sun shone down relentlessly. Then came the chill of the night. The blood oozing from Charles's chest wound colored the muddy ground beneath him a sticky reddish brown. As his life slowly drained away, there was nothing he could do about it. Charles was too weak to move; he could not even cry out. "I thought I was dying," he recalled. "I lay there wishing I would hurry up and die, because it was so cold."[3] By the time a British naval officer—who was himself killed in battle the very next day—chanced to find and rescue him, Charles was delirious and near death. His biggest concern was not dying, but rather the fact that he had money in his wallet. He asked over and over for someone to notify Mickey and let her know that he had $112 for her.

Charles was taken to Queen Mary Hospital, Hong Kong's best. Following emergency surgery, doctors decided Charles might live after all. The Japanese sniper's bullet had passed through the left side of his chest, narrowly missing the lung and other major organs. A fraction of an inch either way and Charles would have died instantly.

Determined to do all that she could for Charles, Mickey arranged to stay at the home of a nurse who lived near the hospital, a woman named Veronica Weill. The fighting was drawing ever closer, and it was now impossible for Mickey to return to War Memorial Hospital, even if she had wanted to do so.

Captain Bill Wiseman, 1946. He's smiling because he has returned home to England following his liberation from a Hong Kong POW camp to find his bank account flush with five years of back pay.
Courtesy Bill Wiseman

Mickey learned that Veronica's mother had taken refuge there and was a member of the Food Control Committee. At Mickey's urging, Veronica phoned her mother to ask about Carola. The news was not reassuring. Ah Cheung and Carola had waited all day for Mickey's friend Vera Armstrong to come for them. When Vera had failed to appear, Ah Cheung and Carola vanished. Veronica rang the Armstrong house to speak with Vera. Over a crackling line, Vera explained that she had been unable to reach the hospital; the ferocity of the bombardment had forced her to turn back. Mickey, sick with worry and guilt, was "ready to tear my hair out by the roots," as she said.[4] She could do nothing other than wait and pray that Carola and her amah were safe.

Mickey spent the next few days at Charles's bedside. Sometimes she helped the nursing staff make bandages for the steady stream of casualties who were arriving. The job helped Mickey keep her mind off her missing baby. It also allowed her to escape Charles's questions. Now that he was becoming more aware of his surroundings, he wanted to see Carola. Each time that he did, Mickey evaded his requests. She could not bear to tell him the truth: she had no idea where their baby was.

This uncertainty lasted for three days. Mickey later would learn how Ah King had saved Carola's life. The baby's amah Ah Cheung wanted to run off in search of her own twelve-year-old daughter, but faithful Ah King had convinced her to stay with Carola. Ah Cheung and the baby hid in a room in the hospital's cellar to escape the shelling. Ah King brought them food and water, which he smuggled out of the pantry under the noses of the nurses and members of the Food Control Committee.

A friend of Mickey's, an American businessman named Bill Hunt, saved the day. Sick with worry, Mickey had called various people to inquire about Carola. Hunt, who was in Hong Kong only because he had missed a plane, was holed up with six other men at a room in the Grips. He volunteered to go to the War Memorial Hospital to look for Carola and her amah. If they were there, he pledged to bring them to Mickey. That was much easier said than done, of course. By the morning of December 24, the battle for Hong Kong was in its final hours. The Japanese now controlled most of the island. From across the harbor in Kowloon came the sounds of Christmas music. "A Merry Christmas to the gallant British soldiers," a Japanese voice intoned over loudspeakers. "You have fought a good fight, but you are outnumbered. Now is the time to surrender. If you don't, within twenty-four hours we will give you all that we've got. A Merry Christmas to the gallant British soldiers. . . ."[5]

The scene in Victoria's streets was bizarre. Shells were exploding everywhere, there was constant gunfire, and Christmas music blared from across the harbor. Bill Hunt dodged the shell fire, wreckage, snipers, and gangs of roving looters to race at breakneck speed to the War Memorial Hospital. When the car he was driving was wrecked, he commandeered Selwyn-Clarke's vehicle. Late that morning, Hunt and his passengers—who included Carola, Ah King, and Ah Cheung—and a load of canned goods arrived at the Weill home. A tearful Mickey was reunited with Carola. Mickey was forever grateful to Bill Hunt, who had bravely risked his own life to save the lives of a child and other people who were strangers to him.

Hilda Selwyn-Clarke, Veronica's mother, and several other people who had been at War Memorial Hospital appeared at Queen Mary not long after Hunt's arrival. The situation on the Peak was deteriorating rapidly, and there were terrifying rumors about atrocities being committed by the advancing Japanese troops. Charles had warned Mickey that it was customary whenever the Japanese army captured a city for the officers to turn their men loose for three days to "enjoy the fruits of victory." Sometimes things got out of control, as they had in Nanking. There were fears that the same kind of frenzied, drunken bloodletting would take place in Hong Kong. All signs pointed in that direction. On that hot, sunny Christmas morning of 1941, Japanese soldiers massacred more than fifty wounded Canadian soldiers at St. Stephen's Emergency Hospital, on the south side of the island. The helpless men were dragged from their beds, their bandages were ripped off, and then they were bayoneted to death. Two attending doctors were cut down at the door; seven nurses were gang raped before being bayoneted to death.

This was no isolated incident. A St. John's Ambulance Corps nurse who survived a similar ordeal recounted to Gwen Dew what had happened at a military hospital near North Point where the Japanese had shot all the doctors and raped the nurses before killing them too. Dew reported that one doctor had "rushed the Jap firing line with bare hands," only to be slashed to bits.[6] Similar atrocities occurred all over Hong Kong.

In the face of such savagery, Governor Mark Young was determined to somehow hold out to the bitter end, as were Maltby's advisors. Another Japanese surrender demand was rejected early on Christmas morning, but by midday, the situation was hopeless; Hong Kong's remaining defenders were badly outnumbered and bone weary after eighteen days of hard fighting and relentless bombardment. Most were down to their last few rounds of ammunition. Japanese troops had begun occupying key buildings on the Peak. The water supplies in most of Victoria had been cut, as had many of the telephone lines, and Major General Maltby could no longer communicate with the defenders of besieged Fort Stanley on the south side of the island.

At 3 P.M., Sir Mark turned off the gramophone in his office at Government House, where he had been listening to Beethoven records. He then strolled around the corner to see Maltby at the underground military bunker. Maltby's aide-de-camp, Second Lieutenant Ian McGregor, saw the governor approaching. He seemed oblivious to the shells and gunfire. Young was dressed in a beautifully tailored light gray suit and a matching homburg hat. His polished black shoes glistened in the sunlight. "He was unconcernedly swinging a malacca walking stick, as if he was playing truant from the Colonial Office and taking a quiet walk in St. James Park," McGregor would remember. "I called out: 'It's getting a bit hot along there, Sir; better take cover.' He smiled and said, 'Hullo McGregor! Lovely day, isn't it.' And he strolled on, neither slackening nor quickening his pace, completely composed and apparently without a care in the world."[7]

Inside the bunker, Maltby repeated the same message a group of fearful civilians had told Sir Mark only a few hours earlier: the only hope for Hong Kong's defenders and for the 1.7 million civilians trapped by the fighting was to lay down their arms and pray that the Japanese commanders could—and would—restrain their troops. Initially, the governor was adamant that the colony's defenders should fight to the end; in his mind, anything else was unthinkable. He changed his mind after a long and very frank discussion with the general. Sir Mark then instructed Maltby to arrange a surrender. In a final dispatch to his troops, Maltby explained the decision, saying further resistance could only mean "the useless slaughter of the remainder of the garrison, risked severe retaliation on the large civilian population, and could not affect the final outcome."[8]

In late afternoon, just before 5 P.M., the remaining defenders began waving white flags. At first, the Japanese troops assumed it was some sort of trick, so the fighting continued. Then two small parties of British soldiers were sent into Japanese lines to announce Maltby's surrender decision. British historian Oliver Lindsay reported in his book *The Lasting Honour* that a Lieutenant-Colonel White led one of the three-man delegations. The other was headed by H. V. M. ("Monkey") Stewart, the commander of the 1st Middlesex Regiment. Bill Wiseman, who knew Monkey Stewart, recalled him as "a very strong character" who kept a Jack Russell terrier. Oliver Lindsay wrote that Stewart was sent out to convey word of the surrender to the Japanese commander in the Wanchai district of town. "Colonel Shoji Toshishige gleefully reported that a military representative of the Governor, a British Lieutenant-Colonel, accompanied by another man with a small dog had arrived by truck," Lindsay said.[9]

Early that evening, Sir Mark, Major General Maltby, and some of his staff boarded a torpedo boat for the crossing to Kowloon. There they met for forty minutes with General Sakai at his headquarters in the Peninsula Hotel. Then in a brief ceremony in a candlelit ballroom, at 7:30 P.M. on Christmas night, the governor of Hong Kong signed a formal, unconditional surrender. More than 10,000 surviving British, Canadian, and Indian troops laid down their weapons. The next morning, most of them were rounded up and marched off to hastily created prisoner-of-war camps. Some British soldiers who were cut off in the hills above Victoria and at Fort Stanley at first did not hear news of the surrender or refused to believe it; they continued fighting for a brief time. For the most part, though, the British guns fell silent.

Casualty figures revealed that 3,445 Allied soldiers had been killed, were missing, or were seriously wounded; 7,500 civilians were dead. On the other side, 675 Japanese soldiers had died in the battle. What the *Times* of London had described as the "valiant defence" of Hong Kong[10] had come to a terrible, bloody, and (some would later argue) inevitable conclusion. The Union Jack that Japanese soldiers tore down from the flagpole at Fort Stanley on Boxing Day was made of a tattered, bloodstained hospital sheet.

• • •

News of the governor's decision to surrender was greeted with shock and disbelief at the Queen Mary Hospital. Mickey and Charles had been celebrating the day with a bottle of whisky when Hilda burst into the room. She was in tears, her voice breaking. Hilda reported that her husband had telephoned to say Sir Mark had surrendered. Bill Wiseman remembered that a continuous stream of visitors, men and women, military as well as civilians, had come by in the two days before Christmas. Most related news of the battle to Charles and sought his reassurances on various matters.[11] Mickey later said that Charles seemed stunned by the decision to surrender, which he had opposed. "They didn't tell me," he muttered.[12]

Mickey wept on Charles's good shoulder while Hilda went off to spread the news. From outside came the sounds of loud explosions; Charles surmised that British troops were destroying their remaining big guns. That may have been so, or else it is possible that they heard British mines exploding. "There was a tremendous roar as the minefields went up, the entire southwest arc of the sea, three or four miles offshore," Bill Wiseman recalled.[13]

Presently, Wiseman reappeared in his wheelchair to ask "C.R.B."—his nickname for Charles—if the rumors of a surrender were true. Charles said he believed they were, and his words were confirmed when a group of Japanese cavalry charged past the hospital. Mickey knew that the enemy infantry would not be far behind. By the time Mickey's friend Veronica came by to suggest it was time to go home, it was already too late to do so. Through the window came a cacophony of excited voices shouting in Japanese, sporadic gunfire, and the roar of truck engines. Veronica went out onto the veranda to see what was happening. "There they are," she said flatly. "Japs. Little beasts. Swarming all over."[14]

Mickey took a look. Down below, the road was filled with Japanese army trucks. They were pulling up to the front doors of the hospital. As the vehicles screeched to a halt, soldiers leaped out the tailgates and raced off in all directions, rifles at the ready. Mickey knew that she was trapped; there was no point in trying to run or hide. "I had seen Japanese armies before," she later wrote. "I saw the Victory March in Shanghai. My stomach felt queasy, and I knew we would have to face it now or I would begin to be really afraid. I picked up my bag."[15]

Mickey bid Charles a tearful farewell as she and Veronica set off for home on foot. Their plan was simple: walk as quickly as possible without drawing attention to themselves. They prayed that the Japanese soldiers outside would be so busy with other things that they would not notice them. Mickey knew that she had good reason to be fearful. That morning, as she and Veronica were en route to the hospital, they had seen a truck full of auxiliary nurses. When it stopped, several of the women tumbled out and staggered into the hospital arm in arm. After speaking with their companions, Veronica commented about how the nurses were in a "bad way." Mickey asked why. The women had been taken prisoner by Japanese troops at a first-aid post at Happy Valley, Veronica explained; all had been raped and beaten.

That terrible memory was still fresh in Mickey's mind as she, Veronica, and another woman beetled out the gates of Queen Mary Hospital. They had gone only a few steps when two Japanese soldiers spotted them. One was an officer with a sword on his belt. The other was a private. "Oy!" shouted the private. The women pretended not to hear and continued on their way. "Oy!" came a second shout, louder and this time edged with anger. The two soldiers ran after the women. As they stopped, the private approached menacingly. He pointed his rifle and motioned toward the women's arms. Mickey was relieved that he only wanted their wristwatches; they were being mugged. The man grinned with a mouthful of crooked, dirty teeth as he then took the watches from Mickey's companions. He missed hers because she wore it high on her right arm, and in his hurry he did not bother to check there. What Mickey remembered most about the soldier as he walked away with his booty was the overpowering stench of body odor.

Mickey and her companions encountered more Japanese soldiers at home. Three officers had already taken up residence in the Weill's living room. Veronica's mother, who spoke some Japanese, had evidently arrived at an accommodation with them. For now, the officers and their men were sober and reasonably well behaved, although one of them had stolen a wristwatch from an elderly woman who was staying in the house. While doing so, the soldier had motioned toward a sofa and made a crude gesture indicating he wanted something more than just the woman's time. Fortunately, she was able to dissuade him.

Mickey, Carola, Veronica, and several other young women who had taken refuge in the house laid low for the next few days. They did so partly for their own safety and partly because they were concealing Veronica's brother, a British soldier who for now had eluded capture. Mrs. Weill did her best to divert the attentions of the Japanese. She strode about the house, talking to the soldiers and doing whatever she could to make them content.

In the long, idle hours that they spent in hiding, Mickey and her companions had lots of time to think and to worry. They worried about loved ones. They worried about what would happen to Hong Kong. But mostly they worried about themselves and the dangers they faced from the Japanese soldiers who seemed so intent on committing mayhem. Mickey wondered if they would be robbed or murdered. Or raped. "When you talk about (wartime) 'atrocities' that is the first thing you think of," Mickey later wrote. "There is a horror about it, and there is also a fascination. . . . We seem to have a sort of race jealousy that is manifested in our lynchings and in special interest people always show in the sex behavior of other races."[16]

Mickey had been in China long enough to know that Japanese officers allowed their men to engage in mass rape for a reason. "They know that it is the quickest, surest way to humiliate a community. I think that they rape almost as a religious duty, a sacrifice to the God of Victory, a symbol of their triumphant power," she wrote.[17]

The more Mickey mused about this, the angrier it made her. After all, she decided, stripped of its psychological terror, battlefield rape is just another physical aggression men commit against women. What gives rape its real impact as a weapon of war is the age-old notion that women are the prized property of men. To the victor go the spoils of war; thus, the ultimate humiliation a victorious soldier can heap on his vanquished foe is to defile that man's wife and daughters. In Mickey's mind, the most effective means of dealing with "the misery caused by war rape" was to change the way we react to it. "My suggestions to alleviate the misery . . . are not too practical," she conceded. "I want us to lift the guilt burden from the minds of victims. To do this we would have to uproot centuries of diametrically opposed ideas. We would have to teach [young women] that rape is simply a physical hazard, one of the penalties of war which might possibly happen to anyone. . . . I realize I am trying to go against nature. We don't scare the girls deliberately; we are scared ourselves, and we just pass it on."[18]

When Mickey wrote those words more than half a century ago, most people had trouble dealing with them rationally. Many people were puzzled, some were outraged. The whole issue of war rape was still too raw, too emotional, and too immediate. Mickey accepted this and did not let it bother her. Holed up in a spare room in the Weill house as she was, powerless, vulnerable, and surrounded by drunken enemy soldiers, Mickey drew strength and courage from her unorthodox views. They helped her survive the ordeal of those dark days.

Later, when she encountered friends, the question that inevitably came up was, "Were you, um . . . Did you have any *trouble* with the Japanese soldiers?" Mickey's answer was no; she escaped being raped, although many other women in Hong Kong were not so fortunate. The situation was at its worst in the Happy Valley section of the island, where some of the fiercest fighting of the Battle of Hong Kong occurred. "(People) who lived there told me they can never forget the screams of the women," Gwen Dew reported. "No woman was respected—Chinese, Portuguese, Filipino, French, and British. Nor was age given any consideration."[19]

Mickey saw none of this where she was, although she did *hear* many stories of Chinese women being raped. Was it because drunken Japanese soldiers found Chinese women more attractive than whites, she wondered? Or had the soldiers been reined in by their officers, who were determined to show the snooty Brits that they, too, could behave as gentlemen? Mickey could not decide.

As Rudyard Kipling had observed, "Oh, East is East, and West is West, and never the twain shall meet."[20] The world was a much bigger place in 1941. Few Westerners ever visited Japan, and vice versa. There was little trade, and little other contact; the era of Japanese-manufactured goods flooding the Western retail market was still a long way off. Prejudice and racism, fueled sometimes by simple ignorance, sometimes by pseudo-scientific or quasi-religious theories of racial superiority, had always been central to the behavior of whites in the Far East. With the war raging, the same antipathies now fed incredible brutality and hatred on both sides.

Fortunately, the situation in Hong Kong calmed down after the first few days. Japanese commanders finally reasserted control over their men. By that time, the jubilant soldiers had begun to sober up after drinking all the liquor they had looted from homes, shops, and restaurants—every bottle that Hong Kong residents had been unable to pour down their drains before fleeing.

Veronica's mother did what she could to placate the Japanese who had taken up residence in her house; when one of the soldiers fell ill with malaria, she located some quinacrine. Her efforts paid off, for the soldiers in the Weill home remained relatively well behaved. Unfortunately, their civility did not extend to the matter of toilet manners. They urinated everywhere in the house, mostly on the floors. One of Mickey's friends reported that when the Japanese soldiers who had occupied her flat moved on, they trashed the place. But not before carefully arranging her best linen doilies on the living room floor and methodically defecating on each little square.

• • •

After several days in hiding, Mickey and her companions gradually emerged. The women found if they stayed together in groups of three or four, dressed inconspicuously, they could make it back and forth to the hospital, usually without any trouble. Initially, the Japanese had not disturbed the patients in the hospital. "The only Nips seen on the wards were offering to buy Parker pens and/or Rolex watches," Bill Wiseman later recorded in an account of those days that he wrote for his sons.[21]

The situation changed soon enough. Enemy officers began coming "in droves" to visit Charles; he still had many friends and admirers in high places. Some Japanese officers came because they knew him from his prewar liaison work with the 38th Infantry Regiment. They were eager to pay Charles their respects, as was required by *bushido*, the ancient code of honor among Japanese warriors. Others came by for "business reasons"—because of who Charles was and what he knew in his work as a British intelligence officer. Some arrived simply because they were curious to see this foreigner who wrote and spoke Japanese like a gentleman. If Charles's visitors came calling while Mickey was at the hospital, she quietly retreated to a corner. Mickey stepped forward to offer a light any time one of the Japanese took out a cigarette. Invariably, someone would ask Charles who Mickey was. There would be much nodding of heads as he explained. Then attentions would turn to Bill Wiseman, lying in the bed beside that of Charles. The Japanese were fascinated by his missing leg.

Wiseman, who spoke no Japanese, wondered what was being said about him. When he found out one day, he also learned that as Charles gained strength he also recovered his sense of humor, which was mischievous at times. Wiseman recalled waking one day to find the room filled with Japanese officers. "I thought, 'Christ, this is a nightmare!' So I went back to sleep again," he said. "I woke up after a bit, and the room *was* full of Nips. Judging by their rank tabs, they were pretty senior. They all stood up and bowed when they saw I was awake. I was dumbfounded. Charles was nattering away in Japanese, and so I lay back and wondered what was going on.

"When they left, several Japanese soldiers brought in canned goods for Charles. He distributed a whole whack of stuff to all of the wounded officers. I said to Charles, 'What was all that about? Why did those Japanese stand up and bow to me?'

" 'Oh,' he said. 'They wanted to know why you had a wooden leg. I told them you'd stopped a German tank at Dunkirk by sticking your foot into the track.'

"Although he was a senior officer, I said, 'You bloody fool!' Charles laughed and laughed. He thought it was very funny. I was horrified. But that was typical of Charles. Fortunately, my 'heroic past' never returned to haunt me, though I was very worried it would."[22]

Wiseman, like all the patients, found there were far more pressing concerns; food was one. Getting enough to eat was a problem. The hospital administrators and staff were rationing supplies. While that in itself might have been justifiable under the circumstances, Mickey could not help but notice it was only the patients who went hungry; the doctors, nurses, and hospital administrators continued to eat well in their own mess. When Mickey complained to Hilda, her protests were ignored. "I shall never, I suppose, stop being bitter about that period," Mickey later wrote.[23]

She was no less distressed by the disappearance of several tins of the powdered milk she was using to feed Carola, and by her own dwindling purse. When Ah King told Mickey that he was broke, she gave him $50 and advised she could no longer afford to pay him; the Japanese had frozen all bank accounts, leaving Mickey with just the $200 she had in her pocket. Ah King smiled wanly; she could pay him whenever she had money again, he said.

Not everyone Mickey encountered was as selfless or accommodating as Ah King, or as the owner of the Grips, who came by the hospital one day to leave off a twelve-pound can of powdered milk. Day-to-day living conditions worsened as the Japanese tightened their grip on Hong Kong. A favorite topic of debate among the British was the reason for the harsh treatment of both the military POWs and the civilians. Some felt it was revenge for the alleged mistreatment of Japanese prisoners by the British; others argued it was simply a case of payback—Asians treating whites with the same disdain with which the Imperial powers had long treated persons of color. When Charles raised the issue with a Japanese consul who visited him at the hospital, the man expressed surprise; all prisoners were being "well treated," he insisted. Mickey decided the consul actually believed that to be the case. "I think the Japanese were that way," she said. "Their prisons were nearly *always* unspeakable."[24]

In the wake of the colony's surrender, the Japanese had confined all British, Canadian, and Indian soldiers to hastily created POW camps. The Japanese were initially too busy to be concerned about Hong Kong's civilian population. As a result, many Europeans and Americans were left free to wander about, although doing so proved risky and sometimes fatal. Foreign nationals who were captured during the battle were held in makeshift jails. What happened to Gwen Dew was typical. She was taken prisoner at the Repulse Bay Hotel, one of the first big buildings on the south side of the island to surrender. Dew and two hundred other civilians—men, women, and children—were marched eight miles at bayonet point to an old paint factory, where they awaited their fate. At one point, the prisoners were paraded through a Chinese neighborhood. "Struggling with our bundles, exhausted, our tongues swollen, our feet blistered, we were the perfect picture of the Fall of the White Man in the Far East," Dew wrote. "A white man lying disemboweled in the dirt, a white woman stretched naked and gang raped, a parade of whites carrying their own pitiful burdens—these pictures delighted the Jap heart."[25]

Perhaps. But if such scenes really did "delight" the Japanese military, it was small consolation. Apart from the plunder, there was little else to recommend Hong Kong to the Japanese as a prize. One of the first things the victors did when the shooting stopped was to compile an inventory of all the buildings and property they had seized. Street and building names were changed, sometimes repeatedly and usually without warning, in an effort to "Japanize" them. The Peninsula Hotel—known affectionately as the Grips—became the *Tao* (which means Great Eastern); Queen's Road, one of Victoria's main thoroughfares, became Nakameiji-dori (central street).

Items of personal property looted from private homes were shipped to Japan as war booty. All bank accounts were frozen and the assets siphoned off as Hong Kong dollars were exchanged for devalued Japanese military yen. Many of the wealthy taipans who had ruled the colony were held prisoner in former brothels and were forced to go to their offices each day to balance the books and sign "duress" currency. Meanwhile, Chinese merchants and industrialists were "encouraged" to join associations that supported Japan's war efforts. Keeping them in business furthered these ends and provided fodder for the Japanese propaganda mill. It also gave the *Kempetai*, the ruthless Japanese secret police, and their friends ample opportunity to engage in the age-old Chinese custom known as "the squeeze." Mickey had seen the same game played in Shanghai, albeit on a lesser scale; the threat of kidnappings, murder, and robbery were used to extort money. No one was immune from the lawlessness. Mickey received a terrifying reminder of this on New Year's Eve.

She, the Weills, and some friends were having a candlelit dinner when armed men burst through the front door. Some wore Japanese army uniforms. The others were dressed in civilian garb. It was apparent to Mickey these men were just "Chinese rabble" who had stolen the Japanese weapons and clothing. They were looking for a large sum of money the leader of the gang was convinced that Mrs. Weill had hidden in her house. After tying up the men, the bandits proceeded to slap the terrified women in an effort to frighten them into saying where the money was hidden. Throughout the ordeal, all Mickey could think of was that her time had come. She was certain that she and the other women in the house would be raped, then killed. From upstairs came the sounds of rooms being ransacked. Carola shrieked. As Mickey rose to run to her, the guards shouted at her to sit back down. Mickey's knees turned to jelly, and she fainted to the floor.

When she awoke, the ordeal was still going on. For two terrifying hours, the men tore the house apart. When finally they left, they did so lugging bags of jewels, clothing, and many personal possessions belonging to the people in the house. Miraculously, no one was raped or killed. Veronica had rescued Carola, and Mickey was relieved to discover that the cardboard box in which she kept her own jewels had been overlooked.

That incident was a stark reminder of how lawless life in Hong Kong was in the weeks after the Japanese victory. Gangs of armed thugs prowled the streets at night. General Rensuke Isogai, the new military governor, had issued an edict in early January of 1942 making robbery and rape punishable by death. However, the ongoing "incidents" underscored the fact that Japanese military planners in Tokyo, who had worked out such a meticulous battle plan to capture the colony, had little idea of what to do with it afterward. Apart from its obvious symbolic value as a war prize, Hong Kong served no real military purpose. "Any supportive role that [the colony] might have played in the battles in Southeast Asia was neutralized in December 1941 by the sinking of the battleships *Repulse* and *Prince of Wales*," historian Alan Birch pointed out. "Hong Kong . . . was not a great asset, and the Japanese did not intend for it to become a liability. Even just to maintain Hong Kong at its pre-war level of existence would have been an unwarranted luxury."[26]

Hong Kong had always been an insatiable consumer of food, goods, and services. In the prewar years, the colony's harbor was one of the world's busiest. Most of the food consumed by residents came from the surrounding hinterland. In the wake of the Japanese occupation of southern China, though, this ended. Agricultural production was seriously disrupted. Crops were razed, livestock were slaughtered, and many farmers fled. Widespread famine was the inevitable result. Hundreds of thousands of hungry Chinese refugees with nowhere else to run had sought haven in Hong Kong. There they lived in makeshift shelters under wretched conditions. The outcome of the battle for Hong Kong made little difference to these people, with one exception: whereas the British policy had been one of benign neglect, the Japanese began a "reign of terror." This ruthless campaign was intended to forcibly depopulate the city of as many of its more than 1.5 million Chinese residents as possible. Japanese propaganda had boasted that the war was being fought to oust the white imperialists and return "Asia to the Asiatics." None of the half a million Chinese who were forcibly evicted would have agreed.

The Japanese made some effort to grow food for Hong Kong's remaining population. British crop experts and administrators were conscripted to advise farmers in the New Territories on how to use night soil—human waste—as fertilizer. The program ultimately failed because as the tide of war began turning against Japan and the officials who had devised the program were posted elsewhere, their replacements proved less committed to its success. As historian Alan Birch noted, "Finally, one Japanese governor is reputed to have shrugged his shoulders and said 'Let them eat grass!' There was plenty of it growing in the empty streets."[27]

Similar efforts to maintain public health in the colony proved more successful. The Japanese, being acutely aware of the dangers of epidemics, enlisted Selwyn-Clarke as an "advisor." He was given an armband to wear and told to go about his old duties as Hong Kong's director of medical services. Selwyn-Clarke did so with an at times manic determination, often working nonstop, without food or sleep. It was the same scenario film director David Lean dramatized in *The Bridge on the River Kwai*, his Oscar-winning 1957 epic movie about British military POWs forced by the Japanese to build a railway through the Burmese jungle. Alec Guinness played the role of a British officer who implored his men to build the best bridge they can. Doing so, he rationalized, would attest to British ingenuity and proficiency and would help his men's morale. However, the other side was that it also helped the enemy. What to do in such a situation was the moral dilemma. Selwyn-Clarke had no doubts about what he would do. "My duty," he told Mickey, "is the population of this town—the Chinese and Indians and Eurasians as well as the whites. I shall continue to do my duty, if it is permitted, to keep them as healthy as possible."[28]

It was not long before Selwyn-Clarke's job became much easier logistically. This was because of a secret decision by the Japanese military that only a few weeks earlier would have seemed too crazy, too impossible for Hong Kong residents to believe. As word of the plan leaked out, wild and crazy rumors spread through the colony. While some had suspected what the Japanese had in mind, most refused to believe it.

24

THE CRYPTIC NOTICES that appeared throughout Hong Kong one morning in mid-January 1942 were the first sign of what the Japanese military had in mind for the colony. The message was ominous. All British, American, Dutch, and Belgian nationals were ordered to report that afternoon to the Murray Parade Ground in downtown Victoria. They were told to bring a blanket and some clothing; that was the only clue to what was planned for them. Those who came lugging suitcases stuffed with whatever they could carry were glad they had done so, for in the coming months they would welcome any creature comforts they could lay their hands on.

The colony's new military overlords had decided to do the unthinkable: intern all white-skinned enemy civilians. The Japanese rallying cry had become "Asia for the Asiatics!" It was time for the imperialists who had exploited Hong Kong to get their comeuppance; they would experience life as Chinese coolies lived it, with daily hardship, deprivation, and humiliation. The irony of a Japanese army that had itself slaughtered and raped hundreds of thousands of Chinese civilians attempting to claim the moral high ground was lost on those in command. No matter. Charles's dramatic prophecy that the "day of the white man is done out here" was about to come true.

The roundup of foreign nationals went ahead more quickly than anyone ever expected. Initially, at least, there were discussions about confining the internees to an area on the Peak. Sir Atholl MacGregor (derisively known as "Sir Alcohol"), Hong Kong's chief justice, pleaded with the Japanese to allow this—mainly, as some people suspected, because his *own* house was there and he wanted to continue living in comfort. In the end, the Japanese military banished the thousands of enemy nationals to a site five miles from Victoria as the crow flies. At Selwyn-Clarke's suggestion, they were loaded onto old harbor boats and ferried around to Stanley, a historic fishing village on the island's windswept south coast.

The decision to do this made sense from the Japanese perspective. Stanley Peninsula was isolated and could easily be sealed off. A British prison adjacent to the village was used as the administrative center for the new civilian internment camp as well as a place where military POWs deemed guilty of various infractions were sent to be punished; many of those who entered the prison's gates did not come out alive.

Just south of Stanley, atop the conical hill at the southern tip of the peninsula, stood Fort Stanley. There Hong Kong's defenders had held out until the bitter end in December 1941. The fortifications, being well located with excellent views in all directions, had been occupied by the Japanese and were made off-limits to all foreigners.

The Japanese dispatched work gangs of American and British citizens to Stanley to bury the Allied war dead and to ready a camp for the arrival of the other internees, many of whom were elderly people, women, and children. Having the able-bodied men tend to this task suited the Japanese military, because it relieved them of a dirty job, and (just as importantly) it pitted the Americans against the British in a scramble for the choicest locations and facilities. By sheer dint of personality, Bill Hunt, the resourceful businessman who had rescued Carola, was put in charge of the American section of Stanley Camp, as the site was called. Using his Yankee ingenuity to full advantage—a few well-placed bribes and some carefully chosen words of flattery helped—Hunt did his job so efficiently that even the Japanese marveled and many British were resentful. It occurred to Mickey that for now the Japanese seemed to be giving Americans preferential treatment, although that would change dramatically as the war progressed and the tide of battle turned. "Not that the Japanese are ever placatory," Mickey wrote, "but I could see, myself, from the way they treated me when they knew I was American, that a prejudice did exist in our favor. I think they felt they would be able to make a deal with the United States later on. But their feeling toward the British was one of ruthless, revengeful hate."[1]

Despite any preferential treatment of Americans, Mickey wanted nothing to do with Stanley Camp. She had seen for herself in Shanghai how the Japanese treated internees; a Japanese prison camp was no place for her baby. "I was in a tremor over Carola, I didn't know what to do," Mickey wrote. "It was out of the question to walk right into it, to take my baby and go into town and throw ourselves in jail. I don't think my legs would have carried me."[2]

Given her relationship with Charles, Mickey knew it would be difficult and dangerous for her to evade internment by hiding out. Nonetheless, she was determined to avoid it, at all costs. Mickey realized she had to act quickly, before Japanese soldiers or the secret police came looking for her. She devised a desperate plan that she hoped would keep her out of prison for now and buy her time to ponder her next move.

She noticed that hospital patients had not been included in the general roundup. With the help of Hilda Selwyn-Clarke and another friend, Mickey got Carola and herself admitted to Queen Mary Hospital. She was supposedly suffering from complications arising from an operation—the cesarean section that she had three months earlier. The ruse worked; Japanese military doctors had not yet gotten around to assessing hospital medical charts. Mickey moved into a four-bed room in the maternity ward, which she shared with just one other woman. This bought Mickey some time to assess her situation. For now, she and Carola were near Charles, and they were relatively safe, even if they were hungry.

When Mickey observed a group of Japanese officers touring Queen Mary Hospital to assess the facilities and equipment, she guessed her days there were numbered. She was right. On January 21, 1942, the Japanese began evacuating the building so they could use it themselves. Within an hour, all the convalescents had been moved out. Later there were reports about the brutality of the Japanese stretcher bearers, who were said to have ripped bandages off Allied soldiers to check their wounds and to have forcibly removed anyone who resisted. Such atrocities may have happened, but if they did Mickey saw none of them.

What she did see was that only the most seriously wounded or ill soldiers—Charles and Bill Wiseman among them—were transferred to the Bowen Road military hospital, on a long cul-de-sac on the hillside below Mount Gough. "Its once immaculate grounds were full of shell holes and obviously some of them had been used as burial pits," Bill Wiseman recalled. "The main buildings had been quite badly damaged, much of the roof had gone and almost all the top floor was unsafe and useless. And it was bursting at the seams with people, having absorbed the staff and casualties from the Wanchai Naval Hospital when already crowded with Army wounded."[3]

Regardless, the patients from Queen Mary Hospital were fitted in. Nearly a dozen of them were put into a cramped psychiatric ward with bars on the windows. "So in little more than a month I had progressed from the mortuary via maternity to lunacy," Wiseman quipped.[4]

The walking wounded who were cleared out of Queen Mary Hospital were interned in the various POW camps that had been set up on Hong Kong Island or across the harbor in Kowloon. Most of the British enlisted men were sent to an old barracks at Sham Shui Po, while their officers were held in a camp on Argyle Street. The Canadian officers and men were interned on North Point and the Indians at Ma Ta Chung. All civilians were shipped off to Stanley Camp. Mickey refused to accept that this would also be her fate, even after Charles declined to use his connections in the Japanese high command to obtain preferential treatment for himself or his family. This refusal angered Mickey, who resolved to do on her own what Charles would or could not bring himself to do.

By Japanese law, a person was considered a citizen of the country in which he or she was born, regardless of place of residence. Mickey knew this law precluded her from claiming to be anything other than American. However, a Russian woman pointed out an intriguing loophole in Japanese law. The provision reflected the same gender bias that prevailed in the East, just as it did in the West at the time: a wife was considered to "belong" to her husband. Thus, when a woman married, it followed that she, too, assumed her husband's citizenship. Hearing this gave Mickey an idea.

Five years earlier, in mid-1937, she had signed a legal document in Shanghai attesting that she was Sinmay Zau's concubine; polygamy was legal in China. At the time, Mickey had regarded this more as a matter of procedure than substance. She knew that the "marriage" was null and void under American law. But by becoming one of Sinmay's "wives," Mickey had become entitled to claim some important legal rights. One of them had been a permit allowing her to reclaim some of "her" valuables from the Zaus' house, which had been confiscated by the Japanese authorities, and to assert title to a printing press Sinmay used to earn a living by publishing books, pamphlets, and soft-core pornography.

Now, in 1942, Mickey told her story with bowed head to a Japanese medical officer, who listened intently. "Chinese husband, eh?" he inquired. "How many children?" When Mickey replied just one, the officer nodded. He then produced a wallet-sized card, which he stamped and initialed. It was a pass permitting Mickey to remain free for two more days. This would give her enough time to apply to the Japanese Foreign Affairs office in Hong Kong for permanent status. Mickey could scarcely believe her good fortune. Neither could Charles when she showed him the pass card that the officer had given her. "God," he muttered. "Do you think you can get away with that?"[5]

Mickey was determined to try. With the help of a Persian businessman friend, she arranged for male escorts to take her to the Foreign Affairs Office downtown; the streets still were unsafe for a woman walking alone. Despite the military high command's efforts to restore order, armed thugs and rogue Japanese soldiers intent on looting the homes of interned foreign nationals were still busy. They were evidently too busy to notice Mickey and her companions, who arrived safely at their destination. Because she was late for registration, Mickey was sent to the office of the Japanese consul, a man whose face she was relieved to discover she recognized. Mickey and Charles had dined with Shiroshici Kimura only a few months earlier; they all had drunk too much that evening, danced, and sung American college songs.

By chance, it was Kimura who drafted the internment regulations for Hong Kong. As they sat down to talk, Mickey sensed that although he was embarrassed and guarded, Kimura was still trying to be friendly. After they had exchanged pleasantries, the consul inquired about Charles. Then he got down to business. He examined Mickey's pass card, nodding as he confirmed that by Japanese law she was considered to be a Chinese national; as such, she could not legally be interned. Interestingly enough, the Japanese authorities also excluded many Eurasians—persons of mixed parentage—as well as the Chinese wives of Westerners. The Japanese were forced to do so by circumstance. When the initial decision was made to intern foreign nationals, the colony's military governors had no idea how many people they were dealing with. "They had assumed that only the haughty whites were British," Mickey wrote. "Naturally [the crowd that turned up at Murray Parade Grounds] was far too big to handle, and besides, [the Japanese] didn't feel prepared to decide at just a moment's notice who was 'Asiatic' and who wasn't."[6]

When Mickey left Kimura's office that day she did so carrying a new pass card, this one adorned with official-looking red seals. However, she also had a new and potentially serious problem. Mickey had two days to produce a marriage certificate or sworn statement proving she really was married to Sinmay Zao. Mickey had neither a copy of the Chinese legal document she had signed, nor the time to try to contact Sinmay—even if he was still alive and was willing to confirm their relationship, which had ended abruptly and with some bitterness. Mickey knew her only hope was to find someone willing to sign a sworn statement that she really was Sinmay's wife (even though she knew the marriage had not been recognized by British or American law). The difficulty, of course, was finding such a person in occupied Hong Kong. "What followed sounds incredible," Mickey later wrote. "That is the trouble with real life: you can't write it down as fiction because it is so impossible. . . . You will have to believe me because this is the truth."[7]

Mickey chanced to encounter a student she knew on a crowded Hong Kong street. Freddie Kwai was one of Sinmay's nephews. When Mickey explained her predicament to him, Freddie agreed to swear she was his auntie, as long as Mickey promised *not* to tell the Japanese that he had fought as a volunteer in the Chinese army. Mickey did so, and she and Freddie visited the Foreign Affairs Office together. There Mickey was issued a new passport showing that she was a Chinese citizen—at least as far as the Japanese authorities were concerned.

• • •

As Mickey was struggling with her passport in occupied Hong Kong, efforts to rescue her were under way back home in New York. Mickey's sister Helen and literary agent Carl Brandt had begun writing letters and inquiring about Mickey's fate. All they knew for certain was that she and her baby had been in Hong Kong when the Japanese attacked on December 8, 1941. No one had heard anything more since then. A fearful Carl Brandt wrote to the Secretary of State in Washington on January 15, 1942, seeking information. Two weeks later, Brandt received a reply from the secretary of state's office informing him that Washington had sent to Tokyo, through the intermediary of the Swiss government, a proposal for the exchange of the "official personnel" the two sides were holding. American officials also requested that all accredited "press representatives" be included in any such swap; Mickey's name had been added to the list of American journalists thought to be in Hong Kong.[8] For now, nothing more could be done. When Helen tried to transfer money to Mickey's bank account through the Swiss-based International Red Cross, she was informed that it was no longer possible.

Mickey knew nothing of any of this. It would have made no difference to her even if she had, for she had other more immediate concerns. When Charles was moved out of the Queen Mary Hospital to the British military hospital on Bowen Road, Mickey was discharged, too. She, Carola, Ah King, and Ah Yuk—a new amah Mickey had hired to help care for Carola—returned home to Mickey's flat on May Road, now officially known as Higashi-Tisho Tori. That was not the only change. Her home was occupied by refugees: two Eurasian women along with their young children, several elderly relatives, and various Chinese servants. There were now a dozen people living in the flat. The Eurasian women, Mickey learned, were sisters named Irene and Phyllis. Both were widows of British soldiers who had died in the battle. Although the apartment building had been damaged in the battle and looters had stolen many of Mickey's belongings, the flat was still habitable. Ah King had seen to that. He had also continued to care for two of Mickey's gibbons; Mr. Mills and a younger animal named Junior had survived. The animals looked on with interest as Mickey, Carola, and Ah King unpacked the three suitcases in which Mickey now carried everything she owned.

Now that she had time to assess her own situation, Mickey realized that being spared internment had created a whole new set of problems. Finding food was one of them. Those who had money or gold could buy food on the black market. Unfortunately, when the Japanese seized the colony's banks, they froze all accounts and issued a new currency—the Japanese military yen (MY), pegged at four to the Hong Kong dollar. In reality it was worthless. Like most foreign nationals, Mickey had been left with only the cash in her pocket. She made do by bartering the contents of her jewelry box piece by piece—a necklace for a bag of rice here, a ring for a can of evaporated milk for Carola there. Mickey knew she could not last long doing this; she was now trying to feed five people: herself, Carola, Ah King, Ah Yuk, and Charles, whom she visited each afternoon. Whenever possible, Mickey took along a food parcel to Bowen Road Hospital. She knew the guards stole whatever items they wanted, but that was the price to be paid. The remaining food in those precious parcels was the difference between life and death for Charles and other patients with whom he shared it.

"It was a nasty period altogether," Mickey later wrote. "On the part of the public there was an eager rush to make friends with the conquerors."[9] Some

Hong Kong women—Russian and Chinese nationals mostly—were stricken with what Mickey dubbed "Sabine complex." Like the women of the ancient kingdom of Sabine, who had became the wives and lovers of the marauding Romans, these Hong Kong women began sleeping with Japanese soldiers, *Kempetai* agents, and other officials. This was one way of finding protectors and providers in these uncertain times. Although Mickey understood the women's motivation, she did not approve. Frankie Zung, a half-American black, half-Chinese hustler whom Mickey knew, insisted he was going to introduce her to a Japanese army major "who likes white women." Mickey was adamant that he would do nothing of the sort. Still, she knew that she too would have to somehow cultivate "friendships" among the occupying forces while maintaining her dignity. Mickey had a headstart in this regard.

Unlike many Westerners in Hong Kong, prior to the war she and Charles had worked and socialized with Japanese officials and army officers. In addition to Mr. Kimura, one of their friends had been the former Japanese consul in Hong Kong, a young American-educated foreign service officer named Takio Oda. In the wake of the Japanese occupation, Oda returned to Hong Kong from Tokyo to help set up the new military administration. Among his duties as the head of the colony's Foreign Affairs Office was to assist the gendarmerie in running the civilian internment camp at Stanley. On the surface, Oda seemed to be as callous and unpredictable as other Japanese occupation officials, and he was hated for it by many Europeans. What few of them realized was that Oda was an old-fashioned man of honor. The brutality and corruption he saw in Hong Kong disgusted him. For that reason, Oda quietly intervened with the gendarmerie on the prisoners' behalf. Unbeknownst to Mickey or Charles, he also had pulled a few strings for Mickey.

"It was the military who decided [who was interned and who was not]," he explained. "But there were two or three important people whom I knew well, and I told them Mickey and Charles were all right."[10] Oda's say-so was enough reason for Kimura to exempt Mickey from internment, even though he must have known—or at least suspected—that her relationship with Sinmay was dubious. The fact that Oda could intervene on behalf of his friends was indicative of the rivalries among the Japanese officials who were now running Hong Kong. It also helps to explain the outcome of a terrifying incident that happened to Mickey a few days after she received her new passport.

She was having breakfast at Hilda's flat one morning, when she received a caller: Mr. Cheng, a flabby, tubercular Chinese man in gray flannels and a striped necktie. Mickey knew Cheng was a supporter of Wang Ching-wei, a pro-Japanese politician who was one of Chiang Kai-shek's main rivals for leadership of the Chinese nationalist movement. Cheng had little interest in politics. Mickey later learned that he had paid the gendarmerie for the "right" to run Stanley Camp and to squeeze its residents. "[Cheng's] object was to make hay while the sun shone," wrote American journalist Joe Alsop, himself a prisoner in the camp, "and besides taking bribes for special favors from the richer internees, Cheng and his gang chiseled on the [camp] rations, keeping back a portion of them and selling it on the rocketing Hong Kong food [black] market."[11]

While Cheng had identified Mickey as a prime prospect for extortion, as yet he dared not squeeze her. It was evident to all that she had friends in high places. Cheng knew he needed permission to work his mischief. With that in mind, he studied the papers that Mickey had been given at the Foreign Affairs Office. As he did so he must have seen that they posed a problem for him. After a few minutes, Cheng rose to leave, asking Mickey to return to Kimura's office that afternoon. She agreed, although she sensed this was an ominous development.

Kimura's behavior further heightened Mickey's anxieties. He sat at his desk, staring down at his hands as he spoke. Kimura was apologetic. Colonel Noma, the feared head of the gendarmerie, had been making inquiries about Mickey's "case," he explained. Now the colonel wanted to see her about "a small matter." She was to go immediately to Noma's office in the former supreme court building. Mickey was filled with dread but knew she must comply with Noma's summons. She was going into the belly of the beast; there was nowhere to hide.

She had heard stories about people who had simply "disappeared" while being interrogated by the gendarmes; others suffered "unfortunate accidents" while being questioned. "[The gendarmes] are the Japanese Gestapo," Mickey explained. "They are envied and enviable, because, officially, they take orders from nobody but the Emperor, and everyone knows that actually they don't even take orders from him. They do just what they like. The chief of the gendarmerie on Hong Kong really rules the roost. There is a Japanese governor, put there for show, but it is always the gendarmerie who make the ultimate decisions."[12]

Mickey discovered that the head of the gendarmes, the man who held the power of life and death over her, was an "extra small goblin in khaki."[13] Colonel Noma sat behind a large desk in a very long room. Because he pretended (not very convincingly) not to speak English, he immediately began barking questions at Mickey through an interpreter. At first, she had difficulty answering. Her mouth was parched and a lump of fear blocked her throat. As the interrogation progressed, it became obvious that Noma knew a lot about Mickey and about her prewar activities in China. She later learned that her *Soong Sisters* book had been translated into Japanese and had been circulated among the Japanese Foreign Affairs staff in China, the senior military, and the

Kempetai. She was unaware of this; what terrified Mickey most was that Noma would question her about her friends in Shanghai, especially Sinmay's brother (a general in the Chinese guerilla army), and about her own occasional work as a Nationalist courier.

Fortunately, the colonel knew none of this, because he had not bothered to ask his counterpart in Shanghai for Mickey's file. Noma smugly assumed he knew everything worth knowing about Mickey: namely, that she was Charles Boxer's lover and that she had spent time in Chungking with the Soongs. It was these two aspects of Mickey's life that Noma questioned her about. He did so at great length, in the process suggesting to Mickey that her loyalties to Charles were wasted because—among other things—he did not really love her and had been unfaithful. Mickey replied that she did not care; after all, *she* was another man's wife. After several hours, Colonel Noma grew frustrated. He was convinced that Mickey was a silly woman who had no useful information. Finally, Noma demanded to know why if she was *really* married to Sinmay she had borne Charles Boxer's baby. By this point in the interrogation, Mickey was so weary and disoriented she was almost giddy. "Because I'm a bad girl!" she blurted.

On that note, the questioning ended. As Noma and his interpreter huddled, talking in hushed tones, fearsome thoughts flashed through Mickey's mind. She was certain her flippancy had been a mistake; she was bound for Stanley Camp or someplace much worse. Then suddenly the interpreter laughed. He clapped Mickey on the back like an old friend and told her she could go home. That was it. As quickly as the questioning had begun, it was over. Mickey could scarcely believe her good fortune. She had not been beaten or abused. Even more surprisingly, she was not being interned. For now, at least.

Charles was incredulous when Mickey told him about her interrogation. He knew the Japanese were intent on learning the details of his intelligence work. Despite various threats, he himself had revealed nothing. He refused to do so, and that was that. Charles was prepared to die and to take his secrets to the grave with him. As the warrior's *bushido* code bade him, he would not beg, nor complain; Charles had resolved to die with honor, like a true samurai.

He had never discussed his intelligence work with anyone other than his superiors, and he had always been careful never to take documents home with him. At first, Charles's interrogators either didn't know or refused to believe it, for the gendarmes had ransacked his flat. In the process, they stole his priceless collection of sword furnishings, some early Dutch drawings from Japan, and many of his precious books. They had also beaten his Chinese houseboy in an effort to extract information. When that failed, the gendarmes tried a subtler approach. They offered the houseboy rice and tobacco to spy on

Mickey in the hope she could provide incriminating evidence. When he told her about it, she advised him to go ahead. Mickey had nothing to hide.

Neither her summons by Noma nor the fact that she was now being watched had any significant impact on Mickey's daily life. The biggest change in her routine came about as the Japanese tightened their grip on Hong Kong. Security at the Bowen Road military hospital was increased, and the daily visiting period ended. Japanese officials claimed this was because of a cholera outbreak, but Mickey learned from Hilda (who heard from her husband) that this was just an excuse. It mattered not. What did matter was that hospital visiting periods were cut back to a couple of hours per week. Visitors were no longer permitted inside the building, and for a time all patients were prohibited from receiving outside food parcels. This latter restriction caused great suffering because food and medical supplies were so scarce inside the hospital. Charles received a small respite from a Japanese guard with a fondness for chocolate. The man turned his back one day when Mickey and Carola came calling. As a result, Charles, Mickey, and the baby had an hour together in private.

Mickey saw that Charles had largely recovered from his chest wound. However, he badly needed rehabilitation therapy for his left arm, which hung uselessly in a sling. As a result, he had difficulty tending to many of the little tasks that are part of daily life—tying his shoelaces and shaving, for example. Nevertheless, Charles refused to complain about his health or about the treatment he was receiving. When asked, he always insisted that others at the hospital were suffering far more. He was probably right. Several of the men remained in perilous shape; others suffered from a variety of painful afflictions.

Bill Wiseman's experiences were typical. He developed a bad case of impetigo, a highly contagious skin infection. His face erupted in painful, oozing sores. Just after that cleared up, his throat became inflamed. British army doctors decided his tonsils had to be removed. The surgeon who performed the procedure eased Wiseman's discomfort using local anesthetic, which was all that was available. This was almost useless, though, and the pain was excruciating. "I was cornered," Wiseman said. "The patient whose turn was next, just let out a screech and bolted from the [operating] theater."[14]

• • •

For all its inadequacies, the treatment afforded patients in Bowen Road military hospital was markedly better than that being meted out in Hong Kong's POW camps, where conditions truly were grim. The men in these camps faced what Gwen Dew called "the twin horrors of hunger and disease."[15] In many ways, the early months of captivity, in early 1942, were among the worst.

The prisoners got used to living in crowded, dirty barrack-style quarters that lacked even the most basic amenities. Medical supplies were scarce or nonexistent. By day, the prisoners sweated in the tropical sun; by night, they were chilled to the bone by cold. Flies, mosquitos, cockroaches, fleas, lice, bedbugs, rats, and a host of other pests spread misery and disease.

Bill Wiseman recalled that when the power failed at the Argyle Street camp, it was not restored. Thus, for the duration of the war, all outdoor activities for the prisoners were restricted to daylight hours, and those days of endless despair began with mornings of mind-numbing routine. Week after week, month after month, the prisoners were roused from their beds, usually about 4:30 A.M. Following morning parade and roll call, they ate a meager breakfast of a cup of rice—"maggotty, moldy, and full of mouse turds," as one POW recalled—washed down by watery tea.[16] Many of the enlisted men struggled to survive on a starvation diet of less than nine hundred calories per day; some who tried to turn the tables by eating rats found to their sorrow that rodent meat was unpalatably greasy and made them violently ill.

After the morning meal, the prisoners went to work; only the most ill were excused. Labor gangs were formed to work on Japanese construction projects, one of which was the expansion of the Kai Tak Airport. At first, the prisoners were paid small amounts for their efforts, but this payment soon ended and the work became forced. As the POWs grew increasingly hungry, enfeebled, and ravaged by diseases, such work became well nigh impossible, but still the Japanese insisted. Hundreds of men died as a result. Later, many of the healthiest men were shipped off to Japan to toil as slave labor in coal mines or locomotive works. On several occasions, Japanese ships loaded with POWs were inadvertently torpedoed by American submarines, resulting in horrendous loss of life. Those POWs who did not toil in labor gangs were responsible for cleaning and maintaining the prison camp and its latrines, a wretched job considering the number of men suffering from dysentery and other diseases.

A second parade and camp roll call were held each evening, usually about 8 P.M. Dinner followed. Invariably it consisted of another cup of rice, more watery tea, and sometimes a thin soup of vegetable tops, which the men dubbed "green horror." Whole fresh vegetables, meat, and protein were as rare in the camps as was privacy.

The inhumane conditions in Hong Kong's military POW camps caused a myriad of health problems. Bill Wiseman eventually dropped to little more than half his usual weight of 180 pounds; others suffered comparable weight losses. Because of the combination of malnutrition and disease, prisoners died by the hundreds. "Everyone was affected," Wiseman noted. "We all made the acquaintance of the various diseases: beriberi, pellagra, vitaminosis, dysentery, and there was the odd cholera scare, too."[17]

Mercifully, conditions were less severe in Stanley Camp, where Hong Kong's civilian internees generally were spared the kind of cruelties, although not the deprivations, meted out to the military POWs. "The real story of the camp must be written around food—for that was the subject of nine-tenths of the conversations and it dominated most of our dreams," one British internee later wrote.[18]

Under the terms of the Geneva Convention for the Treatment of War Prisoners, which the Japanese had not signed but had agreed to comply with, civilian internees were to receive 2,400 calories per day. Initially, most of the civilians in Stanley Camp struggled to survive on less than half of that. "At ten in the morning in the American quarters we received a small bowl of rice and three quarters of a cup of thin gravy," Gwen Dew reported. "At five we received another dose of rice and the same small amount of questionable stew. Many times the small amount of meat in it should have been rejected owing to its bad state, but it meant no food at all if it was sent back."[19]

The reality was that the rapacious Mr. Cheng, Mickey's tormenter, was making a fortune selling stolen prisoners' rations on the black market. The food situation in the camp improved only when Cheng fell from grace in March and was replaced. At that point, Mickey's friend Takio Oda decided to put a Japanese man in charge of Stanley Camp. His choice to be the new supervisor was a "civilian nonentity" named Yamashita, who formerly had been a barber at the Hong Kong Hotel. "When Takio Oda and Yamashita pressed for reforms, the gendarmes objected that we were getting Japanese army rations—an argument often heard, in which the only flaw is that while the Japanese soldier gets approximately the same food, he receives infinitely more of it, and a far higher proportion of meat, fish, and vegetables," journalist Joe Alsop explained.[20]

25

CIVILIAN INTERNEES in Stanley Camp spent their days lining up for food and dreaming of home, yet life behind the barbed wire had a simplicity to it that Mickey sometimes longed for. Her days were an endless struggle filled with dangers and uncertainty. Mickey's health suffered as a result. Stress and dietary deficiencies took a toll; her hair fell out and her teeth were in sad shape. Without a job or the income from articles and stories she could no longer send to the *New Yorker*, Mickey scrambled to live.

Meanwhile, back in New York her agent had arranged for publication of her collected Pan Heh-ven short stories. They had been highly popular with readers when they appeared in the *New Yorker*, and the reviewers, too, liked the book, which was entitled *Mr. Pan*.[1] F. W. Bullock of *Books* called it "a delectable novelized portrait of a modern Chinese gentleman."[2] Marianne Hauser of the *New York Times* observed that Mr. Pan was a "highly individual, well-rounded, and warm-hearted fellow whom one would like to count among one's friends."[3]

Sales of *Mr. Pan* were brisk, but none of the royalties found their way to Mickey. It accumulated in her New York bank account even as she struggled to scratch out a living in Hong Kong. "Our chief difficulty is money," she confided in a letter home, which was smuggled out through Free China.[4] Mickey stayed only "a jump ahead of destitution," as she put it, by selling off the last of her jewelry—a diamond ring, a gold chain, a bracelet, and some French watches.

The money did not go far. The food available on the black market was ridiculously expensive. When it could be found, a pound of rice that cost about three American cents before the war now sold for thirty cents. Other food items were almost beyond reach. Two large tins of powdered milk that Mickey bought for Carola were $35 (U.S.) plus a bribe for the man who delivered them to her. Those who could not afford to pay such inflated prices tried to make do as best they could, which was generally not very well. Many Chinese coolies and their families were starving to death, and there were reports of human flesh being sold in some Hong Kong marketplaces.

Adding to residents' miseries were the growing tensions as the pace of Japanese conquest in the Pacific slowed and American forces began to reclaim lost territory. No amount of radio propaganda or stories in the daily *Hongkong News* about Japan's invincibility could disguise the fact that the war's outcome was becoming much less certain. That uncertainty was reflected in the behavior of the Japanese occupation forces, who were increasingly erratic and vindictive. Random street checks were stepped up, as were the dreaded Japanese "curfews." Mickey explained, "A curfew was called every time an important visitor—a general or admiral from overseas, usually—was in town and moving around on a tour of inspection."[5] These events were a hardship because all traffic was halted and pedestrians were forced to kneel down and remain still. Sometimes the "freeze" lasted only a few minutes; other times it was hours before the "all clear" was given.

Food shortages and harassments aside, Mickey had an even more serious worry: she had been recruited by Hilda and her husband for a secret relief operation to smuggle food, bedding, medicine, mosquito netting, and clothing into the various internment camps and hospitals, both military and civilian. However much she may have been terrified of the consequences of being caught, Mickey's conscience obliged her to do whatever she could to help out.

Selwyn-Clarke received almost $2 million from well-to-do Chinese businessmen in Hong Kong who were appalled by the way the Japanese were treating prisoners. Mickey and a small group of trusted volunteers carried black market goods into the internment camps in their parcels. This was risky. The Japanese gendarmes were already on the alert for Chinese guerillas and some British POW escapees who were staging hit-and-run raids on the colony. Punishment for anyone caught engaging in "subversive activity"—even something as innocuous as bringing in unauthorized relief for starving POWS—was swift and ruthless.

The perils of being involved in Selwyn's group, combined with a growing despair over her own plight, were almost too much for Mickey. It was blind hope alone that kept her going. "I was still held up by that conviction, always held by members of the middle class, that it can't happen to *me*," Mickey wrote. "Hungry and worried, I still had that faith. I don't know why. I had learned that I couldn't and shouldn't expect to depend on friends. We were all in the same boat and with a few exceptions we weren't even friends any more."[6] Ironically, when relief did come to Mickey, it came not from friends, but from the most unlikely of sources: the enemy.

One evening, there was a knock on the door of Mickey's flat. The caller was a Mr. Kung, an interpreter whom Mickey recognized from her visit to the gendarmes' headquarters. Kung had come with an intriguing proposal. He asked if Mickey and her Eurasian housemate Irene were interested in teaching English to a couple of "scholarly gendarmes, real gentlemen," as Kung described them. "He was emphatic about those adjectives," Mickey wrote. "There would be no funny stuff."[7] That being so, she and Irene agreed to discuss the offer further the next day over lunch at a downtown restaurant.

Kung was there to introduce the women to their would-be language students. One was a tall Japanese soldier, dressed for the occasion in a Western-style business suit. He appeared to be in his mid-thirties and had a pencil-thin mustache, like the one Errol Flynn wore in the movies. What Mickey noticed first about him were his eyes; they were the most cunning, piercing eyes she had ever seen. This was Lieutenant Chikanori Nakazawa, although he announced in pidgin English that he preferred to be called "Chick." His companion, another Japanese officer named Yoshida, spoke no English at all, so Chick did all the talking. He proposed that he and Yoshida meet Mickey and Irene each day for a language lesson. They would pay with food: flour, sugar, rice, fruit, and meat, or whatever other commodities the women wanted. Mickey guessed the food cost the gendarmes nothing because they had warehouses full of stolen Red Cross parcels and food pilfered from the stores at Stanley Camp.

Mickey observed how carefully Chick avoided eye contact with her as he spoke; he addressed his words to Irene. "Now and then those eyes flashed over to my face," Mickey wrote. "I knew then what it was about. They thought I was a spy, . . . and [Chick] was investigating me. He looked me up and down in quick stolen glaces: the tired black dress, the runs in my stockings, the mended shoes."[8]

Mickey could only guess what Nakazawa really had in mind. However, she was ready to play the game. Charles had sent word that he did not object to the English lessons, and Mickey herself knew that she and Irene had no real choice in the matter; Chick and Yoshida took their orders from the feared Colonel Noma. That being so, Mickey also knew that tutoring Chick meant that she would be temporarily immune from harassment by the "petty gendarme spies," mostly Chinese collaborators, whom she knew had been watching her like jackals waiting for the opportunity to pounce.

Chick proved conscientious in his duties. He telephoned Mickey each morning to arrange a time and place for the day's lesson. Sometimes the foursome met at a downtown restaurant. Other times, Chick and Yoshida came by the flat. Whenever they did, a supply truck came by beforehand with provisions so that Ah King could prepare a meal. Mickey was not surprised when Chick and Yoshida began bringing guests with them, usually other gendarmes and their Chinese girlfriends. So much for their scholarly interests! Mickey and Irene did not protest, because the arrangement was proving far more beneficial than even they had ever imagined.

When Japanese soldiers began moving into the Tregunter Mansions in March 1942, the foreign tenants were evicted. Most were left to fend for themselves. Not Mickey. Chick protected his interests by relocating her and everyone in her household a few streets farther down the Peak, to another flat on Kennedy Road—now officially known as Higashi-Taisho Dori. Yoshida even arranged for Chinese coolies and an army truck to haul Mickey's belongings and furniture.

Dropping Chick's name around town also helped Mickey find more tutoring work; she began teaching English to a Japanese journalist from the Domei news agency. The extra income made life a little easier; but Mickey was realistic enough to know that her newfound prosperity could not last. She was right, for it took Chick only a few weeks to realize that she was of no real use to him. He continued the "geisha arrangement" only because he delighted in playing the role of big shot. When he was not "educating" ignorant Westerners about the superiority of Japanese culture and customs, Chick boasted of how back home he had owned several nightclubs, which were managed for him by his girlfriends. Even now, he had a Chinese mistress somewhere downtown.

Mickey flattered Chick by placing his photo on a shelf in the living room, front and center among those of Chiang Kai-shek and the Soong sisters. Chick was so pleased that on occasion he provided his "friends" with an army car and driver. Once he even took Mickey, Irene, and Irene's younger sister Phyllis out for an evening at a movie theater, where they watched a Japanese propaganda film. Then they had dinner at the Navy Club. The presence of Chick's photo in the flat paid off in another way too; when a gang of marauding Japanese soldiers invaded the flat, they left in a hurry when one of them spotted Chick's picture.

When the day inevitably came for Chick to end their relationship, Mickey was geniunely sorry. Her "personal spy" was posted out of Hong Kong soon afterward. The transfer came about as a result of intrigues by Yoshida, who had grown jealous of Chick's influence with Noma and who coveted Chick's black-market business connections. "When I next heard of Chick, he was in Canton, trying to get a monopoly on the city's cabaret business, and he also owned two department stores," Mickey wrote. "He was a smoothie all right."[9]

• • •

Chick's departure in the fall of 1942 was only the first of a series of good-byes that eroded Mickey's social safety net and her morale. Not long afterward, Irene, Phyllis, and their families slipped away to Free China via the underground used by Chinese nationalist guerillas to smuggle people and goods in and out of Hong Kong. British authorities had tried to end this clandestine traffic before the war, just as the Japanese tried to now, albeit for different reasons. Neither succeeded. Despite the presence of an occupying army and the best efforts of the gendarmes, Chinese people could still move in and out of Hong Kong undetected.

Leaving the colony for the mainland via the underground, no matter how hazardous that proposition was, suited Irene's elderly mother. Throughout the time she lived in Mickey's flat she scarcely had been able to conceal her scorn for her host's "free-thinking ways." Equally distressing was her daughter Irene's admiration of Mickey. "They got on very well," recalled Irene's eldest daughter Frances, who was born in Hong Kong just a few months before Carola. Until the war, Frances explained, her mother had led "a rather sheltered life." Hers was a traditional Chinese family in which the young women were silent and subservient. The six months that Irene lived with Mickey changed her forever. She envied her new American friend, who had been to college and "was very much her own person," as Frances noted. "Mickey Hahn seemed like a feminist, a true-blue feminist."[10]

Mickey's influence did not end when Irene left Hong Kong. Years later, Mickey learned that once Irene was in Free China, she promptly fell in love with a married British army officer. In September of 1943—just as Mickey had done—Irene gave birth to a baby daughter. "The whole family thought this was because of Mickey, who'd been so 'promiscuous,'" said Frances.[11]

The departure of Irene and her family left Mickey's flat empty, but another leave-taking truly deflated her. This was the long-rumored swap of Japanese and American prisoners in the fall of 1942. "There had been carefully considered deals between warring nations before," explained the Tokyo bureau chief of the Associated Press, Max Hill, one of the lucky ones who went home, "but never on such a scale as this one."[12] The first inkling that Mickey had that this mass exchange might actually occur came the day Takio Oda sent an urgent message summoning her to his office. He confirmed that arrangements had been finalized for a mid-September exchange and that Mickey's name was on the list of American journalists to be repatriated. Unbeknownst to either of them, this was due to the lobbying efforts of Mickey's sister Helen and her friends back home.

Oda seemed almost relieved as he outlined the details of the impending exchange. Mickey listened intently, all the while mulling over the implications of what she was hearing. Finally, Oda suggested that Mickey and Carola go to live with the other American internees in Stanley Camp until the Red Cross ship arrived to take them home. That is when Mickey spoke up. She shocked Oda, and even herself, by announcing that she was *not* going home. She remained adamant in her refusal to take Carola into the internment camp or to abandon Charles—or the other POWs who now shared the food parcels she delivered to the hospital every other week. Since visits were now prohibited and communications forbidden, Mickey could only watch from a distance as Charles and his fellow prisoners walked the hospital grounds.

Mickey agonized over whether or not Carola should stay with her mother or be sent to Chicago to live with the Hahns; friends had volunteered to take her. Mickey rejected these offers after Charles smuggled out a message saying that he opposed sending Carola away. A child's place was with her mother, he insisted; if Mickey was staying, so should Carola. "When you are not sure if you are right or wrong you must take someone else's decision. I was glad to have Charles to guide me, even in retrospect," Mickey wrote.[13]

In many ways, the decision to remain in Hong Kong was easier than living with its consequences; Mickey was left to ponder whether or not she had signed Carola's death warrant. Living conditions remained grim, and the mood of the Japanese took a marked turn for the worse only a few weeks after the departure of the Red Cross exchange ship. This downturn was due to a surprising development: the appearance of American warplanes in the skies over the colony. They came out of nowhere one day and vanished again in a few minutes. Although the air raid caused minimal damage, the mere fact that the planes came at all suggested that Allied military planners had not forgotten Hong Kong. This was a good news/bad news scenario. The good news was that it was an enormous morale boost for Mickey and the thousands of starving British, Canadian, and Indian POWs. The bad news was that the Japanese reacted angrily to the raid, lashing out at those least able to defend themselves.

Charles and other patients at Bowen Road Hospital had gathered on a veranda to watch the attack, cheering loudly as each bomb fell. The next day, the walking wounded were lined up on the veranda to watch as both the attending army surgeon and Charles, as the highest-ranking officer in the hospital, were reprimanded. Both were scolded and slapped in the face by an irate Japanese officer. He then stormed into the adjacent diphtheria ward, where he slapped the faces of the bedridden men who lay sick and dying.

Despite these developments and the new tensions in the colony as the American air raids became more regular, Mickey's life settled back into a routine. She even took in another female boarder, as much for company as to help make ends meet, although doing so was more difficult than ever. The bareness of her cupboards may have been at least partly to blame for what happened to her pet gibbon, Mr. Mills. The mischievous ape had survived the Battle of Hong Kong, the subsequent looting, and numerous brushes with angry neighbors upset by his unannounced visits. He even endured several brushes with death after ingesting various inedible objects. But a meal of paper clips proved too much for him. Mr. Mills's death was a painful one that Mickey could do nothing to prevent.

Around this same time, Charles was finally discharged from the hospital and transferred to the Argyle Street internment camp in Kowloon. Although Mickey now had to take the ferry across the harbor and then ride a crowded bus to visit him, she decided this arrangement was better; at least now she could *see* him. Mickey and Carola could join the crowd of women and children who delivered food parcels to a visitors' center, about three hundred yards from the camp's barbed wire fence. From there they could see and be seen by the prisoners. The armed guards enforced strict rules, which forbade visitors from stopping, waving, shouting, staring, or approaching the fence. That did not matter. Just being able to see Charles was reassuring. As Mickey walked along the street leading to the visitors' center, Charles moved with her step for step from one end of the POW camp to the other. As he did, Mickey could see that his wounded arm was improving, although he still had no use of the fingers. At one point, Charles was allowed to write a short note thanking Mickey for the food parcels, which he advised her he was sharing with seven other men "who would otherwise have nothing." That revelation filled Mickey with tears. She was still doing what she could to supply food parcels to Charles's friends at Bowen Road, and now she faced the daunting task of increasing the size of the parcels she delivered to the Argyle Street camp. "Making sure that [Charles didn't starve] was my whole existence, save for the effort I put in at home to seeing that Carola, too, was adequately fed," Mickey wrote. "My universe shrank to the dimensions of a digestive tube. There was nothing else to think about, no world outside, nothing."[14]

Mickey's own hunger was eased somewhat by Oda's kindness. He and members of his Foreign Office staff occasionally asked Mickey to dine with them. On one memorable evening, she was invited to the Grips to attend a dinner in honor of a Swiss man named Engle, who was in charge of the Far East Red Cross. The other guests were Oda's male subordinates at the Foreign Office, some of whom were accompanied by Chinese girlfriends. As the dinner progressed, Engle gushed about how well the Japanese were governing occupied China, and he spoke favorably of the German community in Shanghai. From time to time, Engle caught Mickey's eye and winked. All this was too much for her; the more she drank, the more hostile and resentful she became. Mickey hated Engle's guts. She wanted to lash out at him. In fact, she wanted to lash out at all of them. But she did not. Instead, she drank and brooded.

Mickey awoke the next morning with a hangover, fuzzy memories of the rest of the previous evening, and an awful sense that something was wrong, terribly wrong. When she rang Oda to thank him for the meal, he was cool. The reason became clear as they talked. Oda and two of his staff had driven a very drunk Mickey home from the restaurant. En route, Oda recounted, Mickey had lashed out at him, finally slapping him in the face. Mickey was incredulous; she had only a vague recollection of the incident. "Why did I slap you?" she asked, a knot of fear tightening her stomach. She knew it was unwise (unless one had a death wish) to slap the face of a Japanese official in occupied Hong Kong—particularly that of the head of the Foreign Affairs Office.

"I don't really know," Oda replied. "But I think it was probably that you had a subconscious desire to slap a Japanese."[15]

True or not, Mickey apologized profusely and vowed to herself to never again be so foolhardy. She well knew it was only because of Oda's goodwill that she had been spared internment, a beating, or much worse. "It is difficult to explain how this man, so much hated by many of the prisoners, so dangerously liable to attacks of conceit, still went on being extraordinarily and subtly decent to me," Mickey wrote. "It was Charles again, I suppose, and a sense of honor that most of his compatriots did not possess."[16]

Given the unique nature of their relationship, Mickey was devastated by the news not long afterward that Oda was being recalled to Tokyo. To show there were no hard feelings, he invited Mickey to a small farewell dinner party he was giving for his friends. She went, determined to be on her best behavior, and was, at least until she had a few drinks. As the evening passed, the conversation turned to the progress of the war, and Mickey found herself loudly proclaiming why the Axis powers were doomed. When Oda objected and calmly began explaining how Japan would one day rule the world, Mickey interrupted him by shouting, "Nuts!"

Oda responded by slapping her hard across the face. "I thought we had better get evened up before I left," he said coolly. There was an awkward pause, then both of them burst out laughing. The party continued as the others in the restaurant joined in.

Oda's farewell party was not the only one that fall. Mickey attended another that proved to be equally memorable and far more dangerous. The Selwyn-Clarkes asked her to a gathering at the Queen Mary Hospital in honor of Colonel Nguchi. Like Oda, their protector and patron had been posted out of Hong Kong. Mickey had not met Nguchi before, which was just as well for she was not impressed by him. He was short, stocky, and loud. The colonel and two companions, who arrived late, were already drunk. Nguchi insisted on kissing everyone flush on the lips, men and women alike; Mickey overheard one man complain when Nguchi French-kissed him.

At first, a large crowd of people were milling around the room with drinks in hand. There were some of Selwyn-Clarke's Chinese doctor friends, many Japanese army officers and gendarmes, and, of course, their "girls"—stylish young Chinese women who before the war had been "the darlings" of British and American bank boys and soldiers. As the party grew louder, Mickey was alarmed to realize that most of the other female guests had prudently slipped away. She could only protest meekly when a Japanese officer to whom she had been talking clapped her on the back and insisted that she accompany him, Nguchi, and some friends to dinner. The seriousness of her predicament became clear to Mickey the instant she realized everyone else in the dinner party had left in an army staff car, whereas she was hustled into the backseat of a smaller vehicle with the amorous Nguchi and two other Japanese officers, all of whom were extremely drunk.

Mickey fended off Nguchi's clumsy advances as best she could until the car stopped outside a popular downtown Chinese restaurant. Mickey recognized the eatery as a place she had often visited with Charles. As they tumbled out onto the pavement, Nguchi and his companions began to argue. Two of them wanted to eat, while the colonel was adamant about first taking Mickey back to his hotel room. She was frantic at the thought. Taking advantage of the confusion, she slipped into the restaurant. There she approached the surprised manager, who stood just inside the front door. To her relief, she realized that she knew the man. He was Ah King's brother! He hid Mickey in a pantry. Seconds later, an angry Nguchi and his companions burst through the door. The manager directed them upstairs, while a couple of Chinese waiters whisked Mickey out the back door and into a waiting rickshaw, which sped her off into the night. Mickey was relieved to hear nothing more from Nguchi before he left town.

• • •

A preoccupation with her own problems explains why Mickey was initially unaware of a subtle but profound policy shift on the part of the Japanese in early 1943. Within weeks of the British capitulation, the new authorities had made it known they intended to reduce Hong Kong's population from 1.7 million to about 500,000; the fewer useless mouths there were to feed, the better. At first, the strategy to accomplish this goal was passive. Conditions were allowed to deteriorate to the point where life was so wretched that many people had no choice but to flee. Disease and hunger fueled the mass exodus that was soon under way. As many as a thousand hungry Chinese refugees per day streamed northward along the Tai Po road toward China. By mid-1943, with the war going badly, the Japanese abandoned all pretense of "Asia for the Asiatics" and launched a ruthless reign of terror intended to speed the refugees on their way. The new strategy was as simple and effective: Japanese soldiers in trucks began snatching people right off the streets, mostly Chinese coolies who had neither the influence nor the money to cause trouble. Thousands of victims were forcibly rounded up and herded onto junks. These boats were towed out to sea, where most were set adrift to reach mainland China as best they could. Sometimes the boats were set ablaze or shot up by Japanese naval guns. The charred and bloated bodies of Chinese refugees regularly washed up on Hong Kong's beaches.

The Japanese euphemistically referred to this process as "repatriation." Mickey learned of it only when she went looking for her dentist, who was

Chinese. She was told the man had disappeared. When his family inquired, the gendarmes offered no explanations or clues as to his fate. Fortunately for him, the dentist was released a month later after his relatives paid a bribe to the right people. He had been beaten, tortured, and starved, but he was alive.

That such incidents were becoming commonplace was worrisome, because they signaled a new escalation in the level of Japanese thuggery. This could not have come at a worse time for Mickey, who was vulnerable once Oda returned to Tokyo. When word got around that her protector had left, those who had been watching Mickey and waiting for their opportunity pounced. Someone tried to blackmail her over a loan for two thousand yen that she had received from Hong Kong Savings Bank chairman Sir Vandeleur Grayburn, who had been implicated in secret relief efforts in the colony. He was arrested and tortured by the gendarmes and died on August 7, 1943, as a result of malnutrition and the injuries he had suffered during his "questioning." Mickey escaped a similar fate only because of the timely intervention of a Japanese journalist friend who appealed to people in high places on her behalf. That put an end to the threat for now, but there was a price to be paid. Mickey was asked to go to Tokyo to write propaganda for the Japanese government. When she declined the "request," she knew there would be more trouble, even though Oda had spoken to his successor on her behalf.

The new head of the Foreign Affairs Office in Hong Kong was a friend of Oda's. Tsuneo Hattori was tall, handsome, and possessed of "beautiful British manners," at least when he was dealing with those he sought to impress. Hattori, who adored Carola, was surprisingly friendly under the circumstances. Mickey was "his responsibility, his legacy [from Oda]," he explained. Nevertheless, Hattori cautioned Mickey that the gendarmes were watching her; if she got into trouble again, he confided, even *he* might not be able to rescue her.[17]

Mickey, already hungry and tired, became increasingly fearful that the gendarmes or their henchmen would come looking for her. No one was safe. With Nguchi out of the picture, even the Selwyn-Clarkes had been interned. Hilda was in Stanley Camp and her husband had been imprisoned in the gendarmerie. Hattori cautioned Mickey that there was nothing she could do for her friends. For once, Mickey paid heed. She remained fearful of the consequences of being taken away, not so much for herself as for those she loved.

Carola was now eighteen months old, having celebrated her first birthday on October 17, 1942. She had spent virtually all her life as a prisoner of circumstance in Hong Kong and, as a result, she was malnourished and spoke only a few words of English. Mickey could not, would not, let her daughter perish in this awful place, as had the children of several of her friends. She was equally determined to do what she could to see to it that Charles survived his ordeal as a POW. There were now persistent rumors that he and other British officers would be moved inland, possibly to Canton or maybe even Japan, where (contrary to the Geneva Convention) they would be forced to work as slave labor—if they made it there alive. On October 1, 1942, more than 840 British POWs on a Japan-bound merchant ship called the *Lisbon Maru* had drowned when the vessel was torpedoed by an American submarine whose captain was unaware the prisoners were on board. Many of those who died were trapped below decks when the Japanese crew sealed the hatches; others who jumped into the sea were shot by Japanese sailors on nearby ships or were torn apart by sharks as they swam for their lives. News of this incident filled Mickey with dread, because she knew that with his injured arm Charles would never survive such an ordeal.

Mickey worked tirelessly on behalf of Charles, doing whatever she could to stay informed about conditions inside the Argyle Street camp. On occasion, she dined with some of the Japanese guards. One, in particular, who was friendly with Charles, conveyed information back and forth to Mickey. Hattori was upset when he learned this; he felt such behavior on Mickey's part might raise suspicions among the gendarmes and create "problems" for both of them.

To avert any notion that he had anything to hide in his own dealings with her, Hattori introduced Mickey and his office secretary to General Suginami, the newly appointed chief of staff to the governor of Hong Kong. Mickey was pleased to learn that the general was an old friend of Charles's, who had known him back in England. Suginami, who had attended Oxford, was taken with Mickey's companion, an attractive young woman named Yvonne Ho. Yvonne refused to see the general alone, so on several occasions Mickey found herself invited to visit Suginami, too. It was on one of these occasions, over coffee in the garden of his house, that Mickey asked the general about the rumors that Charles and other British officers were about to be "sent away." Suginami was taken aback by the question. However, he politely insisted there was no truth to such reports. Later, he mused that once Germany was beaten, he felt the conflict in the Pacific would wind down "within two years." The general, like many Japanese, was still convinced that America really had no stomach for war and would agree to peace terms that allowed Japan to keep Hong Kong, Singapore, and other conquered territories in the Far East.

Despite the general's assurances, Mickey remained fearful that Charles and his fellow prisoners would be moved at any time. If they were, her reason for staying in Hong Kong would be gone; Hattori also knew this. That thought was running through both their minds one day in the summer of 1943, when Hattori summoned Mickey to his office to tell her the news that she had been waiting for: another Japanese-American prisoner exchange had been arranged for September. As this would probably be the last one, Hattori suggested that Mickey take advantage of it. She would not even have to go to Stanley Camp; he would see to that. Mickey remained reluctant, but Hattori finally convinced her to allow him to go to the Argyle Street camp on her behalf to ask Charles what he wanted Mickey to do.

When Hattori did so, Charles's reply was unequivocal: he wanted Mickey and Carola to leave Hong Kong. Charles also vowed that when the war was done, he would come to America to find Mickey and "make an honest woman" of her. This was surely one of the most unusual marriage proposals any woman had ever received.

James Endicott, his wife Mary, and family, c. 1940.
Courtesy Stephan Endicott

Mickey finally conceded it was time for her to go home. She advised Hattori that when the exchange ship left, she and Carola would be on it. The next few weeks were a flurry of activity, tidying up loose ends, saying good-byes, and selling everything that she had left so that she could give the money to Ah King and Carola's amah. Apart from that, there was just one other thing Mickey wanted to do more than anything: to see Charles one last time. Although she knew all visits with prisoners were forbidden, Mickey wrote a "dignified but flowery, and very military" letter to the camp commandant, Colonel Tokunaga.[18] Using all her literary skills, Mickey pleaded for one last opportunity to see Charles, the man she loved and the father of her child. Miraculously, the letter worked. Tokunaga actually cried as his interpreter read Mickey's words to him. Then, after a few minutes' consideration, he agreed to "break the law" just once, providing that General Suginami had no objections. He did not, and Mickey agreed to tell no one else about the arrangement.

So it was that one morning a few days before the scheduled arrival of the exchange ship, Mickey, Carola, and Ah Yuk appeared as instructed at the front gate of the Argyle Street camp. Ninety anxious minutes later, Charles was escorted into an office in an administrative building. He stood at attention behind an officer who was there to oversee the visit. At this point, it had been almost twenty months since Mickey had seen Charles up close or had spoken to him. And now, here he was, dirty, gaunt, and tired, but with that old twinkle

Hong Kong, early 1942 (l–r) Phyllis Bliss and son Brian, Mickey and Carola, Irene Fincher and daughter Frances.

still very much in his eyes; even he could not hide his pleasure at the joy of the moment.

They talked excitedly for half an hour. Afterward, Mickey scarcely remembered a word they had said. But that did not matter. Everything seemed all right now, especially after the Japanese officer turned his back a moment and

Hong Kong street (Kowloon side) circa 1940.
National Archives of Canada, PA 161883

Mickey and Charles exchanged a hasty kiss. Then it was time to go. As Charles turned to leave, Carola began to whimper. "Uncle's gone," she said. When Ah Yuk whispered in her ear, Carola corrected herself, "Daddy's gone."

"Daddy's gone," Mickey repeated. "So now, Carola, we go to America."[19]

As Mickey lay in her bunk aboard the *Teia Maru* the afternoon of September 22, 1943, she recalled that tearful scene, and thought of many other things. The path that had brought her to this time and place had been long and uncertain. It had often been dangerous, but it had never been dull.

Mickey knew she had reached a crossroads in her life. The man she loved, the father of her child, was in a Japanese POW camp, and chances were that she would never see him alive again. After more than eight years in China, Mickey was finally going home. She was thirty-eight years old, a single mother with only her writing to support her. Everything that she owned was in a couple of battered old suitcases. Where would she and her daughter go? What would they do? How could she ever begin all over again?

Mickey hugged Carola close. Then she wiped the tears from her eyes and pulled a blanket over the two of them. She joined her daughter in the sleep of the exhausted. Mickey knew in her heart that she would somehow make do. She always did.

Victoria waterfront, circa 1940. National Archives of Canada, PA 161884

VI

Happily Ever After?

26

THE *Teia Maru*, the ship that carried Mickey and Carola on the first leg of their 18,000-mile voyage home, steamed west out of Stanley Harbor next morning, September 23, 1943. The Japanese-controlled English daily the *Hongkong News* (sic) reported that before the vessel left, the 1,400 Canadian and American repatriates on board had "expressed their *gratitude* to the authorities for the kind treatment and consideration which had been accorded them."[1] The article neglected to mention that Japanese authorities had warned these same people that denouncing the living conditions in Hong Kong's internment camps would affect the treatment of those left behind and might jeopardize any further prisoner exchanges.

If Mickey expressed "gratitude" for anything, it was that her voyage home had finally begun; there could be no turning back for her or anyone else aboard. Their ship stopped briefly at Mormugao, a neutral Portuguese port on India's west coast, south of Bombay, before continuing on to Lourenço Marques—modern-day Mozambique. Here they awaited a rendezvous with a Swedish relief ship, the *Gripsholm*, loaded with Japanese nationals traveling in the opposite direction. Under the circumstances, the repatriation of such a large number of people was an ambitious undertaking.

"The whole of Asia was either at war or not in a position to handle such an exchange," American journalist Max Hill wrote of a 1942 prisoner swap, of which this one a year later was a carbon copy. "That meant the *Gripsholm* had to sail from New York, cross the Atlantic, swing around the southern tip of Africa and bring the Japanese safely into port at Lourenço Marques. [The] American men, women, and children who were leaving the Japanese Empire, Shanghai, Hong Kong, and Saigon . . . had to skirt the coast of Asia, pass through the Sundra Strait in the Netherlands East Indies, cross the Indian Ocean—keeping far out from the shore to avoid war zones—and then tie up in the same port."[2]

Despite their exhaustion, the first day at sea was a restless one for Mickey and her infant daughter. Like most toddlers, Carola crawled for miles in her sleep. Sharing a bunk with her at night was akin to sleeping with a bag of puppies; Mickey drifted in and out of consciousness. When finally she did nod off, her mind was filled with terrible dreams—the face of a starving Charles, torpedoed ships, Carola sobbing, sharks slicing through the roiling ocean waves. . . . It was nearly too much to take.

Despite the presence of red ants and human clutter, both of which were everywhere on the ship, Mickey tried to sleep on a straw mat that she spread out on her cabin floor. The arrangement proved unworkable, and most nights while Carola settled Mickey went up on deck. There she talked with other passengers or paced endlessly around the ship, which was "lit up like a birthday cake" to make it easy for submarines from both sides to identify.

It was on these nocturnal rambles that Mickey discovered the social structure that had already formed. Most of the *Teia Maru*'s passengers were what Mickey termed "ordinary burghers": diplomats, journalists, oilmen, and businesspeople. However, there were a couple of other groups as well. One was a large contingent of nuns and missionaries, who had been trapped at their charges when the war broke out. Then there were about a dozen rough-and-tumble characters whom Mickey dubbed "the Dead End Kids." Some were merchant seamen, some professional gamblers. Others were soldiers who had somehow escaped from the military. The Dead End Kids were ensconced in a couple of cabins in the second-class passenger area. There they played cards, drank, swore, fought, and generally raised hell, although they were friendly toward Mickey. They were amused that she smoked cigars, and one of them took a liking to Carola. Relations between the Dead End Kids and the other passengers were less cordial. "I still can't decide who behaved with less kindness and tolerance—the Dead End Kids or the missionaries. Their attitude towards each other was the same, a fierce hatred," Mickey observed.[3]

In an effort to keep the peace, the ship's passenger organizing committee formed a vigilante group. At first, the Dead Enders ignored—and resented—this "Goon Squad," as they dubbed them. When the Dead Enders ran out of money to buy liquor from the ship's stores, they began stealing from fellow passengers. This was all too much for the organizing committee, who delegated Mickey to deliver an ominous message to the Dead Enders: unless they shaped up, "Washington" had authorized the Goon Squad to use "any means necessary" to restore order. This included literally throwing offenders off the ship. In the face of such a threat, things quickly quieted down. The rest of the voyage was uneventful, apart from an uproar on the last night at sea, when the Dead Enders joined other passengers in looting a supply of saki that the ship's Japanese crew had stashed away for their own repatriates to drink on the return voyage. The raid was carried out with such precision that by the time the crew organized a search of the passenger cabins, it was too late to recover any of the missing bottles or even to seek retribution. The next morning the *Teia Maru* arrived at Lourenço Marques.

There they rendezvoused with the *Gripsholm*, which arrived the next day carrying hundreds of jubilant Japanese nationals who were bound for home. It was an extraordinary scene. The hull of the *Gripsholm* had been painted in the blue and yellow of the Swedish flag and with gigantic white letters that read: "*Diplomat. Gripsholm Sverige.*" As the ship docked, repatriates crowded to the railings of both vessels. Mickey saw how well fed, well dressed, and content the Japanese aboard the *Gripsholm* were. They burst into song as their ship drew near the quay. By comparison, the scene aboard the *Teia Maru* was funereal; people stood in numb silence. "We were refugees from Japan and Japanese-occupied territory," Mickey wrote, "skinny Americans, shabby Americans, brown-paper parcel Americans, in a particularly chastened frame of mind. We were dried out and grimy, on a filthy little ship."[4]

Mickey, Carola, and their fellow passengers waited two more long days to escape the *Teia Maru*. When finally it was time for the exchange, the passengers lugged their belongings down the gangplank, onto the dock, and then onto the other ship. The entire process took only a few minutes. Once it was complete, there was a deafening silence among the passengers aboard the *Teia Maru*; this time it was the Japanese who looked on in stunned silence as the Americans on the *Gripsholm* sang and laughed.

Conditions were heavenly on the ship that was to take Mickey and Carola home. There were no more pesky red ants. The cabins were clean and comfortable. The crew was friendly, the food was good—and there was lots of it. Mickey was delighted to discover there was even a hairdresser aboard. The passengers "wallowed in Swedish luxury." Carola, malnourished and underweight, had never seen such plenty. The *New York Times* would later report how "many of [the passengers] had put on from eight to twenty-five pounds during their voyage on the *Gripsholm*."[5] Mickey used some of her precious dollars to hire an amah for Carola. Kitty Bush was a young Eurasian woman who spoke Cantonese, the dialect Carola had learned.

There was, as Mickey noted, "room at last for our egos to spread out."[6] The passengers began reverting to familiar behavior patterns. The diplomats became aloof. The missionaries preached. And the businessmen began issuing orders to anyone who would listen, while their wives set about organizing social life aboard the ship. Even the Dead End Kids fell into step; as they had aboard the *Teia Maru*, they holed up in a couple of cabins where they again proceeded to enjoy themselves, this time much more quietly.

The *Gripsholm* arrived at Port Elizabeth, South Africa, a week later. From there it was eleven days sailing to cross the Atlantic to the Brazilian city of Rio de Janeiro. At sea on October 17, Carola celebrated her second birthday. Otherwise, it was a quiet voyage. "Nothing ever dragged as much as the two weeks it took to get us from Rio to New York," Mickey wrote. "It wasn't just my own idea; everybody noticed it. Moreover, everybody was feeling the way I was about reaching New York, too. Instead of being impatient and eager to get there, I was afraid. I was appalled at the prospect of diving into life again. I saw freedom ahead of me, days full of my own decisions, a continent to wander in without exit or entry permits and without permits to take my baggage, permits to own my baby. I was scared to death."[7]

The *Gripsholm* steamed into New York harbor the night of November 30, 1943, with all lights blazing. As the big ship glided past the Statue of Liberty on Bedloe's Island, many repatriates braved the cold to gather on the after-promenade deck, where they broke into a loud chorus of "God Bless America." The sound of their joyful voices rang out in the darkness that cloaked the calm waters of the Upper Bay.

It was too late to disembark, so the ship's captain dropped anchor, and everyone spent one more sleepless night aboard. There was a festive atmosphere. The next morning, shortly before 10 A.M., the *Gripsholm* completed its long voyage when tugs guided it to Pier F in Jersey City, just across the river from Manhattan. A noisy throng of cheering friends, families, and journalists awaited the passengers who crowded to the railing or peered out the ship's portholes into a thick morning fog. Newsreel cameras recorded the joyful scene as the repatriates called out to loved ones. Some among the waiting crowd waved little American flags or threw confetti and streamers as the ship docked. Others wept tears of joy. When Red Cross officials boarded the *Gripsholm*, they did so carrying sacks overflowing with 20,000 welcome home letters and messages, as well as new clothes for everyone who needed them. The emotional homecoming was front-page news in the next morning's edition of the *New York Times*.

It was two hours before the first passengers came down the *Gripsholm*'s gangplank and into the welcoming arms of loved ones. The delay was due to customs officials who filled out myriad forms and scanned the passengers' documents. When that was done, agents from Army and Navy intelligence, as well as the Federal Bureau of Investigation (FBI) went to work; they were searching for enemy spies and collaborators. Everyone aboard the ship was interviewed. The process took so long that two hundred passengers, Mickey and Carola among them, were forced to spend yet another night aboard the ship. Thirty of the repatriates, even less fortunate, were taken away to Ellis Island for more extensive questioning.

Mickey also received special attention. American intelligence officials knew little of her life in China. Having lived abroad since 1935, she was a relative unknown to the FBI. Her file initially consisted of no more than a few sheets of paper with the barest of biographical information, most of it incorrect or out of date. All that changed the day that she arrived home. According to declassified government documents, FBI agents sought out at least two "confidential informants" in New York City who provided information about Mickey and her life in China. Thus, although most of the *Gripsholm*'s passengers were asked a few perfunctory questions while their papers were being processed,

Mickey was interrogated at length. She was given a quick physical examination—"height: 5′4½″, weight: 130 lb, hair: dark brown, eyes: hazel," the report noted—and then interviewed by a succession of eight panels of military intelligence officers and FBI agents. The men asked her the same questions over and over, hoping to catch her out. The ordeal lasted all day, although everything became a blur to Mickey after only a few hours. "It was all very confusing," she recalled, "and so very tiring."[8]

At one point, Carola began to cry uncontrollably. This so unnerved Mickey's questioners that they suggested that she and a female customs officer deliver the child to "a relative" who was waiting on the dock. "As I stepped down from the gangplank, a whole lot of lights flared in our faces," Mickey wrote. "Carola screamed, of course, and started hitting out at the world, most of the blows landing on me." A crowd of reporters surged forward, pencils and notebook poised. "What's your name? Who are you?" they shouted. Mickey stood before them dumbfounded, vainly trying to comfort her daughter. Suddenly a woman emerged from the crowd. "I stared at her utterly strange, emotion-suffused face, and then, just before she put her arms around me, she turned into my sister Helen," Mickey wrote. "I almost laughed because I hadn't known her at once, but there was no time to tell her about it."[9] There was also no time to talk; the customs officer tapped Mickey on the arm and reminded her she was obliged to return to the ship.

Later, when she tried to recall other details of the day and of her interrogation, Mickey could not. It had all become an endless swirl of names, faces, and questions. The men asked her about every detail of her life in Hong Kong, her relationships with Sinmay and Charles, and her dealings with Japanese officials such as Takio Oda, Tsuneo Hattori, Chick Nakazowa, Colonel Noma, and General Suginami.

Why hadn't she been interned like other Americans?

Why had she received "favors" from the Japanese?

Why had she fraternized with such high-ranking enemy officials?

Had she been a Japanese spy?

On and on it went. Mickey answered each question truthfully, holding nothing back. She even revealed that she had carried home with her a cryptic note from a Japanese friend in Hong Kong to some people in New York. It read: *"Japanese affection for/ Japanese verse is the/ glowing disk of the rising sun/ over Japan's mountains."* The message had been typed on a tiny piece of cloth that Mickey had sewn into the sleeve of Carola's blue silk dress. This revelation piqued the curiosity of the FBI agents, who were convinced they were onto something big. The dress was dispatched to the agency's headquarters in Washington, where the fabric was examined in the labs and the message was studied by cryptographers.

In the end, the FBI found nothing incriminating. Although they remained suspicious, Mickey was finally permitted to leave the ship late on the afternoon of December 2, 1943. By the time she stumbled down the ship's gangplank, most of the crowd on the pier had gone home. The only one waiting for Mickey was a friend of her brother-in-law, who drove Mickey to Helen and Herbert's downtown apartment. There she found the group of friends and relatives eager to welcome her gathered in the living room. They had a problem. Carola, howling loudly, had scrambled under the sofa and stayed there for several hours. She spoke no English, of course, and did not know her aunt or anyone else who tried to lure her out. Carola was inconsolable. Mickey extracted her daughter, dried her tears, and hugged her. Then she looked around the room at the crowd of smiling faces. There next to Helen and Herbert was Mickey's mother Hannah, who was now a spry eighty-seven-year-old. She had come all the way from Chicago to welcome Mickey home. "Well!" was all Hannah could think to say. "Well!" Now it was her turn to hug and Mickey's to cry. Afterward, they sat down to talk. "How's everybody, and where are they?" Mickey asked. There were two years of family news to catch up on.

• • •

Mickey had last seen her sister Helen on that day in June 1935 when she had sailed from Shanghai, leaving her sister behind in China. It had been even longer since Mickey had seen her mother. Hannah was in New York for her daughter's homecoming because *New Yorker* editor Harold Ross had paid her train fare from Chicago and put her up in a downtown hotel. Mickey never forgot Ross's kindness, which was typical of him.

On the evening of December 2, Ross and his wife Ariane (his third) visited Hannah's hotel room, where Mickey and Carola were spending the night. Ross and Mickey had a long conversation, for he was full of questions about China, a country that fascinated him. For all his presumed worldliness and sophistication, Harold Ross had traveled very little. He had been abroad just once, while serving in the U.S. Army during the First World War.

In the days that followed, John Gunther, Donald Hansen and his wife Muriel, and many other friends and acquaintances dropped by to say hello. Mickey's return to New York was well publicized in the media, although not all the coverage was positive. Publisher Bennett Cerf reported in the gossip column that he wrote for the *Saturday Review of Literature* how "the publicity-wise Emily Hahn" had returned from Hong Kong with her "two-year-old half-Chinese baby" in her arms and "a long black stogie" in her mouth. Cerf added, "There were a lot of other people on the *Gripsholm* . . . who had a darned sight more interesting and perilous time than the photogenic Emily, but who were more or less overlooked in the *Hahnward* rush."[10]

Mickey, who was fast recovering her feistiness despite her recent travails, responded to the column with a snarly letter to the editor. She chided Cerf, whom she suggested should stick to publishing, while the *Saturday Review* should stick to "reviewing." She also complained that Cerf's account of her homecoming "seems to have been thought up by Mr. Cerf himself, perhaps at a nightclub. There were no reporters allowed aboard the *Gripsholm* and I wasn't interviewed at all, by anyone but government officials."[11]

Mickey's friend Katharine White, one of her *New Yorker* editors, insisted on

THEY'LL SPEND CHRISTMAS IN WINNETKA

Emily Hahn and her daughter, Carola, who speaks only Chinese, arrive at the La Salle Street Station to spend Christmas with Mrs. Hahn's mother and sister in Winnetka. They returned to the United States aboard the S.S. Gripsholm after spending two years in Jap-held Hong Kong. Mrs. Hahn's husband is still a Jap prisoner. SUN PHOTO.

Mickey and Carola go home for the Christmas holidays.
Newspaper clipping from the Chicago Sun, *December 22, 1943.*

taking Mickey to consult with "one of the *New Yorker*'s finest attorneys." When she did, the attorney sent Cerf a "threatening letter." He apologized in his next column, conceding he had been wrong about Carola being half Chinese. "He also pointed out that her father was, in fact, a married British army officer who was now a POW in Hong Kong," Mickey recalled with a laugh. "I told Katharine we should have left well enough alone."[12]

Mickey could afford to laugh off the incident. She had other things to worry about as she struggled to rebuild her life. Fortunately, money was not a problem. Carl Brandt had deposited thousands of dollars in royalties from *The Soong Sisters* and *Mr. Pan* books in Mickey's bank account, which Helen had tended to in her sister's absence. Mickey used the money to rent a suite in a downtown hotel and to buy a new typewriter. She was bursting with creative energy. Over the next few weeks, Mickey wrote dozens of short stories and magazine articles about her wartime experiences in Hong Kong. One of the first was a two-part "Reporter at Large" series for the *New Yorker*, which told the true story of her experiences aboard the *Teia Maru* and *Gripsholm*. The articles attracted a wide readership because they were among the most compelling accounts of the wartime repatriation of American civilians from Japanese occupied territories. Other writers have told of similar experiences, but no one has ever written as eloquently or in as much detail as Mickey did. She also began work on a book, a startlingly candid memoir of her eight years in China. Mickey had a phenomenal memory, and she used it to full advantage now. She was determined to hold nothing back, to tell her story as fully and truthfully as she possibly could.

The emotional price she paid for doing so was high. The writing brought back a flood of vivid memories—happy as well as painful—of her life in the Far East. Most acute were her feelings for Charles. Mickey had heard nothing more of him since leaving Hong Kong. Although she remained hopeful, in her heart she despaired of ever seeing him alive again. The thought of Charles dying alone in a dark, filthy prison cell from starvation or torture filled her with longing and smoldering rage. Mickey was angry at the fates who had toyed with her so cruelly, angry with the Japanese and the British for their stupidities, and angry at the war. But most of all, she was angry at herself for being weak and for having left Hong Kong. It mattered little that she knew that she had done what was best for everyone; in her heart Mickey still felt she should have stayed for Charles's sake. Had she done so, Mickey and Carola almost certainly would have perished.

The situation in Hong Kong had continued to deteriorate in the wake of the *Teia Maru*'s departure. As it did, Charles became swept up in deadly prison camp intrigues. The Japanese guards were determined to control the flow of goods and information into and out of the POW camps. The punishments were harsh for those who were caught smuggling messages or listening to BBC war news on makeshift radio receivers. Nevertheless, the prisoners had developed an elaborate underground network that was fueled as much by ingenuity and courage as by sheer boredom and the corruption of many of the Japanese guards and their Chinese and Indian collaborators.

In late September 1943, some of the men in the British POW camps figured out that the supply truck that served them also made runs out to Stanley Camp, the civilian internment facility. Someone devised a way to hide messages inside one of the truck's hubcaps, which was cleverly modified for the purpose. "That was fine," explained Charles's friend Alf Bennett, "but what happened was that those bloody people, instead of using this for good and useful information, began using it to send personal messages to wives, girlfriends, and others at Stanley Camp. Of course, the Japanese found out about this stupid chit chat."[13]

An Indian informer passed on the information to the Japanese. Although he had not been involved directly, Charles was implicated and was "arrested" by the *Kempetai*, along with several other British officers. All were found guilty at a court martial. The *New York Times* and many other American newspapers subsequently carried a wire news service story from the Associated Press that claimed Charles was one of two British officers who had been executed for being caught with a radio receiver.[14] This chilling news fulfilled all of Mickey's darkest fears. When she scrambled to learn more, her frantic phone calls yielded no further information. Mickey spent several tearful and sleepless nights being consoled by family and friends. In her heart, she would not, could not, believe that Charles was dead. When approached for a comment by a *Times* reporter, Mickey put on a brave face. "Unless there is more evidence, I do not intend to believe the rumor," she said.[15] Still, she had only blind faith to sustain her.

Mickey did what she could to get on with her life. She rented an apartment on 96th Avenue East in Manhattan and found a nursery school for Carola. The principal suggested that Mickey have Carola examined by a doctor who was doing some innovative work with young patients. Dr. Benjamin Spock, a native of nearby New Haven, Connecticut, was the first American physician to complete professional training both as a pediatrician and as a psychiatrist. When Mickey and Carola met him, childcare guru-to-be Spock was still developing the ideas he would present to the world in *The Commonsense Book of Baby and Child Care* (1946).

Spock said Carola's lack of hair and her tiny size were related to the nutritional deficiencies she had suffered. Both would correct themselves as her diet improved, he predicted. Her dental problems could be solved by a dentist. As for her fearfulness, Spock prescribed megadoses of maternal affection. "Spoil her. Within reason," he instructed Mickey.

She was more than willing to comply. Here was an opportunity to make up for all the deprivations and hardships Carola had endured in Hong Kong; Mickey might never see Charles again, but she would love their child with all her heart and soul. To the dismay of many of her family and friends, Mickey smothered Carola with affection. She bought her toys and anything else that she wanted. Nothing was too big or expensive. Mickey moved Carola's crib into her bedroom and installed a night-light. She doted on her tiny daughter. The results were wondrous. Just as Dr. Spock had predicted, Carola responded. Soon she was looking and behaving like a normal American three-year-old.

Mickey's own transition to her new life in New York was considerably more arduous. She found that time stretched ahead endlessly with no real rhyme or reason. The uncertainty over Charles's fate left Mickey empty and utterly alone. Nothing else seemed important; she was slipping into a depression. In early December, Mickey, Carola, and Kitty, the new amah, left on an extended Yuletide visit to Chicago. Rose and Mitchell Dawson had offered Mickey the use of a study in their seventeen-room house in suburban Winnetka, where she could work on a planned book about her China experiences. Hannah was also staying with the Dawsons, and Mickey's younger sister Dauphine, who had married and was also living in Winnetka. Sadly, what initially promised to be both a carefree family reunion and a productive work time soon became an unpleasant ordeal for everyone. Rose, who had stepped into Hannah's shoes as the Hahn matriarch, was every bit as adamant as her mother had been in her opinions about family etiquette. This put her on a collision course with Mickey.

Rose and Mitchell Dawson had three children: a son named Greg and two daughters, Hilary and Jill. Mickey's arrival in the house made vivid impressions on all of them. For as long as any of the children could remember, their Aunt Mickey had been someone who sent letters and occasionally a photo from distant China. All that the children knew about her had come from listening to their parents talk. Now suddenly here was Aunt Mickey in the flesh; it was not easy to reconcile expectations with reality. Mickey recalled how disappointed nine-year-old Greg was to discover that she was not a monkey. He had somehow gained that impression. Hilary remembered how her mother was "angered, shocked, and astounded" by Mickey's attitudes and behavior.[16] When they got to know her, the Dawson children decided their aunt was so carefree and exotic she must have dropped in from another planet; Mickey demanded nothing of her nieces and nephew and imposed no restrictions on them.

Greg remembered his Aunt Mickey's "un-Dawsonlike" attitude toward money. "[She] had been deprived of money for so long that when she returned home to the U.S. she went crazy spending the money which had accumulated in her bank account while she was away. Mickey was Lady Bountiful. It was as though she said, 'Let's spoil Carola, and we'll do Greg too while we're at it!' "[17]

Mickey bought the children a pet monkey. For Christmas, she gave Greg an elaborate Chinese warrior costume that he coveted; Rose was shocked at the extravagance. She was no less astounded when she learned that Mickey had bought her son an expensive miniature pipe. Rose, Mickey, and Greg were shopping in Chicago one day when Mickey stopped at a tobacco shop for cigars. There, in a display case, Greg spotted a exquisite Kaywoodie miniature pipe. He had to have it. Rose thought the $10 price ridiculous, and she said so. Mickey was of a different mind; she promptly bought the tiny wooden pipe, which she secretly gave to Greg.

Such gestures heightened tensions between Mickey and Rose, and it was not long before things came to a head. Surprisingly, the trouble began not because of Mickey's relationships with the Dawson children, but rather over her treatment of Carola. A reporter from the *Chicago Sun* came by the Dawson house one evening in late December to interview Mickey, who talked freely about her relationship with Sinmay and about the circumstances of Carola's birth. Mickey also allowed a photographer to take a shot of Carola in her crib. Mitchell, who observed all of this, listened in on an extension when the reporter phoned in his story, the details of which sent Rose into a rage. Mitchell called an editor friend at the newspaper to ask that the article be killed. It was not. The impact was immediate when it appeared in the *Sun* under a headline proclaiming, "I was the concubine of a Chinese!" The Dawson children were delighted to see their cousin Carola's picture in the newspaper; Rose was furious that Mickey had "exploited" her daughter for what Rose regarded as selfish reasons. Mickey took exception, of course, and all hell broke loose. When the shouting ended, Mickey packed up Carola and her amah and moved out of the Dawson house and into a hotel.

• • •

Back in New York, Mickey began working feverishly on her China memoir, which she finished in just a few months. *China to Me* was a book so unflinchingly honest and candid that it sent some people reeling. In it, Mickey related the details of her experiences in China from 1935 through to her 1943 repatriation aboard the *Gripsholm*. It was all there—her "marriage" to Sinmay, her relationship with Sir Victor Sassoon, her opium addiction, and the whole story of her love affair with Charles. She spared none of the details; after all, the book was a "partial autobiography," as Mickey termed it. But it was more than that. *China to Me* was also a wondrous blend of reportage and personal memoir written in Mickey's own inimitable style. Mickey, who insisted she had no political allegiances, nonetheless held strong opinions about what was happening in China, and she was not reluctant to share them. What she had to say put her at odds with a vocal lobby of left-leaning sympathizers who had been working hard to paint the Nationalist forces under Chiang Kai-shek as corrupt and incompetent.

Mickey asserted that the American public had been hoodwinked into believing that the Communist guerillas under Mao Tse-tung comprised the only Chinese military force that was making a stand against the Japanese. While conceding that the efforts of the Communists were "inspiring and invaluable," Mickey argued that much of their effectiveness was lost because of internal squabbles and petty personal jealousies among the leadership. "I am not trying to run them down, Agnes Smedley and Ed Snow and General [Evans] Carlson and the rest of you; I'm only trying to undo some of the harm you have unwittingly done your friends," Mickey wrote. "You have worked people into a state where they are going to be awfully mad pretty soon. They are heading for a big disappointment."[18]

Mickey went on to chide those American journalists in China who "out of a frustrated sense of guilt, a superior viewpoint of things as they are, and of a tendency to follow the crowd," had jumped on the bandwagon and were boosting America's faith in the good intentions of the Chinese Communists. "Most newspapermen don't know any more about the Communists in China than you do," she cautioned her readers.[19]

China to Me caused a sensation when it was published in the fall of 1944. Mickey's candor landed her smack in the middle of a growing public debate about China, and that alienated many former friends. Agnes Smedley, whom Mickey had befriended in Hong Kong, was especially irate. She had taken exception to Mickey's book *The Soong Sisters*, dismissing it as Nationalist propaganda. *China to Me* was the last straw for Agnes, who regarded it as a personal attack and began denouncing Mickey to anyone who would listen. Mickey attended a backstage reception for panelists who had discussed China on the NBC radio show *America's Town Meeting*. Agnes, who had taken part in the program, reported in a letter to a friend that "the bitch Emily Hahn came, and of course we [did] not speak."[20]

Reviewer T. A. Bisson of the *Nation*, a journal that in 1944 strongly supported many leftist causes, led the mob that was counterattacking Mickey. "Her prejudices—the strongest one is against 'leftists,' a term she much affects—are almost as fascinating as her naivete," wrote Bisson. "God rest her soul! Both China and the leftists may, perhaps, manage to outlive even Emily Hahn's commentary."[21]

More typical of the media reception for *China to Me* were the comments of reviewer H. L. Binsse of *Commonweal*, the Roman Catholic weekly. Ironically, he ignored Mickey's amorous adventures, preferring instead to focus his attention on the book's political aspects. Binsse pointed out that in "nine-tenths of its pages" *China to Me* was a "vivid and moving account of life on the China Coast."[22] Most other reviewers agreed, even Adrienne Koch of the *New York Times Book Review*, whose enthusiasm for *China to Me* was tempered; she acknowledged Mickey's storytelling gift. "She's as good as the best over a martini," wrote Koch. "Nobody will be so dour as to resent her autointoxication."[23]

It was not politics as much as Mickey's morality—or perceived *immorality*—that disturbed many readers. As had been the case with her controversial 1935 novel *Affair*, which had dealt with abortion, Mickey's candor in dealing with sensitive issues upset conservatives. Reviewer Katharine Shorey of *Library Journal* noted that "[*China to Me*] will be very valuable for all libraries, but its extreme frankness may unfortunately rule it out of school libraries."[24]

Predictably, all of the controversy and the resulting publicity spurred sales of the book. Despite wartime paper shortages, which delayed reprintings, *China to Me* climbed to second place on the national nonfiction best-seller list. Sales would have been even better—and Mickey's literary career much different—had the Book-of-the-Month Club (BOMC) not opted to take a new book of humor by Mickey's *New Yorker* colleague James Thurber as its selection for the 1944 Christmas season. *The Thurber Carnival* was a much safer choice for middle America than a topical book about politics and love in wartorn China.

Despite the BOMC disappointment, Mickey suddenly found herself in demand for interviews and appearances. She began working with a Broadway producer on a possible play about her adventures aboard the *Gripsholm*. America had finally discovered the literary talents of Mickey Hahn; she had become an instant celebrity. In late 1944, she began a series of lucrative public lectures for which she was billed as "a woman years ahead of her time."

No one was more puzzled by all of this attention than Mickey herself. "The hubhub I have caused surprised even me," she confided in a letter to her old friend Sir Victor Sassoon, who was living in Bombay, India. "I don't consider [*China to Me*] a very shocking book, and I certainly don't think they are justified in assuming that I rolled in the hay with every man I mentioned. After all, I mention only one affair, and Charles was practically legal. American book reviewers, who are obviously the most frustrated people in the world, seem to think if there was so much smoke, there must have been fire, too."[25]

Flush with success, Mickey splurged by renting an eleven-room townhouse on East 95th Street in upper Manhattan. However, despite her newfound affluence, Mickey was deeply troubled. "I am terribly homesick [for China]," she told Sir Victor. "I am working terribly hard—harder than I ever did in my life, but since a good deal of it is only for Carola and me, I feel guilty that I should be doing more about the war."[26]

Mickey's life had taken on an air of fantasy; nothing seemed real, not even the bountiful supplies of food and consumer goods that were available in New York shops. With rationing still in effect, butter and nylons were in short supply, and Mickey began seeking out these items on New York's version of the black market. It was the "old familiar thrill of outwitting authority," as she put it, that inspired her to do so.[27] What's more, she boasted to family and friends of her prowess in finding goods others could not. "I'd come home from Hong Kong wearing a chip on my shoulder, and it wasn't to be jiggled off all that quickly," Mickey later said. "I couldn't have explained any of this to my family—I didn't understand it myself."[28]

Those who were close to her were distressed by Mickey's sometimes outlandish behavior. Her salty language and cigar smoking were the talk of the town, as was her decision to pose in the nude for New York society photographer George Platt Lynnes. Helen and other family members were no less disturbed by Mickey's decision to hire a Dutch-born "artful dodger" named Willy Schumacher as her cook-houseboy. Willy, a friend of the Dead Enders whom Mickey had met aboard the *Gripsholm*, was looking for work and Mickey needed help, so she hired him. "He was small and rat-like, a really rough character," recalled one of Mickey's nephews.[29]

Given Willy's background, it was not surprising that he was adept at securing scarce consumer goods on the black market, particularly prime grade steaks. He was also a good cook, so Willy and Mickey got along well. However, his unpolished demeanor was not his worst shortcoming. Far more ominous was that Willy and his wife were addicted to morphine. It was not long before Willy was supplying the drug to Mickey. She embraced its soothing properties, which helped her to forget her pain. Although morphine initially produces euphoria in its users, chronic abuse has serious physiological and emotional side effects, one of which can be depression. Mickey knew this, and she agonized over the dangers of slipping back into drug dependency. Apart from a few pipes of opium she had shared with friends in Hong Kong, she had been "clean" for almost four years.

The emotional and physical strain were taking a terrible toll on Mickey, who continued her headlong rush toward disaster. She never saw what was coming. Four years of poor nutrition, stress, and troubles all caught up with her during a mid-January 1945 visit home, during which she was to give "a hush-hush" lecture to some officers at the military base in Evanston, Illinois. An army doctor there took one look at Mickey and whisked her to a nearby hospital for a shot of penicillin, which he hoped would relieve her burning fever and the howling pain from two nasty carbuncles. The penicillin proved useless against the fever or the boils. What was wrong with Mickey was far more serious than she or anyone else initially realized. Mickey Hahn was in a fight for her very life.

27

It was sheer luck and nothing more that saved Mickey Hahn's life when she was rushed to the hospital in Evanston that cold day in January 1945. By chance, the pathologist on duty in the emergency department was a German-trained war refugee who had worked in the Philippines. Had he not been, it is unlikely anyone at St. Francis Hospital would have realized in time that Mickey's ailment was *not* a strain of malaria, which was the diagnosis of the army doctor who had sent her for treatment. Nor was it a simple skin condition caused by "worry or celibacy," as Mickey quipped in a letter to Sir Victor Sassoon.[1]

Fortunately for Mickey, the pathologist elicited enough information from her before she passed out from the pain that he was able to diagnose her condition as an attack of Borneo sores. The disease, caused by a virulent streptococcal bacteria, is usually fatal if left untreated. This being only the fourth recorded case of Borneo sores ever seen in the United States at that time, and the first ever in the American Midwest, Mickey certainly would have died from blood poisoning if not for the German doctor's skill. In the operating room, the surgeon discovered that Mickey's carbuncles were gangrenous. Doctors drained three pints of fluid from her wounds during a life-saving operation.

Several anxious days passed before Mickey's family and friends learned she would survive. It was another week before she had the strength to sit up in bed, feed herself, or even dictate a letter. "If you are interested in how I stay comfortable, I will tell you the secret," Mickey confided in a note to Katharine White, one of her editors at the *New Yorker.* "One wound is on the left buttock and the other on the left side of my stomach, so I balance on my right hip. . . . I now weigh less than I had ever hoped to achieve."[2]

The seriousness of Mickey's illness and the three weeks she spent in the hospital were a jolt to her psyche as well as her bank account. The rate of pay for *New Yorker* contributors was based on frequency of contributions and because Mickey had become so prolific, at the time of her illness she was earning $2,000 per article—just $300 less than the average factory worker in the United States earned for a full year's work—and royalty money from various books was rolling in. Mickey earned more than $20,000 in book royalties alone in 1944. The woman who had been a penniless refugee just a few months before was doing very well for herself. Although this amount allowed her to live comfortably, she was not without financial worries, for she was spending money faster than she made it. After suffering through two years of hunger and deprivation in Hong Kong, Mickey was adamant that neither she nor Carola would ever again want for anything. For that reason, as soon as she had the strength to do so, Mickey dictated a letter to Bernice Baumgarten at her agent's office instructing Bernice to seek an advance of $1,000 from George Shively of Doubleday publishing, with whom Brandt was negotiating a new book contract. That money, plus a royalty check from Mickey's English publisher, tided her over until she was back on her feet.[3]

The realization of just how precarious her financial situation was served as a wake-up call. Mickey needed to increase her income; that much was clear. Just as clear was the fact that the easiest way to do so was to write more. Fortunately, in the wake of her recent successes, America was interested in what she had to say. Mickey's public lectures on China drew large crowds, and her books and articles found wide readership. Doubleday sold more than 24,000 copies of *China to Me* in the first two months after the book's publication, and the book continued to sell strongly throughout 1945. As a result, so many people began writing to her that Mickey hired a personal secretary to handle correspondence. Mixed in with all of the mail arriving at her door were letters from friends with whom Mickey had lost touch during the war; no one had trouble finding her now. Dick Smith, a newsman she had known in Shanghai, wrote to say he was now in Chungking, where the two copies of *China to Me* in Chiang Kai-shek's wartime capital were "circulating faster than the currency." China was plagued by runaway inflation, Smith explained; fresh eggs were now selling in Chungking for $25 *each*.[4]

Other friends and acquaintances wrote with news on the rumored fate of Charles. No matter how tenaciously she clung to her hopes, there was growing evidence that the man she loved was dead. American journalist Joe Alsop, a friend with whom Mickey had occasionally smoked opium in Hong Kong, got in touch to say that he had heard that Charles had been killed. Lorraine Murray, a Canadian who had been one of Mickey's housemates in Shanghai, wrote from Australia to share the same news. Murray sent word that newspapers down under had carried an article stating that Charles had been executed by guards at Stanley Prison.[5] David McDougall of the British Foreign Office wrote with the same grim news. He said that a rumor was making the rounds in diplomatic circles in Free China that had it that Charles had died in prison. In the same letter, though, he held out a slim hope. "As you know, unofficial reports cannot be all together disregarded, but they have been many times wrong in [the] past," McDougall reminded Mickey. "I was in Chungking a week ago, and there was absolutely no news there. That is a good sign."[6]

Mickey desperately wanted to believe him. She scanned the daily papers for news of Charles or developments in Hong Kong. Only occasionally did she find anything. One wire-service story quoted "reliable sources" as saying that

Major Charles Boxer was still alive and had been shipped to Japan with other Hong Kong POWs to toil as slave labor. From India, Charles's sister, Beryl Smeeton, wrote to report that she had been told by an escaped British POW from Hong Kong that the Japanese were still holding Charles in solitary confinement at Stanley Prison. Then Mickey received a reassuring letter from a captain in the U.S. Air Force who wrote that he had heard from friends in the French diplomatic service that "Boxer is OK. I don't know how authentic that is, but I pass it along."[7]

Ultimately there were so many conflicting rumors that Mickey found it impossible to know who or what to believe. It was all too much to cope with; life had become an emotional roller coaster. Mickey escaped as she had done so often; she lost herself in her writing, which streamed from her typewriter at a frenetic pace. Mickey continued to spin articles and short stories for the *New Yorker* about her wartime adventures in Hong Kong, but she also had begun writing about a variety of other topics. So prolific was she that Katharine White at the *New Yorker* (which had a contractual first right of refusal on any articles that Mickey wrote) did not object when Mickey's byline began appearing in other national publications such as *American Mercury*, *Good Housekeeping*, *Collier's*, the *New York Times Magazine*, and *Women's Day*, a mass-circulation monthly published by her old friend Donald Hanson.

Mickey also was working on at least three books. At the urging of publisher George Shively, who felt the public still hungered to hear more from her about China, Mickey did the text for two picture books—one for adults and the other for young people. The third book was about Sir Thomas Stamford Raffles (1781–1826), the adventurer turned trader who had founded Britain's East Asian Empire when he raised the Union Jack over Singapore in 1819. The war in the Pacific had heightened America's interest in that British colony and, at Shively's urging, Mickey was back working on the biography *Raffles of Singapore*.

The same creative impulses that shaped her literary output during this period reflected themselves in Mickey's personal life. She was slowly emerging from self-imposed isolation. Mickey and Carola spent July and part of August with Patrick Putnam and his wife at the Putnam family's summer home on Martha's Vineyard. There Mickey worked on the Raffles book and spent many idle hours watching the waves and daydreaming of Charles and of her old life in China.

Mickey's nostalgia was fueled by a letter that arrived from Shanghai in August. It was from another old friend, who had spotted one of Mickey's short stories in the *New Yorker* and had written to her care of the magazine. Sinmay Zau, as canny and resilient as ever, wrote to let Mickey know that he and his wife Zoa had survived the Japanese occupation. "It's about time that we should try to get to know each other again. I am sure it will be safe and pleasant," he assured her.[8] Although Sinmay himself was well, he said the war had been long and hard. He was thirty-nine, a year younger than Mickey, but confided he looked "more than sixty" and "no longer kissed young women" for fear they would slap his face. Like Mickey, Sinmay longed for the old days. He said that he had heard a lot about *China to Me* but had not read it yet; could Mickey somehow find a way to "smuggle" him a copy?

Mickey sent the book by mail. In an accompanying letter she explained how in occupied Hong Kong she had claimed to be "Mrs. Zau," despite her fears that the Japanese would question Sinmay about their relationship. She had told the whole story in *China to Me.* "It will all make sense to you," she assured him. "It seems a perfectly logical and obvious thing to have done, although American minds are not as clear . . . as the Chinese mentality. The government officials here were very puzzled and almost put your former wife into jail."[9]

Sinmay's letter was a siren call beckoning Mickey back to China. The urge to go was powerful, for Mickey was "homesick" for her friends and her old life there. Yet she knew there could be no going back. Not now. Not without Charles. Not with the war still on and a young daughter to worry about.

Mickey sought solace in the company of "old China hands," as the diplomats, journalists, businesspeople, and others who had spent time in the Middle Kingdom were known. To her dismay, she discovered that some of the males among these old China connections had, as she punned it, "rushin' hands and roamin' fingers." Mickey's "literary reputation" preceded her; having read *China to Me,* these men assumed the author would fall into bed with anyone that she met. She would not, of course, and told these would-be Lotharios so in no uncertain terms. Her experiences left Mickey more resentful and embittered than ever. She felt hardened, edgy, even angry—ready to take on the world.

Mickey got into a spirited debate with Randall Gould, editor of the *Shanghai Evening Post and Mercury,* which during the Japanese occupation was published out of New York. As the war in China wound down, supporters of Chiang Kai-shek on the one side and those of the rival Communist leader Mao Tse-tung on the other, began lobbying in an effort to convince Washington to back their side in the postwar world. President Roosevelt and his advisors initially favored the formation of a coalition government in China. With that in mind, in late 1944 the president's special envoy, Major General Patrick J. Hurley, journeyed unannounced to the Chinese Communist headquarters at Yenan. Hurley hoped to negotiate a treaty that would bring the Communists into the war against Japan as full allies. In return, they would receive American military aid and financial support.

Mao's number two man, Chou En-lai, with whom Mickey had sometimes sipped tea in her Shanghai days, met Hurley's plane at the airport. Upon discovering the identity of the American general and the reason for his visit, Chou hastily sent word to his boss. Mao raced to the airport in the only motor vehicle in Yenan—a converted Chevrolet ambulance marked "Gift of N.Y. Chinese Laundrymen's Association." When Hurley succeeded in convincing Mao of his good intentions, the two men reached agreement on a deal to unite the Nationalist and Communist armies under joint leadership. They also proposed to form a coalition postwar government in China. When told of this, Chiang was outraged. He refused to agree to any such deal. As a result, when Roosevelt died suddenly on April 12, 1945, the jockeying for position by Nationalist and Communist Chinese supporters in the United States began in earnest.

China to Me had been read widely by State Department officials and others in Washington, as had *The Soong Sisters.* Unlike many old China hands, Mickey had no overt political motives. In fact, she had friends on both sides of the debate. She also knew, as John Gunther and other American journalists had pointed out, that the Chinese Nationalist government was corrupt and ruthless; as much as 10 percent of Chiang Kai-shek's annual budget—an estimated $25 million (U.S.)—reportedly came from the opium trade. Nevertheless, Mickey felt that as America's ally, Chiang deserved to be treated with respect. In an interview with a reporter from the *New York World Telegram*, she spoke out against the Chinese Communist propaganda that many Americans "had fallen for."[10]

A vocal chorus of American leftists and liberals who supported the Chinese Communists—"stay-at-home experts," Mickey termed them—opposed this view and vigorously attacked anyone who spoke up for the Nationalists. When the *Shanghai Evening Post and Mercury* reported criticisms of Mickey by Agnes Smedley and other leftists, Mickey responded with angry letters to editor Gould. She chided him for adopting a pro-Communist tone that she found troubling. "You, Mr. Editor, have lately been shifting your paper's policies without due warning," she charged. "[The] *Shanghai Evening Post* is known to us China hands as a supporter of our ally, China. This is what the paper has always claimed to be, and part of its popularity is owing, I believe, to that."[11]

Mickey's feistiness spilled over into all areas of her life. She was quick to take offense at any slight, whether real or imagined. After one lively outburst at a cocktail party in June 1945, Mickey received a letter from a cousin of Patrick Putnam, who was distraught about how Mickey had treated her. Mickey's contrite response reveals much about her mind-set at the time. "I am a completely self-centered woman these days," she admitted. "My experiences in China crystalized what was already an abnormal amount of egocentricity; just because it's me, I don't see why I shouldn't be aware of it and admit it. I like people as much as the next person. I suppose I like people *better* than the next person. . . . [But] now I have no time and there are a lot of people trying to eat me up because I have become somewhat notorious. Those people are a sheer waste of time, and worse. I refuse to care what they say about me when they are dissatisfied with the attention I give them because I know from way back . . . that the more one gives them, the more they want. If I cared about the jealous mutterings . . . of the 'public' I would never have accomplished anything that I have done. I believe that if you think it over, it's obvious the whole set-up of my life has been complete indifference to this 'public intrude.'"[12]

• • •

After almost six dark years, the lights went on again all over Europe when Germany surrendered unconditionally on May 7, 1945. Japan's surrender came on August 15. By then, it had been more than eighteen months since Mickey had seen Charles. Despite rumors to the contrary and particularly upsetting reports about the Japanese beheading British officers in Hong Kong, she clung to an unextinguishable hope that somehow he had survived. Even if he had not, Charles would live forever in Mickey's heart; she knew he had loved her as much as she loved him. If Charles *was* still alive, Mickey was certain that he would find a way to contact her.

Mickey's first real hint of Charles's fate came on September 4, 1945. A brief article in that day's *London Evening News* said that Major Charles Boxer had been found "alive and well" in a Japanese POW camp. There were no further details. Mickey's hopes had been dashed too many times to accept such a story until there was more proof. This time was different; this time there was proof. Mickey's family and friends called to say they had heard or read the same news reports. Then from Chicago came a phone call that Mickey had dreamed about for two long years: her sister Rose rang to say that she and her husband Mitchell had received a cable for Mickey. It had been sent from the Portuguese colony of Macau on Charles's behalf by one of Selwyn-Clarke's friends. It said Charles was back in Hong Kong after being liberated from a POW camp in Canton. Mickey, never one to cry easily, wept like a lost child found upon hearing this news. When a *New York Times* reporter called to ask what she thought Charles would do next, Mickey had no doubts. "He'll come home and marry me, of course," she sniffled.

A few days later, Mickey received an airmail letter from the British military hospital in Hong Kong. With trembling hands she tore open the envelope and read the precious words penned by Charles himself on September 11, 1945. The handwriting was faint and spidery, but there was no mistaking that it was Charles's or that his wonderfully dry wit had survived his wartime ordeal.

"I am fit and well," he wrote. "Two years of Colonel Noma's Course for

Backward Boys in Stanley and Canton jails having done me rather good." Then, growing serious, Charles continued, "It is quite impossible to put down in writing all of the million things that I want to ask you and I won't even try, but please let me know: a) do you still feel I am the same as in 1943, or have you got someone else? b) if you still feel the same, where and when shall we meet and marry? c) like Darcy in the trial—or is it the penultimate chapter?—[of] *Pride and Prejudice* (sic), my own sentiments and feelings are unchanged, but one word from you will silence me forever on the subject."[13]

More letters arrived from Hong Kong. As they did and as Mickey talked with friends who had returned from the Far East, the full story of Charles's POW nightmare became clear. The March 1945 wire-service story about two British officers having been beheaded by the Japanese had been incorrect. Charles was not involved in that particular incident but rather in another that happened around this same time and that resulted in his being banished to a cell in Stanley Prison.

Charles and several other officers had been feeding information to British intelligence in Chungking for almost two years. Charles also had been keeping other prisoners informed on the progress of the war by secretly listening to broadcasts on a makeshift radio receiver and by gleaning information from scraps of Japanese-language newspapers smuggled into the Argyle Street camp. He and seven other prisoners were arrested and charged with building the radio set; four of the men were summarily executed; the others were spared only because Charles had used his Japanese skills to persuade a military court to commute the sentences to fifteen years of "penal servitude." After the war, when the British government proposed Charles as a member of the Order of the British Empire for his efforts, the citation noted: "Until liberated in August 1945, Major Boxer served his term in Stanley and Canton prisons suffering continual privations and a starvation diet. During his entire imprisonment [he] never ceased to work for the welfare of his fellow prisoners at risk to his own life."[14] While this was true, Charles refused to accept the award because a colleague whom he deemed equally deserving of the honor was not similarly cited. As one of Charles's friends told author Miles Clark, "[Charles] told them they could stuff it."[15] (Mickey herself was honored by the Hong Kong colonial administration, which in November 1945 presented her with a certificate "in recognition of her gallant sacrifice in bringing food, money, and other necessities to the occupants of Prisoner of War camps and Internment Camps in the Colony of Hong Kong during the Japanese occupation. . . .")

Following his conviction, Charles was transferred to Stanley Prison, within shouting distance of the civilian facility at Stanley Camp. "It was a hell of a place," said Charles's friend Bill Wiseman, who himself spent three weeks in Stanley Prison. Wiseman recalled one unfortunate Sikh officer who had been beaten so badly by his Japanese tormenters that they had torn all the hair from his head. "Mahindar Singh was an absolute lion," said Wiseman. "He and the other Indian officers would scrub the doorstep of my cell and he would shout the news to me. I was down on all fours on the other side whispering, 'Sir! Please piss off or else you'll get us both beaten!' He would say, 'Ho, ho, ho! What's a beating?' "[16]

Like many of the other prisoners, Charles had been confined to a tiny dark cell equipped with only a toilet bucket and a straw mat on which to sleep. The space was infested with mice and rats—so many, in fact, that their constant scurrying about nearly drove him mad. The Japanese were determined to make Charles's existence miserable, and they succeeded. His prewar relationships with high-ranking enemy officers and Foreign Office officials undoubtedly saved him from being tortured to death like so many other POWs. Barbara Ker-Seymer, Mickey's longtime friend, claimed Mickey had once confided to her that she had slept with a Japanese official to buy special treatment for Charles. Asked about this many years later, Mickey smiled enigmatically. "Barbara is a romantic," she said. "It's all right to ask about it, but it wasn't true."[17]

Mickey pointed out that Charles had survived almost two years after she left Hong Kong and that his captors could easily have killed him anytime. Given Mickey's pragmatism where her own sexuality and the whole issue of wartime rape were concerned, there can be no doubt that she would have sacrificed herself and suffered almost any indignity to save Charles. Did she, or didn't she? No one will ever know, but it seems unlikely that she would have kept mum if she had done so; after all, Mickey made no secret of her views on war rape or of her anger with Alf Bennett, who "took advantage" of her one night in Hong Kong when Charles was absent and she and Alf had both had too much to drink. Also, after the war, when living conditions in Japan were hard and food was scarce, Mickey and Charles located Takio Oda and Chikanori Nakazawa and sent them relief parcels. It is doubtful that she would have done so had either of them sexually exploited her.

Mickey always insisted that Charles's survival was due to his language skills, his relationships with the Japanese, and his own resiliency. She correctly pointed out that Charles's death would have served no end; by late 1943 any secrets he may have known were of little military value. The fact was, despite all that had happened, Japanese military commanders in Hong Kong regarded Charles as a brave and honorable man. He was one of their own, *almost*. This was difficult for most Westerners to comprehend. Fraternization with the enemy in wartime was considered treason.

Charles remained an enigma to many of the guards at Stanley Prison, for no matter how much abuse they inflicted on him, he never complained. A British reporter who interviewed Charles in Hong Kong after his liberation told

Mickey in a letter that "[Charles] was perfectly lousy as a source of stories about what the Japs did to our people. Apparently they had given him *a time*, but he kept insisting that he had it coming because, after all, he'd been trying to work a radio deal and that was something you had to pay for if you got caught."[18]

Charles had suffered in silence, as would any true samurai. Unlike most POWs, he admired the Japanese people and culture; his loathing was reserved for only those sadistic officers and guards who had derived a perverse satisfaction out of tormenting and murdering prisoners. Later, Charles even joked about the miseries he had endured. He told a British journalist that he had slept a lot in prison, eaten "simple foods," and lost "his middle-aged ass."[19] The reality was that the hunger and pain he experienced were often unbearable; Charles, who was never religious, at times resorted to prayer. He had no fear of death and prayed it would come to him swiftly and painlessly if he could not be freed.

Charles had passed several months sitting on his haunches on the floor of his bare cell, as was "standard procedure" for prisoners. He stared blankly at the wall, never complaining and seldom speaking. As his body wasted and his hopes flickered, his spirit drifted to places none of his tormenters could follow. Such stoicism confounded many of the guards, who were illiterate farm boys. They were in awe of this British officer who had mastered the ancient martial art of kendo and who spoke and read Japanese like a real gentleman. As Charles got to know his keepers, he became an "expert in jailor psychology," as he put it, and was gradually able to make friends with a few of them. He began reading them stories from the Japanese newspapers. In return, one offered to get him an English-language book. More than anything, Charles said, he wanted a copy of the collected works of William Shakespeare. The Bard's words were "much more consoling [to him] than the horrors in the Old Testament or the impractical—though better—New Testament," as he later explained.[20]

Whether by design or accident, the binding had been torn away on the one book that Charles received in prison. That did not matter. Nor did it matter to Charles that his Shakespeare arrived in installments. He read and reread the well-thumbed pages, passing the long, lonely hours by memorizing complete poems and entire scenes of dramatic dialogue. Shakespeare became his lifeline to rationality.

In May 1945, shortly after the end of the war in Europe, the Japanese moved Charles and other British officers to a POW camp in the nearby city of Canton. The men were dirty, hungry, and plagued with a variety of physical ailments. Charles suffered from beriberi, a nutritional deficiency that results in weight loss, bloating, numbness in the limbs, and other grave symptoms. The inmates in Stanley Prison had been starved for a reason: the Japanese knew that hungry men were less likely to cause trouble. However, the POW camp at Canton was outside in the sunshine and fresh air. Charles made a convincing case to his new guards for letting the prisoners plant a small garden, even though he himself could not work there; his wounded left arm still had not healed properly. "He persuaded the Nips that it was really a waste of time to keep these half-dozen Brits locked up all the time when they could be usefully employed in a garden to supplement the [guards'] rations," said Bill Wiseman. "Charles also said he'd like to make the place a bit tidier, but to do so he'd really need a bonfire. [The guards] said yes. . . . Charles was a master at getting other people to do the work. There were two sergeants there, and it wasn't long before one of them was brewing tea on the fire and the other was actually shaving Charles. . . . Bit by bit things became more tolerable. The Nips overlooked the fact he was clean shaven whereas everybody else [in the Canton POW camp] was as shaggy as hell. I wasn't in there, but these were the tales that circulated."[21]

Charles passed the last four months of the war at Canton. With the cease-fire on August 15, the Japanese guards simply disappeared, and the prisoners were left to fend for themselves. A few days later, Chinese troops arrived on the scene. British soldiers were not far behind. Charles and the other prisoners were transported back to Hong Kong the first week of September. Here Charles was reunited with faithful Ah King, who had used every ounce of his wiles to survive two long, hard years following Mickey's autumn 1943 departure. Apart from the physical destruction he saw in the colony, Charles later joked that what he found most distressing was the high cost and limited availability of alcohol; beer was $15 (U.S.) a bottle! Even that did not stop Charles and his mates from making up for lost drinking time.

Most of the surviving British POWs in Hong Kong had just one thing on their minds: getting home to England. Charles was in no rush to go back. He readily agreed when asked to stay on "for a few weeks" to help reestablish the British military intelligence office and to sit as a member of a committee investigating Japanese war crimes. "I want to ensure that the villains of this piece . . . are brought to trial and don't escape if I have anything to do with it," Charles told Mickey in one of his letters. Almost as important, he also said that he wanted to recover as much of his library as possible, because many of the two thousand volumes looted from his flat were irreplaceable. "I've got about two hundred books back. . . . The remainder are supposed to have been sent to Japan in February 1942," he said.[22]

One other book Charles was especially keen to get his hands on was a copy of *China to Me*, which had caused a great stir among those of his friends who had read it. Charles immediately understood why. He liked what Mickey had written, especially her kind words about Oda and Hattori, but he found other passages disquieting, particularly those that dealt with his own relationship with Mickey. "[The book] is well written, of course. I don't think you could write badly if you tried," he told her. "I never realized before just how elephantine your memory is. I have been staggered to find myself confronted in print by fatuous remarks I have made at some drunken party and I thought you were under the influence. Next time I go out with you, Mickey, I shall take along a rag or a muzzle and ask someone to stuff it into my mouth between drinks."[23]

By mid-October, Charles had done all the preliminary work he could for the Hong Kong war crimes trials. After seeing to it that Ah King got a good job in the officers' mess, Charles quietly took a leave. On October 23 he sailed for San Francisco aboard a British cargo ship called the *Shirrabank*. His mission, he announced, was "to make an honest woman out of Mickey Hahn." Apart from his professed reason—it would no longer be "inconvenient when staying in hotels"—his plan filled his family and friends with misgivings. Charles and Mickey were indeed a strange couple. In British eyes it was the ultimate indiscretion to kiss and tell.

Back From Hong Kong To Wed Author

MAJOR CHARLES BOXER, AUTHOR EMILY HAHN AND THEIR CHILD
Excited cries of "Daddy, Daddy," greeted him.

Charles greeted by a tearful Mickey and a puzzled Carola as he arrived at La Guardia Airport in New York, November 22, 1945.
Corbis-Bettman Photo Archives

Beryl's daughter Clio Smeeton said, "I think the problem, and an understandable one, too, was that Aunt Mickey wrote about herself, about having a child out of wedlock, about Uncle Charlie, and all the British relations. Everyone [Mickey] met was grist to her mill. She thrived on media attention and she garnered as much as she could. . . . She did not appear to have the propriety to protect, or at least not use, the family she married into. That is not, in general, the ideal army wife. Nor does it, in general, help the career of a husband. . . . So, viewed from the outside . . . it was hard for the Boxer relations to perceive, apart from her beauty and charm, what benefits she brought to Uncle Charlie."[24]

None of this mattered to Charles, of course. He was determined to marry Mickey. With that in mind, he arrived in New York on November 22, 1945. It was a Thanksgiving Day like none Mickey had ever celebrated. She, Carola, and their relatives and friends were joined by a throng of reporters and photographers who braved a cool rain and blustery winds on the tarmac at La Guardia Airport. They watched and waited in hushed anticipation as the transport plane carrying Charles taxied to a stop outside the passenger terminal. What happened next was all a blur to Mickey, whose usually infallible memory failed her when she tried to recall this occasion. According to the news story in the next day's *New York Times*, "As Major Boxer's plane came in, Carola, who had been waiting with her mother at the airport, exclaimed, 'Daddy, daddy, here comes daddy!'"[25] In reality, she did not know who "daddy" was.

Although he survived his opium addiction, the hardships of the war years, and political "re-education," Sinmay Zau was a broken man.
Courtesy Dr. Xiaohong Shao

A photo that appeared in the newspapers next day showed Charles being met at the bottom of the boarding ramp by Mickey and by Carola, who had leapt into his arms. Mickey wept tears of joy. Their long ordeal was finally over; they were all together again. As the three of them walked arm in arm to a waiting car, reporters pushed close to fire questions at them. Where were they going? What did they plan to do now? Mickey smiled coyly. Why, they would go home to a Thanksgiving dinner, "if I can find a roasting pan," she added with a laugh.

28

THE PHOTOGRAPH that appeared on page 40 of the December 3, 1945, issue of *Life* magazine was vintage Americana. The black-and-white image that took up most of the page showed a uniformed army veteran down on all fours on the living room carpet. A four-year-old girl enjoying a horsey ride on her daddy's back looked somewhat bewildered, even a little uncertain of just what was happening. Behind the little girl stood her mother, bracing her and beaming an incandescent smile that leapt right off the page. This wonderful family scene could have been photographed almost anywhere in America in the fall of 1945, as sixteen million jubilant GIs returned home from the war. However, appearances were deceiving. The "playful threesome" pictured—Mickey, Charles, and Carola—were certainly not the typical all-American family.

Mickey was a friend of writer Clare Booth Luce, the wife of *Life* magazine publisher Henry R. Luce, so the Luces knew the whole story of Mickey's love affair with Charles. Just minutes after the major arrived in New York, a *Life* photographer knocked on the door of Mickey's East Ninety-Fifth Street home looking for "an exclusive." Mickey could not resist, of course, and so she, Charles, and Carola posed obligingly. So the daddy down on all fours in that famous *Life* slice-of-Americana photo was actually a British officer visiting the United States for the first time. The little girl on his back was his Hong Kong–born daughter, and the child's mother was his globetrotting fiancée. A headline under the photo read, "Boxer's baby." The subheading announced that Charles, recently liberated from a Japanese POW camp, was there to make "an honest woman" of "the handsome, unconventional Authoress Emily Hahn." He would do so, the story noted, as soon as a divorce from his first wife was finalized. It promised to be a fairy-tale outcome to what *Life* termed "one of the best-publicized romances of the war."[1]

What *Life* readers did not know was that by the time that photo was published, Charles and Mickey were already husband and wife. Charles received word from London just a few days after arriving in New York that his divorce from Ursula had gone through. He immediately applied for a marriage license, but the request was denied. New York law prescribed a three-year waiting period for anyone who had been divorced on grounds of adultery; the same held true in neighboring New Jersey. Charles and Mickey got around this problem by driving up to New Haven, Connecticut, on the morning of November 28, 1945. There they applied for and received a waiver on the requirement for blood tests and a five-day waiting period. Charles paid a fifty-cent license fee, then he and Mickey were wed at city hall by a justice of the peace.

Afterward, the newlyweds returned to New York. Charles had a series of appointments with doctors who were assessing his injured left arm, and Mickey was feeling ill. She had told no one that she was suffering from the effects of morphine withdrawal. Charles's arrival had hastened her decision to end her drug dependency, which she knew posed a grave danger; the more one uses morphine, the more one needs to use and the greater the likelihood of a fatal overdose. That was clear from what had happened to the wife of Willy, Mickey's cook-houseboy (and would happen to Willy himself in 1947).

Willy had described to Mickey how he awoke one morning to find his wife lying next to him in bed stone-cold; she had died during the night from a morphine overdose. That news terrified Mickey, who resolved to end her own habit as soon as possible. It was Charles, blissfully ignorant of any of this, who inadvertently helped her to do it. He suggested that because he was now in New York, Mickey no longer needed a cook-houseboy. Initially, Charles had begrudgingly accepted Willy's presence, but that changed as Charles settled in. He was appalled that Willy called everyone by first name and by how casually he treated both guests and family. In Charles's experience, it went without saying that servants—like children—were expected to be seen and not heard. Ap-

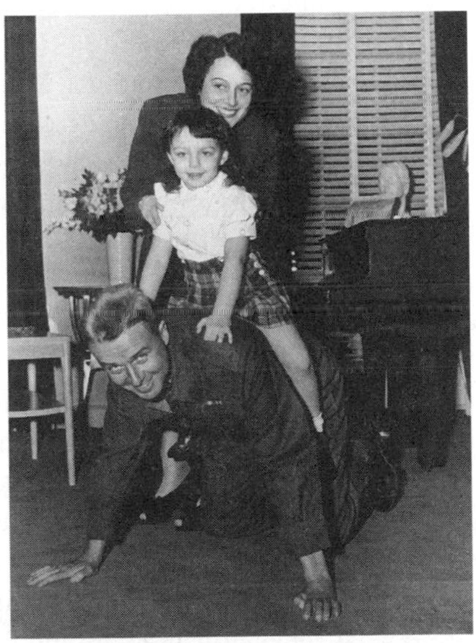

The famous Life *magazine photo of Charles, Carola, and Mickey, taken at her New York apartment on November 22, 1945, the day Charles came to make "an honest woman" out of Mickey.*
Corbis-Bettman Photo Archives

parently not in New York. "Willy would cook dinner and then sit down to eat with us, country style," Mickey explained. "Charles thought America was very odd, indeed."[2]

With Willy's departure, Mickey no longer had easy access to morphine. She quit the drug then and there. "I stopped cold-turkey. It was painful, but quick," she said. "Charles thought I was awfully sick. I *was* awfully sick. I never talked to anyone about it, never sought medical treatment, never wrote about it. Why? Probably because of Carola."[3]

Freed from the demon of morphine addiction, Mickey was intent on becoming a model wife and mother, which for her took no small effort. She joked in a letter to Bill Wiseman that for several weeks after her marriage to Charles she would "jump nervously and look over my shoulder for Ursula"[4] whenever anyone referred to "Mrs. Boxer." The specter of Charles's first wife was still a dark cloud in their lives. Upon his return to freedom he had expected to find £4,000—more than $16,000 (U.S.)—back pay in his bank account. Instead, Charles discovered that Ursula, still bitter about the breakup of their marriage, had spent all but £400, and she was angling for the rest in alimony. If it were not for some *China to Me* royalty money that Mickey had set aside for him, Charles would have been flat broke. He earned just £50 per month in the army. Having no other means to support himself and his family, Charles opted to stay in His Majesty's service. He requested a new overseas posting; Manchuria, Japan, and Singapore were mentioned as possibilities. Until his posting came through, he had been asked to assist the International Military Tribunal for the Far East, which had been set up to prosecute Japanese war criminals.

Charles left on a six-week trip to Tokyo a few days after Christmas 1945. In his absence, Mickey completed her novel about Shanghai and eight chapters of the Raffles book. Her enthusiasm for the latter was waning. "I hate to be typed as a biographer," Mickey explained to her agent. "We don't really know if this odd style of mine is going to be popular in biography. *The Soong Sisters* didn't sell on style, but on timeliness. I can't believe the American public will go on indefinitely buying this sort of book, which I'm fairly convinced they read only to improve themselves and to say they've done it. In fact, lots of them seem to think that when they've paid for the book they've as good as read it. And honestly, I am rather on their side in that. This is not for publication, a remark I seldom make."[5]

Mickey's agent and her publisher, who evidently shared these concerns, were intent on sticking to what they felt was a winning formula: Mickey and China. Thus, she did three China-related books in 1946. One was a children's picture book, for which Mickey wrote the text. The second was a children's alphabet book, for which she crafted rhymes. The third was *Hong Kong Holiday*,[6] a collection of twenty vignettes—some of which had been written for the

New Yorker—chronicling Mickey's adventures in occupied Hong Kong and her 1943 repatriation. This would become a familiar methodology for her: roughly a third of the thirty-seven books she would produce in coming years grew out of articles that she originally wrote for the magazine.

The whimsical title of *Hong Kong Holiday* belied the dark undertone of much of the subject matter; it was Mickey's way of sarcastically poking fun at those who had accused her of receiving special treatment from the Japanese. The book was in many ways a sequel to *China to Me,* but unfortunately for Mickey, its timing was poor. A war-weary America was ready to turn its attentions homeward, and sales of *Hong Kong Holiday* were lower than expected. The public's indifference may have owed something to the tepid critical reception for the book. Russell Maloney of the *New York Times Book Review* seemed to speak for the majority opinion when he dismissed *Hong Kong Holiday* as "a program of cheerful and inoffensive vaudeville."[7] The lone notable exception was the reviewer from *Commonweal,* who enthused, "Miss Hahn possesses an endless facility at this sort of writing; those addicted to it will clamor for more."[8]

Despite the appearance of these three new books, Mickey's main source of income and her creative outlet continued to be the *New Yorker.* However, when Katharine White rejected two of Mickey's short stories, saying they dealt with themes that other writers had covered already, Mickey "began acting wild." She stopped submitting material. This prompted a query from the *New Yorker* managing editor for fiction, Gustave ("Gus") Lobrano. "I never claimed to be able to write anything that hasn't been touched on before in the world of literature somewhere, and if that is going to be Mrs. White's standard from now on I think I'll just have to go on feeling stage fright," Mickey told Lobrano. "Let me know when the rest of the editorial department is back in working order."[9]

Her comments were duly reported to editor Harold Ross, who promptly got in touch with Mickey himself. Ross had been in the hospital when White rejected Mickey's stories. Now he was intent on playing the role of peacemaker and on gently pointing out to Mickey that she was in breach of her "solemn agreement" with the magazine. Ross reminded her that a contract she had signed gave the *New Yorker* first right of refusal on any of Mickey's stories or articles in return for a higher rate of pay than usual. Mickey relented somewhat after a conciliatory meeting with Lobrano. She wrote Ross to assure him, "I never meant to distress or alarm you. I guess it's a matter of my dictating in one tone of voice, and your reading it in another. Read this in a friendly voice, with which I am now speaking it."[10]

That said, Mickey went on to point out that her agreement with the *New Yorker* did not in fact give the magazine first right of refusal on *everything* she wrote; she noted that she was permitted to exempt up to three pieces per year. The incredulous Ross checked the contract, then conceded, "I didn't realize you had this privilege, which is unusual."[11]

The exchange with Ross soothed her ire, and Mickey resumed sending her articles and stories to the *New Yorker.* She had made her point. Besides, she really had no time or stomach for a fight just then. She was preoccupied with family matters. Upon his return from Japan, Charles had surgery on March 22 to repair his injured left arm. For several weeks thereafter, he visited a veterans' physiotherapy clinic on Staten Island for daily treatments. Because the army brass in London had not yet figured out what—if anything—to do with a major with a bad arm, he was granted an indefinite sick leave. Charles decided to use the time to go to England. This seemed like an ideal opportunity to visit relatives and check on the condition of Conygar, the Dorset estate he had inherited from his mother's side of the family in the early 1930s. The forty-eight-acre property, not far from the seaside town of Weymouth, had been leased to tenants until 1940, when it had been taken over by the British army. Troops had been billeted there for five years, and the house now needed renovations before it could be let out again. Charles, who joked that he was a "kept man," was eager to get on with them.

The Boxers sailed from New York aboard the *Queen Mary* on July 28, 1946. The stately Cunard passenger liner was still fitted as a troop ship, with six cots jammed into each stateroom. Mickey and Charles shared a cabin, while Carola and her Danish nanny Margrethe bunked in another. The six-day crossing was smooth and uneventful, apart from the adventure of bringing more than a ton of luggage and household goods through British customs. The Boxers were prepared for a move to the Far East. With wartime rationing still in effect on many items in England, Mickey had stocked up in New York.

"Anything to declare?" an unsuspecting customs official asked the Boxers upon their arrival in Southampton.

"Everything," Charles replied. "We were POWs, and we outfitted again in New York. Every single article in these packing cases is new."

The customs man stroked his chin and stared. Images of the reams of paperwork to be done danced in his mind. "Oh, that'll be all right, sir," he said.[12]

They had missed the afternoon train to Weymouth, so the Boxers hired two taxis to drive them and their mountain of luggage the fifty miles to Conygar. It was dark by the time they arrived. Charles had cautioned Mickey that the house would be a shambles, although it had been tended for him by a couple of elderly retainers who lived in a cottage on the property. Mickey discovered that the Hammonds, who had always treated Charles and his siblings "with a sort of gloomy affection strongly tinctured with disapproval for their youth,"[13] ran Conygar with an iron fist. Mr. Hammond was no Jeeves, his wife no Mary Poppins. Nothing had changed in the decade that Charles had been away; it would take more than a world war and the ousting of Winston Churchill's Conservative government by the Labor opposition to affect the Hammonds' lifestyle.

As Mickey described her, Mrs. Hammond was a tall woman "with iron-grey hair parted faultlessly and severely in the middle, and she grows progressively bigger as the eye follows her downward."[14] Her husband, shorter and wirier, was no less dour and unbending. The Hammonds had been fired and rehired so many times during their thirty-five years at Conygar that they and their "attitude" had almost become fixtures there. There were three other servants at Conygar—a couple called the Adamses and a second cook named Bertha Harvell—but the Hammonds had made themselves indispensible by dint of the fact that no one else knew where everything was.

Miles Clark, the biographer of Charles's sister Beryl Smeeton and her husband Miles, described Conygar as "a monument to architectural indecision with its red brick wall, tall chimneys and sandstone parapets surrounded by terraced lawns."[15] Although the three-story mock-Tudor house with its oak main staircase and huge stained-glass window had thirty rooms, it was modest by the standards of the great homes of the British landed aristocracy. Conygar had been built in 1908 by a well-to-do dog breeder who sold it to Charles's maternal grandmother three years later. Grandmother Patterson had added a wing, installed central heating, and hired young Mr. Hammond as her chauffeur and his bride as the cook-housekeeper.

Mickey's first look at the estate confirmed her worst fears. Even in the dark, she could see that the big old red brick house was overgrown with brush and the county's "finest crop of nettles." The grounds teemed with wild rabbits, who in their own way had made an indelible impression on the place. Rabbits were not indigenous to the British Isles, having been brought over from France by the invading Normans in 1066 A.D. "Cony," the Norman word for rabbit, was still common in the West Country in 1945; "Garth" is the Saxon word for farm. Thus the literal translation of "Conygarth"—which got shortened to "Conygar"—was "rabbit farm." This abundance of bunnies on the property was the partial inspiration for "The Scream," one of the most memorable of the many Conygar stories that Mickey wrote for the *New Yorker*.[16]

In it, she told of being awakened in the predawn of an autumn morning by a bloodcurdling shriek. "*E-e-e-eh!*" With her heart pounding, Mickey leapt from bed, raced across the cold floor, and threw open the window. What she saw—or, to be more precise, did not see—puzzled her.

The eastern sky was awash with a rosy translucent hue. The garden and surrounding countryside were as still and picture-perfect as a John Constable painting. There was no sign of anything amiss, no sign of the person or thing that had emitted the awful shriek. It was not until later, when Mickey voiced her concerns at the breakfast table, that the mystery was solved.

"A rabbit being taken by a stoat," Charles explained as he glanced up from a book he was reading at the table.

Mickey was puzzled. What she heard could *not* have been a rabbit being killed by a weasel, she said; rabbits can only squeak. Charles shook his head. "Rabbits *scream* when stoats are after them," he explained. "They act as if they're paralyzed, but they scream. It's the only time they do."[17] And the last time, he might have added.

Confronted by shrieking bunnies and the perpetual scowls of the hired help, Mickey and Carola found the transition from the bright lights and busyness of New York to "the depths of the Dorset countryside without a car" anything but easy.[18] For Carola's first few weeks there she constantly cried to go "home," even though Mickey bought her a yellow corgi named Fitzroy as a playmate and did everything that a mother could think of to make her young daughter feel at ease. Nothing addressed the main problem: Carola found Conygar terrifying. She was convinced the house was haunted and refused to go upstairs alone.

Mickey empathized. The upstairs of the old house was as uninviting as it was spooky, especially at night. The bedrooms were large, drafty, and dusty. The plumbing leaked. Downstairs, there was no refrigerator or even an icebox. Floors and doors creaked, and the large "public rooms" were packed with generations of clutter. "There were sixty cushions in the drawing-room alone," Mickey later wrote. "There were far too many little bric-a-brac tables, and standing framed photographs, and plush traveling cases, and paintings in heavy gilt frames, and lacquer chests of card sets and piquet and backgammon, and tables like glass-topped boxes full of ivory fans and snuff boxes, and little statues and busts of Negro boys."[19]

One thing she remained adamant about was her refusal to perform the household drudgery that most British wives tackled as a matter of course. Although they could scarcely afford to retain more servants, Mickey convinced Charles to hire a woman named Mrs. Alford to cook and a new nanny for Carola when Margrethe returned to the States. Mickey's rationale was simple. "Give me a house in China and a lot of servants, and a favorable exchange, and I can evolve a pleasant existence," she explained. "Give me a house in New York with Willy—there was a good housekeeper for you, though a ruinous one—and I can do the same. But give me a house all by myself and I let it alone. It isn't that I can't mop and dust and sweep and cook and wash and iron, I can. I even like some of it, the cooking and ironing. It's just that there are often so many other things I would rather be doing at that particular moment. . . . I don't like housework."[20]

• • •

It was inevitable that Mickey and the Hammonds would clash. By autumn, the tensions at Conygar were as ripe as the crops in the nearby fields. It was increasingly evident that the Boxers were going to be there much longer than expected, so Mickey decided to enroll Carola in the local public school. This decision caused an uproar at Conygar, where the Hammonds were aghast that their employers would even consider sending their child to a school attended by the offspring of working-class families; such a thing simply was not done. When Charles sought the advice of neighbors, he learned that the village school provided a good education, although the teacher was hopelessly underpaid and overworked, and books and other classroom teaching aids were scarce. In the end, Mickey relented about sending Carola to Broadmayne when she discovered there would be more than forty children packed into the same classroom. That would never do; like her own mother years before her, Mickey was determined that no daughter of hers would ever be denied access to the best education possible. So "just like any Tory couple," Mickey and Charles enrolled Carola at Four Winds Primary School, a nearby private school attended by just eight other children.

No less disturbing to the Hammonds than the school question was Charles's idea that it would be convenient if everyone at Conygar dined together at lunch, the main meal of the day; England had changed, after all. With the dining room still unusable, Charles decreed they should all eat in the kitchen. The family and any guests would gather at the main table, while the staff would sit at a smaller table next to the window. This experiment in social equality proved a dismal failure. The Hammonds, as uncomfortable as rabbits in a roomful of shoats, sat in grim silence despite the Major's best efforts to bring them into conversations. "The [Hammonds] . . . are too old for Brave New England," Mickey wrote. "Maybe all of Dorset is."[21]

The school incident and the short-lived change in the lunchtime ritual were minor skirmishes compared to the protracted battle with the Hammonds over the Boxers' fondness for inviting guests to stay with them at Conygar. Within a few weeks of their arrival, Charles and Mickey were providing temporary accommodation to a young Polish refugee named Jan and his Scottish wife Nellie. Then came Jenny, a Chinese woman Mickey and Charles had known in Shanghai, and her infant Eurasian son. "Considering that we already consisted of two Americans and a Dane [nanny Margrethe] as well as the English Major and the very English [Hammonds], it is no wonder that Conygar became known in the neighborhood as the League of Nations," Mickey noted.[22] The Hammonds, who had lived a quiet rural life for so many years, were unaccustomed to and uneasy amidst such cosmopolitanism.

None of that deterred Mickey and Charles, who loved having a house full of lively people. By times, Barbara Ker-Seymer and her son Max lived at Conygar, as did the young sons of Geoff Wilson, a former policeman Charles had known in Hong Kong. Mickey welcomed them all. She craved the stimulation that her visitors provided, for she found English country life tolerable only to a point. The "poisons" of monotony, isolation, and parochialism wore her down, as did what she termed the "Grimm's fairy-tale atmosphere" the Hammonds exuded. When Charles's uncle, who had lived at Conygar in the late 1920s, could stand life here no more, he had taken his shotgun out into the field and put an end to his misery. Mickey, who had no intention of following suit, fought back with all her might to remake life at Conygar, and this put her at odds with the Hammonds. Most of their differences were niggling and easily forgotten, but occasionally Mickey blew up. That happened the day she learned that Mrs. Hammond, acting like a prison camp warder, was taking Jan and Nellie's rations and leaving the young couple with almost nothing to eat. Mickey put a stop to this immediately. The atmosphere around the house was even cooler than usual for several weeks afterward.

Charles did little to broker peace in the household. Although he, too, grumbled about "the help," he was largely oblivious to what aggravated Mickey most. "Charles was buried in his books," Mickey's friend Barbara Ker-Seymer recalled. "I don't think he took any notice of what was going on."[23] Indeed, Charles had settled into a routine that centered on the rituals of his brisk thrice-a-day walks with the dogs, teatime, an afternoon nap, and long sessions at his desk where he wrote scholarly articles about seventeenth-century Dutch and Portuguese colonial history.

Observing her husband here in his element, it occurred to Mickey that he had become the archetypal "Edwardian country gentlemen." As a breed, they could be laconic and comically (and at times maddeningly) flighty. As Mickey noted, the Edwardian country gentleman never displayed physical affection in public and other than at lunch seldom conversed with his spouse unless there was a pressing need. During breakfasts and teatime at Conygar, the Boxers and their houseguests routinely retreated behind a newspaper, a book, or even a writing pad. Mickey made light of the lack of discourse and the stiff-upper-lip atmosphere when she mused, "I can imagine the Major saying under certain circumstances, 'By the way, the mortgage has been foreclosed. You had better pack a few things for yourself. Sensible shoes, remember.'"[24]

Mickey thus found the winter of 1946 and 1947 long and hard. It was made even more trying by government rationing of food and fuel. As she worked at her desk, Mickey complained of the bone-numbing cold, which brought on a recurrence of her chilblains. She was filled with a growing resentment at having to live in a house that was literally falling down around her. All repair work required a permit from the local labor council. Mickey, having lots of experience getting around bureaucratic red tape, decided that doing so at Conygar was a challenge that she could not resist. Mickey beat the system by paying the village repairman to drop by at night or on weekends. The only problem with this was that before long he was coming so often that it began to seem like he was a member of the family; Charles had no technical skills and balked at fixing anything. This was yet another source of tension in the house.

One afternoon, as Mickey and Charles were having tea with guests in the drawing room, the sofa legs collapsed. Everyone tut-tutted and scrambled to safety. The "crumbling sofa," as Mickey called it, lay in the middle of the drawing-room floor for months afterward, a poignant memorial to Conygar's decrepitude and of Charles's refusal to tackle even the most pressing household repair work.

Mickey found relief from such irritations and from the insular tedium of life at Conygar by accompanying Charles on his academic research trips to Portugal, and also by concentrating on her own work. This was a productive period for Mickey. She wrote a series of lighthearted *New Yorker* articles about her Conygar experiences and finished *Raffles of Singapore*, her biography of Sir Thomas Stamford Raffles. That book was published on both sides of the Atlantic in late 1946.[25] At more than five hundred pages, it was a weighty tome for the general audience to which it was aimed. Some critics liked what a reviewer for *Time* termed Mickey's informal, "chummy" approach. Others were put off by it. "Miss Hahn has a skittish way with biography," commented Edmund Wilson in the *New Yorker*. "She dominates the book, letting her wit run loose, chiding other biographers and generally enjoying herself."[26]

The reception for *Miss Jill*, a novel that Mickey wrote about an Australian prostitute in Shanghai in the 1930s, was no less ambivalent. As had been the case with her 1935 novel *Affair* (which dealt with young love and abortion), many critics were uneasy with Mickey's casual approach to sex. "At times Miss Hahn's material seems to get a bit out of hand," sputtered the *New York Herald Tribune* reviewer;[27] A. F. Wolfe of the *Saturday Review of Literature* dismissed the book as "the prank of an *enfant terrible*."[28] Some readers evidently shared that opinion, and when the sultan of Jahore threatened to sue over what he considered "offensive passages," British publisher Jonathan Cape suspended sales until the text of the novel could be changed.

Such incidents fueled Mickey's growing indignation over the gender inequalities of life in the postwar world. During the Second World War, thousands of women had volunteered for the armed forces. On the home front, millions more American, British, and Canadian women had relieved the manpower shortage by joining the workforce—albeit at less pay than men received for doing the same jobs. These women had proved themselves to be as hard-working, self-reliant, and capable as any man. But when the war ended and their husbands, fathers, and brothers returned, these same women were expected to go back to raising children and keeping house, no questions asked. Although most of her sisters meekly complied, Mickey and some like-minded women—"radicals," they were branded—demanded the option of being able to pursue a career if they desired. Naturally, Mickey made her feelings known to anyone who would listen. She never hesitated to speak her mind, and while she was at it, she expounded on such diverse topics as the immorality of fox hunting and the politics of Ireland. This and the fact that Fitzroy, her pet corgi, had been killing neighbors' chickens landed her in heated debates whenever she and Charles attended social functions at the homes of neighbors and in the community.

• • •

Life changed forever in the Boxer household one day in the summer of 1947. Charles received a job offer from King's College at the University of London. He was invited to become the Cameons Professor of Portuguese History and Literature. Although he lacked formal academic credentials, Charles was the only English expert in the field. The job was a dream come true for him and for Mickey, as well; with Charles in London, she now had an excuse to spend time there too. As the army processed Charles's discharge papers, he and Mickey sought lodgings in the city and renewed acquaintances with many old friends from the Far East.

Meanwhile, back at Conygar, Carola was now feeling more at ease, although she would always remember her early years in Dorset as achingly lonely. There were seldom other children her age to play with. Her only real playmate was the young son of a woman who worked at Conygar for a while. "And I don't think he liked me much," she sighed.[29] Carola passed her time inventing elaborate make-believe games and spent her days prowling the estate grounds, where she communed with nature. "I became very religious for a time, and I think living there had a lot to do with it," she said. "Jesus was my friend."[30]

Mickey too was feeling reborn as a result of the changes in their lives. The new regimen was much more to her liking. She now spent four days out of every two weeks in London, where she landed occasional work writing radio scripts for the British Broadcasting Corporation. She also resumed a "love affair" that dated from her first visit to London, two decades before. That fall and winter, Mickey retreated to the oak-and-brass intellectual mecca that was the reading room of the British Museum. There was still plaster dust and rubble everywhere, and the ceilings were braced while the damage from wartime bombing was repaired, but otherwise the room was timeless and exactly as

Mickey remembered it. She spent a lot of time there researching a couple of planned books about strong women, kindred spirits who had rebelled against the patriarchal social systems of their days; one was Madame d'Arblay (popularly known as Fanny Burney), a female version and contemporary of the celebrated British diarist Samuel Johnson. The other woman was writer Aphra Behn, who had defied seventeenth-century social convention and overcame the "trifling accident of [her] sex," as Mickey termed it, to become a successful novelist and playwright. "Why must a woman be weak?" Mickey has Aphra Behn demand of her mother in an early scene in the novel. "*I'm* not weak."[31]

Mickey suspended her research on the books in June 1948, when she, Carola, and Charles returned to the States for a visit. At the urging of Charles, who insisted that Carola needed a sibling playmate, Mickey was pregnant again at age forty-four. Charles had been invited to spend the summer as a visiting scholar at the University of Michigan in Ann Arbor, and Mickey wanted to have her second child in Winnetka, where she would be among family; she was also keen to go to New York and meet her sister Helen's new husband.

By now, Helen had divorced Herbert Asbury and was remarried. Husband number three was an advertising executive named Y. Kenley Smith. He "looks like a septuagenarian," Mickey joked in a letter to a friend.[32] The Smiths were living on a farm at Red Hook, in the Catskill Mountains an hour's drive north of New York. Helen had gotten into organic farming and ecology long before such things became trendy or even common. Carola, who spent part of that summer at Red Hook, was fascinated by the contrast between the stuffy rituals she and her family followed at Conygar and the simple laid-back lifestyle of her Aunt Helen.

Carola was back in Winnetka when she heard from one of her aunts that she now had a baby sister. Mickey's second child was named Amanda. She was born several weeks premature while Mickey was visiting in New York City on October 20, 1948. "[She] is very large and pink, anyway she looks huge to me,"[33] Mickey reported in a letter to her sister Dorothy. In fact, Amanda was only a little over four pounds and quite tiny. Mickey, who had made no secret of her wish for a son, could barely conceal her disappointment. Years later, when Amanda asked her mother why she had borne a second child so late in her life, Mickey responded, "You don't understand. Nowadays a woman has a choice."[34] Her response was odd, given her liberal approach to so many other gender issues.

Charles and Carola sailed home to England in early November. Mickey and baby Amanda remained in New York at the home of Mickey's old friend Donald Hanson and his wife Muriel. Mother and daughter returned to England by air a few weeks later because of a strike by the crew of the *Queen Elizabeth II*. It was a memorable journey for two reasons: this was the first time Mickey had flown across the Atlantic—just as her youthful hero Charles Lindbergh had done two decades before—and one of the propeller-driven airplane's four engines quit in mid-ocean, forcing an emergency landing in Gander, Newfoundland.

Mickey and Amanda arrived at Conygar a day later than planned, but otherwise none the worse for their ordeal. Mickey was surprised and pleased to find the house "running far better without me than with me," as she wrote in a letter to Muriel Hanson.[35] Knowing this made it easier for Mickey to turn the care of Amanda over to a nanny. As the euphoria of giving birth gave way to postpartum depression, Mickey's old restlessness returned. When in London, she resumed her daytime visits to the British Museum and sometimes spent evenings "getting drunk with pals."[36] The novelty of commuting into the city had worn thin, and the fortnightly rail trips suddenly seemed tiresome and costly. Even with two incomes, it was a strain to pay for the upkeep and servants at Conygar, a flat in London, and Carola's education at the Hanford Boarding School. Money was a constant worry, and Charles fretted over the bills at the end of each month.

Making matters worse, the British income tax office now considered Mickey a "resident." She was badgered to pay taxes on her income for 1945–1946, and did so only to get into a spirited argument subsequently with His Majesty's tax officials over her 1947 income; Mickey figured it at about $13,000 (U.S.), whereas the tax office claimed it was closer to $52,000. These disputes with the tax man became a source of considerable irritation to Mickey. It did not help the family's financial situation that she was still prone to impulsive spending sprees.

These were not happy times for her. She was torn between wanting to be independent enough to pursue her literary career and wanting to be a good and loving mother. Because Mickey and Charles were away so much, Carola had been sent off to boarding school, and Amanda was being raised by an overly possessive nanny she never really liked—"Nanny Hairybottom," she called her. On one occasion, as Mickey and Amanda were walking in the garden alone, Amanda giggled as she whispered, "Aren't we naughty, Mummy!"[37]

Sometimes Mickey could laugh at such incidents. Other times, she felt profoundly guilty and attempted to make good by buying her daughters presents. Doing so only served to underscore the vague, undefined emotional longing that was there, somewhere deep inside her. "I heard myself saying to [Amanda] the other day when we were unexpectedly alone, 'I wish you were *mine*,'" Mickey confided in a letter to her sister Dorothy.[38]

Under the circumstances, it is not surprising that Mickey's marriage was also showing signs of strain. She and Charles were bickering more frequently, sometimes over the most trivial of things. While at least some of the underlying domestic tensions stemmed from the family's troubled dynamics, the public reaction to Mickey's latest book was also a factor. It was originally to be called *England Journal,* but Mickey's agent and publisher were still intent on trading on the success of *China to Me,* so the new book's title was changed. *England to Me* was a collection of twenty-two lighthearted first-person stories about the follies and foibles of English country life. A few of the pieces had been published in the *New Yorker;* the others were new. This was Mickey at the peak of her form: perceptive, highly readable, and wickedly funny. Many years earlier, Harold Ross had told Mickey that she could "write *cattier* than anyone I know except Rebecca West."[39] It now seemed that she had become West's equal.

The book had an undeniable ring of truth to its observations about the differences between the British and American temperaments. Mickey deliberately had tried not to offend members of her family, the servants at Conygar, or the neighbors. She did not succeed. Her British publisher, Jonathan Cape, informed her that the company's solicitors had red-circled ten possible libels in the manuscript. Mickey made the requested changes, and *England to Me* was published in the spring of 1949.

"This is more like it," enthused reviewer A. F. Wolfe of the *Saturday Review of Literature.* "This is the Emily Hahn of *China to Me* and *Hong Kong Holiday.*"[40] When other American reviewers echoed that praise, the book sold well in the States. However, its reception was somewhat different in England. Initial sales were a modest 16,000 copies, and reader reaction was as passionate as it was swift. In the midst of their postwar hardships, the proud British were sensitive to the comments of foreigners, particularly Americans. The Boxer family could not fathom why Mickey had wasted her time writing about such banalities. British critics attacked Mickey for poking fun at the national eccentricities. "It is my most sincere and earnest wish that one of my countrymen gives Emily Hahn such a clout over the ear with either a rolling pin or a knuckle duster that she will immediately transport herself back to the American Way of Life," one irate reader in Cornwall chided in a letter. "And a sailor's farewell to her, anyway."[41]

Although Charles could not quite bring himself to agree, he would certainly have preferred that his spouse write about matters less contentious and less intimate. Those sentiments underlay some at times pointed discussions between Mickey and Charles. American visitors to Conygar evidently overheard some of these exchanges, for in October 1949 Mickey's agent in New York called to let her know that commentator Walter Winchell, whose daily radio show and newspaper gossip column reached an estimated 25 million people, had reported that the Boxers were about to divorce. Mickey, fuming, immediately phoned Winchell to deny the rumor. "I went downstairs first and verified the denial with Charles at his desk," she told Dorothy, "because after all one never knows, does one? But I bet it makes me a lot of trouble nevertheless. Fantastic notion; what do you suppose started it?"[42]

With all of these issues and concerns swirling in the background in early 1950, Mickey and Charles agreed on an innovative solution to all their problems: a variation of that distinctly British anomaly known as the "open marriage," not in a sexual sense but rather in terms of freedom of movement. Mickey would return to New York, where Harold Ross had offered her a staff writer's job at the *New Yorker*. Charles would stay at Conygar and continue commuting to his teaching job in London. Carola would attend boarding school, while Amanda, who was now a toddler, would remain with her nanny. Mickey would visit England regularly, being careful not to stay in the United Kingdom longer than ninety-one days—the magic number to establish residency for income tax purposes. As peculiar as this long-distance marriage may have seemed to Americans at the time, it was not at all unusual among the upper class in England.

The idea of an open marriage struck Mickey and Charles—and many of their friends and relatives—as perfectly natural. Here were two highly independent people who could neither live together nor apart. Theirs was what

Carola (l) and Amanda (r) at Conygar, circa 1951.
Courtesy Emily Hahn Estate

New Yorker writer Roger Angell termed a "shared preference for intimacy built around absence."[43] It was the easy way out of some complex emotional issues that remained unresolved. Mickey's friend Barbara Ker-Seymer recalled an incident that shed some light on the emotional price that was paid. Compartmentalizing their lives allowed both Mickey and Charles to stay married while pursuing their own careers and maximizing the family's income; by living in the States, Mickey avoided paying the crippling British income taxes.

The only real drawback to this bold plan, one that was either overlooked or dismissed, was its impact on the Boxers' two daughters. In theory, it seemed logical that Carola should attend boarding school while Amanda would remain home with her father, who in his own peculiar way doted on her. But cold logic is one thing, flesh-and-blood emotions quite another; splitting the Boxer girls proved to be far more traumatic than either Mickey or Charles could ever have envisioned.

Barbara, estranged from her own husband, brought her young son Max and came to live at Conygar for a time when Mickey was back in England. One bright summer day, Barbara and Mickey took the three children to the seashore for a picnic. When Amanda announced she had to urinate, Mickey told her to go do so in the sand behind a rock; there was no one else around. "No, No!" Amanda tearfully insisted, "Nanny said I mustn't pee except in a proper lavoratory!" Mickey said nonsense and took Amanda along while she herself proved the point. Amanda remained adamant, even when Carola followed her mother's lead. "We finally had to pack up and go home [to Conygar]," Barbara recalled. "Amanda greeted her nanny by saying, 'Nanny, I didn't do it!"[44]

Sadly, Carola and Amanda grew up leading separate lives and with an unfulfilled longing for the loving presence of the sister whom each of them never really knew. Many years later, in a family photo taken in the garden of their English home one summer day, Charles and Mickey were seated in lawn chairs. Amanda stood behind Charles, Carola behind Mickey, who was sporting a New York Mets baseball cap. The physical gap between the chairs upon which Mickey and Charles sat was mere feet, but as absolutely loving and devoted as they were to one another, the psychological distance between those lawn chairs was unbridgeable; the same gap separated their now-grown daughters. "That's just the way it worked out," Amanda explained wistfully.[45] Her sister Carola could only nod in agreement. "I wasn't involved in Amanda's life very much at all [growing up], which was sad," she said.[46]

29

DURING ITS FIRST decade of existence, the *New Yorker* operated out of cramped offices on the sixth floor of 25 West Forty-fifth Street. In 1935, at the nadir of the Great Depression, many national publications were losing money. The *New Yorker* defied that trend by continuing to prosper. Advertisers wanted to reach the magazine's well-heeled readers, who spent fifteen cents a week for what former managing editor Ralph Ingersoll termed "[a] distillate of bitter wit and frustrated humor."[1]

The *New Yorker*'s circulation that year topped 125,000; about half of the readers were outside the New York City area. Ingersoll marveled that a magazine edited by Harold Ross, who was regarded by many people as a mad genius, "has accomplished what no other weekly has been able to do in a generation: for the first six months [of 1934] it ran more pages of advertising than—hold your breath—the *Saturday Evening Post* itself!"[2] F. R. Publishing Corporation, the company Ross, his wife Jane Grant, and Raoul Fleischmann cofounded in 1925 with $45,000, was worth $600,000 a decade later. "Magazines are about eighty-five percent luck," Harold Ross once quipped. "I was about the luckiest son of a bitch alive when I started the *New Yorker*."[3] What Ross and many other people apparently forgot was that Fleischmann and other investors had pumped more than $700,000 into the *New Yorker* before it began paying its own way in 1928.[4] Harold Ross's "luck" had not come cheaply.

In keeping with its elevated status, the *New Yorker* moved to bigger and better offices in early 1935. Its new home was in a twenty-two-story office building at 25 West Forty-third Street, two blocks south of its original location.

Initially, there was lots of room there. However, as the magazine grew, so too did the number of employees, and before long space was again at a premium. By the time Mickey Hahn arrived in the fall of 1950, many members of the editorial staff were jammed two or three to an office.

There was a definite pecking order at the magazine. The eighteenth floor at 25 West Forty-third Street was occupied by writers, the nineteenth by Ross and his editing staff, and the twentieth mostly by the fiction and art departments. Mickey received special treatment when she was given one of what writer Brendan Gill described in his memoir *Here at the New Yorker* as the "bleak little ill-painted cells"[5] on the eighteenth floor. The space had been vacated a few days earlier by Janet Flanner, the *New Yorker*'s Paris correspondent. Flanner had been visiting New York, and when she returned to Paris, Mickey moved into the office she had occupied. It was opposite the elevator. On the main editorial floor—the nineteenth—visitors stepped off the elevator to arrive unannounced at the doors of editor Ross and his staff. As a result, Ross found himself confronted more than once by disgruntled former employees and frustrated freelance writers who were upset that their submissions had been rejected. After one too many of these surprise encounters, Ross had a table and chair set up in the hallway, next to the elevator. Comely young women from Vassar, Barnard, and other exclusive schools, eager to add to their resumes a stint at the fashionable *New Yorker*, were hired as receptionists. Many came from well-to-do families and did not need the money, so they were paid a pittance.

The appearance of a receptionist was a change, one not everyone applauded—among them Wolcott Gibbs, the magazine's theater critic. Gibbs, a fastidious man who was scornful of Ross's adherence to "insect routine," as Gibbs termed it, preferred to write at home. There, attired in a bathrobe, he composed his reviews while pacing the floor and chain-smoking cigarettes. Ross, who admired and liked Gibbs, used any excuse to get him to come to the office. One of the rare occasions that Gibbs did so was just after the receptionist's table appeared in the *New Yorker* hallway. Gibbs dropped by for an appointment with Ross. As he stepped off the elevator and headed for the editor's office, the startled receptionist called after him, "Sir! Sir! Can I help you?" Gibbs stopped and began muttering about Ross. When the young woman demanded, "Whom shall I say is calling?" Gibbs promptly returned to the elevator and pushed the down button. Sensing she had committed a major faux pas, the receptionist implored, "Sir, is there anything I can do for you?" Gibbs stepped into the waiting elevator without looking back. "No, thanks," he said. "I've lost interest."[6]

Such scenes being played out and the stream of people passing one's office door could have been either a curse or a blessing for Mickey. Given her genial nature, her insatiable curiosity, and her remarkable powers of concentration, she reveled in the bustle. Mickey remained in the same office, opposite the elevator, for most of the next forty years. She even took the equivalent space in 1990 when the *New Yorker* moved to its current home, a few doors up the street at 20 West Forty-fifth Street. In the process, Mickey became one of only a handful of *New Yorker* staff writers to serve under all four of the magazine's editors: founder Harold Ross (1925–1951), William Shawn (1951–1987), Robert Gottlieb (1987–1992), and Tina Brown (1992–present).

In some ways, the location of Mickey's office almost seems symbolic. The impression her coworkers had of her was of a woman ceaselessly on the go. One day, Mickey was rushing off to England to visit her husband and daughters, or else to Chicago to visit her siblings and aged mother. The next, she was headed to the far ends of the globe to research another of her celebrated "reporter at large" articles. In the obituary he wrote for the *New Yorker,* veteran staff writer Roger Angell noted, "What is disconcerting about [Mickey] now that she is gone is how few of us, even among the old timers, can claim a close friendship with her, much as we admired her."[7]

As often as not, Mickey's office door was open. Yet even when she was working hard on an assignment and her door was shut, it was never really *closed.* Colleagues who interrupted the steady *tap-tap-tapping* of her typewriter knew she was always ready to talk about writing, office gossip, or any of her many other abiding passions in life—words, apes, monkeys, and zoos especially. Sometimes she would emerge from the office to beetle down the hall to check the spelling of a word in the big *Webster's Dictionary* that was located on a stand on each editorial floor. She would often call on family and friends whenever something piqued her curiosity and she *had* to know. It might be the location of the island of Diego Garcia (in the middle of the Indian Ocean), the meaning of the philosopher's notion of structuralism (a study of the concepts that underlie other concepts), or maybe the facts about the nerve disorder known as Bell's Palsy, which paralyzed muscles in Mickey's face for a time in 1963. A favorite game that Mickey, Sheila McGrath, and others used to play was to track down the word for some obscure activity; if people did it, the theory was, there must be a word for it. A typical example was the word for the act of inserting one word in the middle of another for dramatic or comic effect—un-bloody-believable! The word is "tmesis."

Mickey also loved to pose provocative questions, as much to stir up debate as out of any real desire for answers. ("Did Shakespeare know he was *Shakespeare*?" she would typically ask.) "Emily Hahn had the most intense love affair with words of practically anyone I've known," recalled Valerie Feldner, a receptionist at the *New Yorker* who became her friend in Mickey's latter years. "[She] made hunting for definitions and meanings an endless game."[8]

Because Mickey Hahn's reputation preceded her at the *New Yorker*, when she arrived many of her coworkers were curious about her. She was already something of an office legend due to her *China to Me* notoriety, her cigar smoking, and her striking good looks. Mickey was someone people talked about. She loved it; like her father Isaac, she craved attention and often played to an audience through her penchant for dramatic entrances. Once, in 1969, Mickey attended a high-profile reception at the New York home of the wealthy Canadian industrialist Edgar Bronfman and his wife Anne. Mickey strode into the crowded salon wearing black leather boots and puffing on a huge cigar. When one of the society ladies stared with mouth agape, Mickey smiled at her and announced in a stage whisper, "Can't smoke opium here, you know."[9]

Cigars were an integral prop in countless other Mickey first sightings. Professor James ("Jimmy") Cummins, one of Charles's former students and one of his closest friends, was a graduate student at the University of London in 1948 and was working for the summer as a waiter in a seaside town not far from Conygar. Someone had asked him to deliver a letter to Professor Charles Boxer, whom Cummins had never met, although they had common scholarly interests. "I hiked over there in the afternoon," Cummins said. "As I was walking up the long driveway to Conygar I saw someone who was smoking a cigar standing on the second-floor balcony in riding breeches. It turned out to be Mickey. She didn't have a horse, but she liked to wear riding breeches."[10]

That is not quite the end of the Cummins story. Although Charles was away, Mickey invited Cummins to stay for a drink with her and Charles's brother Myles, who was visiting. Cummins did, and he so enjoyed himself that he had no recollection of what time he finally went home, or of how he got there. All he knew was that he had made a new friend, a fact that was confirmed when he next met Mickey. It was just before Christmas that year at a lecture in London. When Mickey spotted him, she immediately came over and asked what he was doing for the holidays.

"Staying in my lodgings, I suppose," said Cummins, who had been orphaned at an early age and had no close family.

"Nonsense!" replied Mickey. "Come to Conygar with us." So he did, and that was the start of a beautiful, lifelong friendship.[11]

Given Mickey's outgoing nature, it understandably wasn't long before she knew everyone at the *New Yorker* and everyone there knew her (or knew *of* her). People sought her out. She was *among* them for nearly five decades, but it was never in her nature to be a joiner, and so she was never *really* one of them. Asked about his reminiscences of Mickey, veteran *New Yorker* writer Brendan Gill noted, "We've nodded cordially and exchanged hellos for fifty-odd years, but it is in the nature of *New Yorker* relationships never to progress beyond that point. Professionally friendly, but not intimate; admiring, but almost always silently so."[12]

When the *New Yorker* marked its seventieth anniversary in 1995, it did so with a lavish double issue (February 20–27) in which Mickey's name and byline were conspicuously, inexplicably, and inexcusably absent. If the oversight hurt, which it must certainly have, she never let on.

Despite her longevity, Mickey was never one of the inner circle of cronies at the *New Yorker*—mostly males—who in the old days surrounded editor Harold Ross or his successor William Shawn. "The great, liberal *New Yorker*," like virtually all the national magazines of the day, was owned and managed mostly by men. There were many strong female personalities at the magazine all right—Katharine White being the best known—but for the most part, the *New Yorker* was a "guys-only" club, where a kind of literary locker room mentality prevailed. Mickey, no shrinking violet herself, was regarded as a character by her male colleagues. "She was a sweet-tempered feminist, who didn't dislike men," retired *New Yorker* fiction editor William Maxwell told Roger Angell.[13]

It speaks volumes that Mickey did not receive even a single mention in Brendan Gill's book, or in James Thurber's memoir *The Years with Ross.*[14]

• • •

When Mickey met Harold Ross that long ago summer day in 1929, her relationship with the *New Yorker* editor was distant and businesslike. At first, she hated him. That changed as they came to know one another. Mickey never forgot how Ross had paid her mother's way to New York in September 1943 so Hannah Hahn could be there when her daughter arrived from Hong Kong. Later, when Mickey heard that Charles had been beheaded by the Japanese, she "instinctively" rushed into Ross's office to share her grim news. Ross consoled her by taking her to lunch at the Algonquin Hotel, his favorite haunt. "We talked about a lot of other things, and Ross told me not to believe the rumors. He was right," Mickey said.[15]

Ross was always congenial and warm toward Mickey Hahn, even when they had their differences, as they inevitably did. Mickey sensed from the beginning that there was more to the *New Yorker* editor than met the eye. As dissimilar as they were in many ways, in others they were kindred spirits. Like Mickey, Ross was a complex, contradictory character with a chameleon-like vitality. Like Mickey, he knew many people, but few people really knew him. There were many Harold Rosses, just as there were many Mickey Hahns. "I think we should all write our own books about him," Mickey once said. "We all have Ross stories."[16]

No one ever questioned Ross's talent or his dedication. He had an engaging wit, a nimble mind, and an unequalled eye for literary talent. Writers loved to work for him; Ross was a "writer's editor"—one of the nicest things most writers will ever utter about the people whose job it is to prune and polish their words. As Charles McGrath pointed out in a tribute to Ross, written for the *New Yorker*'s seventieth anniversary issue, "He fussed over your punctuation, but he also brooded about your career—about what you should be writing and how you should be doing it."[17] The point was, Ross had a tremendous respect for creative people, and he genuinely cared about the people who wrote for him.

• • •

Given all of the bizarre tales that such writers as Thomas Kunkel, Brendan Gill, and James Thurber have recounted about how *New Yorker* staff were hired and fired, the story of how Mickey Hahn joined the staff is disappointingly mundane. When she first began writing for the magazine, it was because Katharine White—Angell at the time—had drawn her to Ross's attention. The appearance of Mickey's byline in the *New Yorker* jump-started her literary career, giving her instant credibility. The magazine had become a huge success by 1929. Every writer who was anybody in America dreamed of having an article published there. Mickey was as much at home spinning the offhand "casuals"—a *New Yorker* term for articles and stories—as she was at writing the magazine's trademark hard-edged, yet literate, reportage. A. J. Liebling and Joe Mitchell had perfected the format, and Mickey became one of its most skilled practitioners.

When she inquired in 1950, Mickey was offered a job as a *New Yorker* staff writer. It was as easy as that. Although she had spent a lot of time there following her return from Hong Kong, Mickey had always shared office space with others. That was normal; when fellow staff writer Philip Hamburger was hired in 1939, he was put into a cubicle "roughly the size of a hotel icebox" with two other writers.[18] Things were different for Mickey. In 1950, she got her own office. She also got a typewriter and a pile of yellow copy paper. A window with a partially obstructed view of Forty-fourth Street was the only frill.

In at least one important regard, Mickey was no different from other *New Yorker* staff writers: the terms under which she was hired were vague and informal, at least in her mind. Mickey liked to joke that she had no job guarantee, no security, and no safety net. In a 1988 interview with a reporter from *Publishers Weekly*, Mickey explained her status at the *New Yorker* after thirty-eight years there by noting, "I don't know. They might kick me out any minute. But I'm so old (83) they probably won't."[19]

In actual fact, Mickey and other "fact writers"—as opposed to those who wrote for the fiction department—were considered employees. By the terms of the contracts under which each of them had been hired, they were entitled to a share of the magazine's profits and to coverage under the *New Yorker*'s group health insurance plan. This became an issue in 1978, when Internal Revenue Service (IRS) officials decided that people under contract at the *New Yorker* were not "employees" for income tax purposes. This caused a great deal of upset and anger until U.S. Senators Bill Bradley from New Jersey and Daniel Patrick Moynihan from New York cosponsored a 1979 bill in Congress that specifically exempted the magazine's current contract employees—but no new ones—from this tax office ruling. Despite what Mickey may have said, she literally had the U.S. Congress to thank for her job![20]

In that job, Mickey was encouraged to write about anything and everything that interested her. Given her insatiable curiosity, the range of her literary territory was limited only by her boundless imagination and tireless work ethic.

In return for a right of first refusal on her articles and stories, the *New Yorker* provided Mickey with a weekly draw, picked up the costs whenever she traveled on assignment, and paid her a higher rate for submissions than it otherwise would have done had she not been on staff. The more of her work that appeared in the magazine, the higher her per-article rate. Disliking routine as much as she did, this arrangement suited Mickey perfectly. Others might have been uneasy in such an unstructured environment, but Mickey was in heaven; she had found the job of her dreams.

During her first few weeks back in New York, Mickey stayed at the home of her old friend Donald Hanson and his wife Muriel. Then she sublet an apartment from the estranged wife of writer Nunnally Johnson. The dwelling was a brisk half-hour walk from work. Mickey arrived most days no later than seven o'clock, hours before almost everyone else in the editorial department—the regular office hours being 10 A.M. to 6 P.M. Longtime *New Yorker* staff writer E. J. Kahn, Jr., himself "a morning person," recalled that most days when he got in, there was Mickey "almost always at her desk just off the elevator landing, already into her day's stint. Even if I never went to bed, I would be hard pressed to match her formidable output," he wrote.[21]

• • •

Harold Ross was already in failing health when Mickey joined the *New Yorker* staff. His smoking habit caught up with him the following spring, when he learned that he had cancer of the windpipe and only months to live. At first, Ross did not tell any of his *New Yorker* colleagues. However, speculation about his health grew as his absences from work became longer and more frequent. William Shawn, the managing editor of the nonfiction department (Gus Lobrano held the equivalent job in the fiction department), assumed more and more of the editor's duties.

When Mickey learned of Ross's death on December 6, 1951, she was in Hong Kong. She had gone there with Charles for ceremonies marking the tenth anniversary of the Japanese attack on the city. Ross, in Boston for cancer surgery, died unexpectedly on the operating table. "I cried like an idiot," Mickey recalled.[22] It was only after he was gone that she grasped how much he had really meant to her and to her career. Not only was Harold Ross one of the most remarkable men she had ever met; he had been a good friend, indeed. His death was a huge loss to her and to everyone else who knew him. In many ways, Harold Ross had been the heart and soul of the *New Yorker*.

There was a lot of speculation following Ross's death about whether the magazine he had founded could—and would—continue without him. To the surprise of some observers, the transition was almost seamless. The man who made it happen was Ross's handpicked successor, William Shawn. Mickey had known him for many years, and they had an excellent working relationship. Shawn, two years younger than Mickey, had grown up in the same Chicago neighborhood where the Hahns lived, and for a time he and Mickey had even gone to the same school.

Shawn was ruddy, short, balding, and polite to a fault; he used honorifics with speaking about everyone, even messenger boys and elevator operators. He was born William Chon, but changed his name to Shawn. He thought Chon looked too Oriental on paper, and that Shawn was more befitting a young man with literary aspirations. He must have been right; Harold Ross hired Shawn in 1933 to write for the magazine's "Talk of the Town" section. Shawn, who shunned the limelight as much as Ross did , proved to be more skilled with an editor's pencil than with a writer's typewriter. He edited many of the articles that Mickey sent from China in the late 1930s and early 1940s. That is when she got to know him. "Shawn could not have been more different from Ross," Mickey explained. "He was very gentle and deliberate. He pondered everything a long time. Maybe Ross did, too, but he didn't seem to."[23]

This was not to say Shawn was any easier to work for than Ross had been. Mickey recalled one occasion when she was writing a long article about the Greenpeace environmental group. She had given Shawn portions of the article to read. "He came into my office carrying it all," Mickey recalled. "He was very red in the face as he announced, 'We're not going to do this!' Then he put the papers down on my desk and left. I never had any explanation. The editor who was working with me on the article tried but couldn't get an explanation either."[24]

Such incidents were rare. Mickey generally got along with Shawn as well as she did with most of her *New Yorker* colleagues. Of course, she got along better with some than with others. Among the more high-profile *New Yorker* people for whom she had a special fondness was humorist James Thurber. "Jim," as Mickey called him, had lost an eye in a childhood bow-and-arrow accident, and a degenerative condition had left him nearly blind in the other. Although this prompted his early retirement, Thurber's presence was still felt at the magazine. He still dropped in, and he sometimes prowled the offices in the evenings, after all of the staff had gone home. One of his tricks was to write cryptic graffiti in small letters in the upper corners of the walls, near the ceiling. Writer Joe Mitchell was astonished to look up in his office one day to see the words "Too late!" scribbled in Thurber's distinctive hand. How long it had been there, Mitchell had no idea.[25] Other times, Thurber left cave drawing–like humorous doodles in conspicuous locations, often in the hallways. When the *New Yorker* moved from 25 West Forty-third Street, an entire wall with Thurber's pencil renderings was taken down and carted along.

In the fall of 1950, Thurber was only fifty-six years old, but he was already enfeebled. Tall, graying, and with his once-lean body prematurely gone to an old man's paunch, Thurber was a melancholy figure; the death of his old friend Ross had affected him deeply. He could not get around without his wife or someone else to act as his guide. Nonetheless, when he heard that Mickey was back in New York, Thurber sometimes made his way over to her house to visit. When Thurber's wife Helen discovered he was sneaking out on his own, she followed him one day. She was furious with him for taking such a huge risk.

"I came to know Jim pretty well," said Mickey. "Nobody else can remember what I remember about him. He once took me to have lunch with his mother, and she had a bad eye, too. They say it isn't true, but how could I make that up?"[26]

Mickey recalled another incident a few years later which she said was typical of Thurber and revealed his mischievous side. He loved practical jokes. Sadly, toward the end of his life in 1961, these became increasingly sophomoric, sometimes even cruel. "Thurber and I were out some place one evening and we went to the office to get something. Jim was drunk. I'd had a few drinks, too, but I wasn't drunk," Mickey said.

"They used to push the office mail through a slot in the door in those days, and I remember that Jim picked up the *New Yorker*'s mail that night, and he tore up everything—letters, subscription requests, drawings . . . everything. Why? I don't know, and he never said."[27]

Thurber became increasingly prone to such unpredictable outbursts. Even his family and friends were at a loss to explain why. Some people attributed it to his bitterness at going blind. As it turned out, that was not the case; there was a physiological reason. Mickey recalled how she attended a wake at Costello's Bar, long the favorite after-hours haunt of the *New Yorker* editorial staff. It was not until the next day that Mickey realized that during the entire evening at Costello's, no one had even so much as mentioned Thurber's name. "I told Bill Maxwell about it. He said, 'Of course. Jim (Thurber) was so awful people didn't want to talk about him.' Thurber was making scenes. It turned out that he'd had a tumor on the brain."[28]

Another of Mickey's favorite *New Yorker* personalities was cartoonist Charles Addams, the creator of the Addams family characters. Like Thurber, Addams had a sometimes naughty, off-the-wall sense of humor. In 1969, Mickey had caused an uproar with a *New Yorker* article entitled "The Big Smoke," in which she told the story of her opium addiction. Not long afterward, she chanced to be on a crowded office elevator with Addams. He winked as he flashed a wicked smile, then produced a small box from his coat pocket. On it the word "Opium" was spelled out in big letters. Addams tucked the box back into his pocket, where he had been keeping it in anticipation of this moment. Addams said nothing further. That was his way of having fun.

Another time, after Mickey did a series of articles on communicating with animals, Addams marched into her office with his mongrel dog Alice in tow. He introduced the mutt to Mickey. "Addams told me his dog understood everything you said. He looked at her and announced, "Alice, you're looking dirty. We're going to wash you.' The dog quickly made herself scarce," said Mickey. "So maybe she really did understand."[29]

30

DESPITE ALL OF THE distractions and disruptions of a hectic life, Emily Hahn's literary output during her *New Yorker* years was astounding. This was particularly so between 1950 and 1970, when she was at the height of her creative energy. In addition to the scores of articles and stories she did for the *New Yorker*, she wrote thirty books in an encyclopedic range of subject matters and genres. Included in this literary deluge were titles for young readers and adults alike. Some of Mickey's literary friends were quick to dismiss the former as being slight efforts that were done solely for a quick buck. The income was attractive all right, but Mickey also had a mission: she had been a teacher (and continued to be for she sometimes taught writing courses at universities), and time had not diminished her urge to share with young people her zest for life or her love of knowledge.

Ten of Mickey's books in this period were for young readers. These included three in a series about an adventurous girl named Francie; four biographies of inspiring historical personalities (among them *Aboab: First Rabbi of the Americas* [1959], one of the few things Mickey ever wrote that was rooted in her Jewishness); and three others: a children's book about India and two other stories for girls. If there was a unifying theme that ran through most of these books, it was the need for girls and young women to set their sights high. Mickey spelled out that message in explaining her reasons for writing a biography of Elizabeth Cochrane, a feisty turn-of-the-century American journalist who won fame writing under the pen name Nellie Bly. "Today [1959] girls can be reporters or engineers or officers in the armed forces, if they like. If most of them still prefer to stay at home to raise their children, that is also excellent," Mickey wrote. "Free choice is a very precious thing."[1] It was significant and fitting that Mickey dedicated the Bly book to her daughters Carola and Amanda.

Around the World with Nellie Bly and the other books that Mickey wrote for youngsters were a clarion call for gender equality. In the context of today's public opinion, the "freedom to choose" message is no longer extraordinary or unusual. It was much different in 1959, when few writers or public figures were carrying on the fight, and even few book reviewers bothered to discuss the issues Mickey was raising. Many Americans considered radical, even threatening, a revived women's rights movement—with its roots in the discontent over how women in the postwar era had been shortchanged and in the bitter struggle for black civil rights. *Around the World with Nellie Bly* was published four years before feminist Betty Friedan's 1963 book *The Feminine Mystique* created a furor and placed the issues of women's rights, sexual liberation, and "male chauvinism" squarely on the front burner in a heated national debate.

In addition to her stories for young readers, during this period Mickey wrote two books of humor; novels about Aphra Behn and Mata Hari (two more free-spirited women); nonfiction books about India, bohemianism, the maharajas, diamonds, love ("a glandular history of civilization," as Mickey subtitled it); a history of China from 1850 to 1950; and two *Time-Life* books about Chinese cooking. There were also full biographies of writer Fanny Burney, the nineteenth-century British adventurer Sir James Brooke, and the Chinese Nationalist leader Chiang Kai-shek.

The China books marked a return to familiar themes for Mickey and were reminders of her ongoing interest in that country and its culture. In May 1951, the popular author Pearl S. Buck was on a lecture tour of the American Midwest when she chanced to have lunch one day with an acquaintance of Mickey's. The name Soong inevitably came up, and when it did, talk inevitably turned to Mickey's 1941 biography of the three sisters. Buck reportedly quipped that Mickey's notes had been "more interesting" than her book, which, after all, the Soongs "had paid her to write." When word of these remarks got back to Mickey, she was fighting mad. She dashed off an angry letter to Buck, who responded apologetically and with assurances that her remarks had been misinterpreted.[2]

This incident illustrates the extent to which Emily Hahn and China were—and always would be—linked in the public's mind. A lot had happened in China since the end of the war, and both Mickey's agent and her publisher urged her to write more about it. In 1949, the Communists under Mao Tse-tung had emerged victorious from a vicious three-year civil war. Bloodied but defiant, Chiang Kai-shek and his Nationalist army had retreated to Taiwan (once known as Formosa), one hundred miles off the southeast coast of China. The mountainous island, occupied by Japan for many years until 1945, was a natural fortress. Here, the Generalissimo established his Chinese "government in exile." Chiang vowed that he and his army would one day use Taiwan as their springboard for a victorious return to the mainland. He died in April 1975 before doing so, but his followers and their descendants have remained on the island.

In the summer of 1953, Mickey went on a journalistic expedition to Hong Kong, Tokyo, and Taiwan. She also tried unsuccessfully to obtain a visa to visit Shanghai. Sinmay Zau and his family were still living there in the same house they had moved into in 1937, when the Japanese had dislodged them from their home. After the war, the Communists imprisoned Sinmay because of his opium addiction. Once "re-educated," he was allowed to resume his old life and, for a time, even to travel abroad. In 1948, he came to New York to visit

Mickey. Ever resourceful, he pestered her with pleas for money to finance various "get-rich-quick" schemes; for a while, Sinmay talked about starting a Chinese version of *Life* magazine, then there was his scheme to make movies. Ultimately, Sinmay did none of these things. Following the 1949 Communist takeover in China, he lived quietly, scratching out a living by translating English-language novels and poetry into Chinese for state-run publishers.

Mickey's family and friends who met Sinmay in New York were puzzled about what had ever drawn Mickey to him. The years of opium addiction and the hardships of the war had taken their toll on Sinmay. "He took me to lunch at a Chinese restaurant when he was in New York," recalled Mickey's nephew Charless Hahn. "Sinmay was a small Chinese man. He was bright and charming, but it was a wonderful meal and I remember it better than I do *him*."[3]

Sinmay fell ill with heart disease in 1961. According to his daughter Xiaohong Shao, a retired dentist who lives in Nanjing, he died in May 1968 in poverty.[4] It was an inglorious end for Mickey's gentle Chinese poet. In her memories she always saw Sinmay's beautiful eyes, overflowing with light, mischief, and an unquenchable hunger for life.

Mickey did not see Sinmay on her Asian trip, nor ever again. However, she visited Tokyo and saw Chikanori Nakazawa—"Chick," the *Kempetai* officer who had spied on her in Hong Kong in 1942, and in Taiwan she renewed acquaintances with the Chiangs, after a fashion. The Generalissimo and Madame Chiang declined to be formally interviewed because they were acutely embarrassed at their situation. Undeterred, Mickey met with many of Chiang's lieutenants. She also interviewed captured Red Chinese soldiers and inspected the coastal artillery that was trained on the Straits of Taiwan in anticipation of an imminent attack.

On her return home, Mickey wrote a two-part series of articles about Taiwan for the *New Yorker*. The first of these pieces (October 24, 1953) looked at the mass "schizophrenia" that characterized the Chinese Nationalists. On one hand, Chiang's followers were utterly devoted to preparations for the day "the Old Man"—as they affectionately referred to him—would lead an invasion to drive the Communists from the mainland. On the other hand, the Nationalists were taunted by the realization that the glorious liberation might be a long time coming; for now they would have to be content to stay where they were.

The second part of the series (November 7, 1953) was an intimate profile of the Chiangs and of other Nationalist leaders. In retrospect, what is striking is the casual manner in which Mickey approached her subjects. The personalities and events of postwar China were charged with raw emotion, yet Mickey's profile of the Chiangs portrayed them as flesh-and-blood people, with workaday hopes, fears, and troubles. "Taiwan has not been kind to Mme. Chiang. She suffers from allergies," Mickey noted, "and shortly after she and her husband took up residence on the island, she developed a severe case of an unpleasant skin disease called disseminated neurodermatitis."[5] Of the Generalissimo, Mickey noted that his biggest asset—his unbridled devotion to his cause—was also his biggest liability. "[He] is so obstinate," she quoted one of his commanders as saying, "he won't even stop hoping."[6]

Expanding on the interviews and research that she had done in Taiwan, Mickey spent the next year writing a biography of Chiang Kai-shek. Doing so continued a practice she had started in the mid-1940s, when she began recycling material she had originally written for the *New Yorker*. By fleshing out key themes, she was successful in spinning the articles into books. That routine, which she used with great success, goes a long way toward explaining Mickey's amazing productivity; at least ten of the fifty-one books she wrote came about this way.

What made the Chiang book noteworthy was that despite all of the attention paid to China by the Western media in the postwar years, *Chiang Kai-shek: An Unauthorized Biography* was the first full-length English-language profile of the Nationalist leader to appear in the United States. Many reviewers were befuddled to find that Mickey's perspective on Chiang was more Chinese than American; some were disappointed that she did not focus more on Nationalist corruption. Reviewer Henry Lieberman of the *New York Times* took Mickey to task for failing to place Chiang in "a broad historical context;"[7] H. P. Linton of *Library Journal* chided her for not writing an "objective, unbiased, documented biography."[8]

Mickey, who had aimed the Chiang book at the same mass audience her old friend John Gunther was reaching with his successful series of *Inside* books, was puzzled by much of the criticism thrown her way. "I don't even feel prejudice about Chiang personally, I have no fondness for him. Admiration yes, fondness no," she wrote in a letter to one of her critics. "Of course, it is impossible to write the absolute truth, . . . but I assure you, I try."[9]

• • •

The postal stamps on Mickey Hahn's letters to friends and the datelines on her *New Yorker* articles of the 1950s and 1960s read like the table of contents for a world atlas—Brazil, Malaysia, Hong Kong, Taiwan, the Azores, Turkey, India, Pakistan, Nigeria, South Africa, Tanganyika, Kenya, Japan, and on and on. Even as she was slipping into her role as the *New Yorker*'s "roving heroine, our Belle Geste," as Roger Angell once described her,[10] Mickey was busy sorting out the dynamics of her complicated family life, which remained in a state of flux. She was juggling separate and very distinct lives on both sides of the Atlantic.

Mickey had a comfortable life in New York. She loved her work, had many friends in the literary and show business worlds, and had grown especially close to her niece Hilary and nephew Greg, the two Dawson children who were living in town. Hilary had married Charles Schlessiger, a literary agent in the office of Mickey's longtime agent, Carl Brandt. Hilary also became a writer, which endeared her to Aunt Mickey. "In some ways my relationship with her was ideal because we had none of the emotional baggage that comes between a mother and her daughter," she explained.[11]

In many ways, Greg became the son that Mickey had always wanted. She doted on him, and the affection was mutual. "Mickey was like Auntie Mame to me," said Greg. "Not that she was frivolous or anything like that, not at all. I'm talking about her infectious enthusiasm for life."[12]

Mickey's close relationship with Greg and Hilary was a ready reminder of her family in the Chicago suburb of Winnetka. Her sisters Rose and Dauphine, brother Mannel, and assorted family members had settled there. For that reason, there was always something happening in Winnetka, although not all of it was pleasant. Mickey received word on New Year's Day 1955 that Mannel had died after a brief illness; he was fifty-nine. Another cause for concern was the health of Greg and Hilary's father Mitchell, who had fallen ill with Parkinson's disease and other problems. At age sixty-five, his health was failing fast. Fate was cruel to Mitchell, who gradually lost control of his hands and voice, leaving him unable to write or talk, two things in life that he loved most. "Never finish a letter. That is one of the commandments for Parkinsonians. They think up the damnedest excuses for not mailing," Mitchell quipped in the postscript to a missive to Mickey that he had scratched out, only to forget to mail it for a month. That was one of the last letters Mickey ever received from her beloved brother-in-law, who had believed in her and had been so instrumental in having those first articles published in the *New Yorker*.

Around the same time that Mitchell's health began to go, Hannah Hahn, now a crusty octogenarian, became seriously disoriented and was unable to sleep at night. She had slipped into "her own world," as Mickey put it, and needed constant care. Rose was kept busy tending to both her mother and her husband. Doing so was difficult and costly. Although Mickey and her sisters contributed financially toward Hannah's care, the responsibilities of looking after their mother caused much bickering in the family. When finally the burden became too much for Rose to deal with, she reluctantly put the Hahn matriarch into a nursing home.

That is where Hannah was in the summer of 1956, when Mickey, Carola, and Amanda arrived for a visit. Mickey had decided that her daughters should get to know their American relatives and learn more about their heritage. The latter seemed prudent. For now, the girls had dual American-British citizenship; once they came of age, they would be obliged to choose one or the other.

Carola, fourteen, looked "every inch a Hahn," with her dark hair and intense brownish green eyes. Amanda, seven, was tall for her age. She had fair hair, blue eyes, and a mischievous smile. People said she looked like her father. She certainly had her father's dogged resolve.

Ironically, it was Mickey who learned the most from that summer in Winnetka. Seeing her kin and the land of her birth through the eyes of her daughters gave Mickey a fresh perspective. As was her habit, she wrote about her experiences. Mickey penned a lighthearted memoir called *Kissing Cousins: America Through My Children's Eyes.* The title had a double meaning, because it referred both to her daughters' familial ties and to the peculiar relationship between the United States and England. "Moving back and forth between countries as I do, the contrast often hits me," Mickey wrote. "Once when I was fresh out of a long stay in England I went out in New York for a drink with an old beau from Alabama. Said he as we sat down at the bar, 'Just put your little coat over here.' Little coat? Little woman? I nearly swooned with bliss."[13]

The visit to the States was not entirely happy, however. Mickey, Carola, and Amanda got some sad family news one hot day in early September when they were visiting relatives in Biloxi, Mississippi. A family fishing trip on the Gulf of Mexico was interrupted by one of Mickey's cousins calling on the ship-to-shore radio. She reported that Mitchell Dawson had died. Mickey was too stunned to cry or even to react. While the others continued trolling for fish, she went below to lie down. Mickey suddenly felt numb and very much alone.

• • •

With Mickey living in New York and Charles spending time in London or abroad doing lectures and scholarly research, maintaining Conygar was an extravagance that no longer made sense and which they could not afford. The Boxers sold the estate in September 1954 and purchased a smaller house at Little Gaddesden, near the town of Berkhamsted, Hertfordshire. The new house, known as Ringshall End, was a pleasant hour's drive north of London. It was a relatively modest two-story redbrick dwelling.

As it happened, Ringshall End was within ten miles of where Charles's first wife, Ursula, had settled. The Boxers' move to the area was "not intentional," Mickey assured her friend Muriel Hanson. "We're forgetful, that's all."[14] Exactly how forgetful was made abundantly clear the day that Charles and Jimmy Cummins took Amanda and one of her chums to visit the local zoo. A "spritely dressed" woman approached them and smiled at Charles, who at first ignored her. Finally, she spoke. "Hello, Charlie," she said. "What's happened to your eyebrows? They're so bushy."

"I beg your pardon! I don't believe I know you. Have we met?" Charles replied.

"Oh, Charles, don't be so bloody silly. I'm Ursula," she said. "Ursula!"

"Ursula who . . . ?" Charles muttered. "Oh, my God!" he said as the woman's identity dawned on him.[15]

Charles and his ex-wife talked privately for a few minutes. He never mentioned this incident again, but word of it apparently came to the attention of the wags at *Private Eye,* the well-known British gossip magazine. In it, a cartoon appeared, depicting a tweedy, balding gentleman with drink in hand, chatting with a well-dressed lady at a social function. "It's all coming back to me now," the man was saying. "We were married once, weren't we?" The cartoon may or may not have been poking fun at Charles's absentmindedness, but even if it wasn't, friends assumed that to be the case.

With no need for a lot of servants at the new house, Mickey and Charles let the Conygar servants go, except for Amanda's nanny and the cook, Bertha Harvell. Her husband, Leonard, come along to Little Gaddesden, too, accepting a job as the house handyman-cum-chauffeur. (On Mickey's insistence, Charles had finally agreed to buy a car.) The Harvells remained in the Boxers' employ for many years; the despised "Nanny Hairybottom," as Amanda called her, did not.

One rainy day not long after the move to Ringshall End, Amanda and her nanny went out for a walk. A wet, mud-spattered Amanda returned home alone, looking triumphant. When Mickey and Charles asked where her nanny was, Amanda said she did not know. Amanda had run off, abandoning the woman "to die" in a muddy field. "I never liked her," Amanda said many years later. "After that incident, my parents got rid of her."[16] When they did, Amanda stayed at home with her father and the Harvells until she was nine. In the fall of 1957, Amanda, like her sister, was sent to boarding school. She hated it and tried everything she could think of to convince her parents to withdraw her and let her come home, where she was happiest.

The Boxers' life in Hertfordshire was easier than it had ever been in Dorset. Ringshall End was a more manageable house, and Berkhamsted was close enough to London to allow for quick day trips by rail into the city. Mickey felt at home in the new house as she never had at Conygar, especially after Charles bought the car and, in 1960, had a bright, airy room built on the back of the house so that Mickey and he each had a space in which to write.

In his own inimitable way, Charles was every bit as single-minded and prolific as his wife. In addition to his teaching and lecturing, he maintained a voluminous correspondence. Charles wrote everything in longhand, having never learned to type. He had no patience for things mechanical, and when someone gave him a portable typewriter as he sailed for the Far East in 1930, he got frustrated with the machine and threw it overboard. Despite the handicap of being unable to type, Charles wrote eighteen scholarly books in the years between 1950 and 1988. When these were put on the library shelf next to his earlier efforts, Charles's career output totaled twenty-four volumes.

As his scholarly reputation grew, so, too, did the demands on his time. Although he had no formal academic credentials per se, Charles had become the acknowledged authority in sixteenth- and seventeenth-century Dutch and Portuguese colonial history. Over the years, he was awarded six honorary degrees and was inducted into various international historical societies. He was also invited to serve as a visiting professor at Yale, the University of Indiana, and the University of Michigan, among others. Nevertheless, Charles became disillusioned with teaching. He never regarded himself as a good teacher. Despite his need for an income (for a while in the early 1960s, there was a very real danger that Charles would have to sell his precious library to pay back taxes), in 1965 he turned down a lucrative appointment at New York University. Two years later, he resigned his position at the University of London to devote himself to his own scholarly pursuits. From that time on, he confined himself to accepting only part-time, short-term teaching appointments.

Charles was content to stay home, where he adopted the same military-like routine that he had followed at Conygar. Most days were taken up with reading, monastic contemplation, and work on his writings. Charles took time out only for his meals, drinks, an afternoon nap, and three brisk walks per day—one in the morning, one after lunch, and the other following afternoon tea. "There's something strangely abstract about Charles. He's also one of the most independent people I've ever met," said Jimmy Cummins. "When she was a little girl, Amanda once asked her father, 'Daddy, who's your best friend?' Charles thought for a moment and then answered, 'Oh, I don't think I have one.' Amanda burst into tears thinking he was so deprived. Charles was so alarmed that he said, 'Oh no! I'm wrong. It's Jimmy.' I guess mine was the first name that popped into his head. Amanda was greatly relieved and delighted."[17]

So set was Charles in his ways that he allowed nothing and no one to disrupt his schedule. His former comrade-at-arms Bill Wiseman discovered that the day he arrived at the house just as Charles and Jimmy Cummins were striding down the driveway at the start of a walk. Wiseman, who had not seen Charles for several years, had asked his son Martin to drive him out from London for a surprise visit. As their car drew alongside Charles, he and Wiseman exchanged greetings. When Wiseman announced he had come to visit, Charles told Wiseman and his son to go inside and have a drink until he returned from his walk. Wiseman did not hear it quite that way.

"I can't remember Charles's exact words, but he doesn't mince them," Wiseman said. "I was used to it, so it didn't worry me." Martin was so disgusted that he insisted on leaving, taking his father with him. "[Charles] can be direct. You're either very welcome, or else he tells you to get lost,'" Bill Wiseman explained.[18]

People who knew Charles also knew not to take everything he said seriously. He had a habit of saying things to be provocative or shocking. Other times, he was simply having fun. Mickey's old friend Barbara Ker-Seymer admitted that she never ceased to be amazed by this aspect of Charles's behavior. She recalled hearing him joke to Mickey one evening, "You're a middle-aged Jew from the American Midwest, with a voice like a macaw, but you're a jolly good fuck!" Everyone laughed and took the remark in the spirit of the moment. Said Barbara, "Charles could be so outrageous at times that we knew not to mind him."[19]

• • •

When Charles was absent, it was the Harvells who kept the home fires burning at Ringshall End. Mickey, Carola, and Amanda regularly returned for Christmases and summer holidays. Jimmy Cummins was often there, too, and so was Barbara Ker-Seymer, by now a well-known London society photographer. There was no shortage of guests at Ringshall End—an eclectic mixture of visiting family, Mickey's *New Yorker* friends, Charles's academic colleagues, and other assorted acquaintances. The Boxer house was a lively place; Mickey loved it that way.

She also savored the time she spent with her old friends, particularly the writer Rebecca West, who lived in the neighboring county of Buckinghamshire. Mickey and Rebecca had been corresponding off and on ever since John Gunther introduced them in London back in 1930. When Rebecca learned that Mickey and Charles had moved close by, she wrote to Mickey suggesting that they "cash in" by spending a lot more time together. They did, meeting regularly for lunch or drinks. As a result, Mickey became the recipient of long, sometimes baleful letters in which Rebecca ruminated about family troubles, especially her bitter ongoing battles with her son Anthony. Compared to Rebecca West, any family problems Mickey had seemed minor. "My career is in ruins because I am in ruins," Rebecca wrote in the fall of 1957. "You can't think what it is to have, day after day, evidence coming in that your son is an ill-natured ass."[20] In another letter, written at a particularly difficult time for Rebecca, she confided to Mickey, "You are the only person I can tell the truth to."[21]

What had begun as a student-mentor relationship—with Rebecca, thirteen years Mickey's senior, in the latter role—had evolved into a friendship of equals. At one point in early 1958, Rebecca even proposed to Mickey that they collaborate on a "nice broad-minded tolerant study" of mystery writer Dorothy Sayers, who had died recently. Both Mickey and Rebecca were fans of

Sayers's popular fictional sleuth Lord Peter Wimsey. The book project never came off, which may have been just as well. There was a steep price to be paid for being close to Rebbeca West: the danger of being dragged into her family squabbles. Mickey learned that when Rebecca's son Anthony came to visit her one afternoon at Ringshall End. They went for a long walk during which Anthony complained about how cruel his mother was. He proceeded to prove it by intimating that she had criticized Mickey for "spoiling Carola's life" by writing *China to Me*. Anthony surely knew this would get back to his mother, and it did. When confronted with the allegation, Rebecca flew into a rage and vehemently denied ever having criticized her friend. "Anthony did that sort of thing," Mickey said with a shrug.[22]

Such incidents did nothing to dampen the friendship that Mickey and Rebecca shared. They remained close to the end, and Mickey was one of the last of Rebecca's friends to see her alive. "I saw her [on March 13, 1983] two days before she died," Mickey recalled. "I dropped by at her house pretty often by invitation. I knew Rebecca wasn't well, and she was in bed after a bad fall. 'How did it happen?' I asked. She told me in a voice that quivered with fury at her own silliness. She'd seen a slippery spot on the floor and thought to herself that she shouldn't step there. But she said that she had. Then she began to cry, louder than a baby. Doors popped open everywhere and people came running from all directions. I felt awful. That was it. That was the last time I ever saw Rebecca."[23]

• • •

In the late 1950s and early 1960s, Mickey's relationships with her own children, Amanda especially, were sometimes difficult. The situation was seldom discussed, but in retrospect, the reasons for this are obvious: both girls were still struggling to reconcile themselves to their mother's frequent absences and to the uniquely British custom of sending the children away to boarding school. Neither sister ever really enjoyed being away from home. Even Carola, who grew to accept the system, longed for her parents. When Mickey visited Carola at boarding school, the sweet scent of perfume and cigars lingered in the room long after she had gone, and Carola loved it.

It was Amanda who had the most trouble adjusting to boarding school. She cried to be at home. Whenever Charles was traveling on business during school holidays, Mickey usually arranged to be in England with the girls. Occasionally, she treated them to special trips; she took Amanda to the Soviet Union once, and Carola to Italy. However, none of this was enough to make up for the long, lonely stretches when they were all separated.

Partings were always traumatic; one that stands out was a particularly loud one that took place in early February 1957. Amanda bawled uncontrollably when she and Charles took Mickey to the airport to catch a flight to India, where she was to spend several months gathering information for a series of *New Yorker* articles on tiger hunting and maharajas. When Mickey became frustrated with Amanda's behavior, she scolded her. This argument led to angry words with Charles, and Mickey's departure that day was bittersweet.

Such quarrels were frequent during this period. Minor matters became major, in part because Mickey was feeling blue, as she did periodically throughout her life. In this case, her gloominess was brought on by the death on July 13, 1957, of her mother at age ninety-one. Hannah had always been a towering presence in Mickey's life; for better or worse, in good times and bad, she had been there for her. When Hannah died, Mickey was in England. She had just returned from her trip to India and Pakistan, and she could not be there in Chicago when the end came. Now that Hannah was gone, Mickey felt a great void in her life. She redoubled her own efforts to be a good mother to her own children, whom she loved with all her heart. Given the family's living arrangements and their frequent partings, it was not always easy to convey this.

There were spirited battles with Amanda over sometimes bizarre concerns—for example, her insistence on having her dog Pan, which had been killed by a car, stuffed and put on display in her room. But mostly these quarrels were over what Mickey felt was erratic behavior on her younger daughter's part. Amanda's letters from school to her "dearest mummy" in this period reflect the anguish and rejection that she was feeling. They were penned in a scrawly longhand and filled with spelling and grammatical errors that hint at more than normal teenage rebellion or indifference. It is evident from the tone and content of the correspondence that Amanda was a very unhappy and confused young woman. At the top of one of her letters, she scratched out the name of the school, scribbling the words "the blasted prison."

Carola's relations with her parents, which were generally much rosier, also took a turn for the worse in the fall of 1959. Carola had turned eighteen and was struggling to decide where to go to college. She studied at the Sorbonne in Paris for a month, then went to Italy to learn the language. While studying in the Italian city of Perugia, she met and fell in love with a man fourteen years her senior. Alfred Vecchio, a thirty-two-year-old instructor at New York University, was studying in Florence on a Fulbright Scholarship. When Carola announced that she planned to abandon her education to get married, Mickey was adamantly opposed. She suggested that her daughter forget marriage and simply live with her young man for a while. Carola, who for several years had been delving into various religions in a search for answers to the burning questions in her life, was aghast at the notion. The quirky reversal of the usual dynamics of mother-daughter relations is revealing. It is also comical, in a dark sort of way. Echoes were heard a few years later in a less serious intergenerational debate that took place when Mickey suspected that Carola had disposed of or hid (Mickey said she was never sure which) copies of some of the nude photos for which her mother had posed in New York in 1944.

Charles's reaction to Carola's announcement was less confrontational, but no more favorable. He calmly asked how she intended "to be a Hindu philosopher"—a reference to his daughter's current theological flirtation—if she was married to a Roman Catholic. The sarcasm of his question was not lost on Carola, who would not be deterred from her plans.

For better or worse, most of this mother-daughter debate was carried on long distance. Mickey was in Africa researching a planned series of *New Yorker* articles that she eventually turned into the book *Africa to Me*. It was Mickey's firsthand impressions of a continent where one by one in the early 1960s former colonies were shaking off European domination. In Lagos on October 1, 1960, Mickey was a special guest at the ceremonies that marked Nigeria's independence from Britain. She also visited Tanganyika, Rhodesia, South Africa, and Kenya on her tour. Mickey did not return to the Belgian Congo, where she had lived in 1931 and 1932, but she did renew acquaintances with many people she had known back then. Among them was Kenyan politician Jomo

Mickey (l) having a smoke with King Hussein of Jordan (r) and one of his advisors during a stopover after her 1964 tour of Africa.
Courtesy Emily Hahn Estate

Kenyatta, who in December 1963 became his country's first native-born president. In 1960, Kenyatta was still an opposition politician. When Mickey went to interview him at his home, he was killing termites in his orchard and answered her questions in a perfunctory way. Then Mickey asked if he remembered an incident in a café in the Soho district of London thirty years earlier in which a white woman had struck up a conversation in Swahili with him and his companion. "Jesus Christ!" Kenyatta exclaimed. "Was that you?" When Mickey nodded, he embraced her as an old friend, and they had a long talk about Kenya, the sometimes heated politics of postcolonial Africa, and mutual acquaintances.[24]

Meanwhile, back home, Carola was fighting her own war of liberation. With no money for a wedding or the downpayment on a house she and her fiancé hoped to buy, Carola had asked for money from a trust that Mickey had set up for her daughters in 1956. Under its terms, her old friend Donald Hanson, as trustee, was to deliver money to each of the girls when she turned twenty-one. As Carola was still only nineteen, she was not yet entitled to her share. However, Mickey finally agreed to let her borrow $2,000, using shares in the trust account as collateral. That was enough to meet her needs, and Carola became Mrs. Alfred Vecchio in a ceremony at a Roman Catholic church in Queens one day in September 1960. Afterward, the newlyweds settled at Spring Valley, a bedroom community just north of New York City. The marriage lasted sixteen years and produced two children: Alfia, who was adopted in 1964, and Sofie, who was born three years later. Carola tried being a full-time mother for a while. Then she worked at a variety of jobs, one of which was teaching art at tough inner-city schools in New York. Like her mother, she had a real rapport with young people and loved working with them.

Amanda completed her early schooling in England, then lived with her aunt Helen and her husband for a couple of years while she attended Bard College in Upstate New York. She later worked in stage management before becoming an actress herself. Today, she has a successful career as a stage and television performer in London.

As the Boxer girls grew into adulthood, the nature of their relationship with their mother inevitably mellowed and changed. "Our mother always filled us with a sense of youth and wonder. She was an amazingly brave and strong person," Carola said in late 1997. Amanda agreed. "She really showed us how to be true to ourselves."[25]

31

ON JANUARY 14, 1970, Emily Hahn and a small group of family and friends gathered at Ringshall End to celebrate her sixty-fifth birthday. At a time of life when most people are easing into retirement, Mickey showed no signs of slowing down. She had done three books in the previous three years and was busy working on another, her forty-second. This was intended to be her memoir, a life's story filled with rollicking adventures, love affairs, memorable characters, and Mickey's own larger-than-life accomplishments. It did not turn out that way.

Mickey had already written four semiautobiographical books—*China to Me, Hong Kong Holiday, England to Me,* and *Kissing Cousins.* When her agent told her that publisher Thomas Crowell was eager to have her do a single volume of tell-all memoirs, she was enthusiastic, at first. Mickey was feeling introspective. Although she was still in good health, she had reached the age when she was beginning to ponder the inevitability of her own mortality. After all, both her parents were now dead, as was her brother Mannel. Her sister Dorothy, gravely ill with the diabetes that ran in the Hahn family, had been confined to a wheelchair for almost three years; Dot was virtually blinded by the disease that would claim her on January 1, 1971. Mickey's brother-in-law Mitchell was dead, as was her sister Helen's second husband, Herbert Asbury, who had succumbed to heart troubles in 1963. Sinmay had died in 1968; Mickey's old friend Sir Victor Sassoon had fallen victim to heart failure in 1961, Patrick Putnam to malaria in 1953, John Gunther to cancer in 1970 . . . and the list went on. "There you have it," Mickey would often say with a wry smile. "Everyone I knew is dead."

The more she thought about writing her memoir, the less ardor Mickey had for the project. She was vaguely uneasy about it for reasons only she knew, and in the end she made only a perfunctory effort to fulfill the terms of the contract she had signed. The result was a curious little book called *Times and Places,* which was published in the fall of 1970. On the front cover, beside the script title was an asterisk that referred readers to the words "a memoir," which appeared below in slightly smaller script. This odd typography was no accident. What had originally been intended as Mickey's memoir ended up as an anthology of twenty-three articles that she had written for the *New Yorker* from 1937 to 1970.

Times and Places was a collection of entertaining and revealing literary snapshots of Mickey's life. She did not bother tying together the chapters in any kind of cohesive narrative. There was no introduction, no index, and Mickey did not reveal—if she could even remember—the identities of some of the characters she wrote about.

Patrick Putnam (the "Murray Den" of Mickey's 1933 book *Congo Solo*) remained "Stewart Cass," as he had been when her story about the Belgian Congo appeared in the October 22, 1966, edition of the *New Yorker*. Mickey had shielded Patrick's identity as a favor to his widow, who was terminally ill with cancer at the time. By 1970, Anne Putnam had been dead for three years, and there was no further reason to continue the ruse, but Mickey did. The identities of others who were mentioned in the book were also obscured.

For all the book's shortcomings, it received surprisingly good reviews. "If you would like to travel practically all over the world, [and] do offbeat things, well, sit down in your favorite chair and read this fascinating [auto]biography," said reviewer Marie Leary of *Bestsellers*.[1] Janet Freedman of *Library Journal* offered this praise: "While some of the anecdotes are merely amusing, most contribute to an extraordinary self-portrait of a determined woman who refused to let her sex or society's conventions block her aspirations."[2]

Freedman's comment was very much a reflection of the mood of the day. Mickey, who had often been vilified by conservative critics and readers alike for her "immoral and amoral" behavior, suddenly found that she was no longer as far from America's cultural mainstream as she had once been.

Mickey had come of age in the 1920s at a time of great social ferment. Women had been given the right to vote when the 19th Amendment was passed in August 1920, but many feminists were dismayed by the widespread apathy toward further reforms; most women seemed content to live as their mothers had and to accept traditional roles as wives and homemakers. About 43 percent of American women were working, yet the results of a 1970 Harris poll indicated that more than 70 percent of all women felt that taking care of a home and raising children was more rewarding than having a career. Mickey had never accepted the idea that it was a woman's "duty" to stay home, to raise children, and to be only a wife and mother. This helps to explain the vehemence with which she objected to her daughter Carola's 1960 marriage plans.

Mickey had no patience for the arguments that a man, for no other reason than his gender, should be paid more than a woman who did the same work. She got into heated arguments over this issue, usually on her visits to England, where many people refused to accept the notion that she could lead two very separate and successful lives: she was Emily Hahn when she was in New York and Emily Hahn Boxer when she was at Ringshall End in England. "Woman after woman comes into this house . . . and tells me women oughtn't to have equal pay because their place is in the home, and a man has commitments and women aren't really any good at their jobs in any case, and if you give equal pay it will only do a lot of them out of jobs because people will only hire men," Mickey had fumed in a letter to her friend Muriel Hanson at one point in 1954. "Every . . . female says the same things in the same order. Every now and then a man says it as well, but it is usually some flat-faced English nag."[3]

The fact that Mickey dared to be different had always befuddled most people and enraged others. All that changed in the late 1960s, as the pendulum of social reform swung back to where it had been forty years earlier. The 1960s saw antiwar protests, women's liberation, black power, and sexual revolution. "Do your own thing" became a slogan to live by. In 1967, Mickey wrote a book celebrating that very notion. *Romantic Rebels* was a survey history of American bohemianism, from Edgar Allen Poe—the original American bohemian—down to such modern-day writers as Henry Miller, Mabel Dodge Luhan, Floyd Dell, Jack Kerouac, and Allen Ginsberg. Fittingly enough, Mickey had met and personally knew many of the characters she wrote about.

By 1970, America's political epicenter had shifted to the Left, and Mickey Hahn, like many other free thinkers of earlier times, basked in a newfound respectability. Mickey had become an "authority." Journalists sought her out for her opinions on social trends. The publisher of *Encyclopedia Americana* asked her to write an essay on bohemianism for a new edition of that reference publication, and Mickey found herself being invited to teach creative writing seminars and courses at American universities. In 1965, when Charles accepted a part-time continuing position as a visiting professor at the University of Indiana, Mickey accompanied him to Bloomington. There she worked with student writers. She later did the same thing at Yale, the University of Wisconsin, and the University of Missouri, in her hometown of St. Louis. "Like daddy, I've always loved an audience," she explained, although she did have to admit that she was sometimes befuddled by things that happened in the classroom. Mickey was taken aback by the students' masochism in wanting to read their stories aloud so they could receive criticism, and their preoccupation with writing about their sex lives. "One day I found myself writing in the margin of a story, in editorial comment, 'A small point, but how does one hiss [the word] prick?' "[4]

Mickey had always found that being around a university campus and having easy access to library research facilities sparked her intellect. Nothing had changed in that regard. Her interests were as eclectic as ever. Mickey's agent, her publisher, and the book-buying public never quite knew what to expect next from her. In 1971, she wrote *Breath of God*, a slim volume in which she delved into the mythology of angels, demons, and ghosts, which had always fascinated her. The book was scarcely noticed by the general public; it was reviewed in only a handful of specialized publications and sales amounted to no more than a few thousand copies. None of that mattered to Mickey, who refused to settle into a routine or became predictable. "That's no accident," she once told an interviewer. "As an actress might, early on, I made a decision to avoid being typecast."[5]

In retrospect, even Mickey admitted that this attitude hurt sales of her books. It also played a large part in her frequent quarrels with publishers and agents. Still, she never let any of this bother her. "I've heard people say, 'Oh, she's had a lot of publishers!' Well, I think that's all right," she said. "I never wanted to be typed. So I always did my best not to be."[6]

As esoteric as a study of angels and devils was, Mickey's next book was topical and timely. *Once Upon a Pedestal*, which appeared in the fall of 1974, was an informal survey of the history of the women's movement in the United States.[7] As Mickey saw it, American women had climbed down from the pedestal upon which men had put them. "It took . . . years to achieve this goal, but in the end [reformers] got the vote," Mickey wrote. "And if even now we do not live in the utopia they promised themselves, it is not for lack of trying. Pedestals are definitely out."[8] To Mickey, this alone was progress; she argued that life on a pedestal, no matter how lofty or gilded, is ultimately dehumanizing. A statue is an object to be admired and enjoyed; it's not a flesh-and-blood human being with real hopes, fears, loves, hates, dreams, and passions.

In offering an informal survey of the history of American feminism, Mickey reminded readers that every right and every advance in the cause of gender equality had been won the hard way. Nothing had come easy, and if the momentum for change was to continue it would do so only with vigilance. "If . . . progress is maintained, there will come a time when men can forget the old days when women were stuck up on their pedestals, out of the way, and women can take the chips off their shoulders and learn to walk around like everybody else," Mickey wrote. "We have a long time to wait, of course, before everything is all right—I find it impossible, myself, to keep out of my approach to life anger against men—but utopia is on the way, given luck and vigilance."[9]

Despite the unusually strident tone of some of Mickey's words, *Once Upon a Pedestal* was a refreshingly light, moderate, and reader-friendly look at a subject many observers felt was in danger of becoming bogged down in emotion, polemics, and rhetoric. The book profiled some of the women who had played pivotal roles in the history of the American women's movement from colonial times to the first half of the twentieth century. The book looked at the debates over some key milestones during that period—the suffrage movement, birth control, abortion, the Equal Rights Amendment of 1972, and the push for women's education.

"Who's going to read a book that declares itself an informal history of women's lib, but dares to have a humorous title?" mused reviewer Eden

Lipson of the *New York Times Book Review*. "Emily Hahn fans. Also, women curious about the American female experience but bored or offended, or both, by the righteous pedantry and relentless solemnity of *Ms* and other less slick, more militant journals."[10]

A reviewer for *Publishers Weekly* noted that "Foreigners love to ask why Women's Lib has taken off in the United States when American women are more spoiled and have more power than any other women in the world. Emily Hahn tried to answer that question by looking at the lives and work of women in America."[11]

Such skepticism was widespread, but what such conservative critics failed to deal with was the essence of the argument. Comparisons between the lot of American women and those in other countries were irrelevant; what Mickey and others like her were arguing for was the need for the equality of *American* men and woman. That was the real issue.

Some more radical feminists chided Mickey for devoting only a few pages to contemporary developments in the gender rights battle. It was true that she ignored the plight of African-American women and only mentioned in passing some pivotal events of the day. Mickey did not deal at all with the impact of recent books by a whole new generation of feminists, people such as Gloria Steinem, Betty Friedan, and Germaine Greer. These women were the intellectual successors to Mickey and the other women of her generation who had fought the good fight for so many long, lonely years. "One thing that Emily [Hahn] shares with other early feminists is that whole 'say it as you see it attitude.' She was pretty gutsy, and other early feminists were that way, too. Gloria Steinem was outspoken in her early years," said Valerie Feldner, one of Mickey's young friends and admirers at the *New Yorker*.[12]

Mickey never got involved in the feminist movement for one simple reason: it was not in her nature to do so. It was fitting that she hailed from St. Louis, the gateway to the American frontier, for she was the archetypal rugged American individualist; she preferred to lead by example rather than by organized political involvement. Mickey was honored in May 1976 by her alma mater, the University of Wisconsin. She received an honorary Doctor of Humane Letters for being "a true pioneer in establishing the right of women to have their own careers." When the University of Missouri at St. Louis followed suit in 1977, Mickey was lauded as a "nationally prominent author." It was true that during the course of her career, she wrote about many vital issues that women are still grappling with today. Her articles about female unemployment, poverty, and other social ills during the Great Depression and her neglected novels from the 1930s—*Affair* and *With Naked Foot*—await rediscovery and evaluation by feminist literary scholars. Mickey also wrote about most aspects of her own life, but she was never one to trumpet her own accomplishments; she was a woman totally without affectation. "She always had great strength of character, but she had no ego. What you saw with Mickey was what you got," said her friend Muriel Hanson.[13] "She had no pretensions, none at all," agreed Barbara Ker-Seymer.[14]

That she did not become more engaged in women's issues is unfortunate in some regards because Emily Hahn was the type of feminist role model the women's movement in America so badly needed. Writing in the preview issue of *Ms*, the feminist magazine she founded in 1972, Gloria Steinem might well have been thinking about Mickey when she wrote, "I have met brave women who are exploring the outer edge of possibility, with no history to guide them and a courage to make themselves vulnerable that I find moving beyond the words to express it."[15]

• • •

Mickey's articles and short stories continued to appear regularly in the *New Yorker* throughout the 1970s and early 1980s. Between 1971 and 1981, she astounded even her family and closest friends by writing nine more books. Such a pace would have been impressive for a writer half her age; for someone in her so-called golden years, it was astounding.

She wrote books on angels and on feminism; there was one on the history of Ireland, one on man's love affair with gold, and one tracing America's in-

Mickey receiving an honorary degree from the University of Missouri–St. Louis, May 1977.
Courtesy Western Historical Manuscript Collection, University of Missouri-St. Louis

volvement in the Philippines. There were also full biographies of writers D. H. Lawrence and Mabel Dodge Luhan, both of whom Mickey had met during her time in New Mexico back in 1927. Two other books dealt with a subject that had always fascinated Mickey: zoology.

Animals were one of the abiding passions in Mickey's life. Some of her earliest and fondest memories were of animals, though her parents forbade her to have a real pet of her own; she had made do with teddy bears. Mickey always remembered how as a girl she had chased after the huge draft horses that pulled delivery wagons through the streets of St. Louis. Other times, she had played with dogs and cats she encountered in the neighborhood. Mickey delighted in telling a story about how she and a stray cat she encountered in the alley behind her parents' house had become pals and had gone for a walk together. When they did, they came across a plump, freshly killed rat. The hungry feline dined on the corpse. "I knew that the cat thought I had helped it find the rat, and liked me for it," Mickey wrote.[16]

In the late 1920s, when Mickey was living in New York and struggling to become a writer, she bought a monkey that she called Punk. Mickey loved the attention she got whenever she went out with the creature perched on her shoulder. "People who see us register something, attraction, or perhaps, irritation—the kind of irritation one might say, being aroused by modern painting or sculpture," Mickey explained.[17] Later, while living at Penge in the Belgian Congo and in Shanghai and Hong Kong, she had kept apes as pets. She wrote several hilarious stories about life with her gibbons, particularly the mischievous Mr. Mills.

Mickey indulged her passion for animals in 1967 when she wrote a two-part series for the *New Yorker* on zoos and animal conservation. The subjects are as timely and as contentious today as they were back then. "I like zoos," Mickey confided. "Some people, as soon as they arrive in a city they have never visited before, rush off to an art museum; I go to the zoo." Acknowledging that animal rights advocates make good arguments against keeping animals in captivity, she spoke in favor of zoos for their educational and scientific contributions. Besides, she noted, "[the animals] are the only representatives of wildlife that we are likely to have around at all in the future. If man goes on increasing at the present rate, the question of wildlife conservation will one day be academic. The wilderness is shrinking, many of its animals are on the way to extinction and soon the sole survivors will be those living in zoos and other protected areas."[18]

Mickey so enjoyed doing the *New Yorker* articles that she expanded her research into a book. The result was *Animal Gardens,* which was published in the fall of 1967. Most of the book's four hundred pages were a survey of the history of zoos and interviews with noted zookeepers from around the world.

Animal Gardens was vintage Emily Hahn: informative, casual, and lots of fun to read. Reviewing the book for the *New York Times Book Review*, British zoologist Gerald Durrell praised Mickey's "refreshing, down-to-earth attitude." At the same time, however, he chuckled that "her innocence must on occasion have made her the ideal subject for a leg pull."[19]

Other reviews were positive. Yet the book was not as successful as Mickey had anticipated, despite being chosen as a Book-of-the-Month Club alternate. Mickey complained to Doubleday, her publisher, that the company's salespeople had not promoted the book enthusiastically or well. Total sales were less than six thousand copies, and booksellers quickly consigned *Animal Gardens* to their remainder bins, where it sold for bargain prices that earned Mickey almost nothing in royalties.

Sluggish sales were a source of intense frustration and disappointment for Mickey. They also highlighted what had become a recurring problem: her versatility, which enabled her to write authoritatively on almost any subject, befuddled her publishers. They seemed at a loss as to how to promote or market an Emily Hahn book. She did not fit into any of the usual categories when she moved effortlessly, as she did, from genre to genre. When *Love of Gold*, her fiftieth book, was published, the milestone was virtually ignored by Mickey's publisher, her agent, and many others in the literary world. It was her nephew

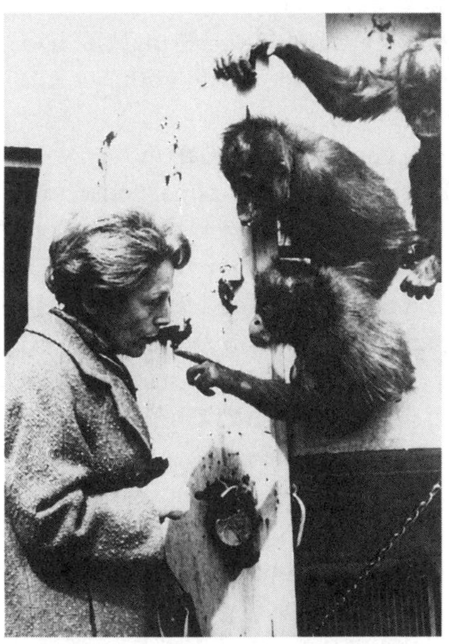

Mickey conversing with some simian subjects while researching her 1978 book on animal communications, Look Who's Talking.
Courtesy Emily Hahn Estate

Greg Dawson who threw a party in his Aunt Mickey's honor at a downtown restaurant-cabarét that he ran.

Mickey dealt with animal themes for a second time in *Look Who's Talking*, a 1978 book that investigated the controversial area of animal-human communications. Of all her thirty-eight nonfiction books, this was Mickey's personal favorite. Once again, what began as an article for the *New Yorker* grew into a book-length exploration of a topic that had long fascinated her. Mickey had always been puzzled by the realization that the world is full of creatures with whom she could not talk. It was obvious to her that animals communicated among themselves. Why, then, she wondered, could we not learn animal languages the same way we learn to speak Swahili, Chinese, or any other foreign tongue? Implicit in the inquiry was an almost childlike faith in the power of science to unlock the mysteries of nature. Scientists today have a better understanding of how different species of animals communicate, but in 1978 research into this area was still in its early stages.

What Mickey discovered from her own inquiries was that she was not the only one who mused about such things. Whether or not humans could learn to "talk to the animals" was an age-old question, as was the even more basic matter of *how* humans themselves learn to speak. What if you could experiment with a "hypothetical baby," what sort of language would such a child develop by itself? We now know that babies learn to speak through a complex process of mimicry and their own genetically programmed instincts. In 1978, our understanding of this subject was much more vague. Mickey's research found that on at least four occasions, powerful men in history had conducted their own experiments to answer this very question. The ancient Egyptian pharaoh Psamtik, King James IV of Scotland, an unnamed Indian emperor, and Frederick the Great of Prussia had each arranged for a newborn baby to be isolated in an effort to discover what language—if any—the child would speak. "Unfortunately, in each case the baby died before it could prove anything except the fact that infants need company, and without it fade away," Mickey wrote.[20]

She spent several busy months researching and interviewing scientists, animal care experts, zoo officials, and zoologists around the world on the topic of animal-human communications. Mickey delved into studies that probed the possibility of talking with our closest relatives among the higher primates—chimpanzees and gorillas. She also looked into experiments to unlock the mysteries of how to communicate with dolphins, birds, dogs, cats, insects, and a host of other creatures. Her conclusion: while the results of studies to that point were inconclusive, there were encouraging signs that one day people and animals would indeed learn to talk.

Look Who's Talking appeared just as the work of Jane Goodall, Dian Fossey, and other high-profile primatologists was beginning to capture the public's imagination. People were interested in animal communications and in the burgeoning ecological movement; they *wanted* to believe that it was possible to talk with the animals. *Look Who's Talking* struck a responsive chord, and the book's enthusiastic reception by critics and the public reflected this. "Readable and entertaining as well as informative," said a reviewer from *Library Journal*.[21] "As an experienced journalist . . . Hahn balances her enthusiasms for the unknown with a reverence for the facts and, when necessary, the lack of them," R. Z. Sheppard of *Time* pointed out.[22]

Mickey stuck with an animal theme in her fifty-second, and final, book. *Eve and the Apes* was published in 1988 when Mickey was eighty-three. It recounted the stories of nine little-known female primatologists. In some ways, the book was an exercise in self-discovery for Mickey, who had long puzzled over her own fondness for animals in general, and for apes in particular. Mickey correctly noted that most of the world's leading authorities on apes were female. She rejected the notion that this was because of "sheer maternal instinct." The reasons were a lot more complex than that, she concluded. Some women—herself among them—found it easier to get along with animals than with humans. Some, especially the pioneers in the field, got involved at a time when opportunities for women in scientific research were limited. It was generally assumed that all females were nurturing. "That a woman should be good at rearing an exotic [childlike] creature like an ape was accepted as natural, even as a safe means of self-expression," Mickey noted.[23]

• • •

The late 1980s were a time of profound change in Mickey's life. Her sister Rose died in Winnetka in the spring of 1988, and on Christmas Eve 1990 her sister Helen died of cancer in New York. Mickey and Helen had shared an apartment in lower Manhattan for the previous fifteen years, and although they were sometimes antagonistic housemates, Helen's death left a gap in Mickey's life.

With Helen gone, Mickey and her sister Dauphine, who was living with her infirm husband in Tucson, Arizona, were the last of the six Hahn siblings. Everyone else in the family was dead. Mickey, never one to be maudlin about such things, could not help but cast her mind back to a memorable 1982 article that she had written for *American Heritage* magazine. In it she recalled her childhood memories of St. Louis. She told of riding the trolley cars, of dress-buying expeditions with her mother in downtown shops, of the wilting midsummer heat, and of carefree picnics with her sisters Helen and Dauphine in Fountain Park. Mickey, who had gone to St. Louis to do some research, used the opportunity to return to the house on Fountain Avenue where her family had lived from 1898 to 1920. Her concluding paragraphs described that visit to her childhood home, a place she had not set eyes on for sixty-two years. That article was one of the most beautiful and moving things Emily Hahn ever wrote; it was a marvelously clean and precise piece of writing, yet it was filled with haunting, evocative images. Mickey, the master traveler, used her imagination and her awesome powers of recall to take us back in time with her.

Mickey and one of her cousins drove over to 4858 Fountain Avenue one sunny afternoon. The neighborhood, like so many other inner-city neighborhoods across America, had deteriorated in recent years. The prosperous middle-class burghers and the Irish and German immigrant families had long since moved to suburbia, their places taken mostly by poor African Americans. "It was not easy to recognize our house, because the porch had been removed and there was a new facade," Mickey wrote. "But the old number was still tacked up on the door in metallic letters—4858. The 5 now hung upside down, dangling." When Mickey went to the front door, she noticed there were doorbells for three apartments. She rang one, and a young African-American woman came to the door.[24]

Mickey explained who she was and why she had come. The woman said that she was babysitting on the second floor and was the only one home. She agreed to let Mickey come in to look around. Like a specter, Mickey floated through the scenes of her early life. The very room where her parents had slept and where Mickey had been born that frosty January day an eternity ago was tired, but clean. On the way out, Mickey paused at the bottom of the stairs to look back and thank her guide one last time. "Until that moment I had no nostalgia, none of the Proustian feelings one might expect to entertain," she wrote. "The whole experience had been—well, almost antiseptic. It was at the front door, after I called one more good-bye that it happened, when I pulled the door shut behind me and the number 5 in 4858 swung a little, but it wasn't the number 5 that did it. It was that *my hand on the doorknob remembered the door.* My arm remembered its weight and the way it felt being pulled shut.

"They talk about the years dropping away, sensations flooding over one, all that stuff. They are right."[25]

It was significant that Mickey's St. Louis article appeared in *American Heritage* magazine. She had begun "to lose her feeling" for the *New Yorker* and no longer even had an agreement with them to give the editors there first call on whatever she wrote. Times and faces had changed and were changing. Mickey's old friend William Shawn was forced out of his job as editor in early 1987, after S. I. Newhouse, Jr., bought the magazine. Mickey retained her office there, but she wrote fewer and fewer articles. This was a function of the passing of the torch to the new editors and of Mickey's advanced age. When she was in New York, she still came into the office most mornings and she still wrote for a few hours. Now that her income was lower and taxes were less of a concern, she was spending much more time with Charles in England. She no longer felt the same urgency to rush back to New York.

In late 1991, Mickey and Charles took a long trip together to the Far East for ceremonies and an academic conference marking the fiftieth anniversary of the Japanese attack on Hong Kong. Jimmy Cummins went along, too, to help out. He was an interested spectator when Charles attended a function in Tokyo where he met with many of the enemy officers he had known during the war years; among them were men who had been his former jailors. Charles and Mickey had kept in touch over the years with Takio Oda, Chikanori Nakazawa, and other Japanese they had known in occupied Hong Kong. Unlike so many former Hong Kong POWs, Charles bore no ill will toward the Japanese people. He never felt the urge to seek revenge; the war was over and done with. "Most of them were just doing what they were supposed to do," he said. At one point in the 1950s, Oda had come to pay his respects to the Boxers at Conygar. Mickey had not seen Oda in more than ten years, the last time being in Hong Kong the night he slapped her face at his farewell dinner. It was Charles who broke the ice in what could have been an awkward moment. "He met Oda at the car with a shot of whisky. 'Nobody passes over the threshold of my house unless he drinks one of these!' Charles said. Oda downed the whisky, and we all laughed. That was that."[26]

Mickey shared her husband's dispassionate outlook on the passing of time and on her own place in the grand scheme of life, whether it involved her memories of the momentous events that took place in wartime Hong Kong or the mundane details of her own life and work. She felt no ill will or anger, just a profound sadness at the inevitability of change. That was how she felt about her final years at the *New Yorker*.

The reign of Robert Gottlieb, William Shawn's successor, as editor of the magazine came to a dramatic end in 1992. S. I. Newhouse, Jr., the owner of Advance Publications, the *New Yorker*'s parent company, made changes in an effort to reverse the magazine's long slide into mediocrity and debt. Newhouse gave the editor's job to thirty-eight-year-old Tina Brown, an energetic Briton who had turned around the fortunes of the new *Vanity Fair*, also owned by Newhouse.

Brown's appointment signaled big changes in the sixty-seven-year-old *New Yorker*. Under William Shawn, the magazine had become quieter and more reflective than it had ever been under founding editor Harold Ross; it had become a literary magazine with a social conscience. It had also become ponderous and, at times, downright dull. Michael Kinsley, the former editor of *New Republic* magazine, put his finger on it when he said that the *New Yorker*'s "besetting sins" were "the accretion of tiny detail, the endless length, the deadening and unenlightening pieces."[27] Tina Brown arrived intent on changing all that and on restoring some of the magazine's original spirit, which she felt had atrophied over the years. Under Brown, the *New Yorker* became hipper, more topical than ever. She brought in new writers, updated the design, introduced new departments (among them a "letters to the editor" page in 1993), and made more and better use of photographs (even some in color).

From afar, Mickey watched this process of renewal and revitalization with approval. However, she also felt some "personal trepidation." After all, how could she not? The *New Yorker* had been the focus of her life for more than forty years. Mickey was allowed to keep her office under the new regime, though no one ever called or wrote to clarify her role in the editorial organization, or even to advise her if she *had* one. Mickey never dared to ask; she did not know *whom* to ask. Her friend Sheila McGrath left in 1991, and most of her other coworkers for so many years were by now dead, retired, or had moved on as a result of all of the changes that were taking place. Theater critic Edith Oliver, staff writers Joe Mitchell, Philip Hamburger, E. J. Kahn, Jr., and Brendan Gill were among the last of the old guard. Mickey saw them only rarely. For the most part, she felt like a ghost at the *New Yorker*, just as she had during her visit to the old Hahn family home in St. Louis: she had caught a glimpse of the future, and there was no spot in it for her. Mickey was neither bitter nor surprised by her nonstatus. "The magazine had to change. It was falling asleep," she said matter-of-factly. "There you have it."[28]

Mickey (l), Jimmy Cummins, and Charles (r) during a May 1991 visit to Japan.
Courtesy Jimmy Cummins

Mickey did not meet Tina Brown until more than a year after she became editor, and then it was only because they happened to be in an elevator together. Many of the other new staff did not know Mickey either. Most of those who encountered her were only dimly aware of her history at the magazine and of her amazing accomplishments. To them, she was a spry little old lady in running shoes and windbreaker who sometimes sat in the office opposite to the elevators tapping away at her typewriter. Mickey still came in each weekday when she was in New York; it was a habit she retained almost to the end. Mickey remained as quick and alert as ever; she could quote lines of poetry and prose she had written (or read) half a century before. She could recall names, places, and dates with microchip speed and accuracy. Mickey did so with the same ease and gentle good humor with which she talked about the latest book she had read or social trend that she had heard about. She remained vitally interested in the latest developments and fashions; she was fascinated by computers and the Internet.

Mickey Hahn was not one to sit around feeling sorry for herself or telling "war stories" about the old days, although if asked—as she often was by authors who interviewed her for various projects—she was a ready, willing, and eminently reliable source. Mickey was especially kind to young writers who sought her out or asked her opinions. When an interviewer asked her to assess her own writing, Mickey responded with typical candor. "I liked writing biographies," she explained. "I was not too keen on novels—writing them, I mean. . . . I [didn't] write very good ones except for an early one, *With Naked Foot*, which *is* good."[29]

Mickey's daily routine changed abruptly one cool morning in November

The Boxer family all together (l–r): Mickey, Carola, Amanda, and Charles, summer 1992.
Courtesy Emily Hahn Estate

1991. She was returning from an appointment with her eye doctor when she took a fall on a busy downtown street. Passersby must have helped her up, for she made her way to her office at the *New Yorker.* Still unable to see because of drops in her eyes, she fell again. This time, Mickey was rushed by ambulance to the hospital. Mickey's daughter Carola realized that her mother now needed some extra help. She arranged for a nurse-companion on weekdays, when Carola was working at the American Cancer Society and could not be with her mother. The person they hired was a genial, soft-spoken Guyanese woman named Hyacinth Wilkie. She and Mickey hit it off and became instant friends. Hyacinth cared for Mickey until she was well enough to travel to Ringshall End. She remained there while she recuperated.

Even when she returned to New York, Mickey spent most of her time at home, reading, watching mystery shows on television, and trying in vain to write. Through it all, her spirits stayed high, and her enthusiasm for life never waned. Hyacinth recalled how one evening in the fall of 1996 she and Mickey were watching a country music awards show on television, when Mickey suddenly leapt up from the sofa and began singing and dancing her way around the living room. She reached out for Hyacinth's hand and pulled her up, too. The pair took an impromptu whirl around the living room, laughing and giggling. "She loved life," said Hyacinth. "She was always singing. She used to

At work to the end: Mickey writing in her New Yorker *office, summer 1995.*
Ken Cuthbertson

sing the old songs I knew from my childhood. I couldn't open a song that she didn't know. We'd walk around the apartment humming together."[30]

It was not until many months after her fall that Mickey was well enough to return to her office at the *New Yorker*. When she did, it was by taxi each day and in the company of Hyacinth, who now escorted her everywhere. Remarkably, Mickey's indomitable spirit gradually rebounded. It was no coincidence that it did so around the time that she developed a friendship with Valerie Feldner, an aspiring screenwriter who was working at the *New Yorker* as a sort of "jack-of-all-trades" receptionist. "It was a gradual thing. She was very quiet and went about her business each day. I saw her come and go like clockwork," Feldner recalled. "Like Joe Mitchell, she was just there. They were the nice old people 'down the hall.' I slowly began to read their work and to realize who it was that I was working with. It was like these people were almost in disguise."[31]

Feldner found that she and Mickey shared a love of animals; their relationship started there. Before long, Feldner was asking for and getting Mickey's advice on her writing projects. What astounded Feldner was how nonjudgmental her newfound mentor was; Mickey treated her like a peer. That was at once flattering and daunting.

With Feldner's help and encouragement, Mickey began proposing articles to the *New Yorker*'s editors. In the old days, she would simply have pitched the idea to Harold Ross or William Shawn in person; now she was obliged to wait in line like everyone else. Mickey sometimes waited weeks for a response. Sometimes she did not hear back at all. Mickey shrugged it off, but she began referring to the *New Yorker*'s editorial approval process as "the black hole" in which ideas were swallowed up without leaving a trace. Occasionally, one of her suggestions found favor, and she was asked to go ahead with the article. Mickey's byline reappeared in the magazine in the July 31, 1995, issue after an absence of more than four years. She wrote again about her experiences in a "far-off time," the early 1930s in the Congo and of the role of women in tribal society. Mickey conceded that the status of native women there "may well have changed completely," but she added, "somehow I doubt it. Changing the name of a country is simpler than changing the way women are treated."[32]

That article, which attracted a lot of reader attention and favorable comment, proved to be the last of the 181 that Mickey wrote for the *New Yorker*, although her byline did appear one last time, in the December 2, 1996, issue. Ironically, Mickey's final contribution to the magazine that she so loved was an eleven-line poem entitled "Wind Blowing." It was one of the first pieces of verse she had ever written, back in 1917, when she was just twelve. The final lines read:

Nothing, nothing, anywhere, night and day and night,
Poor wind blowing, looking for a fight,
Nothing left to blow against, nothing left to bite.

In some ways, the spent wind that Mickey alluded to was a metaphor for her own energy and vitality, which waned in the late months of 1996. Her life came crashing to a halt one evening a week or so before Christmas. Mickey fell in her apartment, breaking her left arm. "I don't recall falling, only that I hit my head and found myself on the floor," she said later.[33] Mickey was rushed by ambulance to the hospital, where doctors applied a cast and sent her home after a few days.

Mickey never really recovered from that fall. Her doctor gave her a walker to help her get around—"a birdcage," she called it. When visitors were present, she made a show of shunning it. "It's for old ladies," she scoffed. When no one was watching, it was another story; she practiced with it, and soon became as adept as a gibbon on a swing. But there was really nowhere to go, so most of the time she watched television or sat on her bed reading. All the while, she grew more and more frustrated with the slow pace of her recovery. Writing had always come to her as naturally as breathing, and as long as she could do one, the other followed. Now that she was having difficulty typing, she was frustrated and angry. "Why is it taking me so long to get well?" she asked a visitor. They both knew the answer.

Early on the morning of February 8, Mickey rose from her bed to go to the bathroom. As she did so, she slipped and fell, badly breaking her right leg. Hyacinth rang Carola, who called for an ambulance. Mickey was raced to nearby St. Vincent's Hospital on West Eleventh Street. When doctors there operated to reset the shattered femur, the strain on Mickey's heart was too much. She was a fighter to the end, but it was a struggle no one her age could win. Mickey lingered for ten long days with her daughters, Carola and Amanda and other family and friends keeping vigil at her bedside; Charles was too infirm to be there.

When the end came for Mickey, it was just before 3 A.M. on the morning of February 18, 1997. Carola was there as her mother went away for the last time. Mickey Hahn was ninety-two years old.

Afterword

IN THE DAYS FOLLOWING Emily Hahn's death at age ninety-two, obituaries were published in the *New York Times,* the *London Times,* the *New Yorker,* and many other prominent publications around the world. The news was even carried in Chinese newspapers, and Sinmay's daughter wrote a tribute to Mickey that appeared in a Chinese-language literary journal in Shanghai called *Century.* In addition, novelist Hortense Calisher, a friend of Mickey's, read a glowing tribute to her at the 1997 spring meeting of the American Academy and Institute of Arts and Letters.

In England, word of Mickey's death was delivered to Charles by Jim McDonald, a man hired to help out at Ringshall End. This was a particularly difficult task because Mickey's body was cremated the same day that she died, and so there was no funeral. For Charles, ninety-three and himself in failing health, that meant there was no real sense of closure to his fifty-six-year relationship with Mickey. In his mind, she had gone away as she had so often in the past. But this time, Mickey was not coming back. Jimmy Cummins talked with Charles about the circumstances of Mickey's death. "He asked me repeatedly if Mickey had been in any pain when she died," Cummins said. "I assured him that no, she was not in pain. That seemed to provide him with a measure of relief."[1]

Charles was unable to travel to New York on March 1, 1997, when a group of Mickey's family, friends, and *New Yorker* colleagues gathered in a salon at the Algonquin Hotel for a memorial service. The setting was appropriate, given the hotel's legendary association with the *New Yorker,* especially in the old days when editor Harold Ross and his celebrated round table had gathered there to take meals, have drinks, play cards, and share good times. There were laughs and some tears at the Algonquin on that cool, rainy Saturday afternoon as one by one the invited speakers shared their memories of Mickey. Veteran *New Yorker* staff writer Roger Angell read from a splendid obituary of Mickey that he wrote for the March 10, 1997, edition of the magazine. Other speakers that afternoon included Mickey's daughters Carola and Amanda, nephew Greg Dawson, niece Hilary Schlessiger, *New Yorker* staffer Charles McGrath (who read a reminiscence on behalf of Mickey's former editor William Maxwell, himself too old and frail to attend), and Mickey's dear friend Sheila McGrath. Carola read two moving eulogies written by her daughters Sofia

Veçchio and Alfia Vecchio Wallace, which touched on the personal side of their grandmother's sometimes very public life.

"When I was little, I knew my grandmother was special," wrote Sofia. "And as a child, I perceived this specialness as a strong presence upon which I could rely. I knew she was a successful writer, but as a child, I never felt pressured to be as grand as she was. To me, she was fun, and funny, and always there."

Alfia echoed those sentiments. "Chances are that your grandmother didn't smoke cigars and let you hold wild role-playing parties in her apartment. Chances are that she didn't teach you Swahili obscenities. Chances are that when she took you to the zoo, she didn't start whooping passionately at the top of her lungs as you passed the gibbon cage. Sadly for you . . . your grandmother was not Emily Hahn."

Afterward, the invited guests stayed for drinks and they talked about Mickey. There was a lot to talk about. The quiet little girl from St. Louis—who had never intended to become a writer—had left behind an impressive literary legacy of fifty-two books, hundreds of articles, short stories, and poems. In the process, she had thumbed her nose at convention and was one of those who had helped blaze a feminist trail that other free-spirited women who came after her have followed. Mickey herself was born and raised in an era when women were expected to, and did, marry and stay home, raise children, and cook for a husband. Mickey steadfastly refused to do what society expected of her. The durability and success of her long-distance "open marriage" confounded many people at a time when such things simply "weren't done"; the two-career family is today nothing unusual.

There was, of course, a price to be paid for such independence of spirit: Mickey was vilified by those who were scandalized that she dared to assert her own sexuality. Her relations with her own family were certainly not always as warm as they might have been had she led a more conventional life. Then, too, she never achieved the degree of fame or credit that she so richly deserved either as a writer or as a pioneer in the struggle for women's rights.

"Mickey was a truly liberated human being. She always lived life as *she* wanted," said her nephew Greg Dawson. "But what was especially important was that she lived without hurting other people. It's a rare thing to do that. Mickey showed us how to live life on one's own terms. That's her legacy to us."[2]

Notes

Introduction

1. Rebecca West to EH, June 15, 1960.
2. As cited in the *New York Times*, February 19, 1997, p. B-7.
3. *Times and Places* by Emily Hahn (Crowell, 1970), p. 262. (Cited hereafter as *Times and Places*.)
4. Ibid., p. 7.
5. As quoted in *Contemporary Authors*, NRS Volume 27, p. 209.

Chapter 1

1. *Hong Kong Holiday* by Emily Hahn (Doubleday & Company, 1946) p. 275. (Cited hereafter as *Hong Kong Holiday*.)
2. Hahn family history by Isaac Hahn, unpublished, May 18, 1925, p. 1. (Cited hereafter as *Isaac Hahn memoir*.)
3. Ibid., p. 1.
4. Ibid., p. 6.
5. Ibid., p. 7.
6. Ibid., p. 7.
7. *Times and Places* , op cit., p. 1.
8. Ibid., p.1.
9. Author interview with EH, Ringshall End, Little Gaddesden, Berkhamsted, Hertfordshire, England, Oct. 22, 1992. (Cited hereafter as EH Ringshall End interview.)
10. *Isaac Hahn memoir*, op cit., p. 8.
11. EH Ringshall End interview, op cit.
12. Ibid.
13. Ibid.

Chapter 2

1. Ibid., pp. 47–48.
2. *Times and Places*, op cit., p.7.
3. Author interview with Josephine ("Dauphine") Arthur, from Tucson, Arizona, November 18, 1992. (Cited hereafter as Arthur interview.)
4. EH Ringshall End interview, op cit.
5. *Times and Places*, op cit., p. 3.
6. *Times and Places*, op cit., pp. 32–33.
7. Ibid., p. 5.
8. EH Ringshall End interview, op cit.
9. Ibid., p. 32.
10. Ibid., p. 28.
11. *Kissing Cousins* by Emily Hahn (Doubleday & Company, 1958), p. 19. (Cited hereafter as *Kissing Cousins*.)

Chapter 3

1. Ralph Crowley to EH, fall, 1919.
2. Dr. Miner Evans to EH, Dec. 7, 1919.
3. EH Ringshall End interview, op cit.
4. *Kissing Cousins*, op cit., p. 19.
5. *Kissing Cousins*, op cit. p. 19.
6. EH Ringshall interview, op cit.
7. *Jean Toomer, Artist: A Study of His Literary Life and Word, 1894–1936* by Nellie Y. McKay (University of North Carolina Press, 1984), p. 180.
8. *Cane* by Jean Toomer (Boni and Liveright, 1923).
9. Ibid, Introduction, p. ix.
10. EH Ringshall End interview, op cit.
11. Author interview with EH, New York City, January 3, 1997.
12. Ibid.
13. *Times and Places*, op cit., p. 20.
14. Ibid., p. 11.
15. Ibid., p. 14.
16. *Kissing Cousins*, op cit., p. 14.
17. Ibid., p. 22.
18. EH Ringshall End interview, op cit.
19. Ibid., p. 21.
20. *Times and Places*, op cit., p. 38.

21. The *New Yorker,* Aug. 20, 1947.
22. Arthur interview, op. cit.

Chapter 4

1. *Times and Places,* op cit. p. 46.
2. EH to the author, Nov. 6, 1992.
3. "B.SC." The *New Yorker,* June 15, 1946, p. 22.
4. Ibid.
5. Ibid., p. 23.
6. EH to Dorothy Hahn, undated letter, 1925.
7. *Times and Places,* op cit., p. 63.
8. Ibid., p. 68.
9. *Wisconsin Literary Magazine,* June 1923.
10. *Times and Places,* op cit., p. 70.
11. Author interview with Dorothy Miller (nee Raper), from Salt Lake City, Utah, Nov. 16, 1992. (Cited hereafter as Miller interview.)
12. EH to Dorothy Hahn, undated letter, late 1925.
13. Arthur interview, op cit.
14. Ibid.
15. Author interview with EH, New York City, July 12, 1993.
16. Ibid.
17. Miller interview, op cit.
18. Ibid.
19. *Times and Places,* op cit., p.73.

Chapter 5

1. *Kissing Cousins,* op cit., p. 74.
2. Author interview with EH, New York City, Dec. 14, 1992.
3. *Times and Places,* op cit, p. 73.
4. Isaac Hahn to EH, June 26, 1924.
5. *Times and Places,* op cit., p. 74.
6. Trip Journal kept by Dorothy Raper. (Cited hereafter as Trip Journal.)
7. Ibid.
8. *Times and Places,* op cit., p. 81.
9. EH to her parents, July 4, 1924.
10. *Times and Places,* op cit., p. 79.
11. *Albuquerque Morning Journal,* July 10, 1924.
12. EH to her parents, July 24, 1924.
13. *Times and Places,* op cit., p. 82.
14. EH to the author, Feb. 27, 1995.
15. Arthur interview, op cit.
16. *Kissing Cousins,* op cit., p. 24.
17. Isaac Hahn to EH, June 8, 1926.

Chapter 6

1. Helen Hahn to EH, April 25, 1926.
2. *Times and Places,* op cit., p. 86.
3. Ibid., p. 90.
4. Interview with EH, Dec. 14, 1992, New York City.
5. Ibid.
6. Noel Stearn to EH, undated 1927 letter.
7. Dorothy Raper to EH, April 18, 1927.
8. Interview with EH, Dec. 14, 1992, New York City.
9. *Times and Places,* op cit., p. 93.
10. *Times and Places,* op cit., p. 99.
11. Ibid., p. 101.
12. *Santa Fe New Mexican,* Saturday, Sept. 8, 1927.
13. *Times and Places,* op cit., p. 101.
14. EH to Hannah Hahn, Nov. 16, 1927.
15. EH to Hannah Hahn, Aug. 2, 1927.
16. *Times and Places,* op cit., p. 103.
17. Ibid., p. 107.
18. Ibid., p. 108.

Chapter 7

1. EH to Hannah Hahn, Feb. 17, 1928.
2. EH to Hannah Hahn, Jan. 31, 1928.
3. EH to Hannah Hahn, March 3, 1928.
4. The *New Yorker,* Aug. 3, 1929, p. 15.
5. EH to Rose and Mitchell Dawson, May 17, 1928.
6. Author interview with EH, New York City, July 12, 1993.
7. *The Brownings: A Victorian Idyll* (Brentano, 1929).
8. *New York Sunday World,* June 17, 1928.
9. EH to Hannah Hahn, June 17, 1928.
10. EH to Hannah Hahn, July 1, 1928.
11. Author interview with EH, New York City, May 16, 1995.

12. EH letter to the author, Oct. 4, 1995. Carl Van Doren worked for a time as literary editor of the *Nation* and then *Century Magazine*, before becoming editor of the Literary Guild from 1926 to 1934. Over the years he wrote many books of criticism as well as several literary biographies, one of which was a 1938 Pulitzer Prize–winning biography of Benjamin Franklin.
13. Ibid.
14. Ibid.
15. *The Barbary Coast: An Informal History of the San Francisco Underworld* by Herbert Asbury (Garden City Publishing, 1933). Asbury dedicated this and several other books "To Helen."
16. *Chicago Daily Times*, April (undated) 1930.
17. The book was published as *Seductio Ad Absurdum: The Principles and Practices of Seduction, a Beginner's Handbook* by Brewer and Warren Inc. of New York in May 1930. Mickey dedicated the book to Herbert Asbury, "Who told me to write it."
18. EH to the author, Oct. 24, 1995. Mexican-born Miguel Covarrubias arrived in New York in 1923 as a twenty-one-year-old art student on a limited scholarship from the Mexican government. His bold use of color and his strong style caught the eyes of critics, and he quickly established a name for himself as one of New York's brightest and most versatile young artists. Over the next four years Covarrubias designed three ballets, did scenery and costumes for Broadway plays, did hundreds of caricatures for the *New Yorker* and *Vanity Fair*, for which he was a regular contributor, illustrated one book and published two of his own. One of them, *Negro Drawings* (1927), was a collection of drawings of black musicians, artists, blues singers, flappers, and preachers from Harlem. The book was widely praised, and Covarrubias was acknowledged for raising awareness of the culture of black Americans, much as French artist Gauguin had for that of the native people of the South Pacific islands. In his later life, Covarrubias turned to a serious study of ethnology. His extraordinary career was as brief as it was brilliant, for when he died in 1957 he was just fifty-three.
19. EH letter to the author, April 24, 1995.
20. EH to Hannah Hahn, Oct. 11, 1928.
21. EH to Hannah Hahn, Oct. 18, 1928.
22. EH to Hannah Hahn, Nov. 14, 1928.
23. EH to Hannah Hahn, Dec. 1, 1928.
24. EH to Hannah Hahn, Dec. 2, 1928.
25. Rebecca West to EH, Jan. 3, 1959. Fortunately, Emily Hahn did not dispose of all of Rebecca's letters, and they are available to literary scholars as part of the Hahn papers at the Lilly Library, University of Indiana, Bloomington, Indiana.
26. EH to Hannah Hahn, Dec. 28, 1928.

Chapter 8

1. EH to Isaac Hahn, Feb. 12, 1929.
2. EH to Hannah Hahn, Apr. 24, 1929.
3. EH Ringshall End interview, op cit.
4. *Fortune*, August 1934, p. 92. The text of "The first successful *New Yorker* advertisement" was reproduced in an anonymous eighteen-page article. That article, the first to probe the secrets of the *New Yorker*'s astounding success, was full of revealing inside information about the F-R Publishing Corporation, the magazine's parent company. In reality, the article's author was former *New Yorker* managing editor Ralph Ingersoll, who became the editor of *Fortune* after being fired by Harold Ross. Ingersoll had detailed first-hand knowledge of the *New Yorker*'s corporate structure, as well as its personalities. (Cited hereafter as *Fortune* article.)
5. *The Years with Ross* by James Thurber (Little Brown & Co., 1957), p. 20. (Cited hereafter as *Thurber*.)
6. *Genius in Disguise: Harold Ross of the New Yorker* by Thomas Kunkel (Random House, 1995), p. 94. (Cited hereafter as Kunkel.)

7. Author interview with EH, New York City, May 16, 1995.
8. *The Last Days of the New Yorker* by Gigi Mahon (McGraw-Hill, 1988), p.31 (Cited hereafter as *The Last Days of the New Yorker.*)
9. *Fortune* article, op cit., p. 73.
10. "Lovely Lady," the *New Yorker,* May 25, 1929, pp. 79–80.
11. Author interview with EH, New York City, May 16, 1995.
12. "The Stranger," the *New Yorker,* Aug. 3, 1929, p. 15.
13. *Thurber,* op cit., p. 144.
14. Kunkle, op cit., p. 79.
15. *Tales of a Wayward Inn* by Frank Case (Frederick A. Stokes Co., 1938), p. 227.
16. *Fortune* article, op cit., p. 74.
17. Author interview with EH, New York City, Nov. 16, 1993.
18. Ibid.

Chapter 9

1. EH to the author, March 14, 1995.
2. EH to Hannah Hahn, May 20, 1929.
3. Mitchell Dawson to EH, Nov. 15, 1929.
4. *Times and Places,* op cit., pp. 113.
5. Ibid., p. 120.
6. Ibid., p. 123.
7. Author interview with Barbara Ker-Seymer, London, U.K., Oct. 26, 1992. (Cited hereafter as the Ker-Seymer interview.)
8. Ashton began choreographing in 1926 with a revue called *A Tragedy of Fashion.* After a twenty-five-year career as a dancer and choreographer, he was appointed associate director of the Royal Ballet in 1952, and headed the company from 1963 to 1970. Ashton was knighted in 1962. He died on August 18, 1988.
9. Author interview with EH, New York City, Dec. 14, 1992.
10. EH to the author, Oct. 4, 1995.
11. Ker-Seymer interview, op cit.
12. EH to Hannah Hahn, Dec. 21, 1929.
13. EH to Hannah Hahn, Jan. 3, 1930.
14. EH to Hannah Hahn, Jan. 8, 1930.
15. Ibid.
16. "Life with Africa's Little People" by Anne Eisner Putnam, *National Geographic,* Feb. 1960, p. 279.
17. EH to the author, July 3, 1995.
18. The *New Yorker,* Oct. 22, 1966, p. 208.
19. *Times and Places,* op cit., p. 142.
20. Ibid., p. 138.
21. EH to Hannah Hahn, March 1, 1930.
22. *Times and Places,* op cit., p. 126.
23. EH to Hannah Hahn, February 26, 1930.
24. Ibid.
25. EH to Hannah Hahn, March 28, 1930.
26. EH writing in her diary. Undated entry, early 1930, London, U.K.
27. Mitchell Dawson to Emily Hahn, March 1, 1930.
28. EH to Hannah Hahn, March 21, 1930.
29. *Books,* June 22, 1930, p. 14.
30. *New York World,* April 14, 1930, p. 14.
31. *Chicago Daily News,* April 2, 1930.
32. Author interview with EH, New York City, Nov. 16, 1993.
33. EH to Hannah Hahn, March 21, 1930.
34. *New York Sunday World,* April 27, 1930.
35. Ibid.
36. *Chicago Daily Times,* undated clipping, May 1930.
37. *Chicago Evening Post,* May 7, 1930.
38. William Benét to EH, June (undated) 1930.
39. William Benét to EH, June 30, 1930.
40. William Benét to EH, July 12, 1930.
41. The *New Yorker,* September 27, 1930, p. 45.
42. EH to Hannah Hahn, Aug. 6, 1930.
43. EH to Hannah Hahn, Dec. 3, 1930.
44. *Harper's Magazine,* October 1930, pp. 631–33.
45. EH to Hannah Hahn, Oct. 10, 1930.
46. EH to Hannah Hahn, Sept. 7, 1930.
47. EH to Hannah Hahn, Dec. 7, 1930.
48. EH to Hannah Hahn, Dec. 14, 1930.

49. EH to Hannah Hahn, Dec. 23, 1930.
50. EH to Hannah Hahn, Nov. 4, 1930. Mickey related the substance of the cables in this letter to her mother.

Chapter 10

1. *Times and Places,* op cit., pp. 138–39.
2. *Congo Solo: Misadventures Two Degrees North* by Emily Hahn (Bobbs-Merrill, 1933), p. 15. (Cited hereafter as *Congo Solo.*)
3. EH to Hannah Hahn, Dec. 30, 1930.
4. *Congo Solo,* op cit., p. 21.
5. EH to Hannah Hahn, Jan. 20, 1931.
6. Ibid.
7. *Travels in the Congo* by André Gide (Knopf, 1929). (Cited hereafter as *Travels in the Congo.*)
8. EH to Hannah Hahn, Jan. 26, 1931.
9. Ibid.
10. Ibid.
11. *Congo Solo,* op cit., p. 39.
12. Ibid.
13. EH to Hannah Hahn, Feb. 1, 1931.
14. EH to the author, Aug. 2, 1995.
15. *Congo Solo,* op cit., p. 43.
16. *Travels in the Congo,* op cit., p. 14.
17. EH Ringshall End interview, op cit.
18. "Forest trails in the Congo," *Travel,* July 1933, pp. 12–15.
19. *Congo Solo,* op cit., p. 48.

Chapter 11

1. *Times and Places,* op cit., p. 148.
2. The *New Yorker,* February 28, 1931.
3. *The King of the World in the Land of the Pygmies,* by Joan Mark (University of Nebraska, 1995), p. 53. (Cited hereafter as *The King of the World.*)
4. *Our Camp on the Epulu in the Belgian Congo* by Patrick Tracy Lowell Putnam and Mary Farlow Linder Putnam, 1933 (privately published).
5. The *New Yorker,* Oct. 22, 1966, p. 214.
6. EH letter to the author, Sept. 7, 1995.
7. *Through the Congo Basin,* op cit., p. 23.
8. *Times and Places,* op cit., p. 153.
9. EH letter to the author, Sept. 7, 1995.
10. *Beginner's Luck* by Emily Hahn (Brewer, Warren and Putnam, 1931).
11. *New York Times,* Aug. 30, 1931, p. 6.
12. *Saturday Review of Literature,* Sept. 12, 1931, p. 8.
13. The *New Yorker,* Oct. 22, 1966, pp. 222–23.
14. *Times and Places,* op cit., p. 160.

Chapter 12

1. The *New Yorker,* April 15, 1967, p. 48.
2. EH letter to the author, Sept. 7, 1995.
3. *Travels in the Congo,* op cit., p. 93.
4. *Times and Places,* op cit., p. 169.
5. *Congo Solo,* op cit., p. 290.
6. Ibid., p. 171.
7. The *New Yorker,* April 15, 1967, p. 52.
8. The *New Yorker,* May 20, 1967, p. 156.
9. *Out of Africa* by Isak Dinesen (a.k.a. Karen Blixen) (Random House, 1938).
10. The *New Yorker,* May 20, 1967, p. 157.
11. Ibid., p. 166.
12. Author interview with EH, New York City, December 14, 1992.

Chapter 13

1. *Africa to Me: Person to Person* by Emily Hahn (Doubleday and Company, 1964), p. 253. (Cited hereafter as *Africa to Me.*)
2. Author telephone interview with EH, from New York City. Oct. 3, 1995.
3. Barbara Ker-Seymer interview, op. cit.
4. EH to the author, Oct. 24, 1995.
5. Author telephone interview with EH, from New York City, Oct. 3, 1995.

6. *The New Republic,* May 31, 1933, p. 65.
7. EH to the author, Oct. 24, 1995.
8. Ibid.
9. *Books,* July 30, 1933, p. 12.
10. *New York Times,* July 30, 1933, p. 4.
11. *Forum,* Nov. 1933.
12. Eddie Mayer to EH, May 13, 1933.
13. Eddie Mayer to EH, May 23, 1933.
14. Eddie Mayer to EH, May 23, 1933.
15. Ibid.
16. EH Ringshall End interview, op cit.
17. *Kissing Cousins,* op cit., p. 25.
18. Author interview, op. cit.
19. EH to author, Oct. 24, 1995.
20. Ker-Seymer interview, op cit.
21. *Books,* Sept. 30, 1934, p.3.
22. *Boston Transcript,* Oct. 3, 1934, p.3.
23. Author interview with EH in New York City, Dec. 14, 1992.
24. EH to the author, Oct. 24, 1995.
25. Eddie Mayer to EH, March 6, 1935.
26. Eddie and his wife Frances got back together; however, they split again before long and were divorced in 1937. Mayer died in New York in 1960 after a brief illness.

Chapter 14

1. *Times and Places,* op cit., p. 212.
2. Ibid., p. 213.
3. *Shanghai* by Harriet Sargeant (Jonathan Cape, 1991), p. 2. (Cited hereafter as *Shanghai.*)
4. Ibid., p. 9.
5. *Shanghai,* op cit., p. 2.
6. *China to Me,* op cit., p. 14.
7. EH to the author, Dec. 6, 1995.
8. *Memoirs of an Aesthete* by Harold Acton (Methuen and Co., 1948), p. 287. (Cited hereafter as *Memoirs of an Aesthete.*)
9. "Cosmopolitan Shanghai, Key Seaport of China," by W. Robert Moore, *National Geographic,* Sept. 1932, p. 326.
10. *Shanghai: City for Sale* by Ernest Hauser (Harcourt, Brace and Co., 1940), p. 265. (Cited hereafter as *City For Sale.*)
11. *China to Me,* op cit., p.3.
12. EH to the author, Dec. 6, 1995.
13. *The Sassoons* by Stanley Jackson (Heinemann, 1968), p. xi. (Cited hereafter as *The Sassoons.*)
14. EH Ringshall End interview, op cit.
15. *Shanghai,* op cit., p. 133.
16. EH to the author, March 4, 1996.
17. EH to Hannah Hahn, June 12, 1935.
18. Ibid.
19. *China to Me,* op cit., p. 18.
20. Ibid., p. 5.

Chapter 15

1. *Steps of the Sun* by Emily Hahn (Dial Press, 1940). (Cited hereafter as *Steps of the Sun.*)
2. EH Ringshall End interview, op cit.
3. Xiao-hong Shao letter to the author, Feb. 12, 1993.
4. "Mother-in-law's Joke," by EH, *New Yorker,* July 2, 1938.
5. *China to Me,* op cit., p. 9.
6. *Times and Places,* op cit., p. 222.
7. *North-China Daily News,* June 13, 1935, p. 13.
8. *Times and Places,* op cit., p. 225.
9. Ibid.
10. Ibid., p. 227.
11. EH to Helen Hahn, July 24, 1935.
12. *China to Me,* op cit., p. 8.
13. EH to Hannah Hahn, Feb. 11, 1936.
14. EH to Hannah Hahn, Aug. 26, 1936.
15. *New York Times Book Review,* May 23, 1942, p. 19.
16. "Revolt in Shanghai," *Harper's,* March 1936, p. 455.
17. EH to Helen Hahn, Aug. 16, 1935.
18. EH to Hannah Hahn, Oct. 1936.
19. *China to Me,* op cit., p. 65.
20. Ibid., p. 12.
21. *Shanghai,* op cit., p. 292.
22. EH to Hannah Hahn, Dec. 27, 1935.
23. "Gibbons and Interactions with Man in Domestic Settings" by Emily Hahn, *Gibbon and Siamang,* vol. I, 1972, p. 250. Cited hereafter as "Gibbons and Interactions."

24. EH to Hannah Hahn, Sept. 10, 1937.
25. *Eve and the Apes* by Emily Hahn (Weidenfeld and Nicolson, 1988), p. 5. (Cited hereafter as *Eve and the Apes.*)
26. "Gibbons and Interactions," op cit., p. 256.
27. Ibid., p. 103.
28. Ibid., p. 56.
29. *Affair* by Emily Hahn (Bobbs-Merrill, 1935).
30. *New York Post,* April 13, 1935, p. 7.
31. *New York Times Book Review,* April 14, 1935, p. 20.
32. EH to Helen Hahn, July 24, 1935.
33. EH to Helen Hahn, June 12, 1935.
34. Ibid.
35. EH Ringshall End interview, op cit.
36. EH to Helen Hahn, Sept. 16, 1935.

Chapter 16

1. EH to Hannah Hahn, Oct. 18, 1936.
2. *Times and Places,* op cit., pp. 261–62.
3. EH to Hannah Hahn, March 6, 1937.
4. EH to the author, Feb. 20, 1996.
5. EH to Hannah Hahn, April 15, 1936.
6. EH to Hannah Hahn, Oct. 18, 1936.
7. *China to Me,* op cit., p. 40.
8. *Saturday Review of Literature,* March 26, 1955, p. 13.
9. *China to Me,* op cit., p. 73.
10. Ibid.
11. Ibid., p. 80.
12. Ibid., p. 61.
13. Ibid., p. 51.
14. *Times and Places,* op cit., p. 257.
15. EH to Hannah Hahn, July 10, 1936.
16. EH to Hannah Hahn, Aug. 24, 1937.
17. EH to Helen Hahn, April 20, 1936.
18. Patrick Putnam to EH, Jan. 21, 1938.
19. EH to Helen Hahn, April 1, 1937.
20. Ibid.
21. EH interview with the author, Nov. 16, 1993, New York City.
22. *China to Me,* op cit., p. 70.

Chapter 17

1. The *New Yorker,* August 23, 1947, p. 33.
2. EH to Hannah Hahn, April 11, 1938.
3. Carl Brandt to EH, Aug. 4, 1938.
4. Frances Gunther to Jawaharlal Nehru, April 14, 1938, as quoted in *Inside: The Biography of John Gunther* by Ken Cuthbertson (Bonus Books, 1992), p. 172.
5. Author interview with EH, Dec. 15, 1986, from New York.
6. *New York Times,* April 7, 1938, p. 8.
7. EH to Hannah Hahn, June 3, 1939.
8. EH to Hannah Hahn, Mar. 25, 1938.
9. EH to Carl Brandt, Aug. 20, 1938.
10. EH to Hannah Hahn, Aug. 25, 1938.
11. *China to Me,* op cit, p. 86.
12. Ibid., p. 88.
13. EH to Hannah Hahn, June 3, 1939.
14. *Times and Places,* op cit., p. 282.
15. Ibid., p. 279.
16. Ibid., p. 104.
17. Author interview with EH, New York City, November 16, 1993.
18. EH to Hannah Hahn, April 4, 1939.
19. *China to Me,* op cit., p. 104.
20. *Times and Places,* op cit., p. 231.
21. EH to the author, April 17, 1996.
22. *Times and Places,* op cit., p. 238.

Chapter 18

1. *China to Me,* op cit., p. 108.
2. Ibid., p. 106.
3. Ibid., p. 109.
4. EH letter to the author, May 21, 1996.
5. Sinmay Zao to EH, Dec. 23, 1939.
6. Ibid., p. 113.
7. Ibid.
8. *The Soong Sisters* by Emily Hahn (Doubleday, Doran and Company. 1941), p. 297. (Cited hereafter as *The Soong Sisters.*)
9. Chinese place names from the old Wade-Giles Chinese transliteration system have been changed on modern maps

and in reference books. Under the modern Pinyin system, Szechuan Province is now called Sichuan; Chungking is known as Chongqing, and the Yangtze River is the Chang Jiang River.

10. *China to Me,* op cit., p. 118.
11. *The Soong Sisters,* op cit., p. 179.
12. *China to Me,* op cit., p. 122.
13. Ibid., p. 123.
14. *The Soong Sisters,* op cit., p. 300.
15. Author telephone interview from Toronto, Ontario, with Stephen Endicott, February 22, 1994.
16. The *New Yorker,* March 15, 1941, p. 23.
17. *China to Me,* op cit., p. 151.
18. Ibid., pp. 151–52.
19. Author telephone interview with Alf Bennett from London, U.K., March 6, 1994. (Cited hereafter as Bennett interview.)
20. *China to Me,* op cit., p. 153.

Chapter 19

1. EH to Hannah Hahn, Feb. 22, 1940.
2. *China to Me,* op cit., p. 154.
3. Ibid., p. 156.
4. Ibid., p. 161.
5. Ibid., p. 182.
6. Ibid., p. 191.
7. Ibid. p. 186.
8. Ibid., p. 194.
9. *The King of the World in the Land of the Pygmies,* op cit., p. 95.
10. *Steps of the Sun,* op. cit.
11. *New York Times,* September 29, 1940, p. 21.
12. *Boston Transcript,* September 28, 1940, p. 2.
13. *China to Me,* op cit., p. 197.

Chapter 20

1. *China to Me,* op cit., p. 201.
2. Jimmy Cummins to the author, July 9, 1996.
3. Ibid.
4. Clio Smeeton E-mail to the author, March 5, 1997.
5. *High Endeavours: The Extraordinary Life and Adventures of Miles and Beryl Smeeton* by Miles Clark (Grafton Books, 1991), p. 7. (Cited hereafter as *High Endeavours.*)
6. Charles Boxer to the author, June 23, 1993.
7. Bennett interview, op. cit.
8. *China to Me,* op cit., p. 153.
9. *The Commentaries of Ruy Freyre de Andrade* (1929); *The Journal of M.H. Tromp, Anno 1639* (1930); and, *Jan Compagnie in Japan, 1600–1817* (1936).
10. *Times of London,* May 23, 1996, p. 23.
11. *High Endeavours,* op cit., p. 189.
12. Patrick Putnam to EH, Oct. 24, 1940.
13. EH to Hannah Hahn, Nov. 27, 1940.
14. "Major Told Me," by Emily Hahn, *New Yorker,* April 1, 1944, p. 23.
15. *China to Me,* op cit., p. 202.
16. Ibid., p. 202.
17. *Hong Kong: The Colony That Never Was* by Alan Birch (Guidebook Company, 1991), p. 62. (Cited hereafter as *The Colony That Never Was.*)
18. *The Fall of Hong Kong* by Tim Carew (Anthony Blobd, 1960), p. 29. (Cited hereafter as *The Fall of Hong Kong.*)
19. Bennett interview, op cit.
20. Author interview with Bill Wiseman, from St. Albans, Herts., U.K., Jan. 11, 1994. (Cited hereafter as Wiseman interview.)
21. EH to Hannah Hahn, Nov. 27, 1940.

Chapter 21

1. Author interview with EH, from New York, January 25, 1997.
2. Lt. Joseph L. LaCombe to EH, Dec. 23, 1940.
3. Wiseman interview, op cit.
4. *China to Me,* op cit., p. 215.
5. *New York Times Book Review,* April 20, 1941, p. 9.
6. *Atlantic Monthly,* June 1941.
7. The *New Yorker,* April 9, 1941, p. 88.
8. *Nation,* April 19, 1941, p. 478.
9. EH to the author, July 10, 1996.

10. "Gibbon vs. Tenant" by Emily Hahn, the *New Yorker,* July 19, 1941, p. 44.
11. *Agnes Smedley: The Life and Times of an American Radical* by Janice R. MacKinnon and Stephen R. MacKinnon (University of California Press, 1988), p. 230. (Cited hereafter as *Agnes Smedley: The Life and Times of an American Radical.*)
12. *China to Me,* op cit., p. 229.
13. Ursula managed to escape capture when Singapore fell to the Japanese in February 1942. She made her way to Ceylon and could have returned home with other British expatriates. Instead she chose to stay in the Far East, where she worked for the British military as a cryptographer. After the war, she returned to England, where in 1947 she married I. A. R. Peebles, the renowed English cricketer and *Sunday Times* journalist. Following Pebbles's death in 1980, Ursula remarried. Her third husband, Montague Churchill-Dawes, died in 1991. Ursula herself passed away on April 26, 1996, at age eighty-six.
14. *High Endeavours,* op cit., p. 191.
15. *China to Me,* op cit., p. 244.
16. Ibid., p. 246.
17. EH to Hannah Hahn, July 28, 1941.
18. *The Fall of Hong Kong,* op cit., p. 27.
19. Ibid.
20. "1940 Paradox in Hong Kong" by Frederick Simpich, *National Geographic,* April 1940, p. 531.
21. *China to Me,* op cit., p. 217.
22. Author interview with Stephen Endicott, from Toronto, Ontario, Feb. 22, 1994.
23. James Endicott to EH, Aug. 21, 1941.
24. Ibid., p. 250.
25. *China to Me,* op cit., p. 250.

Chapter 22

1. EH to Helen Hahn, Nov. 1, 1941.
2. *China to Me,* op cit., p. 251.
3. Ibid., p. 252.
4. Ibid.
5. *Hong Kong Holiday,* op cit., p. 16.
6. Sir Victor Sassoon to EH, Autumn 1941.
7. *China to Me,* op cit., p. 257.
8. FDR's letter to Hirohito is in *Memoirs* by Cordell Hull (Macmillan, 1948), Volume II, pp. 1094–95.
9. File 106/2400, Public Records Office, London, U.K., as cited in *The Lasting Honour: The Fall of Hong Kong, 1941* by Oliver Lindsay (Hamish Hamilton, 1979), p. 25. (Cited hereafter as *The Fall of Hong Kong,* 1941.)
10. *China to Me,* op cit., p. 257.
11. Ibid., p. 258.
12. *Long Day's Journey into War,* op cit., p. 165.
13. *China to Me,* op cit., p. 258.
14. Ibid., p. 260.
15. *Prisoner of the Japs* by Gwen Dew (Knopf, 1943), p. 52. (Cited hereafter as *Prisoner of the Japs.*)
16. Ibid.
17. Ibid., pp. 54–55.
18. Ibid., p. 261.
19. Ibid., p. 262.
20. "1940 Paradox in Hong Kong," op. cit.
21. *China to Me,* op cit., p. 267.
22. Ibid., p. 271.

Chapter 23

1. *China to Me,* op cit., p. 273.
2. Ibid., p. 274.
3. Ibid.
4. *China to Me,* op cit., p. 278.
5. *The Lasting Honour,* op cit., p. 143.
6. "Horrors of Hong Kong" by Gwen Dew, *American Mercury,* November 1942, p. 560. (Cited hereafter as "Horrors of Hong Kong.")
7. *The Lasting Honour,* op cit., p. 149.
8. *Desperate Siege,* op cit., p. 215.
9. *The Lasting Honour,* op cit., p. 150.
10. *The Times of London,* December 24, 1941, p. 4.
11. Bill Wiseman to the author, October 7, 1996.
12. *China to Me,* op cit., p. 285.
13. Wiseman interview, op. cit.
14. Ibid, p. 285.

15. Ibid.
16. Ibid., pp. 287–88.
17. Ibid.
18. Ibid., p. 288.
19. "Horrors of Hong Kong," op cit., p. 562.
20. "The Ballad of East and West" by Rudyard Kipling.
21. Wiseman to the author, October 7, 1996.
22. Wiseman interview.
23. *China to Me,* op cit., p. 294.
24. "Horrors of Hong Kong," op cit., p. 562.
25. *Hong Kong: The Colony That Never Was,* op cit., p. 66.
26. Ibid., p. 67.
27. *China to Me,* op cit., p. 296.

Chapter 24

1. *China to Me,* op cit., p. 306.
2. Ibid., p. 302.
3. Bill Wiseman memoir, cited hereafter as Wiseman memoir.
4. Ibid.
5. *China to Me,* op cit., p. 312.
6. Ibid., p. 301.
7. Ibid., p. 323.
8. Joseph C. Green, special assistant to the Secretary of State, to Carl Brandt, January 28, 1942.
9. *China to Me,* op cit., p. 328.
10. Author interview with Takio Oda, from Tokyo, August 12, 1993.
11. "City in Prison," op cit.
12. *Hong Kong Holiday,* op. cit., pp. 158–59.
13. *China to Me,* op cit., p. 334.
14. Wiseman interview, op. cit.
15. "Horrors in Hong Kong," op cit., p. 563.
16. *Where Life and Death Hold Hands* by Wiliam Allister (Stoddart, 1989), p. 51.
17. Wiseman interview, op. cit.
18. "Stanley Military Internment Camp: Hong Kong" by Lancelot Foster, *Contemporary Review,* January 1946, p. 38.
19. *Prisoner of the Japs* by Gwen Dew, op cit., pp. 236–37.
20. "City in Prison," op cit., p. 422.

Chapter 25

1. *Mr. Pan* by Emily Hahn (Doubleday, Doran and Co., 1942).
2. *Books,* May 24, 1942, p. 4.
3. *New York Times,* May 24, 1942, p. 7.
4. EH to her family, Aug. 8, 1942.
5. *Times and Places,* op cit., p. 294.
6. *China to Me,* op cit., p. 342.
7. Ibid., p. 345.
8. *Hong Kong Holiday,* op cit., p. 162.
9. *China to Me,* op cit., p. 350.
10. Author interview with Frances Zainoeddin, July 19, 1993, New York City.
11. Ibid.
12. *Exchange Ship* by Max Hill (Farrar and Rinehart, 1942), p. 19. (Referred to hereafter as *Exchange Ship.*)
13. *China to Me,* op cit., p. 368.
14. Ibid., p. 386.
15. Ibid., p. 375.
16. Ibid., p. 397.
17. Ibid., p. 407.
18. Ibid., p. 423.
19. Ibid., p. 424.
20. Now known as Maputo, Mozambique.
21. *Exchange Ship,* op cit., p. 23.
22. *Hong Kong Holiday,* op cit., p. 275.

Chapter 26

1. *The Hongkong News,* September 25, 1943.
2. *Exchange Ship,* op cit., pp. 19–20.
3. *Hong Kong Holiday,* op cit., p. 282.
4. Ibid., p. 292.
5. *The New York Times,* December 2, 1943, p. 18:1.
6. The *New Yorker,* December 11, 1943, p. 24.
7. *Hong Kong Holiday,* op cit., p. 305.
8. Author interview with EH, New York City, January 3, 1997.
9. *Times and Places,* op cit., p. 287.
10. *Saturday Review of Literature,* Jan. 15, 1944.
11. *Saturday Review of Literature,* January 22, 1944.
12. Author interview with EH, New York City, January 3, 1997.
13. Bennett interview, op. cit.

14. *New York Times,* March 15, 1945.
15. Ibid.
16. Author interview with Hilary Schlessiger, New York City, November 16, 1993.
17. Author interview with Greg Dawson, New York City, November 16, 1993.
18. *China to Me,* op cit., p. 199.
19. Ibid., p. 200.
20. *Agnes Smedley: The Life and Times of an American Radical,* op cit., p. 291.
21. *Nation,* January 27, 1945, p. 108.
22. *Commonweal,* December 29, 1944, p. 281.
23. *New York Times Book Review,* December 10, 1944, p. 5.
24. *Library Journal,* November 15, 1944, p. 998.
25. EH to Sir Victor Sassoon, February 3, 1945.
26. Ibid.
27. *Times and Places,* op cit., p. 293.
28. Ibid., pp. 292–93.
29. Author interview with Charless Hahn, from Winnetka, Ill., June 1, 1993.

Chapter 27

1. EH to Sir Victor Sassoon, February 3, 1945.
2. EH to Katharine White, January 31, 1945.
3. EH to Bernice Baumgarten, January 30, 1945.
4. Dick Smith to EH, April 2, 1945.
5. Lorraine Murray to EH, May 1, 1945.
6. David McDougall to EH, April 14, 1945.
7. Captain Robert B. Ekvall to EH, April 1945.
8. Sinmay Zau to EH, Aug. 1, 1945.
9. EH to Sinmay Zau, January 26, 1946.
10. *New York World Telegram,* November 20, 1944.
11. EH to Randall Gould, May 1, 1945.
12. EH to Patrick Putnam's cousin Lillian, June 29, 1945.
13. Charles Boxer to EH, September 11, 1945.
14. *High Endeavours,* op cit., p. 248.
15. Ibid., p. 248.
16. Wiseman interview, op. cit.
17. Author interview with EH, New York City, December 14, 1992.
18. "DC" (an otherwise unidentified British journalist) to EH, September 12, 1945.
19. Ibid.
20. Ibid.
21. Wiseman interview, op. cit.
22. Charles Boxer to EH, September 15, 1945.
23. Charles Boxer to EH, September 27, 1945.
24. Clio Smeeton E-mail to the author, March 6, 1997.
25. *New York Times,* November 23, 1945, p. A-25.

Chapter 28

1. *Life,* December 3, 1945, p. 40.
2. Author interview with EH, New York City, December 14, 1992.
3. Ibid.
4. EH to Bill Wiseman, December 31, 1945.
5. EH to Bernice Baumgarten, February 6, 1946.
6. *Hong Kong Holiday,* op. cit.
7. *New York Times Book Review,* June 23, 1946, p. 5.
8. *Commonweal,* August 16, 1946, p. 438.
9. EH to Gus Lobrano, February 11, 1946.
10. EH to Harold Ross, February 16, 1946.
11. Harold Ross to EH, February 19, 1946.
12. *England to Me* by Emily Hahn (Jonathan Cape, 1950), p. 2. (Referred to hereafter as *England to Me.*)
13. Ibid., p. 23.
14. Ibid.
15. *High Endeavours,* op cit., p. 19.
16. The *New Yorker,* April 15, 1950, p. 82.
17. *England to Me,* op cit., p. 23.
18. *Kissing Cousins,* op cit., p. 66.
19. Ibid., p. 21.
20. Ibid., pp. 32–33.

21. Ibid., p. 26.
22. Ibid., p. 35.
23. Barbara Ker-Seymer interview, op. cit.
24. Ibid., p. 124.
25. *Raffles of Singapore* by Emily Hahn (Doubleday and Company, 1946).
26. The *New Yorker,* November 30, 1946, p. 143.
27. *New York Herald Tribune,* November 30, 1947, p. 19.
28. *Saturday Review of Literature,* December 6, 1947, p. 40.
29. Author interview with Carola Vecchio, New York City, December 15, 1992.
30. Ibid.
31. *Aphra Behn* by Emily Hahn (Jonathan Cape, 1950), p. 31. Also published as *Purple Passage: A Novel about a Lady Both Famous and Fantastic* (Doubleday & Company, 1950). (Cited hereafter as *Aphra Behn.*)
32. EH to Patrick Perry, March 21, 1946.
33. EH to Dorothy Larson, January 21, 1949.
34. Author interview with Amanda Boxer, from London, April 13, 1997.
35. EH to Muriel Hanson, November 21, 1948.
36. EH to Muriel Hanson, December 12, 1948.
37. Author interview with Amanda Boxer, from London, U.K., April 13, 1997.
38. EH to Dorothy Larson, November 24, 1949.
39. Author interview with EH, New York City, Nov. 16, 1993.
40. *Saturday Review of Literature,* January 15, 1949, p. 28.
41. Sydney Horler to Doubleday and Company, February 1, 1949.
42. EH to Dorothy Larson, October 17, 1949.
43. "Ms Ulysses," the *New Yorker,* March 10, 1997, p. 52. (Hereafter cited as "Ms Ulysses.")
44. Barbara Ker-Seymer interview, op. cit.
45. Author interview with Amanda Boxer, London, U.K., October 25, 1992.
46. Carola Vecchio interview, op. cit.

Chapter 29

1. "The New Yorker," *Fortune,* August 1934, p. 73.
2. Ibid, p. 74.
3. *Genius in Disguise,* op cit., p. 241.
4. *Magazines in the 20th Century* by Theodore Peterson (University of Illinois Press, 1956), p. 237.
5. *Here at the New Yorker* by Brendan Gill (Random House, 1975), p. 5. (Cited hereafter as *Here at the New Yorker.*)
6. Author interview with Sheila McGrath, from New York City, April 10, 1997.
7. "Ms Ulysses," op. cit.
8. Valerie Feldner to Roger Angell, February 20, 1997.
9. *Chicago Tribune,* December 1, 1967.
10. Author interview with Jimmy Cummins, from London, U.K., June 17, 1996.
11. Ibid.
12. Brendan Gill to the author, March 17, 1994.
13. "Ms Ulysses," op. cit., p. 52.
14. *The Years with Ross,* op. cit.
15. Ibid.
16. Ibid.
17. "The Ross Years" by Charles McGrath, the *New Yorker,* February 20–27, 1995, p. 185.
18. *Curious World* by Philip Hamburger (North Point Press, 1987), p. xi.
19. *Publishers Weekly,* March 18, 1988, p. 63.
20. For a more detailed account, see *The Last Days of the New Yorker,* op cit., pp. 109–11.
21. *About the New Yorker & Me: A Sentimental Journey* by E. J. Kahn, Jr., (Penguin, 1979), p. 399.
22. Ibid.
23. Author interview with EH, New York City, November 16, 1993.
24. Ibid.
25. Author interview with Sheila McGrath, from New York City, May 9, 1997.
26. Ibid.
27. Ibid.
28. Ibid.
29. Author interview with EH, New York City, November 16, 1993.

Chapter 30

1. *Around the World with Nellie Bly* by Emily Hahn, with illustrations by B. Holmes (Houghton Mifflin Company, 1959).
2. EH to Pearl S. Buck, June 23, 1951.
3. Charless interview, op. cit.
4. Xiaohong Shao to the author, March 3, 1997.
5. "The Old Boys," the *New Yorker,* November 7, 1953, p. 125.
6. *Chiang Kai-shek: An Unauthorized Biography* by Emily Hahn (Doubleday and Company, 1955), p. 365.
7. *New York Times Book Review,* March 27, 1955, p. 3.
8. *Library Journal,* March 1, 1955, p. 558.
9. EH to unnamed recipient, July 5, 1955.
10. "Ms Ulysses," op. cit.
11. Author interview with Hilary Schlessiger, New York City, November 16, 1993.
12. Author interview with Greg Dawson, from New York City, May 10, 1997.
13. *Kissing Cousins,* op cit., p. 132.
14. EH to Muriel Hanson, September 3, 1954.
15. Author interview with Jimmy Cummins, from London, England, May 27, 1993.
16. Author interview with Amanda Boxer, from London, May 18, 1997.
17. Author interview with Jimmy Cummins, from London, England, May 27, 1993.
18. Wiseman interview, op. cit.
19. Barbara Ker-Seymer interview, op. cit.
20. Rebecca West to EH, winter 1957.
21. Rebecca West to EH, June 15, 1960.
22. Author interview with EH, New York City, July 12, 1993.
23. Ibid.
24. *Africa to Me,* op. cit.
25. Author interview with Carola.

Chapter 31

1. *Bestsellers,* December 15, 1970, p. 393.
2. *Library Journal,* December 15, 1970, p. 4252.
3. EH to Muriel Hanson, March 29, 1954.
4. *The Barrytown Explorer,* March 1971, p.2.
5. *Publishers Weekly,* March 18, 1988, p. 62.
6. Author interview with EH, New York City, July 12, 1993.
7. *Once Upon a Pedestal* by Emily Hahn (Crowell, 1974). (Cited hereafter as *Once Upon a Pedestal.*)
8. Ibid., p. 4.
9. Ibid., p. 263.
10. *New York Times Book Review,* September 29, 1974, p. 20.
11. *Publishers Weekly,* May 27, 1974, p. 63.
12. Author interview with Valerie Feldner, New York City, November 15, 1993.
13. Author interview with Muriel Hanson, from Wellfleet, Massachusetts, January 21, 1993.
14. Barbara Ker-Seymer interview, op. cit.
15. *Moving Beyond Words* by Gloria Steinem (Simon and Schuster, 1994), p. 14.
16. *Look Who's Talking* by Emily Hahn (Crowell, 1978), p. 2. (Cited hereafter as *Look Who's Talking.*)
17. *Publishers Weekly,* March 18, 1988, p. 62.
18. The *New Yorker,* Sept. 2, 1967, p. 38.
19. *New York Times Book Review,* Nov. 19, 1967, p. 18.
20. *Look Who's Talking,* op cit., p. 8.
21. *Library Journal,* May 1, 1978, p. 985.
22. *Time,* June 26, 1978, p. 75.
23. Ibid., p. 6.
24. *American Heritage,* August/Sept. 1982, p. 53.
25. Ibid.
26. Author interview with EH, New York City, January 7, 1997.
27. *New York Times,* July 1, 1992, p. C-20.
28. EH Ringshall End interview, op cit.
29. EH to the author, June 29, 1992.

30. Author interview with Hyacinth Wilkie, from New York City, April 2, 1997.
31. Valerie Feldner interview, op. cit.
32. The *New Yorker,* July 31, 1995, p. 35.
33. Author interview with EH, New York City, January 7, 1997.

Afterword

1. Author interview with Jimmy Cummins, from London, February 23, 1997.
2. Author interview with Gregory Dawson, New York City, November 16, 1993.

Bibliography

Books by Emily Hahn, 1930–1988

Legend

A = Autobiography	B = Biography	F = Fiction	H = Humor
J = Juvenile literature	N = Non-fiction	S = Short stories	T = Travel

Seductio Ad Absurdum: The Principles and Practices of Seduction—A Beginner's Handbook (1930) H

Beginner's Luck (1931) F

Congo Solo: Misadventures Two Degrees North (1933) T

With Naked Foot (1934) F

Affair (1935) F

Steps of the Sun (1940) F

The Soong Sisters (1941, 1970) B

Mr. Pan (1942) S

China to Me: A Partial Autobiography (1944, 1975, 1988) A

Hong Kong Holiday (1946) A

China: A to Z (1946) J

The Picture Story of China (1946) J

Raffles of Singapore (1946) B

Miss Jill (1947) Published in the U.K. as *House in Shanghai* (1958) F

England to Me (1949) A

A Degree of Prudery: A Biography of Fanny Burney (1950) B

Purple Passage: A Novel About a Lady Both Famous and Fantastic (1950) Published in the U.K. as *Aphra Behn* (1951) F

Francie (1951) J

Love Conquers Nothing: A Glandular History of Civilization (1952) N

Francie Again (1953) J

Mary, Queen of Scots (1953) J

James Brooke of Sarawak: A Biography of Sir James Brooke (1953) B

Meet the British (with Charles Roetter and Harford Thomas) (1953) N

The First Book of India (1955) J

Chiang Kai-shek: An Unauthorized Biography (1955) B

Francie Comes Home (1956) J

Spousery (1956) H

Diamond: The Spectacular Story of the Earth's Greatest Treasure and Man's Greatest Greed, (1956) N

Leonardo da Vinci (1956) J

Kissing Cousins: America Through My Children's Eyes (1958) A

The Tiger House Party: The Last Days of the Maharajas (1959) N

Aboab: First Rabbi of the Americas (1959) J

Around the World with Nellie Bly (1959) J

June Finds a Way (1960) J

China Only Yesterday, 1850–1950*: A Century of Change* (1963) N

Indo (1963) N
Africa to Me (1964) A
Romantic Rebels: An Informal History of Bohemianism in America (1967) N
Animal Gardens (1967) N
The Cooking of China (1968) N
Recipes: Chinese Cooking (1968) N
Times and Places (1970) A
Breath of God: A Book about Angels, Demons, Familiars, Elementals and Spirits (1971) N
Fractured Emerald: Ireland (1971) N
On the Side of the Apes: A New Look at the Primates, the Men Who Study Them and What They Have Learned (1971) N
Once Upon a Pedestal (1974) N
Lorenzo: D. H. Lawrence and the Women Who Loved Him (1975) B
Mabel: A Biography of Mabel Dodge Luhan (1977) B
Look Who's Talking! (1978) N
Love of Gold (1980) N
The Islands: America's Imperial Adventures in the Philippines (1981) N
Eve and the Apes (1988) N

Index